BUILDING AND THE LAW
4th edition

BUILDING AND THE LAW

4TH REVISED AND EXPANDED EDITION | DAVID KEANE

RIAI

THE ROYAL INSTITUTE OF THE ARCHITECTS OF IRELAND

BUILDING AND THE LAW
(4th revised and expanded edition)

DAVID KEANE
B.Arch. (NUI) FRIAI, MCI Arb, Barrister-at-Law
KMD Architecture

Published by the Royal Institute of the Architects of Ireland

First edition – July 1993
Second revised edition – September 1994
Third revised edition – January 1998
Fourth revised edition – January 2003

ISBN 0948037 008

Design – John O'Regan (© Gandon, 2003)
Production – Nicola Dearey
Produced by Gandon Editions, Kinsale, for the RIAI
Printing – Betaprint, Dublin

THE ROYAL INSTITUTE OF THE ARCHITECTS
OF IRELAND
8 Merrion Square, Dublin 2
tel: 01-6761703 / fax: 01-6610948 / e-mail: info@riai.ie

Contents

Foreword

It has given me great pleasure to be invited to introduce this book by David Keane, a detailed and scholarly companion volume to his authoritative book on RIAI Contracts.

In this book, BUILDING AND THE LAW, David Keane has applied his extensive knowledge of the law to the architectural and building professions. He has started with the Constitution and guided the reader through the law relating to Local Government in Ireland and on to an overview of all the major legislation affecting the practising architect in Ireland.

In addition to reviewing national legislation, David Keane has set out clearly how European regulations and directives enacted under the Treaty of Rome and other treaties have had a major influence in this country since we first joined the European Community.

Up to relatively recently, building was regulated by a range of legislation going back over 120 years, but since the enactment of the Building Control Act 1990 which repealed Building Bye-Laws enacted under the Public Health Acts of the late nineteenth century, the Local Government (Planning and Development) Act enacted in 1963 is now the starting point for the majority of legislation affecting building in Ireland.

Most of the significant legislation has been enacted in the last ten years, and David Keane's text brings together in a coherent and comprehensive way the essential legal elements affecting the practicing architect, whether brought about by national legislation or by the transposition into Irish Law of European Regulations and Directives.

Not alone has he succeeded admirably in this monumental task, but in addition he has examined the prospect for the future, set out European trends in a number of key areas, and has summarised the essential details of attempts to harmonise liability within all EC States.

I believe that this book will be of great assistance not alone to architects, but will benefit all those whose professions are directly or indirectly affected by law as if affects planning, the environment, and building in Ireland. He has clarified the gen-

eral application of European and Irish legislation, and has made a substantial contribution to the science or knowledge of law as it affects the architect in Ireland and in
Europe.

I have pleasure in expressing the compliments and gratitude of the Council of the
Royal Institute of the Architects of Ireland to David Keane for this work, and recommend it without reservation.

PETER J HANNA
B.Arch (NUI) FRIAI, RIBA
President, Royal Institute of the Architects of Ireland, 1993

Preface to First Edition

The introduction to Chapter 1 describes the purpose of this guide. Basically it is intended as a work of reference, so that the law relating to a particular problem can be readily identified. There are a good many books dealing with particular areas of the construction world such as planning, the contract, the environment and so on, but it seemed that there was a need to provide a source which would identify, in a general way, the laws in question and enable a detailed answer to be found by reference to the piece of legislation itself.

Even though this guide is not intended to be a formal textbook, I have listed all the cases referred to in the text so that anyone interested in any particular subject can refer to the reports of the cases in the legal journals.

The law relating to design and construction is now extremely complex and some areas of this law are not as certain as they might be. When a problem seems to be entering more the world of law than that of building, formal legal advice should be sought.

When, some years ago, I was writing THE RIAI CONTRACTS – A WORKING GUIDE, it fell to me to thank a number of people who had made the task easier. Their support and encouragement continue: John Graby, General Secretary of the RIAI, Judge Ronan Keane of the High Court, the partners of Keane Murphy Duff, and Ian Duff in particular, past president of the RIAI John O'Reilly for help on Europe and syntax, and to Hilary Kirk for again unravelling my handwriting. My wife, Dr Maureen Keane, was a continuing help. Finally I would like to put on record my indebtedness to the late Judge Niall McCarthy of the Supreme Court. In an expert and analytical way that masked a kindness and an interest he added an extra dimension of enjoyment to the work required both on this book and on my previous one. I am far from alone in missing him.

The information contained in this book is up to date, as far as I am aware, to the 1st July 1993.

DAVID KEANE   October 1993

Preface to Fourth Edition

The event which gave rise to this edition was the passing fully into law on the 11th March 2002 of the Planning and Development Act 2000 together with the Planning and Development Regulations – S.I. 600 of 2001. These two pieces of legislation consolidated, with some significant changes and additions, the previous nine planning acts and innumerable regulations. Naturally there has not been any significant case law arising yet from this legislation.

It does, however, seem to me that the legislation concerning planning has now reached a stage of complexity as to make it almost unworkable. It cannot have been the intention of the framers of the 1963 Planning Act that changing the tiles in the bathroom of a small terraced house would require planning permission. In 2001 the Ombudsman gave it as his opinion that the whole planning system was near collapse. In my view, this is largely as a result of our unique, and virtually unlimited, right of third party appeal. More recently the Comptroller and Auditor General was very critical of the lack of consistency in planning decisions. I must agree with both of these comments.

Over the years since the first edition of this book in 1993 quite a number of organisations have changed their names. A good Example would be the recent re-naming of the former Department of Arts, Heritage, Gaeltacht and the Islands which is now the Department of Community, Rural and Gaeltacht Affairs. The name current at the date of the legislation being discussed is used in the book. All amounts referred to in legislation as being in Irish pounds have been converted to euro.

When writing the third edition in January 1998 I said that an event which might have a significant effect on the future of many aspects of the construction field was the publication in June 1997 by the Department of the Environment of the report of the Strategic Review Committee of the building industry, entitled BUILDING OUR FUTURE TOGETHER. The dealt with the very wide range of issues and made very firm recommendations, incorporating a timetable for the various actions required. This report led to the establishment of the Forum for the Construction Industry, a body representative of all interested parties in the building industry drawn from both the private and the public sectors. The objective of the Forum is to oversee and monitor the recommendations of the Strategic Review Committee. In turn, the Department has indicated that it intends to implement this report as fully as possible. Many of the recommendations have already been implemented. Some, such as the production of national standard forms of contract, registration of the title 'architect', and others are well advanced.

I would like to thank, at this stage, the former Minister of the Environment, Noel Dempsey, and his Department for encouragement generally over the years, and in particular Michael McCarthy of the Construction Division for help and assistance in producing this edition in a comparatively short space of time.

The information in this edition is up to date to the 1st December 2002.

DAVID KEANE   December 2002

Chapter 1 – **The Framework**

1.1   **Introduction**

Over the years the practice of designing and of building has become more and more regulated until, at the present, there is a bewildering array of legislation to control the entire process from before the start until after the finish. The various Acts, and the Regulations issued under them, are not listed or scheduled by reference to construction and it seemed that a guide to this body of law would be of considerable benefit to anyone concerned in the building industry. The designers, that is the architects and engineers, and the contractors are those who would primarily benefit from such a guide but solicitors and barristers dealing with conveyancing and contracts are affected in their day to day work with many of these areas. So too are quantity surveyors.

The word 'practitioner' has been used generally to describe the participant in the process as the activity being described might involve any of those who engage in construction. Where it would normally and properly be the architect or some other professional who would be particularly involved then the word 'architect' or other professional title is used as appropriate. The fact that there is as yet no such thing in Ireland as a registered architect, is commented on later in this chapter.

The regulators of the system, that is the staff of the local authorities, are similarly affected not only by the matters dealt with in this guide but also by a further comprehensive range of legislation dealing with the administration of local authorities. This legislation is only referred to when it impinges on construction or planning legislation.

The guide is divided into ten chapters, each dealing with a separate section of various laws and controls, and it is emphasised that the main purpose of the guide is to lead the practitioner through the legal and administrative framework and not to deal with the substance of planning or building detail. In this way, the procedures to be followed with regard to, for instance, the Building Regulations are dealt with, but the Regulations themselves are not considered. In each section, further guidance is given by reference to standard works which will contain any necessary detail. Each chapter has a contents page and, in addition, chapters 2, 3, 4 and 5 dealing with planning, the environment, the Building Regulations and Safety at Work have a checklist of questions that might naturally arise in the course of a project.

The Acts and Regulations are rarely quoted in detail. The laws themselves must always be referred to. As is mentioned more than once in this guide, one of the difficulties experienced by the practitioner is the fact that many statutes have been amended or partly revoked and one of the primary purposes of this guide is to list and describe all of the relevant and up to date Acts and Regulations.

Because of the complexity of the subject some omissions may have occurred and observant readers are asked to bring any such items to the attention of the publisher. Where relevant, cases are mentioned and references given so that those interested in specific subjects can do further reading. A list of cases is set out at the end of each chapter.

A particular difficulty relates to on-going changes. At any one time there are proposed alterations, or rumours of alterations, to many areas of legislation. There is always the on-going EU legislation which is becoming more and more relevant and which, at the time of the first edition was in a state of considerable confusion due to the fact that the High Court had held that regulations made under the European Communities Act 1972 were unconstitutional. That decision was reversed by the Supreme Court (par.1.4).

1.2 Local Government in Ireland

Most of the contact that practitioners in the construction industry will have with the apparatus of state will be through the local authorities, acting in their varying capacities. There will be exceptions, such as dealing with An Bord Pleanála, but by and large, the local authorities are the bodies charged with implementing legislation in the built environment, and because of this, it is useful for the practitioner to have an overall idea of the structure of local government in Ireland. Those interested in reading further on the subject are recommended THE LAW OF LOCAL GOVERNMENT IN THE REPUBLIC OF IRELAND by Judge Ronan Keane, which is published by the Law Society and although now twenty years in existence is still a useful overall guide.

The country is divided at present into 29 county councils (which are the 26 counties, with 2 councils in Tipperary and 3 in Co Dublin) and 5 county boroughs or corporations. The corporations were altered to City Councils in the Local Government Act 2001. The City Councils are Dublin, Cork, Limerick, Waterford, and Galway. These 34 authorities act in different capacities, and can be variously described when they are carrying out different functions. Acting in their primary capacity and carrying out their basic administrative function they are described as local authorities. They are also sanitary authorities, but most of their powers in this area were transferred to the Health Boards in 1970. The functions that they retained as sanitary authorities after 1970 principally related to the provision of sewers, water supplies, refuse collection, street lighting, the control of dangerous buildings, burial grounds and, until 1992, building bye-laws. They act as housing authorities under the various housing Acts, as fire brigade authorities under the Fire Services Act 1981, as planning authorities under the Planning Acts, and finally, as building control authorities under the Building Control Act 1990.

Their role as housing authorities derives mainly from the Housing Act 1966, which charges them with providing housing for those unable to make such provision themselves. This Act is referred to in par 6.3 where standards relating to habitable rooms in houses are set out.

The same overall management controls each of these functions, but with separate specialist staff for each function. The three new Dublin authorities, Fingal, South Dublin and Dun Laoghaire / Rathdown, established under the Local Government (Dublin) Act 1993, will all function in these roles but it is proposed that a common fire service will be provided for all Dublin.

Subsidiary to these 34 major local authorities are 49 urban district councils. These would be managed by the county manager of the county in which they are situated but would have their own elected representatives. They act as sanitary authorities, housing authorities and planning authorities. Finally there are 29 towns which have town commissioners. They are in the same management framework as the urban district councils but act only as housing authorities, and even here often delegate these powers to the appropriate county council.

All of the local authorities referred to have elected representatives who have powers called reserved functions. The managers have specified powers called executive functions. There is a separate manager for each county council, and city council. The reserved functions of a council are numerous, but the most important, as far as construction is concerned, is the power to make a development plan under the Planning Acts and the power to revoke a planning permission. Any power which is not specified in the various Acts as being reserved to the elected members is an executive power. The granting, or refusing of a planning permission is an executive function and this power has long been an object of envy by the elected representatives. They frequently used a power given to them under Section 4 of the City and County Management (Amendment) Act 1955, which enabled them to direct the manager, as far as the carrying out of his executive functions is concerned, to grant planning permissions against the advice of the planning officials and the manager That particular act has now been revoked, and this power of direction is now contained in Section 140 of the Local Government Act 2001. This practice became so widespread that it has now been curtailed. Chapter 2, which deals with planning, goes into this matter in greater detail at pars 2.4.9. and 2.4.10

The framework of local government set out above results in 88 planning authorities, which may seem too detailed a framework for such a small country. Admittedly, a large number of these, particularly in the case of the urban districts, share their technical staff, but the number of elected representatives involved in the process must inevitably lead to great pressure on some of the staff involved to make decisions based on factors other than those of a strictly planning nature.

A fairly recent development in local government administration has been the establishment of regional authorities. These have been set up under the Local Government Act 1991 and S.I. 394 of 1993 – The Regional Authorities (Establishment) Order 1993. The date of their establishment was 1st January 1994. There are eight regional authorities: Dublin, South East (Kilkenny, Carlow, Wexford, Waterford and Tipperary SR), South West (Cork and Kerry), Mid West (Clare, Limerick and Tipperary NR), West (Galway, Mayo and Roscommon), Border (Donegal, Leitrim, Cavan, Monaghan, Louth and Sligo), Midlands (Offaly, Longford, Westmeath and Laois) and Mid-East (Kildare, Meath and Wicklow). The Regional Authorities are referred to in the Planning and Development Act 2000 in respect of the making of regional plans (Part II – Chapter III).

The general function of the regional authorities is stated, in the statutory instrument, to be the promotion of co-ordination of the provision of public services in the authority's region. They will also have responsibility for monitoring and advising on the implementation at regional level of the various operational programmes under the EU Structural and Cohesion Funds. They have no statutory powers and can only advise. Their members are drawn from the local authorities in their region.

1.3   The Legal System

While a detailed knowledge of the legal system in Ireland is not necessary to enable a practitioner to find his way around the law affecting construction, it is useful to be aware of the basic framework. Almost all the relevant legislation referred to in this guide sets out enforcement procedures and penalties to which architects and clients might relate and this necessarily very condensed description of the Courts system is concerned primarily with these enforcement procedures and penalties. This is where the practitioner is most likely to become involved in the legal system. The range of these penalties now runs from a fine of €25.39 under Section 32 of the Office Premises Act 1958 to a fine of €12,697,380 under Section 9(1) of the Environmental Protection Agency Act 1992.

To be found guilty of a breach of an Act is a criminal offence and the following notes deal with the Courts when exercising their criminal jurisdiction. The civil role of the Courts is set out briefly in chapter 8 which deals with dispute resolution. The District Court is the lowest of the Courts of first instance, that is a Court where the offence will be heard for the first time. The country is divided into 23 District Court areas, and cases are heard by a district judge sitting alone without a jury. This lack of a jury restricts the District Court to hearing what are called minor offences, as anything that is not classed as a minor offence entitles the accused to the right of trial by jury, as provided for in Article 38.2 of the

Constitution. A difficulty is that a minor offence is nowhere defined but it has been suggested that if the penalty is greater than a term of imprisonment of one year, or a fine of €1,270 then the offence can no longer be considered minor.

The jurisdiction, or range of cases, that the District Court can hear is very wide but its powers of sentence are limited. This brings us to the distinction between summary and indictable offences. A summary offence is one heard by the District Court without a jury and for which the maximum punishment is six months imprisonment and/or a fine. An indictable offence entitles the accused as of right to trial by jury and would normally be heard in the Circuit Court. Certain cases of indictable offences can be heard by the District Court if the accused consents, and in these cases the punishment is limited to twelve months imprisonment and/or a fine. An appeal against a decision of the District Court lies to the Circuit Court.

The Circuit Court is the next Court in the hierarchy above the District Court. In criminal matters it hears indictable offences sent to it by the District Court and can impose any penalty that the law allows. It can deal with any criminal offence except murder, treason, piracy, genocide and rape. The country is divided into eight circuits, with permanent Courts in Dublin and Cork. An appeal from a decision of the Circuit Court lies to the Court of Criminal Appeal in criminal cases and to the High Court in civil cases.

The High Court is the superior Court of first instance and, while it is invested with full original jurisdiction to determine all questions whether of law or fact in civil matters, its criminal jurisdiction is confined to treason, murder, genocide and rape. The Supreme Court is the Court of final appeal. An appeal to the Supreme Court lies from a decision of the High Court, which is known as the Central Criminal Court when exercising its criminal jurisdiction. An appeal to the Court of Criminal Appeal lies from a decision of the Central Criminal Court. A further appeal may be heard by the Supreme Court from decisions of the Court of Criminal Appeal but only where an important point of law is involved.

In planning matters the Courts can be called in to stop unauthorised works, or prevent an unauthorised use, even where no enforcement notice has been issued. Possibly the best known provision in this regard was Section 27 of the Local Government (Planning and Development) Act 1976, which allowed any person to apply to the High Court to prevent unauthorised development. This section has now been repealed and replaced by Section 160 of the Planning and Development Act 2000 and is described in par. 2.4.13. One of the major amendments has been to allow such actions to be taken in the Circuit Court, which is much more accessible than the High Court.

The process used under the provisions of Section 160 of the 2000 Act referred to above is known as *injunction*, and is an order of the Court directing a party to do, or cease doing, a certain thing. The injunction may be interim, which is for a specified time, or interlocutory where the injunction lasts until a full hearing of the action. Under both the Planning Acts and the Building Control Act there are procedures whereby the local authority can issue enforcement notices requiring certain things to be done, for instance, the removal or cessation of specified works, or the discontinuance of a use.

Other legal processes which the practitioner might meet in his work would be what are called state side orders, and these are obtained by the process of judicial review, which is normally a much quicker route than the usual Court hearing as they are determined on affidavit and not by the evidence of witnesses. The orders that occur most frequently in the construction world are *certiorari*, where the Court will review, and possibly quash, decisions of inferior Courts and other bodies, and *mandamus*, where the Court requires an inferior Court, or any person or body, to perform a legally imposed duty.

The reader will, on many occasions throughout this book, be referred to interpretations by the Courts as to the meaning of certain documents. The position as far as statutes are concerned can vary. If there is a penal or taxation liability involved, as there is in most planning and construction legislation, the words must be construed strictly and the intention of the parliamentary draughtsman is not relevant. What the words say is the law. In other circumstances the words can be interpreted as to their ordinary or colloquial meaning. (*Inspector of Taxes v Kiernan* [1982] ILRM 13). However in planning documents, as opposed to legislation, McCarthy J. held: 'Certain principles may be stated in respect of the true construction of planning documents: (a) to state the obvious they are not Acts of the Oireachtas or subordinate legislation emanating from skilled draughtsmen and inviting the accepted cannons of construction applicable to such material: (b) they are to be construed in their ordinary meaning as it would be understood by members of the public without legal training as well as by developers and their agents, unless such documents read as a whole, necessarily indicate some other meaning.' (*XJS Investments v Dun Laoghaire Corporation* [1987] ILRM 659).

The role of Statutory Instruments should be raised here. Many Acts give the relevant minister power to make regulations to deal with what should be merely regulatory matters in relation to the basic legislation. Over the years, however, more and more important areas of legislation were being controlled by statutory instruments. This was restricted by the case of *Laurentiu v The Minister for Justice and Others* [2000] 1 ILRM 1. The Supreme Court laid down limits on the use of delegated ministerial powers and quoted a previous case with approval: 'In the view of this Court, the test is whether that which is challenged as an unauthorised delegation of parliamentary power is more than a mere giving effect to principles and policies which are contained in the statute itself. If it be, then it is not authorised, for such would constitute a purported exercise of legislative power by an authority which is not permitted to do so under the Constitution. On the other hand, if it be written within the permitted limits – if the law is laid down in the statute and details only filled in or contemplated by the designated minister or subordinate body – there is no unauthorised legislation of legislative power.' The status of statutory instruments was previously questioned in *Meagher v The Minister for Agriculture* [1994] ILRM 1 (see pars 1.4 and 2.3.1 for further observations on the role of statutory instruments).

Some Regulations are regarded as being more important than others and it might be appropriate at this stage to comment on how the Courts view the relative importance of the various Regulations. In some cases the requirements are said to be 'obligatory' or 'imperative', and failure to observe these requirements will invalidate the procedure. In other cases the Regulations may be regarded as 'directory' and are generally held not to be such as to cause an application to be rejected, as in the case of *Molloy v Dublin County Council* [1990] IR 90, where minor inaccuracies were discounted. There is no hard and fast rule. In the Molloy case, which dealt with notices, the Court quoted with approval the Judge's remarks in *Monaghan UDC v Alf-a-Bet Promotions* [1980] ILRM 64: 'What the legislation has, either immediately in the Act or mediately in the Regulations, nominated as being obligatory may not be depreciated to the level of a mere direction except on the application of the de minimus rule' (*De minumus non curat lex* – the law does not concern itself with trifles). The comments of the Court in *Liverpool Borough Bank v Turner* [1851] 30 L.j.Cr.379 were quoted with approval in *Frank Dunne Ltd v Dublin County Council* [1974] IR 45 'No universal rule can be laid down for the construction of statutes as to whether mandatory enactments should be considered directory only or obligatory with an implied nullification for disobedience. It is the duty of the Courts of Justice to try to get at the real intention of the legislature by carefully attending to the whole scope of the statute to be considered.'

1.4 European Union Law

The primary law of the European Union is contained in the treaties and in particular in the originating Treaty of Rome (Jan 1, 1958). Under this primary law is the secondary legislation which consists mainly of Regulations and Directives. The Treaties and the Regulations made under them are binding in their original form on the whole Union. A Directive binds only in that the objective set out in the Directive must be achieved, but each Member State can decide the details as to how the objective may be achieved. A Directive can be brought into force in Ireland by Ministerial Regulation as provided for in the European Communities Act, 1972.

As mentioned above, the validity of these Regulations was questioned in the case of *Meagher v The Minister for Agriculture* (1994 ILRM 1) where the High Court held that a particular regulation made under the 1972 Act was unconstitutional. This decision, however, was reversed by the Supreme Court thereby removing the possibility of considerable legislative complications. One of the objectives of the Treaty of Rome, amended by the Single European Act, 1987, is to ensure the free movement of goods, services, persons and capital, together with the guarantee of free and fair competition. Of the hundreds of Directives issued by the Union and of which the practitioner should be aware are 85/337/EEC (Environmental Impact) – par. 2.3.3; 89/106/EEC (Construction Products) – par. 4.4; 92/50/EEC (Award of Public Service Contracts); 92/57/EEC (Safety on Construction Sites) – par. 5.1, and the 'Seveso', or major acidents hazard directive (96/82/EC). The directives on Architectural Qualifications (85/384/EEC; amended by 2001/19/EC) – par. 1.5, and Freedom of Information (90/313/EEC) – par. 3.5, are also of interest.

1.5   Registration of the title 'Architect'

At the time of writing this edition, the position of the registration of the title 'Architect' is delicately balanced. After many years of discussions with both the Department of the Environment and various architectural and surveying bodies, an agreed report was forwarded in October 1999 by the RIAI on behalf of all bodies representing architects to the Department for consideration. As a result of this, and following on the recommendation made by the Forum for the Construction Industry, a draft bill to be called The Building Control Bill 2001 has been prepared and it is understood that it is hoped to introduce this to the Dáil in the autumn of 2002. The main outlines of the proposed Bill are dealt with below.

In previous editions of this book reference was made to the question of unqualified persons practicing as, and calling themselves, architects. The other building professions did not seem to be troubled to the same extent by this phenomenon and this appears to be because the practice of architecture is regarded almost as a pastime in which anyone can indulge. At the moment, planning applications are being lodged and buildings designed, on a widespread scale, by woodwork teachers, assistant county engineers, engineers in the ESB, and guards, to name but a few. Private houses are a particular source of work to these dilettantes and it is estimated that only 10% of all one-off private houses in Ireland are designed by architects, that is qualified architects and not people who just call themselves architects. That this occurs seems to be a source of astonishment even to people who would be expected to be aware of it. For as long as can be remembered successive governments, until the present one, have set their face against any action to reduce the exposure that the public has to these unqualified people. This is partly due to pressure from special interest groups and partly due to a complete misunderstanding of what a professional service endeavours to offer.

In 1985 the European Union produced the Directive entitled 'On the mutual recognition of diplomas, certificates and other evidence of formal qualifications in architecture, including measures to facilitate the effective exercise of the right of establishment and freedom to provide services' (85/384/EEC). This Directive was amended in May 2001 (2001/19/EC) allowing member states to recognise qualifications from outside the Union. The original Directive was brought into effect in Ireland through the European Communities (Establishment and Provision of Services in Architecture) Regulations 1989 – S.I. 15 of 1989. The primary purpose of the Directive was to permit any architect properly qualified in his own country to practice in any other member state. The Commission indicated in the Directive how important this particular field of expertise is:

'Whereas architecture, the quality of buildings, the way they blend in with their surrounding, respect for the natural and urban environment and the collective and individual cultural heritage are matters of public concern; whereas, therefore, the mutual recognition of diplomas, certificates and other evidence of formal qualifications must be founded on qualitative and quantitative criteria ensuring that the holders of recognised diplomas, certificates and other evidence of formal qualifications are able to understand and give practical expression to the needs of individuals, social groups and communities as regards spatial planning, the design, organisation and construction of buildings, the conservation and enhancement of the architectural heritage and preservation of the natural balance.'

The Directive recognised that not all the Member States required registration of architects, either by way of protecting the title of architect, or by protecting the practice of architecture but it did assume that all the member states would eventually produce some measure of control. To quote the Directive again:
'Whereas, in some Member States, the taking up and pursuit of the activities of architects are by law conditional upon the possession of a diploma in architecture; whereas, in certain other Member States where this condition does not exist, the right to hold the professional title of architect is none the less governed by law; whereas, finally, in some Member States where neither the former or the latter is the case, laws and regulations are being prepared on the taking up and pursuit of these activities under the professional title of architect;'

The basic objective of the Directive is set out in Article 2: 'Each Member State shall recognise the diplomas, certificates and other evidence of formal qualifications acquired as a result of education and training fulfilling the requirements of Articles 3 and 4 and awarded to nationals of Member States by other Member States, by giving such diplomas, certificates and other evidence of formal qualifications, as regards the right to take up activities referred to in Article 1 and pursue them under the professional title of architect pursuant to Article 23(1), the same effect in its territory as those awarded by the Member State itself.'

Article 1 referred to says that the Directive 'shall apply to the field of architecture'. Article 3 sets out the criteria which diplomas must meet (and continue to meet) if they are to obtain and retain recognition. Article 4 deals, primarily, with the length of courses. The requirements are detailed and of a high standard. They require the course to be pursued at university level; to cover, amongst other subjects, design, theory, history, fine arts, urban design, planning, structure and regulations; to be at least four years full time study, or six years of which three must be full time; and to conclude with the successful completion of an examination of degree standard.

Article 23(1) referred to above can require an architect from one Member State to undergo practical training experience in another Member State before being allowed to use the professional title of architect. This is only sensible where laws, rules and regulations will vary considerably from country to country.

The various diplomas and certificates which are the object of mutual recognition by the Member States (and which meet the criteria of Article 3) are published from time to time in the Official Journal of the European Communities, and those currently listed for Ireland are:

i) the degree of Bachelor of Architecture awarded by the National University of Ireland (B.Arch. NUI) to architecture graduates of University College Dublin

ii) the diploma of degree standard in architecture awarded by the College of Technology, Bolton Street, Dublin (Dip. Arch.)

iii) the Certificate of Associateship of the Royal Institute of the Architects of Ireland (ARIAI)

iv) the Certificate of Membership of the Royal Institute of the Architects of Ireland (MRIAI)

At the time of writing, there is a proposal before the European Union to repeal the Architects Directive and to incorporate its provisions into a new directive that would regulate professional recognition for over four hundred professions across Europe. The RIAI, through the Architects Council of Europe, is opposed to this proposal as it will weaken the present protection given to qualified architects throughout the Union. It could be some time before this matter is resolved.

Some unease had been caused in the 1990s by a proposal on the part of the Government to add some further categories to the list of approved Irish qualifications. This initially arose as a result of a decision by the Incorporated Law Society to recommend that their members should only accept opinions of compliance from the four categories of qualified architects listed in the Directive and this was perceived to be anti-competitive. The organisations which the Government wished to add to the list were the Irish Architects Society, The Architects and Surveyors Institute, and the Incorporated Association of Architects and Surveyors (which has since changed its name to the Association of Building Engineers). The Department of the Environment advertised for applications by architects to be included in a list which might eventually serve several functions as, for instance, being used by the Government as a form of informal recognition or, eventually, being used for the purposes of registration. A panel, appointed by the Minister for the Environment, reviewed these applications and those accepted have been included on a list which forms part of the recognised qualifications referred to in the proposed registration bill currently under consideration.

It is only very recently that this problem of registration has been seriously addressed. In 1996 the Minister for the Environment set up a committee to review and report on all aspects of the building industry. The report, entitled IRELAND – BUILDING OUR FUTURE TOGETHER was published in June 1997. The comments of the report on registration are worth quoting in full: 'The Committee has come to the view that there is a strong case for the protection of the titles of those qualified and legitimately practicing as architects, engineers and quantity surveyors within the construction industry. Those entitled to use these titles should be registered. The main reasons for this are the need to protect clients from the danger of inadequate service from those who describe themselves as professionals but are not professionally qualified and the need to maintain high standards within the industry.'

The Committee then went on to make formal recommendations as follows:
'The Royal Institute of the Architects of Ireland and the Society of Chartered Surveyors should develop proposals for a technical basis for assessing qualification for registration for submission to the Department of Enterprise and Employment. The proposals should be formulated in consultation with other bodies representing architects and engineers, and should acknowledge the established right of those in practice, without formal qualifications, for many years (via a 'grandfather clause').'

The register for architects should be administered by the Royal Institute of the Architects of Ireland and that for quantity surveyors by the Society of Chartered Surveyors.

The main headings of the Building Control Bill 2001, which will be the vehicle for introducing registration, are as follows:

1   Registration would be restricted to protection of title, that is, only properly qualified architects acceptable to be included on a register would be entitled to describe themselves as architects, or use any term including the word

architect or architectural. Exceptions would be the use of the terms landscape architect, naval architect or architectural technician.

2   The register would admit

    a)   graduates of the School of Architecture of the National University of Ireland and of the Dublin Institute of Technology who have passed an approved competence examination or can show seven years post graduate experience of professional practice

    b)   Fellows or Members of the Royal Institute of the Architects of Ireland

    c)   persons recognised by the Minister for the Environment and Local Government in connection with the proposed amendment to the Architects Directive

    d)   architects holding a recognised qualification in another Member State

    e)   persons practicing as architects for more than ten years and accessed by a panel to be set up under the Act.

3   The register would be administered by the Royal Institute of the Architects of Ireland as recommended in the Forum report referred to earlier.

4   Persons would be removed from the register for

    a)   failing to pay the appropriate subscription

    b)   for professional misconduct by a professional conduct committee.

In addition to registration, an associated area of difficulty with officialdom is fees.

In the past, governments seemed to imagine that a total ban on any form of qualification requirement together with a progressive dismantling of any form of fee scale would result in greater competition and that the public would benefit. Those involved in the litigation end of the construction industry are only too well aware that a very large number of disputes over building defects arise because of design by incompetent amateurs, or by fee-cutting on such a scale as to prevent the provision of an adequate professional service. The concept of consumerism has probably done as much damage as good, and the standard of service provided in former years by architects, in particular, is becoming more and more difficult to offer as fees become the subject of unlimited competition, including competition from the unqualified sector.

The surrender to popular and incorrect attitudes towards the imagined advantages of unlimited fee competition in Ireland can be contrasted with that of our partners in the European Union where there are minimum fee scales established by law in

Belgium, France, Germany, Greece, Italy, the Netherlands, Portugal and Spain. In Denmark and Luxembourg there are recommended fee scales. Interestingly, the Brookes Act in the United States prohibits fee tendering and architects must be chosen on merit. The Brookes Act states that only after an appointment has been offered can negotiations over the fee take place. One spectacular, and tragic consequence of what unqualified advice can produce was the Stardust disaster of 1981 where 48 people lost their lives and 128 were seriously injured. The Tribunal of Enquiry commented as follows: 'The low level of professional expertise availed of by the owners contributed specifically to the scale of the disaster' (par. 8.3), and again 'The owners failed to ensure that the preparation of drawings for the conversion and supervision of the work of conversion itself was undertaken by properly qualified and experienced persons' (par. 9.70). The Tribunal also criticised the Government's failure to introduce Building Regulations as provided for in the Local Government (Planning and Development) Act 1963.

It is evident that the issue by the Department of Arts Culture and the Gaeltacht in May 1997 of a government policy on architecture was an indication that progress was being made towards the acceptance of the importance of architecture in a nation's culture and of the merit of controlling those who produce it. This publication was followed in 2002 by the publication by the Department of Arts, Heritage, Gaeltacht and the Islands (as the Department was then called) of the document ACTION ON ARCHITECTURE 2002-2005. This publication emphasises the importance that the Government places on good architecture: 'Government policy on architecture aims to place architecture higher on the political and cultural agenda and in so doing to remove impediments to the achievement of a built environment of good quality'

1.6   RIAI Documents and the Architect's Appointment

The Royal Institute of the Architects of Ireland now publishes many standard documents relating to virtually all aspects of architectural practice. Quite apart from the standard forms of contract (dealt with in Chapter 7) there are forms dealing with appointments, opinions on compliance, warranties, etc. A full list of these documents can be obtained at the RIAI website: www.riai.ie.

Perhaps the most basic of all the Institute documents is the GOOD PRACTICE GUIDE. This comprehensive document sets out, in considerable detail, all the information required and the procedures used in every aspect of architectural practice. It is referenced to ISO 9001 which is the international standard used to regulate and control quality management in professional practices. It is indispensable in these days of complex building legislation and of very extensive responsibility.

This might be an appropriate place to deal with the retention of documents. As is commented on in detail in par. 9.5 the position with regard to the Statute of Limitations may well change, but at the moment a period of six years after a contract ends (or twelve years in the case of a contract under seal) is the extent of liability. It is unusual for an architect's appointment to be sealed. It is suggested that, say, seven years would be an appropriate period to retain documents. The accepted view seems to be that if a firm has a rational document retention policy that a Court is unlikely to be critical in cases were documents had been destroyed before they were required for the purpose of litigation.

Perhaps it would be appropriate to examine firstly the documents dealing with differing forms of appointment. At the time of writing, there are five such forms. The first is for general works and will be examined in detail. The other forms of appointment deal with domestic work, commercial small works, private sector estate housing and private sector apartment development. The first mentioned form sets out in detail the various services that can be offered together with a suggested scale of charges. This document is reproduced at the end of par. 1.7 and it is strongly recommended that this form be used in appointments if possible. The preamble to the form explains the basic position and the document then goes on to define the architect's responsibility and duty with regard to each area of the service being offered. Some of these are areas which have given rise to disputes and misunderstandings in the past, and a clear exposition of the scope of the commission and the limitations on the duties and responsibilities being accepted, is helpful in avoiding misunderstandings which might ultimately result in conflict or, even, litigation. Fees seem to figure very largely in these disputes. The fees should always be agreed in advance and in writing. It is well known that fees cannot now be set out in a scale, but the Institute can indicate what would be considered an appropriate fee needed to provide a proper professional service. The comments which follow would apply, generally, to all the forms of appointment.

A question often asked is whether the architect's appointment can be terminated. If no specific provision is made in the contract of appointment it is normally accepted that the appointment is meant to cover the full range of services from start to finish. In that case, if the architect is dismissed at any stage during the course of the work it is generally accepted that in addition to any fees that would be due, the architect would also be entitled to compensation for the loss of the anticipated profit on the remainder of the work.

If, however, the appointment contract provides for stages of work as in the RIAI agreement, it could be argued that either the architect or the client could terminate the agreement on completion of any of the stages. Each case must be judged on the facts. The latest (11th) edition of Hudson on BUILDING AND ENGINEERING CONTRACTS, published in 1995, which is the leading authority on all aspects of building, says at p.265: 'Unless there is disagreement to the contrary, an appointment in explicit, and unqualified terms for a particular project cannot be determined until the purpose of the appointment has been achieved. However, it is not unusual for the contract of employment to contain provisions dividing the duties to be performed by the architect in accordance with various stages of progress of the contemplated project, and to give either party, in effect, the power of termination at the end of the various stages. An important example is the Conditions of Engagement contained in the scale of professional charges of the RIBA. Indeed, this arrangement recognises the reality of the transaction between the parties, since even if nothing specific were said when an architect was first employed to get out plans and advise on a project, it would not necessarily follow that his employer required his services in letting the contract, if there was to be one, or in the supervision of the work. In fact, in the absence of express provision, an architect engaged informally on a particular project will usually owe his employment to a series of informal appointments rather than one appointment covering the whole project from start to finish. In general, until the time that the decision is taken to prepare contract documents with a view to obtaining a tender, the project is frequently of a tentative or exploratory character, and the architect is likely to be employed almost on a day-to-day basis. At that stage the owner is certainly authorising, for the first time, substantial expenditure and, usually, the engagement of other persons, such as the quantity surveyor. But not until tenders are received, and the owner is in a position to k now what his financial commitments are likely to be and to make arrangements for finance, that is to say, at the time of the decision to accept the tender and place or 'let' the contract, has the point of no return, and therefore of a possible anticipatory breach by the owner of the architect's contract of employment, really arrived.' Earlier English cases such as *Edwin Hill and Partners v Leakcliffe Properties* [1984] 29 BLR 43 and *Thomas v Hammersmith Borough Council* [1938] 3 AER 201 took the view that an architect, once appointed, was to be retained until completion of the project, but the Hudson view is now generally accepted.

This book deals with most aspects of the architect's appointment in differing chapters as follows:

Architect's Commission	par. 9.2
Architect's Authority	par. 7.7
Architect's Responsibility	par. 9.2
Consultants	par. 9.2.1
Contractor	chapter 7
Sub-contractor and Suppliers	par. 7.10
Inspection	pars 7.7, 9.2
Client's Instructions	par. 7.7
Copyright	par. 6.7

Agreement between Client and Architect for the provision of Architectural Services

Terms and Conditions of the Agreement

1 Architect's warranty

The Architect warrants that s/he is a Registered Member of the Royal Institute of the Architects of Ireland.

2 Architect's duties

The architect will:

- exercise reasonable skill and care on the project in accordance with the normal standards of the architect's profession, and will provide the client with the services agreed

- not start any Work Stage without the client so requesting

- take account of the client's budget

- make only such alterations, additions and omissions to the agreed drawings and specifications as s/he considers are in the client's interest, and inform the client of such alterations, additions, omissions and of their cost implications

- keep the client informed of any significant increases in cost during construction

- act on the client's behalf in the matters set out in this agreement

- administer the building contract as the client's agent, while acting impartially between the client and contractor.

3 Client's duties

The client will:

- provide the architect with all the information necessary to enable the appropriate design to be prepared

- employ a contractor under a separate agreement to undertake building or other works

- hold the contractor (and not the architect) responsible for the supervision of construction work, for the operational methods, techniques, sequence of procedures and safety precautions, for the proper execution and completion on time of the building work, for any design work the contractor undertakes, and for the remedying of defects in accordance with the terms of his contract with the client

- not engage anybody to do any work on the project unless the architect so agrees, as this may have implications for the building contract

- make a separate appointment for Project Supervisor (Design Stage) and Project Supervision (Construction Stage).

4   Consultants, subcontractors and suppliers

Specialist consultants, sub-contractors or suppliers may be appointed on the architect's recommendation in relation to specialist trades and/or goods or services forming part of the building works. Where such persons design part of the work, the client shall separately engage and pay those people and shall hold them solely responsible for the performance of their design.

5   Inspection of building work

During Work Stage 5 the architect will visit the site at intervals s/he considers appropriate to the stage of construction to inspect the progress and quality of the work and to determine that the work is being carried out generally in accordance with the contract documents. Frequent or constant inspection does not form part of the standard services at [A]. It is the contractors responsibility to supervise the building work.

6   Charges and costs incurred

Percentage charges are calculated on the VAT exclusive value of the building, including fitting-out and loose furniture work with which the architect is involved. Before tenders are obtained, that value is the architect's estimate of cost. After tenders are obtained, the value is the tender(s) recommended to the client. After building work is done, the value is the final account(s) for the work.

Where no building contract is to be entered into, the costs of the work will be calculated using the RIAI Cost Data Base figures for such work. Where costs cannot be agreed at Stage 1, the RIAI cost Data figures shall be used.

Time charges are based on hourly rates for principals and other professional and technical staff. The architect will keep records of time spent on any services performed on a time charge basis, and make such records available to the client on reasonable request.

The estimates of costs which will be incurred at [C] are provisional and subject to recalculation on the basis of the actual cost. Where the architect is being reimbursed for costs incurred, s/he will maintain records of all such costs, and make such records available to the client on reasonable request.

Invoices are to be paid no later than 29 days after they are received by the client. The architect will not start work on a Work Stage until any invoices for work on previous Work Stages have been paid in full.

Where the amount shown as due on any charges/expenses accounts has not been paid in full within one calendar month of the date of the relevant account, the client will be liable for interest thereon at the current AA overdraft rate calculated monthly from one month after the account date.

7 Omitted work and Changes

The architect will be entitled to charge in accordance with [B] for work done to Work Stage 4 in respect of all work included in the tender or estimated cost which the client subsequently omits from the project, and to charge at hourly rates for any changes at the client's request of designs which the client has previously approved.

8 Architect's Liability

The architect's liability shall extend:

- to a term of six years beginning on (a) the architect's issue of the Certificate of Practical Completion under the building contract, (b) the conclusion of the service or (c) the termination of the commission as the circumstances dictate, and the architect's liability shall terminate as soon as any one of these terms has expired, and

- to the cost of making good any construction defects which are established as being caused by the architect's negligence or breach of contract, but not to the cost of making good any loss consequential on such defects.

9 Copyright

Copyright in all drawings and documents prepared by the architect and in any work carried out from those documents shall remain the architect's property. The architect grants the client a licence to use, for this project only, the designs which the client has commissioned, provided that the charges to the appropriate Work Stage have been paid by the client.

10 Suspension and termination

The client may suspend the architect's performance of any or all of the agreed services, and either party may terminate the architect's appointment, on the expiry of reasonable notice given in writing.

11 Disputes

The client and the architect agree to seek to amicably resolve any disputes of misunderstandings between them. They note the informal mediation services which the RIAI may provide in this regard.

Any dispute as to the proper interpretation of this document may, by agreement between the client and the architect, be referred to the President of the RIAI or to the President's nominee for a ruling, provided that such a ruling is sought on a joint statement of undisputed facts and the parties undertake to accept the ruling as final and binding.

Any dispute relating to any of the provisions of this agreement may be referred to conciliation in accordance with the conciliation procedures published by the RIAI. If a settlement of the dispute is not reached under the conciliation procedures either party may refer the dispute to arbitration. These procedures are described in the RIAI Building Contract Forms.

Any other dispute, provided that notice of such dispute shall have been referred by either party to the other in writing, shall be referred to the arbitration and final decision of such person as the parties may agree to appoint as Arbitrator, or failing agreement within 14 days of a request in writing by one party to the other to concur in the appointment of an Arbitrator, by a person to be nominated by the President of the RIAI on the application of either party. The award of such arbitration shall be final and binding on the parties. Every such reference shall be deemed to be a submission to Arbitration within the meaning of the Arbitration Acts 1954/1998 or the Arbitration (Northern Ireland) Act 1957 or any Act amending the same or either of them.

(Insert any agreed amendments to the Terms and Conditions:) ....
....
....

1.7   Cases Referred To   *par.*

Edwin Hill v Leakcliffe [1984] 29 BLR 43	1.3
Frank Dunne v Dublin County Council [1974] IR 45	1.3
Inspector of Taxes v Kiernan [1982] ILRM 13	1.3
Laurentiu v Minister for Justice [2000] 1 ILRM 1	1.3
Liverpool Borough Bank v Turner [1851] 30 Lj Cr 379	1.3
Meagher v Minister for Agriculture [1994] ILRM 1	1.4
Molloy v Dublin Corporation [1990] ILRM 13	1.3
Monaghan UDC v Alf-A-Bet Promotions [1980] ILRM 64	1.3
Thomas v Hammersmith Borough Council [1938] 2 AER 203	1.3
XJS Investments v Dun Laoghaire Corporation [1987] ILRM 659	1.3

Chapter 2 – **Planning**

2.1 The Law

2.1.1 Background

Planning in Ireland can be said to have commenced on the first day of October 1964. That was the day which brought into effect most of the provisions of the Local Government (Planning and Development) Act 1963 which was referred to in the subsequent planning legislation up until now as the 'Principal Act'.

Before 1964 there was no effective planning control. Private developments very often had restrictive covenants in leases which would have acted as a form of localised planning control. The Pembroke Estate in Dublin would be a good example of this type of control. The Dublin Corporation Act 1890 was ahead of its time in dealing with the height of buildings, limiting the height to the equivalent of the width of the street onto which they faced. A next step in the direction of planning control was the Dublin Reconstruction Acts of 1916 and 1924 which gave the City Architect control of rebuilding after the damage caused by the 1916 Rising and the Civil War. Earlier in Britain the subject had been addressed in the Housing, Town Planning, etc, Acts of 1909 and 1919 and then in a series of pre-war enactments which set the basis of the present arrangements. The first such attempt to legislate for planning in Ireland was the Town and Regional Planning Act of 1934 and the Town and Regional Planning (Amendment) Act 1939. They were peculiar pieces of legislation in that it was up to each local authority to decide for itself whether or not the provisions of the Act would be adopted in the area. While a number of local authorities did decide to adopt the provisions of the Act, by 1952 no single planning scheme had been produced and it was only as a result of a case taken by a builder (*The State {Modern Homes (Ireland)} Ltd v Dublin Corporation* [1953] IR 202) that Dublin Corporation eventually produced the first plan under the Act. This plan, which had been initiated by the appointment of Sir Patrick Abercrombie as consultant to the Corporation, was never approved by the Minister for Local Government (as was required by the 1934 Act), and was eventually overtaken by the introduction of the 1963 Act.

The details of the 1934 Act in some ways foreshadowed the later Acts, with its provisions for 'general' and 'special' permissions which roughly equated to 'outline' and 'permission' in the Act. It is interesting to note that the expression 'full permission' does not appear in any of the legislation; the correct expression is merely 'permission'. There were virtually no sanctions in the 1934 Act with regard to enforcement and, generally speaking, not much importance was attached to the subject.

It was evident, however, by 1963 that large scale development was not far off in urban areas of Ireland, and Dublin in particular was seen as very susceptible to large-scale rebuilding. To this end the 1963 Act is described as 'An Act to make provision, in the interests of the common good, for the proper planning and development of cities, towns and other areas, whether urban or rural (including the preservation and improvement of the amenities thereof)...' While primarily concerned with planning, this Act mentions, for the first time, the subject of Building Regulations and gives the Minister power to make such Regulations. It was to be another twenty-eight years before any Regulations were actually made.

The 1963 Act was followed by a considerable number of new, or amending, Acts and by an equally impressive number of Statutory Instruments, nearly all of which were consolidated into a single Statutory Instrument in 1994. All of this legislation, totalling nine acts, was repealed by the Planning and Development Act 2000 (generally referred to in this book as the 2000 Act or simply the Act) which came fully into force on the 11th March 2002, with the exception of Section 281 dealing with the control of quarries and Section 239 relating to funfairs. It is believed that regulations are being drafted to bring these sections into effect. The only sections of previous acts remaining from the old legislation are Section 6 of the1982 Act dealing with the validity of pre 1977 appeal permissions and Section 4 of the 1993 Act which retrospectively validated all state building carried out before 15th June 1993.

All previous statutory instruments issued before the introduction of the 2000 Act have been revoked and replaced by S.I. 600 of 2001 (generally referred to in this book as the 2001 regulations) which introduces new articles and generally revises and consolidates all previous and relevant instruments. Life for practitioners became much simpler on the 11th March 2002 with, generally speaking, just one Act, the 2000 Act and one Statutory Instrument, 600 of 2001 to be consulted. It should be noted that S.I. 1 of 2001, which revoked S.I. 193 of 1998, dealing with retail shopping areas, is still valid, and that since 11th March 2002, two new statutory instruments, S.I. 70 of 2002 dealing with the scale of maps submitted with a planning application and S.I. 149 of 2002 dealing with advertisement fees have been published.

For further reading consult IRISH PLANNING LAW AND PRACTICE by O'Sullivan and Shepherd published by Butterworths and IRISH PLANNING LAW AND PROCEDURE by Eamon Galligan published by Sweet & Maxwell / Round Hall Press. Also recommended is the recently published KEY ISSUES IN PLANNING AND ENVIRONMENTAL LAW by John Gore-Grimes (Butterworths). Although weighted in the direction of legal practice, it is simply set out for reference purposes.

2.1.2 **Statutes**

The Planning and Development Act 2000.

2.1.3 **European Directives**

79/409/EEC	The Birds Directive
85/337/EEC	Environmental Impact (amended by 97/11/EC)
92/43/EEC	Natural Habitats (amended by 97/62/EC)
96/82/EC	Major Accident Hazards

2.1.4 **Statutory Instruments**

S.I. 59 of 1990	Special Amenity Area Order – Liffey Valley
S.I. 70 of 1995	Special Amenity Area Order – North Bull Island
S.I. 133 of 2000	Special Amenity Area Order – Howth
S.I. 1 of 2001	Retail Shopping (revoking S.I. 193 of 1998)
S.I. 272 of 2001	Strategic Development Zone – Adamstown, Lucan
S.I. 273 of 2001	Strategic Development Zone – Hansfield, Blanchardstown
S.I. 274 of 2001	Strategic Development Zone – Clonmaggadon Valley, Navan
S.I. 525 of 2001	Fees changed from Irish Pounds to Euros
S.I. 600 of 2001	The Planning Regulations
S.I. 70 of 2002	Scales of Site Maps, etc
S.I. 149 of 2002	Advertisement Fees

2.1.5 **Previous Acts and Regulations**

Because previous Acts and Regulations might be referred to in older planning decisions or Court cases, a full list of all these issued between 1963 and 2001 is given below:

a)   Previous Planning Acts

The nine acts which were repealed by the 2000 Act were all described as Local Government (Planning and Development) Acts. In this book, for simplicity, they are referred to as the 1963 Act, the 1976 Act, etc. A considerable number of the provisions of the 2000 Act is based on previous provisions contained in these revoked acts.

1963 – Known previously as the 'Principal' Act and the basis of most previous planning legislation.

1976 – This Act set up An Bord Pleanála. Previously the Minister has absolute discretion regarding appeals and it was felt that such important decisions should be more independently decided.

1982 – Until this Act there were no fees for planning applications. Time limits on the validity of permissions were introduced.

1983 – The independence of An Bord Pleanála was further strengthened under this Act.

1990 – Case law had complicated the administration of the compensation provisions set out in the 1963 Act, and this Act was an attempt to regularise the position.

1992 – This Act amended the appeals procedure and altered penalties

1993 – When the Supreme Court decided that State projects needed planning permission, some tidying up was required and this Act provides it (see par. 2.2.5).

1998 – This short Act dealt mainly with the recomposition of An Bord Pleanála

1999 – This Act dealt with protected structures and heritage generally and was incorporated in its entirety into the 2000 Act.

b) **1963 to 1977 Regulations** (Commencement Orders not listed)

S.I. 216 of 1964   Appeals and References
S.I. 217 of 1964   Compensation
S.I. 219 of 1964   Prescribed Documents and Authorities
S.I. 221 of 1964   Permission
S.I. 236 of 1964   Exempted Development
S.I. 76 of 1965   Licensing
S.I. 72 of 1966   Licensing
S.I. 154 of 1967   Development Plans
S.I. 176 of 1967   Exempted Development
S.I. 230 of 1967   Prescribed Documents and Authorities
S.I. 210 of 1968   Licensing
S.I. 260 of 1968   Exempted Development
S.I. 219 of 1976   Exempted Development
S.I. 226 of 1976   Section 25
S.I. 65 of 1977   (this Statutory Instrument revoked all previous ones)

c) **1977 to 1994 Regulations** (Commencement Orders not listed)

S.I. 231 of 1980   Fees for Licenses
S.I. 154 of 1981   Exempted Development
S.I. 264 of 1982   Policy Directive
S.I. 342 of 1982   Duration of Permissions
S.I. 285 of 1983   An Bord Pleanála
S.I. 403 of 1983   Exempted Development
S.I. 348 of 1984   Exempted Development
S.I. 358 of 1984   Fees

S.I. 130 of 1985	Exempted Development
S.I. 287 of 1987	Bord Gais Éireann
S.I. 317 of 1988	Policy Directive
S.I. 338 of 1989	Fees
S.I. 25 of 1990	Environmental Impact Statements
S.I. 144 of 1990	Compensation
S.I. 187 of 1991	Fees
S.I. 3 of 1992	Fees
S.I. 209 of 1992	Environmental Impact Statements
S.I. 222 of 1992	An Bord Pleanála
S.I. 343 of 1993	An Bord Pleanála
S.I. 349 of 1993	Fees
S.I. 402 of 1993	EIA in Dublin Counties
S.I. 86 of 1994	(this Statutory Instrument revoked all previous ones except S.I. 264 of 1982, S.I. 317 of 1988 and S.I. 243 of 1993)

d) 1994 to 2001 Regulations

S.I. 69 of 1995	Exempted Development
S.I. 75 of 1995	Availability of Bord Pleanála Documents
S.I. 100 of 1996	EIS Forestry Thresholds Reduced
S.I. 101 of 1996	(similar to S.I. 100 above when dealing with the EPA Act 1992)
S.I. 78 of 1997	Exempted Development
S.I. 121 of 1997	Notifiable Bodies
S.I. 261 of 1997	Waste Management Act 1996

In addition to the Statutory Instruments which deal with the planning process, there are three further Instruments which would concern only the practicing lawyer. They are S.I. 149 of 1970, titled The Circuit Court Rules (No. 1) 1970 and S.I. 190 of 1982, the Circuit Court Rules (No. 4) 1982, both of which deal with the procedures and forms relevant to legal actions being taken under the 1963 and 1976 Acts. The third instrument, S.I. 215 of 1995 (Circuit Court Rules No. 1) introduces new rules to deal with the availability of the Circuit Court for actions involving Section 27 (as amended) of the 1976 Act.

Finally, mention should be made of S.I. 349 of 1989 and S.I. 84 of 1994 which were issued by the Minister under powers which derive from the European Communities Act 1972. They dealt with the requirements for environmental impact assessment, and have now been incorporated into S.I. 600 of 2001.

2.1.6 **Summary**

This completes the Acts and Statutory Instruments which combine to form the law of planning. The entire corpus of legislation is collectively referred to as the Planning and Development Act 2000 and the Planning and Development Regulations 2001.

2.2 **When is Permission Required?**

2.2.1 **Development**

Permission is required for development. That simple statement needs a very considerable amount of explanation. The Act defines development as 'the carrying out of any works on, in, over, or under land or the making of any material change in the use of any structures or other land'. The insertion of the word 'over' is new in the 2000 Act. The Act, and subsequent Regulations then go on to say what development is exempt from the requirements of the Act. Exemption as it affects building works, and as it affects changes of use, is dealt with at 2.2.2 and 2.2.3 of this section.

It is important to remember that a project might incorporate works that might be exempt, and a material change of use that would not. Similarly, certain changes of use would be exempt but the accompanying works would not be.

The Act at Section 3(3) also makes it clear that sub-dividing a single dwelling is development, even though no external works might be carried out, and the use is not being altered. There are still areas of doubt even though that particular sub-section starts with the words 'For the avoidance of doubt'. In *Ealing Borough Council v Ryan* [1965] 1 137 QBD the comment was made: 'Multiple occupation, as it is sometimes called, is not enough in itself to bring the subsection into play. The dwelling house and houses formed out of the building previously used as a single dwelling house must in truth be separate. In many cases of which the present case is an example, the question whether there has been a change of use within the ambit of the subsection is one of fact and degree. The existence or absence of any form of physical reconstruction is a relevant fact; another is the extent to which the alleged separate dwellings can be regarded as separate in the sense of being self-contained and independent of other parts of the same property.' The sub-section of the UK Act of 1962 was in effect similar to sub-section 3(3) of the Act.

It must be remembered that a site, or premises, can simultaneously enjoy a number of different permissions. It would be possible, for instance, for a city centre site to have separate permissions for office, residential or shopping uses, subject to the time limitations set out in the Act. When any one permission has been implemented the others will naturally run out of validity in time. Similarly a number of permissions for differing uses in an existing premises can exist at the same time. A fundamental feature of the planning system is that the permission is attached to the land, not to the applicant or owner, and transfers automatically on any sale of the property.

2.2.2 Exempted Development – Works

Development, therefore, is either works or a change of use, and requires permission unless it is exempt. It is necessary now to examine the exempted development provisions of the Acts and Regulations, but before dealing with exempted development it is necessary to define 'works'. The Act defines 'works' as being 'any act or operation of construction, excavation, demolition, extension, alteration, repair or renewal'. The new Act, it should be noted, has added 'the replacement of a door, window or roof' to the definition of alterations. The definition also now contains a new phrase, i.e. 'and, in relation to a protected structure or proposed protected structure includes any act or operation involving the application or removal of plaster, paint, wallpaper, tiles or other material to or from the surfaces of the interior or exterior of a structure'. This latter provision is very draconian and is dealt with in par. 2.3.2 dealing with protected structures. The definition is very comprehensive and it can be seen that almost every building operation would be so covered. An architect should assume that permission is required unless the proposed works are clearly exempted development.

It should be noted, however, that even if an architect makes an application for permission where the proposed works are, in fact, exempt, the exempted status is not endangered (*Westmeath County Council v Moriarty* [1991] High Court, 30th July. This decision differs from the view taken in the Tallaght Block case (*Dublin County Council v Tallaght Block Company* [1983] Supreme Court, 17th May) where the Court took the view that in an application for permission for retention of a structure, it cannot be subsequently argued that the development was exempt. As the *Westmeath* case is later, it can be taken generally to apply.

There have been some confusing signals from the Courts as to the interpretation of the exempted development regulations, but the Supreme Court held in *Dillon v Irish Cement Ltd* [1986] 26th November that Regulations conferring exemptions 'should be strictly construed in the sense that for a developer to put himself within them he must be clearly and unambiguously within them in regard to what he proposes to do'.

Exempted development is, obviously, a key area as far as the practicing architect is concerned. There are two separate places in the Act and regulations where exempted development is defined. One is Section 4 of the Act, and the other is in S.I. 600 of 2001 issued under the powers granted to the Minister by virtue of Section 262 of the Act. Care must be taken to ensure that the overall restrictions concerning exempted development, as contained in Article 9 of S.I. 600 of 2001, do not affect the proposal in question. A non-exhaustive list of these restrictions includes the contravention of a condition, interference with the character of a landscape in a preservation area, the interference with archeological items, works to an unauthorised structure, works in an architectural conservation area or a special amenity area order and finally, if the works would either require an environmental impact statement or would be affected by a 'major accident hazard' (par. 2.3.4 for details of this last item).

Some significant changes have been made with regard to exempted development in the 2000 Act and these would include the training of horses and the rearing of livestock in the definition of 'agriculture' making these two activities exempt, and the removal of turbary (turf cutting, etc) and forestry from exempt status. The general maintenance of forestry is still exempt. The further restrictions on turbary and afforestation were introduced as a result of a case taken by the European Commission (Case C-392/96 *Commission v Ireland* [1993] 3 CMLR 727) which decided that Ireland had not properly transposed the 1985 EIA Directive (85/337) into Irish law.

The majority of buildings constructed in connection with agriculture are exempt, and the details are given in the Second Schedule, Part 111: Exempted development – Rural of S.I. 600 of 2001. Buildings for housing cattle, donkeys, sheep, horses etc, generally are exempted up to an overall size of 200 square metres, subject to restrictions listed in the schedule, such for instance being limited to an aggregate exemption limit of 300 square metres, being a certain distance from a public road etc. The aggregate limit of 300 square metres is increased to 900 square metres in the case of barns etc, not used for housing animals. Buildings for housing pigs, mink or poultry are only exempt up to 75 square metres and are subject to a number of conditions.

Golf courses and burial grounds are not exempt. Bord Pleanála, in a Section 5 reference (21.RF.0776) held that the provision of halting sites, where they conform to zoning provisions, was exempted development under Section 4(1)(b) of the 1963 Act, Article 130 of S.I. 86 of 1994 and section 13 of the Housing Act 1998. Section 4(1)(b) of the 1963 Act exempted development by a county council or a corporation in its functional area. This is repeated in the same section of the 2000 Act. The position is still the same although if any development costs more than 126,000 it is not exempt. Par. 2.2.5 deals with this latter subject in more detail.

Exempted development affecting works as defined in the Act (as opposed to the

Regulations) does not affect the architect to any great extent except for one sub-section. Section 4 says, broadly, that the use of land for agriculture, development by a local authority, or development for land reclamation is exempt. As mentioned above afforestation was hitherto exempted development, but is no longer so. A new sub-section 4(1)(i) exempts the thinning, felling and replanting of trees, forests and woodlands, but does not include the replacement of broadleaf high forest by conifer species. Trees generally are dealt with by Section 205 of the Act, where a planning authority may issue orders relating to the preservation and management of trees and woodlands. The section also deals with the details of the orders and matters relating to them. Trees are also protected by the Forestry Act 1946. The basic provision affecting development is that the Garda Síochána must be notified if it is intended to cut down a tree which is more than ten years old. There are a large number of exemptions, the most significant one being that the requirement does not exist in an urban area. It must be remembered, however, that this exemption is of no benefit where the tree or trees are scheduled in a development plan.

The sub-section mentioned above as most affecting the architect was one of the most familiar sections of the old 1963 Act was Section 4(1)(g). This has now become 4(1)(h) but the wording is identical. It must be particularly noted that the sub-section is now restricted by Section 57 of the Act which says that the exemption will not apply to protected structures, or proposed protected structures, where the works proposed would materially affect the character of the structure or any special elements. The unchanged section is worth quoting in full: 'Development consisting of the carrying out of works for the maintenance, improvement, or other alteration of any structure, being works which affect only the interior of the structure or which do not materially affect the external appearance of the structure so as to render such appearance inconsistent with the character of the structure or of neighbouring structures' shall be exempted development.

This, in my view, allows considerable scope. It is important to note that the external appearance of the building may be altered materially, provided that the alteration does not result in the new appearance of the building being inconsistent with the original character of the building, or perhaps more interestingly, not being inconsistent with the character of neighbouring buildings. This interpretation is upheld in a Bord Pleanála reference under Section 5 of the 1963 Act (065.RF.1022). The Supreme Court has held (*Cairnduff v O'Connell* [1986] ILRM 465) that building a first floor balcony and staircase, and opening a new window, in a terraced house was exempted development. The Court held in the *Cairnduff* case that the character of a structure related to the shape, colour, design, ornamental features and lay-out of the structure concerned. It is a matter of considerable irritation to practitioners that planning authorities and An Bord Pleanála consistently interpret this sub-section very narrowly. As an example, the provision of an obscured bathroom window in the side wall of a dormer bungalow in a Dublin suburb was held to be development in a Section 5 reference (06 DRF 0827). These works were very much less significant than those approved of by the Supreme Court in *Cairnduff*. Architects should examine this particular section of the Act when minor alterations are being planned. In my view, architects do not avail sufficiently of the scope given by this judgement. After all, as mentioned before, *De minimus lex non curat* – the law does not concern itself with trifles.

A decision by An Bord Pleanála under Section 5 of the Act to the effect that changing timber sash windows to aluminium windows is development seems to fly in the face of both the *De minimus* rule and of the Supreme Court judgement in *Cairnduff*, even though the building in question was in a sensitive area (see 2.2.4 for a review of decisions by the Board under Section 5 of the Act). In taking this decision the Board seems to be following the view of most planning authorities that everything requires planning permission unless the contrary can be shown. Experience indicates that almost any planning authority will recommend that a permission is required even in the most trivial of proposals, but this was clearly not the intention of the Act. On the other hand, the Board has held that rendering external walls, demolishing an annex, adding a front window and two Velux roof lights to a house does come within the scope of the old Section 4(1)(g) and thereby supports the *Cairnduff* view. An extraordinary decision made by a planning authority in imposing a condition covering the interior layout behind a shop front for a distance of 6 metres was clearly *ultra vires*, and has been thrown out by An Bord Pleanála as a result of an appeal.

A number of decisions by the Board have established, under Section 5 references, that alterations made during construction, even where the changes would be exempt in a completed building, are not exempt where the planning permission contains a condition requiring the development to be built in accordance with the lodged drawings. Some of these, i.e. ref. 24 RF 0859 dealt with window alterations and 58 RF 0836 with the installation of Velux lights. Planning authorities should be encouraged to drop this condition as the resulting situation is farcical. It is significant to note that this narrow and illogical view was not followed by the Supreme Court in *Smyth v Colgan* [1998] Supreme Court, 15th July, where one of the judges said: 'Undoubtedly, if a developer before selling the houses for which he has planning permission decides to carry out a further development for which he has no permission, he appears prima facie to be contravening something for which he has no permission. However, the regulations do not say who may carry out an exempted development ... So long as it is an extension which comes within the exempted development regulations, I can see no reason why it should not be permitted merely because no one has yet lived in the house. *It does not break the planning code* [author's italics]. What is done could lawfully be done at any time after the purchaser had gone into occupation.' If planning authorities, and the Board, took the same relaxed view, as they should in law, there would be less of a workload on architects and on them.

Some planning authorities take the view that internal alterations to a shopping centre, even when they do not intensify the use, are not exempt. An Bord Pleanála in a Section 5 reference (29N.RF.0756) has upheld this view. In the author's opinion they are both wrong.

The exempted works in the Regulations are in addition to those contained in Section 4 of the Act. They are set out in Part I of the Second Schedule of S.I. 600 of 2001.Those which most affect the architect would be:

1   The vexed question of exempted extensions was addressed in S.I. 181 of 2000, eventually revoked and replaced by the provisions set out in S.I. 600 of 2001 in the Second Schedule, Part I. The basic size limit of an extension has been increased from 23 to 40 square metres where the house has never been previously extended. The restriction on retaining 25 square metres of open space to the rear of the house is unchanged. The floor area at first floor in any extension shall not exceed 12 square metres in a terraced or semi-detached house, or 20 square metres in a detached house. The difficulty raised by previous extensions has to some extent been addressed. Any previous extension, whether with or without permission, must be included in any aggregate which may not exceed 40 square metres. The first floor areas of 12 square metres and 20 square metres are similarly controlled as far as aggregates are concerned. There are also minimum distances for windows from boundaries and it is prohibited to use the roof of any extension for a balcony or roof garden without obtaining permission. It is submitted that it is safe to assume from the wording of the regulations that any extension completed before 1st October 1964, with or without permission, is not to be included in any calculation. It is clear from the regulations, which refer only to an extension or to the conversion of a garage, store, etc, that attic conversions are exempt and do not count in any aggregate of area. However, beware of the Velux problem – see 6 in this list.

A conservatory extension would be included in the 40 square metre limit but a greenhouse would not. This immediately raises the question as to what is the difference between a conservatory and a greenhouse. It is possible that habitability and maybe attachment to the house would be a clue. A recent Section 5 reference to the Board (ref: 06D. RF. 0800) decided that a building described as a greenhouse was in effect a conservatory and in this case the structure was attached to the house.

The Regulations also limit the size of any greenhouse, store, garage etc, so that taken with any other such structures of a similar sort previously erected, the aggregate area shall not exceed 25 square metres. There had been an anomaly in the previous Regulations which placed no size restriction on garages leading in certain cases to some rather odd developments. This 25 square metre restriction is not aggregated to any extension covered by the 40 square metre limit. Caravans or boats can be kept or stored at a house, but limited to one caravan or boat.

2   The conversion of a garage into a habitable room, where the garage is attached to the house, and is either at the side or at the rear of the house, is exempt. The limit of 40 square metres referred to above still applies.

3   The addition of a porch of not more than 2 square metres is exempt. In this case the general prohibition of not infringing the building line has been waived provided that a distance of 2 metres is retained between the house and any road.

4   Some confusion can arise between Class 5 and Class 9 of the Exempted Development Regulations. Class 5 deals with gates, railings, walls, etc, 'within or bounding the curtilage of a house', that is attached to or around the house, and Class 9 deals with the same items 'other than within or bounding the curtilage', that is walls around separate outbuildings and the like. The word 'curtilage' is causing many problems, particularly in relation to pro-tected structures (see par. 2.3.2).

5   The erection of a TV or wireless aerial, but only on a dwelling house, is exempt. The regulations also allow the erection of a satellite TV dish, but in both cases, if the house is a protected structure, or a proposed protected struc-ture, the aerial or dish would have to comply with the restrictions in Section 57 of the Act.

6   It is regrettable that the thorny problem of Velux-type lights was not addressed in the new legislation. It is a source of on-going frustration to own-ers and architects and, it is submitted must be a source of unnecessary work to planning officials to have to deal with matters of such planning irrele-vance. Decisions of the Board on the matter only add to the general air of fog and confusion. The lack of any consistent approach makes it impossible for a practitioner to give satisfactory advice to clients. The writer's view is that such lights should almost invariably be permitted under Section 4(1)(h) of the Act. They were, for example, allowed in a Section 5 reference (06D.RF.1041) to the Board, but it would be very useful if the reasons behind such decisions were given.

7   It is often asked if re-plastering or re-painting is exempt, and the answer is, generally, yes, except in any case where a plastering or painting scheme was being proposed that would make the building in question stand out in a noticeable way. Bord Pleanála, in a reference to it under Section 5 of the 1963 Act, decided that a mural painted on to the gable wall of a hotel was not

exempted development (see 2.2.4 for details of Section 5 of the 2000 Act) but that the straightforward plastering of a brick facade was exempt.

8   Advertisements generally are exempt. These Regulations are quite complex and now embrace eighteen different classes (Part II – Second Schedule – S.I. 600 of 2000). The Regulations allow a total area of advertisements on business premises to be exempt up to a maximum of 5 square metres. Only one 'For Sale/To Let' sign will be allowed on any property in the absence of a specific planning permission for signage.

9   Use of a house for 'bed and breakfast' purposes up to a limit of four bedrooms will be exempt provided there is no planning permission condition restricting such a use and also provided that each bedroom is limited to 4 persons.

10   A new provision in the 2001 regulations is the exemption where a house is used for childminding, provided that the number of children, including the minders own children, does not exceed six.

11   Normally, demolition is exempt, but demolition of a habitable house, a building which forms part of a terrace, or which adjoins another building in separate ownership is not exempt. In this regard there is a curious judgement reported in the ARCHITECTS' JOURNAL of 13th March 1997. (There was no legal reference given.) The House of Lords ruled in a dispute between a developer and Westminster City Council that, even in the case of a listed building, demolition means the demolition of the entire building. In the case in question, the front wall and most of the interior was demolished. This could not happen in this jurisdiction under the provisions of the 2000 Act.

12   The use of land for a golf course or as a burial ground will no longer be exempted development.

13   The exemptions dealing with masts and antennae are set out in Class 31 of the Second Schedule (Part 1) of S.I. 600 of 2001. It would be prudent to obtain specialist advice when dealing with this complex subject. Basically, the original exemption of antennae support structures has been removed. In its place the attachment of additional antennae to existing antennae support structures, or the replacement of existing antennae support structures, or the provision of high capacity transmission links to existing high capacity antennae support structures are all now exempt but subject to a number of restrictions. The attachment of antennae to existing buildings, poles, pylons, etc, is also exempt. The conditions and restrictions are set out in Class 31 of Part I of the Second Schedule to S.I. 600 of 2001.

2.2.3 Exempted Development – Use

i) Change of use

A material change of use as mentioned in Section 3 of the Act would seem to be, at first sight, a simple concept but there are some pitfalls. There must be a change of use, and the change must be material.

The Courts have looked at the meaning of 'material' in a number of cases, and have decided that the material aspect of the change of use must be tied to planning considerations. In *Galway County Council v Lackagh Rock Ltd* [1985] High Court, 22nd May, it was observed: 'To test whether or not the uses are materially different it seems to me that what should be looked at are matters which the planning authority would take into account in the event of a planning application being made both for the use on the appointed day and for the present use. If these matters are materially different, then the nature of the use must equally be materially different.' In *Monaghan County Council v Brogan* [1986] High Court, 26th November, the Court held that 'material in this context means material for planning purposes'. These two cases differed on other aspects of the law, but these are not relevant at this particular point. The changes which must occur to cause a material change of use must be physical. For instance a change in the ownership of a business is not material, neither are trivial changes.

ii) Specified uses as development

Certain uses are specified in the Act as being development, and these are:

a) where advertisements are exhibited. (but see previous page, item 8)

b) where vans, tents, etc, are used for caravanning, camping, or for the sale of goods

c) the storage of caravans or tents

d) the deposit of car parts or bodies, industrial waste, builders' rubble, etc (but see par. 3.4 on waste disposal)

e) the sub-division of a dwelling.

iii) Changes of use which are exempt

Then there is the question of changes of use which are exempt. The first group are set out in the Regulations (S.I. 600 of 2001 – Second Schedule – part 1 – class 14) and are:

a) from use for the sale of hot food for consumption off the premises, or for the sale or leasing or display of motor vehicles, to a shop

b) from use as a public house to use as a shop

c) from use for the direction of funerals, as a funeral home, as an amusement arcade or a restaurant, to a shop

d) from use to which class 2 of Part IV of the Schedule applies (this generally covers financial, professional or other services provided principally to visiting members of the public) to use as a shop

e) from use as two or more dwellings to use as a single dwelling of any structure previously used as a single dwelling

f) from use as a dwelling house to use as a residence for up to six persons with an intellectual or physical disability and for two persons providing care for such persons.

The second category of changes of use which are exempt are the changes which might occur within the classes of use listed in Part IV of the Second Schedule to the Regulations. Changes of use within these classes are exempt by the provisions of Article 10 of the Regulations. It should be noted that this exemption would not exclude any building works that would otherwise need permission. Neither would the change be exempt if a condition on a previous permission imposed any restriction. The question of differing uses within a single industrial complex, and the matter of ancillary uses is also addressed in Article 10. The Regulations clarify the fact that an ancillary use is not excluded merely because it is specified in the Schedule. However, certain uses which might have been considered as ancillary uses in certain cases have been specifically excluded and will of themselves require permission. They are listed as:

- an amusement arcade
- a motor service station
- the sale or leasing of motor vehicles
- car hire or a taxi business
- a scrap yard
- the storage or distribution of minerals
- a supermarket exceeding 3,500 square metres in Dublin or 3,000 square metres elsewhere
- a retail warehouse exceeding 6,000 square metres
- a shop associated with a petrol station where the net retail area exceeds 100 square metres.

Some further comments on ancillary uses are given in the sub-heading 'Partial Change of Use' in this chapter.

The definitions of the various classes of use are contained in Article 5 of the Regulations. This list is somewhat incomplete, particularly in regard to developments in the area of certain residential concepts. A more complete list would relieve An Bord Pleanála of a number of references to it under Section 5 of the Act from proposers who find difficulty in interpreting the Regulations. The definitions contained in various development plans issued by planning authorities are obviously helpful in dealing with that particular local authority, but the statutory definitions are those contained in Article 5 and it is suggested that a common list which would apply to Statutory Instruments and development plans would be a useful addition to the Regulations. This list could also be used in relation to the Building Regulations (see par. 4.6). A selected list of definitions contained either in the Act or in the Regulations is given in par. 2.8.

iv) Partial change of use

It can be imagined that a change of use in part of a premises will lead to problems in trying to establish whether or not a material change of use has occurred so as to necessitate an application for permission under the Act. This brings in the concept of the planning 'unit', which has no agreed definition and therefore leads to some uncertainty. It has been said that it is a matter of common sense as to what is or is not a planning unit and the matter has been considered in some Irish cases. An attempt at a definition comes in *Burdle v Secretary of State for the Environment* [1972] 3 AER 24). The importance of the planning unit is that a material change of use only occurs when the planning unit is materially changed. The Burdle case considered three distinct possibilities: 1) if the occupier uses the land for one main purpose, then the entire premises is one unit. The case of *Carroll, Colley v Brushfield Ltd* [1992] High Court, 9th October, held that converting a hotel garage to a public bar was not a change of use as the planning unit, in this case the hotel, allowed for a wide variety of uses such as bars, restaurants, etc, 2) if the occupier carried on a number of different uses, the entire premises is still a single unit even if the uses have no connection with one another, 3) if the same occupier uses physically distinct premises for different purposes, separate planning units exist. This view was expanded in the case of *Dublin Corporation v Regan and Others* [1989] IR 61. At the High Court hearing it was stated: 'It may be a useful working guide to assume that the unit of occupation is the appropriate planning unit, unless and until some smaller unit can be recognised as the site of activities which amount in substance to a separate use both physically and functionally.' In the case in question, a wall of a premises was used for general advertising purposes which had no connection with the business being carried on inside the premises, and the Court held that the advertising was a separate planning unit.

The concept of a planning unit becomes relevant when considering the use of, say, one room in a house for professional purposes. If a professional uses a room for his own professional purposes, but does not invite clients to visit him there, or put up a plate, it is taken that no change of use has occurred.

But if the premises is clearly used as a professional base, for example, as a doctor's surgery, then a change of use has occurred and permission is necessary. An Bord Pleanála has held this view in a reference to it under Section 5 of the 1963 Act.

A premises can, obviously, be used for a primary purpose, and for one or more ancillary uses. In the *Dublin Corporation v Regan* case mentioned above, an original sign advertising the use of the premises was held to be ancillary, but advertising not connected with the use of the premises was held clearly to be a separate use, or planning unit. In *Williams v Minister for Housing and Local Government* [1967] 65 LGR 495, a separate shop building was used to sell produce from a nursery garden. When the shop began to sell goods not connected to the garden it was held that the ancillary connection was broken, and that permission was required for the new use. An ancillary use must obviously be connected to, and dependant on, the primary use in question.

Can two uses be carried on in respect of the same piece of land? This further complication as far as uses are concerned is discussed in *Mountcharles v Meath County Council* [1997] 1 ILRM 268. The case itself was an application by way of judicial review to quash a warning notice issued under Section 26 of the 1976 Act over the holding of open air concerts at Slane Castle. The application was refused for reasons not relevant to the principle here and the judgement of the court commented with approval from an English case which dealt with differing uses from time to time on the same land: 'The normal use of a piece of land is to be found by looking at its use from year to year over a considerable period. If you were to ask Mr. Webber (the owner): 'What do you normally use this field for?' he would reply 'In the summer months for camping and in the winter months for grazing.' In short, for two purposes. So long as he continues that normal use from year to year there is no material change of use. Similarly, when a shop keeper in a seaside town has a forecourt and during the summer he places stalls on it for selling goods but during the winter months he leaves it empty. The normal use of the forecourt is for two purposes, for access to the shop throughout the year and for trading during the summer months. So long as he continues that normal use from year to year there is no material change of use.' (*Webber v Ministry for Housing and Local Government* [1967] 3 AER 981).

In the case of *(Butler) The Irish Rugby Football Union v Dublin Corporation* [1999] 1 ILRM 481 the same problem arose, and it was eventually decided that no planning permission was required for occasional concerts at the Lansdowne Road ground. In the third edition of this book it was suggested that this type of problem could be solved by a licensing system separate from the planning acts. This has now been addressed in Part XVI of the 2000 Act where a system of such licenses is set out.

Events and funfairs are defined and licenses will be required for them. The events referred to will be generally along the lines of the concerts which led to the above mentioned court cases, and the funfairs referred to are the traditional mechanical amusements seen at carnivals and seaside fairgrounds. The local authority will be responsible for issuing the licenses and Section 231 goes into considerable detail as to the requirements. Most notably, however, is Section 240 which states that the holding of an event to which Part XVI applies shall not be 'development' for the purposes of the Act. There are detailed regulations covering every aspect of these events and they are contained in Articles 182 to 199 of the the 2001 regulations. These provisions have yet to come into force.

v) Intensification of use

A material change of use can occur when the use becomes sufficiently intensified. A number of cases have established that intensification has occurred when, firstly, the nature of the operations being carried out had altered somewhat, or secondly, the amount of the activity has increased significantly. In *Patterson v Murphy and Trading Services Ltd* [1978] ILRM 85, quarrying operations increased in both nature and quantity. In *Dublin County Council v Tallaght Block Company* [1983] Supreme Court, 17th May, a similar decision was reached. This case also dealt with the abandonment of a use. In a third case, *Monaghan County Council v Brogan* [1986] High Court, 26th November, the Court said it was satisfied that 'not merely has there been a significant increase in the amount of slaughtering going on, but that the object of the operation now is the supply of food for human consumption. It is also clear that the activity now being carried on is essentially a commercial operation in contrast to the relatively modest and intermittent slaughtering which went on prior to 1983.' The Court held that the resulting intensification was a material change of use.

In IRISH PLANNING LAW AND PRACTICE by O'Sullivan and Shepherd a chapter entitled 'A Practical Guide' is provided by Fergal McCabe and he suggests four useful questions which might be asked to establish whether or not an intensification has occurred. They are:

1　Has there been a change in the kind of products previously made, e.g. from manufacturing concrete blocks to making entire sections of prefabricated buildings?

2　Is the production method more intense by reference to an increase in the workforce or the introductions of more modern machinery?

3　Has there been an intensification in the output of the operation or the volume of customers attracted, e.g. has there been an increase in traffic with attendant parking problems and noise? An increase in the intensity of emissions from a factory would be another relevant factor.

4   Has the area of activity increased or differed? This is a common feature of quarrying operations.

The concept of intensification of use is not one which would normally affect the ordinary increase or development of a business or profession, and it is unlikely that the Courts will allow the doctrine of intensification to act as an inhibiting factor on the growth of economic activity.

vi) Resumption of an abandoned use

If a use of land has been abandoned, it will be necessary to apply for permission for a resumption of the use, as this is regarded as a material change of use. Whether or not the use was actually abandoned or merely suspended is a matter of fact to be decided by the circumstances. The intention of the owner of the land would be important. A comment by an English Court was adopted in the case of *Dublin County Council v Tallaght Block Company* [1983] Supreme Court, 17th May: 'When a previous use of land had not merely been suspended for a temporary and determined period, but had ceased for a considerable time with no evinced intention of resuming it at any particular time, the tribunal of fact was entitled to find that the previous use had been abandoned, so that when it was resumed the resumption constituted a material change of use.' In *Westmeath County Council v Michael F. Quirke* [1966] IPELJ 3 181, the Court held that the removal of plant from a quarry, and a lack of use for nine years, constituted the abandonment of a use.

When adopting the same attitude in *Meath County Council v Daly and Others* [1988] ILRM 274, the Court made the important distinction that a permission cannot be abandoned during the term of its validity by the conduct of the occupier. It is only a use that has been commenced and then abandoned that gives rise to the material change of use. The general principle of abandonment was upheld in the case of *Kildare County Council v Goode Concrete* [2000] 1 ILRM 346. Maintenance and upkeep of an unused premises would be seen as evidence of an intention to maintain the validity of the use. On the other hand, the removal of fixtures, fittings or machinery would normally be regarded as evidence of an intention to abandon the use.

If a use has been extinguished, normally in the case of a building destroyed by fire, a permission is required to resume the use. However, Section 193 of the 2000 Act provides that compensation will be paid where permission is refused to replace a building destroyed by fire or otherwise, or where a condition is imposed which restricts the original use, provided the application is made within two years of the building having been destroyed.

2.2.4 **Disputes as to Development**

The procedure regarding disputes as to whether some proposal is or is not exempted development has been radically altered under the 2000 Act. Previously the matter was referred directly to An Bord Pleanála but now the initial enquiry is to be made to the Planning Authority, who must reply within four weeks. There is a fee and a further information provision of three weeks. An applicant, on payment of another fee, may appeal any decision to the Board and may also apply to the Board for a decision if the Planning Authority does not reply within the specified time. Article 66(2) of S.I. 600 of 2001 requires the National Authority for Occupational Safety and Health to be informed where the development might be affected by the Major Accidents Directive (96/82/EC).

The original process under the 1963 Act has been under way now for almost 30 years, and it was a matter of considerable inconvenience to practitioners that no comprehensive list of decisions is available. Starting in 1986, the Board has listed in its annual report the Section 5 decisions of the year in question. Section 5 of the 2000 Act now requires Planning Authorities to enter any decisions regarding disputes on the register and Section 6 requires the Board to keep and make available a record of decisions. An important point to note is that each reference is taken on its own facts and no precedent can be taken to have been created unless the circumstances are almost identical. Some of the decisions most relevant to practitioners would be: (The Bord Pleanála reference is given so that the full decision can be examined. A fuller list is available in Chapter 10 of O'Sullivan and Shepherd's IRISH PLANNING LAW AND PRACTICE mentioned in par. 2.1.1.)

1   Subdividing a shop is not development (39/8/397)

2   A dormer extension is development (6/8/467). However, and generally speaking, the installation of Velux roof lights is not development. Neither is the conversion of an attic space to a bedroom (28.RF.0784). As pointed out above it must be again stated that each case is decided on its merits but, obviously, a previous Board decision is a weighty argument when a planning authority is seeking an application.

3   Providing two dormer windows to the front of a house is not exempt (Pl06D.RF.0999).

4   The use of townhouses as holiday homes on a commercial basis is development (29/8/479). This decision probably results from a condition that is often attached to residential permissions, prohibiting the use of houses as holiday homes. The intention seems to be to prevent a very frequent turnover of residents, but there are obvious difficulties in trying to draw a firm line between frequent changes of tenants in flats, and a possible more frequent change of holiday visitors. The Board decision resulted in a judicial review application to the High Court (*McMahon and Others v The Right Honorable the Lord*

Mayor, Aldermen and Burgesses of Dublin [1997] 1 ILRM 227). The Court refused to alter the Board's decision on the grounds that Section 28(6) of the 1963 Act provided that 'if no purpose is specified [in respect of development] the permission shall be construed as including permission to use the structure for the purpose for which it was designed.' Associated with this decision is PL 6/8/222 which decided that change of use from a private dwelling to use as a town house providing board and lodging is development and requires permission. Again this seems to be creating a grey area. What is the length of stay that constitutes a change of use? It is hardly contemplated that a decision to lease a house for a number of years to the same person is a change of use requiring permission. Some guidelines would be useful.

5   Changing timber sash windows to aluminium windows is development (29/8/561). Even though the house in question was listed, this decision seems to be bringing very minor and insignificant matters into the realm of planning control. It is difficult to see how these details can affect 'the proper planning and development of the area',

6   The rendering of external walls, demolition of a front annex, provision of an additional front window and two Velux roof lights at the rear of a house is exempted development. This decision was made under Section 4(1)(g) of the 1963 Act and accords with the *Cairnduff* decision referred to in par. 2.2.2. (PL295/RF/681).

7   The use of lands by a private flying club was held to be exempted development under Class 26(d) of Part 1 of the Third Schedule to the 1977 Regulations. The reference was made in July 1994 but the use had commenced before the issue of the 1994 Regulations (16th May 1994) and this exemption class does not now exist.

8   The use of part of a bar for dancing is development (24/8/40).

9   The use of land for a motor cycle scrambling event is exempted development (5/8/491) but the use of lands for hot-rod racing is not (28/8/517). The case of *MCD Management Services v Kildare County Council* [1995] 2 ILRM 532 held that the staging of a concert at Mondello racing circuit required permission and is dealt with more fully at par. 2.4.2. (Conditions).

10   The keeping of greyhounds is development (RF 3/8/558).

11   Internal changes in a shopping centre is development (29N.RN.0756) (see par. 2.2.2).

12   The spreading of topsoil is development. This must clearly relate to the magnitude of the operation and would presumably not apply to residential gardening operations. The proposal in question involved spreading soil along a riverbank.

13 The use of land for sports and for the provision of flood lighting is not exempt (11.RF.0878).

2.2.5 Development by the State and Local Authorities

In May 1993 the Supreme Court decided that the State, acting through the Office of Public Works, was subject to the provisions of the planning acts. Prior to that decision the State had taken the view that Section 84 of the 1963 Act was to be understood as meaning that the State was exempt from the provisions of the planning acts.

It had been long accepted, as a general rule of law, that the State was exempt from its own legislation unless a particular act specifically indicated that the State was to be included within the scope of that act. Section 84 referred to required the State 'to consult with the planning authority to such an extent as may be determined by the Minister'.

The cases before the Supreme Court (*Byrne and Others v the Commissioners of Public Works in Ireland* and *Howard and Others v the Commissioners of Public Works in Ireland* [1993] ILRM 665) were taken in relation to two particular developments, interpretative centres at Mullaghmore in Co Clare and at Lugalla in Co Wicklow, but the decision of the Supreme Court put in doubt the planning status of any building which had been constructed by the State since 1st October 1964 when the 1963 Act came into effect.

To regularise the position the 1993 Act was introduced. The main provisions were:

1 Permission would now be required for any development by the State or any State authority. A State authority is defined as either a Minister of the Government or the Commissioners of Public Works in Ireland.

2 Developments previously carried out by the State were deemed not to have required permission, and

3 The Minister may, by regulation, exempt buildings from the provisions of the Act for reasons of security, public safety, etc.

Section 181 of the 2000 Act continues the provisions of item 3 above which were contained in Section 2 of the 1993 Act. The regulations referred to are Articles 86 to 91 of the 2001 regulations. They detail the developments which shall be exempt from any of the provisions of the 2000 Act and the list is quite extensive. Public notice, except in the case of certain national security requirements, is required both in a newspaper and on site. Drawings are to be made available for inspection but not, as in the case of private sector development, for purchase. The local authority concerned, and in protected structure cases the Minister for Arts, Heritage, Gaeltacht, and the Islands, must be notified. In mid 2002 the functions formerly carried out by this department in the sphere of construction and development were transferred to the Department of the Environment and Local Government. Submissions may be made by members of the public and regard must be taken in coming to a decision of these submissions and of any submissions made by the local authority or the Minister. Notice of the decision shall be sent to those who made submissions and a notice must be published in an approved newspaper.

Development by local authorities is covered by sections 178 and 179 of the 2000 Act. The basic position is set out in Section 4(1) of the 2000 Act at sub-sections (b), (c) and (d) which exempts works carried out by a local authority in its own functional area. Sub-section (e) exempts works concerned with new roads or road maintenance. However, notwithstanding these provisions, section 179 of the Act provides that the Minister may, by regulation, specify certain works which will have to comply with section 179, and may also regulate the process by which the authority will deal with such non-exempt works.

Section 178 states that a local authority cannot carry out any development work which contravenes its own development plan. The detail is set out in Articles 79 to 85 and 145 of the 2001 regulations. Article 80 lists all the non-exempt works and the list is so extensive that Section 4(1) of the Act referred to above applies to very little in the way of development. The provision at sub-article (1)(k) that any development costing more than 126,000 is not exempt would in any event, bring almost all proposed local authority development into the net.

Notice, both on site and in an approved newspaper is required. Submissions may be made not less than two weeks after the end of an inspection period, which is to be not less than four weeks. A large number of prescribed bodies are listed as are the circumstances where they must individually be consulted. On completion of this process the Manager reports to the members of the authority with a recommendation as to whether or not the development should proceed and the members may, by resolution, accept, modify or reject the report.

Section 179 shall not apply to maintenance or repair (except in the case of protected structures), in urgent situations, where the authority is required by statute or by a court order to undertake certain works and, finally, whenever an environmental impact assessment is required. In this latter case section 175 specifies that where any development by a local authority requires an EIS then this shall be prepared as set out in that section and in Articles 92, 122, 123 and 144 of the 2001 regulations. In addition the general regulations affecting an EIS also apply. The EIS is submitted to An Bord Pleanála for approval and the development cannot proceed unless this is obtained with or without modifications. Section 175 also sets out the process of notice, inspection and purchase, submission, further information, oral hearings and decision. Interestingly, the difficulties that arose from overlapping areas of jurisdiction as far as a planning authority and the Environmental Protection Agency are concerned (see par. 3.3.2) are addressed at sub-section (10)(a) where it states that the Board shall not, by condition, control emissions where an integrated pollution control licence or a waste licence is concerned, making it clear that the area of emissions is for the jurisdiction of the Environmental Protection Agency and of the Agency alone.

A related area is that of taking estates in charge. Over the years a substantial number of residential developments were never properly completed to the major inconvenience of the residents. The practice over recent years of requiring security from developers has improved matters but where the estates were not properly completed, local authorities were naturally reluctant to take them over. Section 180 of the 2000 Act requires a local authority to take an estate in charge where the development conforms to a permission granted under either the 1963 Act (as amended) or the 2000 Act, and where a majority of the residents so request. However, even if the development has not been properly completed, and where no enforcement proceedings were taken by the local authority against the developer within seven years after the expiry of the permission and, again, where a majority of the residents so requests the local authority must take the estate in charge.

2.3 Making an Application

2.3.1 The Development Plan and other Plans

Having decided whether or not a planning application is necessary, the next step is to decide what sort of application to make and to be aware of the various regulations which set out the procedures which must be followed. The relative importance of differing regulations is commented on in par. 1.3. It is also essential to be aware of the various contingent matters which might affect a planning application. Apart from the various plans which are mentioned in the following paragraphs, the applicant must consider the legislation affecting Protected Structures, Environmental Impact Assessments, Major Accident Hazards, the Habitats Directive, National Monuments, the Foreshore Acts, Social and Affordable Housing and Strategic Development Zones. These subjects are dealt with in subsequent paragraphs.

The initial area that must be addressed at this stage are the various statutory plans. The plans will, amongst other things, provide the essential information to allow applicants to judge whether or not any particular application will be deemed by the authority to conform to these plans, and so obtain a permission.

The 2000 Act contains new and radical changes in the position regarding the various plans which are now required as part of the planning structure. There are now five types of plans or guidelines. Still of primary importance, and the first to be dealt with here, is the Development Plan. The requirements set out in previous planning legislation down the years were followed with varying degrees of compliance by different planning authorities and a revised system was clearly needed. It is provided in Part II of the 2000 Act. The core provision is that 'Every planning authority shall every six years make a development plan' [Section 9(1)]. A planning authority may combine with other adjoining authorities to produce a single development plan and can be required to do so if directed by the Minister. In any event all planning authorities must have regard to the plans of adjoining authorities. The section dealing with the contents of a development plan (Section 10) no longer distinguishes between urban and rural areas. An interesting new provision [Section 10(8)] states that there is no presumption in law that any land zoned in a development plan will remain so zoned in any subsequent plan. This is to encourage development. A development plan must be positive rather than negative. A development plan which banned all mining was held to be *ultra vires* on these grounds. (*Glencar Exploration v Mayo County Council* [1994] 2 IR 237). A planning authority is normally bound by its own development plan (but see par. 2.4.9 – Material Contravention). An Bord Pleanála, on the other hand, is not so strictly confined (Section 37(2)(b) – 2000 Act). The 2000 Act, however, imposes restrictions that did not exist in earlier legislation. The Board can only give a permission which contravenes a development plan where the proposed development is of strategic or national importance, where the development plan is not clear or where guidelines or policy directives might favour the development. The case of *The Village Residents Association v An Bord Pleanála* [2000] 2 ILRM 59 said that where An Bord Pleanála gave a permission which contravened a development plan it must give clear reasons for so doing.

The timetable for making the plan has been tightened up. Within four years of making a plan, a planning authority must give notice of its intention to review the plan. A newspaper notice is required seeking submissions in a period which cannot be less than eight weeks and the prescribed authorities (of which there are now 26) must be informed. Not later than 16 weeks after the notice the Manager must prepare a report for the members who can then issue directions to the Manager within ten week of receiving the report. Again, not later than twelve weeks after receiving the directions referred to, the Manager shall prepare a draft development plan and submit it to the members, and unless within eight weeks the members amend it, it becomes the draft development plan. This whole process could occupy one year.

The draft development plan is then exhibited for at least ten weeks and submissions are invited from the public. Not later than twenty-two weeks after the start of the exhibition the Manager must prepare a report for the members on the submission received and the members consideration of the plan and of the report must be completed within twelve weeks. At this point the plan is either adopted or amended. If it is to be materially amended, there is a fourteen week period for exhibition, comment and adoption of the amendments. Finally the plan is adopted. This section has taken nearly another year. There is, however, a 'longstop'. If the members have not adopted a plan within two years of the start of the process, the Manager is empowered to make the plan. Section 13 of the Act details the mechanism for varying a plan during its lifetime.

Any practitioner who is retained on a regular basis by the owner of any property would be prudent to inspect any such draft revisions and notify the owner in question of any changes. Property values can be very significantly altered by revisions to development plans.

The importance of the right of the public to comment on the development plan at draft stage was emphasised in *Keogh and Others v Galway Corporation* [1995] 1 ILRM 141 where the comment by the late Mr Justice Niall McCarthy was quoted: 'The development plan is a statement of objectives; it informs the community, in its draft form, of the intended objectives and affords the community the opportunity of inspection, criticism, and, if thought proper, objection. When adopted it forms an environmental contract between the planning authority, the council and the community, embodying a promise by the council that it will regulate private development in a manner consistent with the objectives stated in the plan and, further, that the council itself shall not effect any development which contravenes the plan materially. (*Attorney General (McGarry) v Sligo County Council* [1989] ILRM 768).

A tendency for some planning authorities to anticipate a draft development plan when making decisions has been held to be unlawful. The case of *Tom Chawke Caravans v Limerick County Council* [1991] High Court, July, held that a planning authority was bound by its current plan and could not have regard to a draft development plan which would come into effect two months after the application was made. A planning authority is however entitled to add buildings to the lists of protected structures during the lifetime of a development plan and any such decision confers immediate protection on the structure in question.

A further area involving development plans, and which has generated a number of cases, is the location of halting sites for Travellers. A number of planning authorities have been prevented from siting these in areas not specifically zoned for them. What has become known as the 'O'Leary test' was set out in *O'Leary v Dublin County Council* [1988] IR 150: 'If the application were made by a private developer to develop part of the lands of an area zoned as a High Amenity Area by the erection of five dwellings for private residential accommodation, I have no doubt that it would be resisted strenuously by the Planning Authority on the basis that it would amount to a material contravention of the County Development Plan.' This case, and the case of *Keogh v Galway Corporation* [1995] 1 ILRM 141 which also dealt with halting sites, emphasises the determination of the Courts to see that the planning laws apply equally to planning authorities as they do to private developers. Again, the case of *Byrne v Fingal County Council* [2002] 2 ILRM 321 emphasises the determination of the courts to protect the status of the development plan. As was pointed out in par 2.2.2 Bord Pleanála has held in a Section 5 ref (21.RF0776) that the provision of halting sites, where they conform with the zoning provisions was exempted development under Section 4(1)(b) of the 1963 Act, and Article 130 of S.I. 86. This is now covered by section 179 of the 2000 Act and Articles 80, 84 and 145 of the 2001 Regulations.

Development plans are required to make provision for Architectural Conservation Areas and for Areas of Special Planning Control as set out in Part IV, Chapter II of the 2000 Act. If the planning authority is of the view that any 'place, area, group of structures or townscape' requires preservation, then it shall declare the area to be an architectural conservation area. The effect, as far as practitioners are concerned, is that the exemption conferred by Section 4(1)(h) on the exterior of the structure is restricted.

Similarly, where a planning authority considers that part or all of an architectural conservation area is of special importance as far as civic life, architectural, historical, cultural or social factors are concerned, it shall make a scheme for the enhancement or preservation of that area called an area of special planning control. The detail as far as the making of the plan, inspection by the public, submissions, timescales, variations and reviews, etc, can be best described as a 'mini' development plan scenario. As in the case of an architectural conservation area, practitioners should be aware of Section 87(1) of the 2000 Act: Notwithstanding Section 4 and any regulations made thereunder, any development within an area of special planning control shall not be exempted development where it contravenes an approved scheme applying to that area.

Finally, in the area of development plans, it should be noted the constitutionality of such plans has been confirmed. In *Central Dublin Development Association v Attorney General* [1975] 109 LTR 69, the Court held that the fact that the plan was for the common good and that safeguards by way of public involvement and compensation provisions were included ensured their validity.

Related to the Development Plan is the Special Amenity Area Order and the Landscape Conservation Area Order. Where a planning authority, as empowered

by Sections 202 and 203 of the Act, decides that a particular area is one of outstanding natural beauty or has special recreational value, then they have the
power to issue a Special Amenity Area Order. There then follows the fairly standard procedure of public notice, the opportunity for public objection and the
holding of a public enquiry. The Minister may also require a planning authority
to issue an order for a particular area. There have been three of these orders
issued. These are S.I. 59 of 1990 – Liffey Valley (Lucan Bridge to Palmerston),
S.I. 70 of 1995 – North Bull Island, and S.I. 133 of 2000 – Fingal County Council
(Howth). The main practical effects of any special amenity area order is that a
very large number of the exempted development classes listed in the Second
Schedule to S.I. 600 of 2000 are no longer exempt, and that compensation is not
payable for a refusal of permission in such an area (Third Schedule, 2000 Act).

Previous acts had included in the Special Amenity Area provisions that an area
could be included if it were designated a nature conservation area. This specific
item has now been provided for in Landscape Conservation Areas as detailed in
Sections 204 and 205 of the Act. Again, this has restrictions as far as exempted
development is concerned. An associated provision (Section 205) restates previous legislation regarding tree preservation orders. These may be made in respect
of one or more trees or groups of trees.

The position of the Local Area Plan, the second of the plans now involved in the
process, has been formalised. Detailed local plans existed under the previous system but without any statutory basis, except that Scheduled Towns were required
to be zoned. The 2000 Act (sections 18 to 20) provides that a planning authority
'may' prepare such plans and that such plans must be taken into account when
considering applications for permission.

At the same time any Integrated Area Plan, which is the third plan, made under
the Urban Renewal Act 1998 must also be taken into account. The optional nature
of making a Local Area Plan is removed in the case of any area which is designated as a town in the most recent census, has a population in excess of 2000 and
is situated in the functional area of a county council, when a planning authority
must make such a plan. The legislation deals with the procedure involved and
with the contents of such plans [Section 18(1)(b)].

The fourth plan or guideline is the Regional Planning Guideline. The regional
authorities, eight in number, were set up under the Local Government Act 1991
and S.I. 394 of 1993. They were empowered, but now required unless directed by
the Minister, to make regional planning guidelines. The position of the original
eight authorities was modified in Section 21 of the 2000 Act to allow the strategic planning guidelines already made by Dublin and adjoining areas to form part
of this new arrangement. The objective of regional planning guidelines is to provide a long term strategic planning framework for the development of the region

for a period of not less than twelve or more than twenty years. The main impact of these guidelines will be that all planning authorities in the area must have regard to the guidelines when making a development plan.

Fifthly, and lastly, are the Ministerial Guidelines and Directives. The guidelines must be regarded by all planning authorities and, where applicable, An Bord Pleanála. Equally, any Ministerial Policy Directive must be complied with by both the authorities and the Board, but the Minister cannot exercise any power in relation to any particular case. The Minister can also issue directions in respect of development plans.

2.3.2 Protected Structures

It would be appropriate at this point to examine the latest legislation dealing with what used to be called listed buildings. Some planning authorities had a number of lists generally ranged in order of importance. Some planning authorities had none. Very stringent legislation in the area of preservation and conservation was introduced in the Local Government (Planning and Development) Act 1999. This Act has been revoked and is incorporated in its entirety in the 2000 Act. All section references which follow refer to the latter Act. It is submitted that the absence of any grading or preference regarding protection is unrealistic in view of the very severe and strict provisions of the new legislation. It is quite absurd to impose the same level of protection to an ordinary small terraced house in Dublin suburbia as to that imposed on the Casino at Marino. This new legislation gives an enhanced role to the Minister for the Environment and Local Government, by way of guidelines and recommendations. Associated with the 1999 Act is the Architectural Heritage (National Inventory) and Historic Properties (Miscellaneous Provisions) Act 1999. This Act provides a statutory basis for the National Inventory of Architectural Heritage. The inventory will be used by the Minister as a basis for recommending to planning authorities what buildings should be included in that authority's list of protected structures. After the 2002 general election, all the heritage functions previously under the control of the then called Department of the Arts, Heritage, Gaeltacht and the Islands, including Dúchas, were transferred to the Department of the Environment and Local Government. The Department of Arts, Heritage, Gaeltacht and the Islands was renamed the Department of Community, Rural and Gaeltacht affairs.

Another connected piece of legislation is the Heritage Act 1995. In essence this Act establishes a Heritage Council whose function shall be 'to propose policies and priorities for the identification, protection, preservation and enhancement of the national heritage including monuments, archeological objects, heritage objects, architectural heritage, flora, fauna, wildlife habitats, landscapes, seascapes, wrecks, geology, heritage gardens and parks and inland waterways'

(Section 6(1)). Section 10 of the same Act gives power to the Council to require public authorities to consult with the Council in respect of works to heritage buildings. Such a building is defined in Section 2 of the Act as including 'any building or part thereof, which is of significance because of its intrinsic architectural or artistic quality or its setting or because of its association with the commercial, cultural, economic, industrial, military, political, social or religious history of the place where it is situated or of the country or generally, and includes the amenities of any such building.'

It seems to the author that the reader is now entitled to be confused. The number of acts dealing with the matters set out in the previous paragraph includes the Planning and Development Act 2000, the Architectural Heritage (National Inventory) and Historic Properties (Miscellaneous Provisions) Act 1999, the Wildlife Acts 1976 to 2000, the Heritage Act 1995, the National Monuments Acts 1930 to 1994 and various other pieces of legislation such as the Local Government (Sanitary Services) Act 1964. There are also European directives. It is obvious that a unifying Act would be timely.

Before the introduction of the 1999 Act exempted development was covered either in Section 4 of the 1963 Act or in Part 3 of S.I. 86 of 1994. The provisions contained in Section 4 of the 1963 Act were not restricted in any way as regards listing for preservation or protection and the interiors of such buildings were only to be preserved or protected if such items were specifically listed in the Development Plan. However, exemption under the Statutory Instrument was only available where the buildings were not listed.

Definitions are important and in the Act a 'structure' includes not only the interior of that structure but the land lying within the curtilage of the structure and any other structures lying within that curtilage and their interiors and finally all fixtures and features which form part of the interior or exterior of any of the above structures. This raises the meaning of the word 'curtilage' and there is, unfortunately, no precise or universally accepted legal meaning of the word. In *McAlpine v Secretary of State for the Environment* [1995] JPL 843 it was held that it was 'not necessary for there to be any physical enclosure with the house and overall the term has a restrictive meaning'. In another English case, *The Attorney General v Calderdale Borough Council* [1983] 46 P& CR 399, three criteria were set out: a) the physical layout of the listed building and the structure, b) their ownership, past and present, and c) their use and function, past and present. A third, and final, English case, *Skelitts v Secretary of State for the Environment, Transport and the Regions* [2001] QB 59 concluded that 'this case demonstrated that not even lawyers can have a precise idea of what curtilage means'.

It is respectfully submitted that the definition in the Architectural Heritage Protection Guidelines (still in draft at the time of writing) issued in 2001 by the

Department of Arts, Culture, Gaeltacht and the Islands is not of much help. It is stated there that 'the curtilage of any protected structure can be taken to be the parcel of land immediately associated with that structure or in use for the purposes of that structure'. This is all very perplexing, but the word is in the legislation and it won't go away. It is submitted that, for the present purpose, it is generally accepted to mean anything within the boundaries of the land surrounding the structure (usually a house).The standard reference work, A DICTIONARY OF IRISH LAW, defines curtilage as 'a courtyard, garden, yard, field or piece of ground lying near and belonging to a dwelling house'. It is safe to assume therefore that anything up to and including the boundary walls of a property will be protected.

But in addition to curtilage there is the matter of the 'attendant grounds'. If curtilage is not defined in the act attendant grounds is but not, it is submitted, very clearly. In relation to a structure it includes 'land lying outside the curtilage of the structure'. The lack of definition of 'curtilage' taken with the imprecision of the definition of 'attendant grounds' that is given is bound to cause problems in trying to decide what is protected. The whole area will be resolved on a totally subjective basis until the courts intervene which they will certainly be invited to do. Attendant grounds lying outside the curtilage of a structure could, in a *reductio ad absurdam*, mean the remainder of the country.

The other definition which is important is that of 'works', which is very comprehensive and can include any operation involving the interference with items as detailed as the paint, wallpaper or tiles of the interior of any protected structure. Any works which could affect the character of a protected structure will require planning permission. It would, of course, be up to any practitioner to decide what proposed works would, or would not, materially affect either the structure itself or any element of the structure which contributes to its special architectural, historical, archeological, artistic, cultural, scientific, social or technical interest. It would probably be safer to apply to the planning authority, as set out in Section 57(2), for a declaration as to what features they consider to be included in the protection.

The mechanism involved as far as a Planning Authority is concerned is that protected structures, are, in effect, anything that is listed in an existing Development Plan or anything that it is proposed to list in any future Development Plan. A planning authority may at any time add to or delete buildings from such protection and it is extremely interesting to note that this part of the Act is a reserved function of the planning authority, that is, it is a function which will be in the hands of the elected representatives.

As far as notifying owners is concerned, Section 55 of the 2000 Act requires that where it is proposed to either add or delete a structure, other than during the course of making a development plan, the planning authority must notify the owner and there is the usual arrangement for submissions or observations. A period of twelve weeks after an initial six-week inspection period is allowed to the planning authority to make a decision. The legislation goes on to deal with the safeguarding of protected structures by way of requirements to maintain and repair them, and giving power to the planning authority to take over such duties where necessary. Grants may be made available to owners or to the planning authority (Section 80). Whether the failure of the planning authority to notify owners of such inclusion would have any effect on the protection is uncertain but it is doubtful that it would invalidate the protected status even though the Act says 'shall'.

The effect that this legislation has on exempted development is radical. Section 4(1)(h) of the 2000 Act allows material alterations to the exterior of a building providing it does not render the building inconsistent with the character of the structure or of neighbouring structures but, unlike the previous legislation, nothing, in effect, can be done to a protected structure until the owner of any such structure enquires of the planning authority what specific parts of the structure are to be protected [Section 57(2)]. The planning authority must reply within twelve weeks of receiving such a request. There is, regrettably, no default mechanism and some planning authorities are taking over a year to respond to such requests. Indeed, in some cases no response of any sort could be obtained. The planning authority, before coming to a decision, must have regard to any guidelines issued by the Minister for Arts, Heritage, Gaeltacht and the Islands with regard to policy generally or indeed, to individual structures. A planning authority may only give permission to demolish a protected structure ' in exceptional circumstances' [Section 57(10)(b)]. The Board is similarly restricted. This was seen in a case involving the demolition of St Anne's Hospital in Dublin where local residents obtained a High Court Injunction halting the demolition.

There is a provision that where a building is regularly used as a place of public worship, the planning authority in coming to any decisions with regard to exempted development must 'respect' liturgical requirements. This has already caused problems and an argument as to whether or not liturgical requirements take precedence over planning views has yet to be resolved.

Finally, in the area of protected structures there is a restriction in that an outline application may not be made in respect of a development involving works to a protected structure or a proposed protected structure.

2.3.3 Environmental Impact Assessment

a) General

Before making the planning application it is necessary to establish whether or not the proposed development is affected by the requirements for an envi-

ronmental impact assessment. A very significant change in the overall legislation relates to the position of Environmental Impact Assessment. The original requirements for an Environmental Impact Statement were contained in
S.I. 349 of 1989 which brought into effect in this jurisdiction the E.I.A.
Directive – 85/337/EEC (amended by 97/11/EC). The projects which require
an EIS and the contents of an EIS were originally set out in S.I. 349 of 1989
but these have now, by virtue of Section 176(3) of the 2000 Act been transferred to S.I. 600 of 2001.

The concept of some form of requirement on behalf of developers to show
that their proposals would not harm the environment seems to have appeared
first in the United States towards the end of the 1960s. The first Irish reference to the matter is contained in Section 39 of the 1976 Planning Act which
amended Part IV of the 1963 Act so that a planning authority might, but was
not required to, ask for a written study of the effect of the proposed development on the environment if a) the proposals involved the emission of noise,
vibration, fumes, other effluents, etc, and b) would cost more than IR£5 mil-
lion. This was set out in detail in Article 28 of S.I. 65 of 1977, but this has
been revoked by the new legislation.

The Directives and the regulations referred to deal with the assessment of the
effects of certain public and private projects on the environment. It is referred
to in matters dealing with this subject simply as the 'Council Directive'. In
European law, a Directive of the Community binds the Member State only in
that the objective set out in the Directive must be achieved, and the Member
State can decide on the details of how this objective can be achieved. The
original Directive was amended by the Council Directive 97/11/EC to bring
into effect the requirements of the Directive 96/61/EC on integrated pollution
control, and also expanding the list of development which will now be covered by this new amendment. Member States were required to implement this
Directive by the 14th March 1999.

b) **Projects affected**

The first thing, then, to establish is what proposals will be required to be supported by an environmental impact statement. Article 93 of S.I. 600 of 2001
defines the basic requirements, which, as far as the practising architect is
concerned, are set out in the Fifth Schedule of the same statutory instrument
and can be separated into those projects which would normally involve the
practising architect, and those that would not involve an architect at all, or at
best in only a peripheral way.

Paragraph 10 of Part 2 of the Fifth Schedule lists at sub-paragraph (a) and (b)
what might be called the ordinary building projects which are subject to environmental impact assessment requirements. These are:

a)   Industrial estate developments of an area greater than 15 hectares

b)   A development of more than 500 houses

c)   A car park of more than 400 spaces except where the car park is ancillary to a development

d)   A shopping centre of greater than 10,000 square metres

e)   Urban developments greater than 2 hectares in a business district (i.e. where the predominant use is retail or commercial), greater than 10 hectares in other parts of a built-up area, and 20 hectares elsewhere.

Tourism projects included would be marinas exceeding 100 berths (fresh water) and 300 berths (salt water), holiday villages of more than 100 homes, hotels in rural areas of more than 20 hectares or 300 rooms, camp or caravan sites of more than 100 units and, finally, theme parks of greater than 5 hectares.

The remainder of the Fifth Schedule lists the proposals which would rarely involve the architect acting in a primary role, if at all. The list covers oil refineries, power stations, steel works, chemical plants, airports, seaports, railway lines, mining, processing of nuclear fuels, shipyards, etc.

In fact almost all industrial uses are listed and should be checked in cases of doubt. There are also sections dealing with agriculture, the food industry and other sectors. The agriculture section lists area limits for proposals involving intensive agriculture, water management projects for agriculture, afforestation, and reclamation. It also sets limits for poultry rearing, pig breeding and salmon breeding, above which limits an environmental impact statement must be provided.

The section dealing with the food industry defines the limits for processing of raw materials, for brewing, slaughter of animals, and production of sugar, dairy products, starch, fish meal etc.

Care must be taken in the case of planning applications that might have a significant environmental impact even though the project does not come within the schedule in the Regulations, as either Bord Pleanála (Article 109 of S.I. 600 of 2001) or the planning authority (Article 103 of S.I. 600 of 2001) can require the submission of an environmental impact statement where they are satisfied that such a course could be appropriate. The application date for 'sub-threshold' planning applications runs from the date of the receipt of the EIS. The question as to whether a planning authority was remiss in not requiring an EIS for a project which, was under the threshold was addressed in the case of *Lancefort v An Bord Pleanála* [1998] 2 ILRM 401. The Court did not make a judgement on the precise issue but refused to invalidate a permission where an EIS was not so sought. Bord Pleanála can, on the other hand, waive the requirements for an EIS on written application (section 172). The Board can also be asked for an opinion as to what the EIS should contain (section 173).

As is only to be expected, this area of planning has been the subject of a number of court cases. The first of these, *Michael Browne and Others v An Bord Pleanála* [1989] ILRM 865 sought to overturn a permission granted to Merrill Dow to build a pharmaceutical plant in Cork. The basis of the case was that the developers did not submit an environmental impact statement in accordance with the terms of the Council Directive. The High Court held that it was a matter for the planning authority to decide whether or not the information before it was sufficient to enable it to come to a decision. The decision was appealed to the Supreme Court but does not appear to have been decided. The project was abandoned by Merrill Dow perhaps in view of the delays involved.

The second case was another lengthy legal wrangle, again over a pharmaceutical plant in Cork (Sandoz) and involved a number of issues, including a dispute over the adequacy of the environmental impact statement. The question of the *locus standi* of the plaintiffs was questioned in the Supreme Court and confirmed by that Court. The substantive issues do not seem to have been decided. (*Chambers v An Bord Pleanála* [1992] ILRM 296)

Section 175 of the 2000 Act requires a local authority to prepare an environmental impact statement for work carried out by or on behalf of that local authority. The transboundary provisions, i.e. developments affecting neighbouring EU States, will not trouble many architects.

Finally, it must be remembered that where a licence is required under Part IV of the Environmental Protection Agency Act 1992, then an environmental impact statement is required even if the project does not come within the limits set out in the Fifth Schedule to S.I. 600 of 2001.

c) Planning requirements

Points to be remembered in relation to the submission of an environmental impact statement as part of a planning application are (references are to the articles in S.I. 600 of 2001):

a) The newspaper notice must state that the application will be accompanied by such an EIS [17(1)(a)] and that it may be inspected and purchased.

b) Where Bord Pleanála grants an exemption from the requirement to provide an EIS [Section 172(3)] the Board can apply other requirements.

c) Where a planning authority received a planning application for a development which is below the stated thresholds but where the development

would be located in
i) a European site under the Habitats Directive or
ii) an area covered by Sections 16, 18, 26, 27 or 28 of the Wildlife (Amendment) Act 2000

then they may decide to require an EIS (Article 103).

d) The date of a planning application affected by c) above will run from the time of the receipt of the EIS.

e) Any request under Article 103 is automatically cancelled by an exemption granted under section 172(3).

f) If an EIS is required under Article 102, then a newspaper notice is required (Article 105).

g) If the planning authority considers the EIS inadequate, or that it does not comply with the information requirements sought under Article 94, it may require further information (Article 108).

h) Most of the provisions affecting an EIS in relation to a planning authority also apply to the Board when it considers the matter (Articles 109-116)

i) Outline applications may not be made in cases where an environmental impact statement is required (Article 96).

d) Necessary information

Having established whether or not an impact statement is required, it is then necessary to find out what information is required. This is contained in the Sixth Schedule to the Instrument (S.I. 600 of 2001). At the time of writing the Statutory Instrument sets out all the information needed to prepare an environmental impact statement but it must be remembered that the Environmental Protection Agency Act 1992 at Section 72(1) empowers the Agency to issue guidelines as to what information is to be contained in any environmental impact statement and no doubt these guidelines will be issued in due course by way of regulation.

In summary what is required is:

1 A description of the development, i.e. size, site, design.

2 Where significant adverse effects are identified, the proposed measures to reduce or remedy those effects, and

3 The data necessary to identify and assess the main effects that the development is likely to have on the environment.

4 An outline of the alternatives considered

All of the information listed above is mandatory in every case, and the following may be required in certain cases.

5   Physical characteristics, and land use requirements both during construction and operation.

6   The main characteristics of production process, and the nature and quantity of materials to be used.

7   The estimated type and quality of any emissions, i.e. physical, noise, radiation, etc.

8   A description of the likely significant effects, direct and indirect, of the development on: human beings, flora, fauna, soil, water, air, climate, the landscape the inter-action between any of the foregoing material assets, and cultural heritage.

9   The likely significant effects resulting from the use of natural resources, or emissions, etc, and the forecasting methods used for this assessment, and

10 Any difficulties encountered in providing the necessary information.

2.3.4 Major Accident Hazards

Another factor that must be considered when making a planning application is to discover whether or not it might be affected by the 'Seveso' legislation arising from the European Directive 96/82/EC on the control of major accident hazards involving dangerous substances. This has been transposed into Irish law by S.I. 476 of 2000 – The European Communities (Control of Major Accident Hazards Involving Dangerous Substances) Regulations 2000.

In summary, there is what is called an 'establishment'. These are set out in Table 2 of the Schedule to the Regulations. They are facilities like LPG storage, oil refineries, chemical warehousing, etc. The establishments must be located a specified minimum distance from any development categories which are set out in Table 1 of the same schedule. These latter developments range from housing, holiday accommodation, educational establishments, etc, to car parks, transport links, shopping centres, etc. Table 1 also sets out these minimum distances, which range from 100 metres to 2,000 metres, measured from the perimeter of the establishment.

The planning implications are set out in Articles 133 to 155 of S.I. 600 of 2001. They involve, basically, notices of various sorts including a newspaper notice and notification to the National Authority for Occupational Safety and Health, and any application must contain the detailed information regarding the proposed establishment which is set out in the Third Schedule of S.I. 476 of 2000. No outline application may be made where the 'Seveso' legislation applies. The regulations also deal with appeals, development by local authorities and the State and, finally, the position where a Section 5 declaration involves an establishment.

A problem that is bound to occur would arise from the fact that there is no national register of these establishments and proposals could be well advanced for developments which might be within the various parameters defined without the proposers being aware of the situation.

2.3.5 The Habitats Directive

Another complication in the planning process that practitioners have to deal with before making a planning application is the Directive 92/43/EEC known as the Habitats Directive (amended by 97/62/EC). This was published on the 21st May 1992 and was brought into effect in this country on 26th February 1997 by means of S.I. 94 of 1997 and amended by S.I. 233 of 1998 updating the annexes listing habitat types, animal and plant species The overall purpose of the directive is the protection of certain scheduled flora and fauna and this is done by designating certain areas as 'European Sites'. Such a site is one that is listed as an area of special conservation, a site of Community Importance on the list referred to in the third paragraph of Article 4(2) of the Habitats Directive, or finally, an area classified in accordance with paragraph (1) or (2) of Article 4 of the Directive 79/409/EEC (the 'Birds Directive'). The first two classes above are defined in greater detail in the statutory instrument.

There is a fairly involved procedure for listing these sites and the details need not concern us here but practitioners will be relieved to know that it is a requirement of S.I. 94 of 1997 that the Minister for Arts, Culture, Gaeltacht and the Islands notify all landowners, if any, if their property has been scheduled. Again the protection matters that follow are not relevant here but what is important is the effect that such listing has on any planning application.

Article 27 of S.I. 94 of 1997 requires a planning authority or An Bord Pleanála to make an appropriate assessment and to take regard of the impact that a proposed development might have on a European site. The procedures set out in S.I. 600 of 2001 with regard to environmental impact assessments will be regarded as adequate as far as those regulations are concerned. Even in the case of a negative assessment a planning permission may be granted if there are imperative reasons overriding public interest to justify the decision.

The planning authority may cite reasons for coming to a decision in relation to human health, public safety or beneficial consequences of primary importance for the environment. The planning authority, or the Board, may also apply to the Commission, through the Minister for the Environment, for an opinion with regard to other imperative reasons. If this is done, the time taken to obtain this opinion does not count as regards either the eight-week planning decision limit, or the recommended eighteen-week appeal time.

Sections 28 and 29 deal with the same requirements in respect of developments carried out by or on behalf of local authorities. Section 32 deals with the situation which arises under, amongst other enactments, the licensing provisions of the Environmental Protection Agency Act 1992 and the Waste Management Act 1996.

2.3.6 National Monuments

A further item to be checked before making an application is the legislation affecting national monuments. There is a commentary on the relationship between various 'heritage' Acts and protected structures in par. 2.3.2. At the moment the legislation is in the process of being reviewed and updated. The pres-ent legislation is the National Monuments Acts 1930-1994. Under the existing legislation a monument qualifies for protection in one of four ways: if it is listed in the Register of Historic Monuments (RHM): If it is listed in the Records of Monuments and Places (RMP): if it is subject to a preservation order: and final-ly, if it is in the care of the State or a local authority. The proposed legislation will simplify this and set up a Register of National Monuments. There will be two lev-els of protection. Part 1 will automatically include every monument already on the RHM or the RMP lists and will continue the provisions of section12 of the National Monuments (Amendment) Act 1994 requiring two months notice of any proposed works at or near any such monument. Part 2 will automatically make any monument listed in that part a protected structure and will require the approval of the Minister before carrying out any works.

National Monuments are protected by Section 5 of the Architectural Heritage (National Inventory) and Historic Properties (Miscellaneous Provisions) Act 1999 from the powers given under the Local Government (Sanitary Services) Act 1964 to Sanitary Authorities to require owners to demolish dangerous structures, or if the owners do not to demolish such structures themselves. The particular provi-sion that might affect development is Section 12 of the National Monuments (Amendment) Act 1994, referred to in the previous paragraph, which requires that any person who proposes to carry out works 'at or in relation to such monuments' shall give notice to Dúchas and shall not commence any works for a period of two months after giving notice.

Under the various Acts, that is the National Monuments Act 1930 and the

National Monument (Amendment) Acts 1954, 1987 and 1994 there was a requirement on the Commissioners of Public Works to maintain a National Monuments Register (Section 5(1) of the 1987 Act) They were also required under section 12(1) of the 1994 Act to maintain a record of where they believe there are monuments. The functions of the Commissioners in the area of National Monuments were transferred, under Section 24 of the Heritage Act 1995, to the Minister for Arts, Heritage, Gaeltacht and the Islands and, since 2001, to the Department of the Environment and Local Government. These functions within that department are carried out by Dúchas. In addition to a register of national monuments Dúchas maintains a Sites and Monuments Record (SMR) for each planning authority area which should be consulted by anyone proposing to make a planning application in an area where there is reason to believe that a national monument might exist.

2.3.7 The Foreshore and other Acts

There are a number of acts which impinge to some extent on the planning process but which could in certain circumstances affect a planning application. Some are mentioned in the 2000 Act. The most notable of these are the Foreshore Acts 1933 to 1998. The Foreshore is defined in the 1933 Foreshore Act as 'the bed and shore below the line of high water of ordinary or medium tides, of the sea and of every tidal river and tidal estuary and of every channel, creek, and bay of the sea or any such river of estuary'. This definition is extended in Section 2.2.4 of the 2000 Act as to include 'land between the line of high water of ordinary or medium tides and land within the functional area of the planning authority concerned that adjoins the first-mentioned land'. Section 2.2.5 goes on to say that permission will be required for any development on the foreshore that is not exempt under the Act or the regulations. The section concludes by saying that this particular section is in addition to, and not in substitution for, the Foreshore Acts. The original provisions in the Foreshore Act 1933 regarding development was that the Minister (at that time for Industry and Commerce) could lease portions of the foreshore and could issue licences for structures.

Other acts which might, in rare cases, involve planning matters would be such as the Harbour Acts 1946 to 1996, the Gas Act 1976, the Fisheries (Amendment) Act 1997 and the Turf Development Act 1998. If there is a possibility that any proposed development would impinge on the subjects covered by this legislation, formal planning advice should be sought.

2.3.8 Social and Affordable Housing

The next matter that must be addressed before making a planning application for a development that contains a residential content is the question of social and affordable housing. It would be fair to say that the most radical and controversial aspect of the Planning and Development Bill when it appeared in August 1999 was Part V which dealt with this subject. What had started in the early years of the state as the provision of what was known as Housing for the Working Classes (an unacceptable description to-day) had led to what can only be described as ghettos where enormous developments consisting solely of state financed houses were built on the outskirts of cities and towns. Some, such as Ballyfermot in west Dublin were as large as cities like Limerick and the very nature of the planning of these developments, the size of the schemes and the necessarily similar circumstances of the people living there led to community problems. The lack of reasonable transport systems and very poor community facilities exacerbated the problem.

It was clear that the size of these housing schemes and the lack of variety in the social circumstances of people living in these areas would need to be addressed in future developments if past mistakes were not to be repeated. Part V of the 2000 Act is an attempt to do this. It can be argued that a planning act is not the ideal locus to deal with what is primarily a social problem but that is what has been done and the task now for those working in the area of planning and construction is to understand and operate the legislation.

In simple terms the core of the requirements of Part V is that in future up to 20% of all housing developments or developments with a residential content must consist of 'social and affordable' housing. When the Bill was published in August 1999 a very intense debate commenced with all the various interested parties setting out their stalls. The provisions in the Bill were vigorously debated in the Oireachtas and the Bill was eventually passed on the 15th May 2000. Under the provisions of Article 26 of the Constitution, the Bill was referred by the President to the Supreme Court for a decision on the constitutionality of Part V. A full report of the Court's decision is available at [2000] ILRM 81. A summary can be obtained in Vol. 7, No. 3 of the IRISH PLANNING AND ENVIRONMENTAL LAW JOURNAL. The purpose of Part V was set out succinctly by the Chief Justice: 'It is clear that the purpose of the statutory scheme is to facilitate the purchase of houses by people who would not otherwise be in a position to buy houses and to ensure, as far as possible, that housing developments of this nature are not isolated from the general community.' On the 28th August 2000 the Court issued its judgement saying that none of the provisions of Part V was repugnant to the Constitution. The effect of this judgement is that Part V, unlike the rest of the Act, cannot be again questioned as to its constitutionality.

However, in August 2002 the Department sought submissions from various bodies in connection with a proposal to review Part V. It had become obvious due to a number of factors, such as the reluctance of developers to speculate on the commercial prospects of 'Part V developments' and also the changing economic cli-mate, that Part V as originally envisaged by the legislation was not giving the desired result. It remains to be seen what will emerge.

Part V was brought into force by the Planning and Development (Regulations) Order – S.I. 349 of 2000. In December 2000 the Department of the Environment and Local Government issued guidelines for planning authorities with regard to Part V. This is recommended reading for anyone involved. At the same time the Department published a MODEL STRATEGY AND STEP BY STEP GUIDE. Co Louth was taken as a model county, and the guide explains the factors and background to be considered. The legislation, at Article 50 of the 2001 regulations also sets out minimum sizes for houses ranging from single person houses up to houses for seven people or more.

The essential basis of the Part V scheme is the Housing Strategy. Section 94 of the Act requires that 'each planning authority shall include in any development plan it makes (in accordance with section 12) a strategy for the purpose of ensur-ing that the proper planning and sustainable development of the area of the devel-opment plan provides for the housing of the existing and future population of the area in the manner set out in the strategy'. The Act required that all planning authorities have these strategies in place by 1st August 2000 and it is understood that this requirement was fulfilled. So what is the basis of such a strategy? The second guide referred to in the previous paragraph goes into considerable detail on this but, in essence, the strategy will set out the proportion of future housing that will be required to conform to the Part V requirements. Section 94(4)(a) requires any strategy (amongst other provisions).

i)   to take into account existing and future housing needs

ii) to ensure that differing income levels are catered for

iii) to counteract undue segregation of differing social backgrounds

iv) to estimate the need for social and affordable housing

It would be appropriate at this stage to define what is 'social' and 'affordable' housing. Social housing is, in effect, housing provided by the State under Section 9(2) of the Housing Act 1988 or by housing associations. The Section 9(2) referred to provides that when assessing housing needs, a housing authority shall have regard to the situation of the differing categories of persons mentioned. Included in that section are those that are homeless and also Travellers as defined in section 13 of the same Act. Affordable housing means houses or land made available to 'eligible' persons under the provision of Part V. An eligible person is one whose income would not be sufficient to meet the mortgage repayments required for suitable accommodation.

An essential factor of any realistic housing strategy is the need to take account of the differing circumstances in the various areas covered by the remit of the planning authority. It is obvious that an area which consists at the moment entirely of social housing needs no further such housing and that any planning permissions granted should recognise that. Equally, an area that at the time of the planning application contained no social housing at all, then the planning authority would be justified in calling for the maximum figure of 20%. Each area should be considered separately. This is provided for specifically in Section 95(1)(d) of the 2000 Act.

Housing strategies have until now been largely incorporated into development plans by way of a variation. The Act requires that in future, because of the volatile nature of the housing market and other factors, development plans be reviewed after two years. In addition, any development plan must ensure that sufficient land is zoned to meet residential needs. It is important to note that Part V applies, not only to land zoned for residential use, but also to land zoned for a mixture of residential and other uses.

The mechanism of how Part V will operate is set out in Section 96. Essentially any person receiving permission for a residential, or a mixed, development will be required to enter into an agreement with the planning authority to:

a) transfer to the planning authority ownership of the land based on the specified percentage required for social and affordable housing or

b) transfer ownership of the appropriate percentage of completed houses to either the planning authority or to nominated persons at a price calculated as set out in sub-section 96(3)(a)(ii), or

c) the transfer of the appropriate percentage of serviced sites, again either to the planning authority or to specified persons.

An applicant for permission may indicate which of these options is preferred and the planning authority shall 'have regard' to any such preference. The final option in this area is that if the planning authority decides that none of the three options above is appropriate, a planning condition may require a sum of money to be paid equating to the value of the land set out in sub-paragraph a) above. The planning authority is required to keep this money in a separate account and to use it only for the exercise of its functions under the Housing Acts 1966 to 1998. It has been argued that by signing an agreement the recipient of the grant of a permission could be required under contract law to implement the permission. This could, it is suggested, be described as a fine point.

Any disputes which arise from any agreement required on foot of a planning permission shall be referred to An Bord Pleanála for a determination except in the case of disputes regarding the cost of transferred land, costs of completed houses, costs of service land or sums in lieu of an agreement, all or which shall be referred to a property arbitrator. The value of the land transferred will be determined differently depending on the date of purchase. Land bought before 25th August 1999 will be paid for on the basis of the cost of the land plus interest, whereas land bought after that date will be paid for on the existing use value on the date of the transfer of ownership assuming that no permission was available for development.

Planning permissions granted after 25th August 1999, and provided that a housing strategy was in place at the time of the grant will cease to have effect after 31st December 2002, or two years from the date of the grant, whichever is the later. Any part of a scheme which is complete, including any houses where the external walls are complete, is not affected by this provision. It could well be that this sub-section will cause some short-term problems. It is believed that the current review by the Department of Part V will lead to an abandonment of this provision.

The basic provision of Section 96, that is, the requirement that permission granted for residential or partly residential development shall contain a certain proportion of social and affordable housing shall not apply to:

a) a body approved under Section 6 of the Housing (Miscellaneous Provisions) Act 1992, such as a housing association

b) the conversion or reconstruction of an existing building to create one or more dwellings where 50% or more of the existing external fabric is retained, or

c) carrying out works to an existing house.

Further exemptions to the provisions of Part V are contained in Section 97 where, firstly, the development consists of four or fewer houses and, secondly housing development on sites of 0.2 hectares (0.45 acres) or less but in both cases if, and only if, the applicant can produce a certificate from the planning authority stating that Section 97 will not apply.

The rules governing the issue of such certificates are carefully framed to exclude collusion and other forms chicanery from the process. Apart from the requirements of the Act, Articles 48 and 49 of the 2001 regulations set out further details needed when applying for a certificate. The obvious evasions that would be tried might be, firstly, the splitting up of larger sites into areas of 0.2 hectares or less, or secondly, the splitting up of ownership so that applications from people acting in concert would not be connected. Every applicant will be required to swear a statutory declaration that they are not aware of any circumstance that would prevent the planning authority from issuing such a certificate. There is a four-week default provision if the planning authority does not respond, and a three-week period after the decision for the applicant to appeal against a refusal to issue a certificate to the Circuit Court.

The penalties for deceit or other offences under the section are very severe. On indictment fines of up to €634,869 and/or imprisonment of up to five years is specified. In addition, any gain made by false certificates or other irregularities shall be forfeited on order of the Court.

Finally in this part are the sections dealing with eligible persons (Section 98) and the resale of houses (Section 99). Each planning authority is required to arrange a scheme establishing the priority to be given to eligible persons. There are seven criteria listed to be taken into account by the planning authority. The process is a reserved function of the authority, that is, exercised by the elected members. To cover the resale of houses which were originally sold under the Part V provisions a formula has been devised so that if the house is resold before twenty years the planning authority shall to some extent benefit from any profit.

As a postscript it must be said that initial indications are that Part V could have, in different circumstances, gone a fair distance to balance the needs of society generally. To quote the Chief Justice in the case of In the Matter of Article 26 of the Constitution and in the matter of Part V of the Planning and Development Bill [2000] ILRM 81: 'The objectives sought to be achieved by Part V of the Bill are clear: To enable people of relatively moderate means or suffering from some form of social or economic handicap to buy their own homes in an economic climate where housing costs and average incomes make that difficult and to encourage integrated housing development so as to avoid the creation of large scale housing developments confined to people in the lower income groups.'

2.3.9 **Strategic Development Zones**

The final matter to be addressed when researching the requirements of a planning application is the new provision in the 2000 Act establishing strategic development zones. Over the years concern had been expressed over the length of time required to achieve a planning permission particularly for large industrial or infrastructural projects. The odds were far too favourably tilted towards the objectors and against the proposers of nationally valuable investment. Objections at both outline and approval stages, appeals to the Board and judicial review proceedings often resulted in, literally, years being required to commence work on a project that would be clearly beneficial in national terms. The merits or otherwise of the appeal arguments did not affect the time scales. Some form of fast-track provision was required and this is now provided in Part IX of the 2000 Act – Strategic Development Zones.

Readers who have had experience of the Dublin Docklands Development Authority will recognise the basic framework: 'Where in the opinion of the Government, specified development is of economic or social importance to the State, the Government may by order, when so proposed by the Minister, designate one or more sites for the establishment, in accordance with the provisions of this Part, of a strategic development zone to facilitate such development.' The order will, amongst other things, specify the type of development that may be permitted. Before the legislation was published it was the intention that such zones would be primarily industrial but there is now no such restriction. Sub-section 166(5) is central to the concept and allows for the specifying of development that will require no planning permission. There are wide compulsory purchase powers given to planning authorities to acquire land that is the subject of a strategic development zone order.

The 'developer' referred to in this Part could be a local authority, the IDA and other state agencies, and the developer is required to prepare a planning scheme for any specified zone. sections 168 and 169 of the 2000 Act set out the detail for the making of the plan and the provisions for notice, appeal, etc. Many of these provisions reflect the procedures relating to the making and adoption of a development plan. The draft planning scheme for the zone is submitted to the relevant planning authority and can be appealed to An Bord Pleanála but only by those who made submissions. When it is in place, the planning scheme will take precedence over the development plan where there is conflict. A planning application made under Section 34 for a development in a strategic development zone 'shall' be granted permission if the planning authority is satisfied that the proposal would be consistent with the planning scheme. There is no appeal to An Bord Pleanála from any decision to grant permission. At the time of writing three orders have been made designating specific zones. These are S.I. 272 of 2001 (Adamstown, Lucan), S.I. 273 of 2001 (Hansfield, Blanchardstown) and S.I. 274 of 2001 (Clonmaggadon Valley, Navan).

2.3.10 Types of Application and Consultation

There are in effect four types of planning application which can be made, depending on the nature of the permission being sought.

a) Permission

This is the most common form of application, and is used where sufficient detail can be supplied to the planning authority to allow it to make a decision. It is often referred to as 'full planning permission' though this term does not appear in the Act or in the regulations. It is normally valid for five years (see par. 2.4.6).

b) Outline Permission

The original intention behind the concept of an outline application was that it would allow a proposer, particularly in the case of a large or complex project, to obtain the views of the planning authority as regards the principle of the development proposed without the necessity of going to the expense of preparing detailed plans. This would be particularly useful if the application contained any contentious proposals. An outline permission is converted into a permission by a Permission consequent to an Outline Permission (formerly known as an Approval). An outline permission lapses after three years (or five years if agreed by the planning authority) unless an application for subsequent permission is made during that time.

An outline application cannot be made

i)   for the retention of a structure or for the continuance of a use (Article 21 – S.I. 600 of 2001)

ii) where the building is a protected structure or a proposed protected structure (Article 21 – S.I. 600 of 2001)

iii) where an environmental impact assessment is required under Schedule V of S.I. 600 of 2001

iv) where a licence is required under part IV of the Environmental Protection Agency Act 1992 (Article 21 of S.I. 600 of 2001), or

v)   where the 'Seveso' legislation applies (Article 134 of S.I. 600 of 2001).

Previously outline proposals were not popular and mainly for three reasons. The first was the fact that the appeal provisions allowed third party objectors to appeal against an outline decision and then to lodge, in effect, the same appeal against the approval decision. This double jeopardy has been removed by Section 36(5) of the 2000 Act.

The second factor which formerly discouraged the use of an outline application was the size of the application fee. In the case of a large development the maximum fee for an outline application was €9,523 whereas the maximum fee for a permission application was €12,697. Taking into account the cost of two possible appeals, and the very long delays which might result, the intended advantages of the outline application were considerably restricted and the extra €3,174 fee might well have been offset by avoiding these other costs. The position is now modified so that the combined fee for an outline permission and for a permission subsequent to an outline permission does not exceed that for a permission.

Thirdly, planning authorities were entitled to use provisions in previous legislation to refuse to accept outline applications because in their opinion it 'would be likely to have significant effects on the environment' even if not exceeding the stated limits. This power is still available under Article 96 of the 2001 regulations.

Another aspect of an outline application which caused concern in the past was the doubt as to whether an approval (as it was then known) was bound to follow the grant of an outline permission. This was debated in a number of court cases. It had been thought as a result of comments made by the Court in *The State (Pine Valley Developments Ltd) v Dublin County Council* [1984] IR 407 that an outline permission guaranteed a subsequent permission, and the second edition of PLANNING AND DEVELOPMENT LAW (Walsh and Keane) states: 'the law on the matter is now as stated by Barrington J. and, accordingly, neither the planning authority nor the Board are entitled, in considering an application for approval, to reopen the question as to whether the development is acceptable in principle.'

However, in *The State (Kenny and Hussey) v An Bord Pleanála* [1984] Supreme Court, 20th December, a cautionary note was struck; 'Different considerations would apply if in the interval between the grant of outline permission and the application for approval there had been a significant change of circumstances in the area of the planning authority relevant to the application for approval.'

Two subsequent cases relied on these last comments to uphold the right of a planning authority not to grant approval on foot of an outline permission where the circumstances had indeed changed. These cases are *The State (Tern Houses (Brennanstown) Limited) v An Bord Pleanála* [1985] IR 725 and *Irish Asphalt Ltd v An Bord Pleanála* [1996] IPELJ 3 182

The 2000 Act clarifies the position with regard to outline permissions and subsequent applications for a permission following the outline permission. The Act, at Section 36(4), states that a refusal cannot be issued in respect of any matter which had been approved in the grant of an outline permission. This is comforting, and it may be speculated that the new restriction on the life on an outline permission to three years (or a maximum of five years if agreed by the planning authority) results from other Court comments made in the cases mentioned above referring to a long time lapse between an outline permission and a subsequent application for an approval.

c) Permission consequent on the grant of an Outline Permission

As mentioned above, a permission consequent on the grant of an outline permission converts an outline permission into a permission. It must be based rigidly on the outline permission and must be applied for within three years (or five years if agreed to by the planning authority) from the date of the grant of the outline permission.

d) Permission for Retention of Development

An application which might previously been made either for a retention of a structure, or for the continuance of a use is now described in both cases as permission for retention of development. The provision that the fees for any retention application be three times the ordinary fee reflects the official disapproval of these applications. In the case of large developments the maximum fee for retention is 125,000 as opposed to 38,000 for a standard application.

e) Pre-application consultation

At this point, the matter of pre-application consultation should be considered. Until now considerable frustration has been caused to applicants and their agents by the difficulty, or in some cases the outright denial, of consultation with a planning authority so as to attempt to establish the general parameters affecting any particular application. In such a subjective area as planning these discussions are essential. Section 247 of the 2000 Act deals with this but unfortunately the requirement is not mandatory. 'A person who has an interest in land and who intends to make a planning application *may, with the agreement of the planning authority concerned (which shall not be unreasonably withheld)*, enter into consultations with the planning authority in order to discuss any proposed development in relation to the land and the planning authority may give advice to that person regarding the proposed application.'

Sub-sections go on to emphasise that such discussions do not bind the authority, to permit the authority to list times and places where such consultations may be held, and also to require the authority to record such meetings and to keep such records with the planning file. What concerns many practitioners is the phrase above in italics. Some planning authorities (albeit a small minority) behave in a generally unreasonable manner and it will be interesting to see how they react to sub-section 247(1). John Gore-Grimes in KEY ISSUES IN PLANNING AND ENVIRONMENTAL LAW feels that this section will be used as a further curtailment of reasonable discussion. Time will tell.

The various steps in the application process are as follows:

2.3.11 Giving Notice

An important feature of the planning code is the giving of appropriate notices. As shall be seen later on the Courts interpret these requirements very strictly. Under previous legislation, it was acceptable either to publish a newspaper notice or to fix a notice on the site, but the 1994 regulations required that both of these methods be used and this requirement is continued in the present legislation. An exception to this requirement is that in the case of a planning application for the erection of overhead transmission or distribution lines by either an electricity or telecommunications undertaking, a site notice is not necessary.

a) Newspaper notice

The Regulations (Articles 17 and 18, S.I. 600 of 2001) require that the notice state the name of the applicant, whether the application is for a permission, an outline permission, or for a permission consequent on an outline permission, the location of the proposal, the nature and extent of the proposal, and, in the cases of retention or continuance, the nature of the use. In the case of a residential development the number of houses must be stated. If the proposal affects a protected or a proposed protected structure this must be stated. If an environmental impact statement is being submitted, or if a licence is required under the Environmental Protection Agency Act of 1992, this must also be stated in the notice. Similarly, if the proposal is in a strategic development zone, or is affected by the Major Accidents Directive, this must be stated. The notice must be headed by the name of the planning authority of the city, town, or county concerned. The whole original page containing the newspaper notice must be submitted with the application. The application must be made within two weeks of the appearance of the notice. While the 2001 regulations provide that a standard format be used for site notices, this is not a requirement for a newspaper notice. This is unfortunate as the Courts are constantly being asked as to the validity of newspaper notices. (see subsection c) of this part).

Article 18 also requires that the notice must be published in a newspaper approved by the planning authority. This is a welcome change. The previous legislation required that the newspaper must circulate in the district and this gave rise to a number of slightly bizarre decisions. Somewhat to the irritation of a number of people living in the south, the CORK EXAMINER was not regarded as a national newspaper, but to balance this a local authority in the west refused a planning application on the grounds that the Irish Press was not a national newspaper either. The High Court declared otherwise.

An innovation in Article 18 is that the notice must state that the planning application may 'be inspected or purchased' at the planning authority's office and also that submissions or observations may be made to the planning authority within five weeks of the receipt of the application. The provision, contained in Section 38 of the Act that the application, including drawings, may be purchased is causing copyright difficulties. It is obvious that unscrupulous people will buy and copy architects' drawings and will use them for their own purposes. There seems to be no way in which this can be prevented as proposals for the making of a statutory declaration by purchasers that the drawings will not be copied or used for other projects,will be treated as lightheartedly as the law of perjury is currently treated.

b) A site notice

The requirements are set out in Articles 17 and 19 of S.I. 600 of 2001. Previous editions of this book commented, with some despair, on the difficulties which these provisions had caused but there has been an improvement. Over the years the proliferation of these notices has either worn out the vandals or caused indifference, although some problems remain. The requirements regarding the validity of a planning application are now very severe and, at the time of writing, very many planning applications are being returned as invalid. The power of a planning authority to invalidate a previously judged valid application for up to five weeks after receipt of the application because of, say, the disappearance of the site notice will be resented by very many innocent parties. The fact that Article 26(7) allows a planning authority to accept that a site notice has been destroyed and that an application will not be retrospectively invalidated is not much comfort if past experience is to be considered. The last edition of this book appealed for some regulations to simplify the application process and Article 19 of the 2001 regulations now provides that the standard notice form as set out in Schedule 3 of S.I. 600 of 2001 must be used. The form sets out all the information that must be exhibited and is accompanied by helpful notes on the correct way to complete the form.

The notice must be erected in the two week period before making the application. It must be on a white background. An interesting new provision [Article 19(4)] requires that where a further application is made in respect of the same site within six months of the first application, the notice must be on a yellow background. No size is specified for a site notice and A4 seems generally acceptable. It should be fixed 'in a conspicuous position on or near the main entrance to the land or structure concerned from a public road, or where there is more than one entrance from public roads on or near all such entrances'. A planning authority may require more than one site notice if it considers this appropriate.

c) Interpretation of notices

It was pointed out in the introductory paragraph to this section that the Courts interpret the Regulations with regard to notice in a very strict way, and exact compliance is necessary, although minor and unimportant mistakes are allowed (*O'Donoghue v An Bord Pleanála* [1991] ILRM 750). Four instances will suffice to show how strictly the requirements are observed. In *Readymix (Eire) Limited v Dublin County Council and the Minister for Local Government* [1974] Supreme Court, 30th July, a newspaper notice said that permission was being sought 'to erect a replacement concrete plant in substitution for existing plant'. In fact the proposal was for a considerable expansion of the business being carried out and the Court held that the notice was misleading. In *Keleghan and Others v Dublin Corporation and Hilary Mary Corby* [1977] 111 ILTR 144 a newspaper notice indicated that permission was being sought for the erection of 'three classroom prefabricated extension to St Brigid's Secondary School, Killester' but did not say that a new access road was being provided through an existing cul-de-sac. The permission subsequently granted was held to be invalid. The Judge said: 'The purpose of notice is to give members of the public who may be concerned with the development an idea whether the development looked for is the kind that may affect their interest.' The Judge said that the residents of the cul-de-sac were given no such idea. The third case, *Monaghan Urban District Council v Alf-a-Bet Promotions Ltd* [1980] ILRM 64 dealt with a newspaper notice that referred to 'extensions and improvements of a premises at the Diamond, Monaghan'. The actual proposal was to convert an existing drapery shop into a betting office and amusement arcade. The application was held to be invalid. The last case illustrates how far the Courts will go to ensure exact compliance with the regulations. In *Crodaun Homes Ltd v Kildare County Council* [1983] ILRM 1 the applicants used the name 'Leixlip Gate' to indicate a site. This was a name known locally, but the Supreme Court (by three to two) decided that the more precise name of 'Kilmacradock Upper' should have been used.

The fashion of having long detailed descriptions of the works in newspaper notices is both unnecessary and expensive. This was well put in the case of *Springview v Cavan Development Ltd* [2000] 1 ILRM 437 where the Court said where some details of a proposed development were not listed: 'The notice would, as required, have alerted any vigilant or interested party to what was being contemplated and that person, if they wanted further information as to precisely what was envisaged could have inspected the plans submitted with the application.'

Though it is not required either by the Acts or Regulations, most planning authorities, and An Bord Pleanála, require a notice to state if a habitable building is being demolished even where the development could, quite clearly, not proceed without such demolition. This view was not approved by the Courts in two cases, *Cunningham v An Bord Pleanála* [1990] High Court, 3rd May, and *Molloy and Walsh v Dublin County Council* [1990] ILRM 663, where they refused to quash permissions where the demolition of habitable houses was not referred to in the newspaper notices.

While it may be suspected that some notices are intended to mislead, the majority of notices are rejected because the applicant has not fully appreciated the requirements. The consequences can be very serious. Where a planning authority refers a notice back on receipt of the application, not much harm is done, but where a planning decision is held to be invalid after construction has commenced and when interested parties first become aware of the proposal, the problem is very serious and no architect should ever take the risk of being involved in this type of problem. The 2001 regulations alter the previous provisions, and now provide that if a planning authority is of the view that the notice requirements are not met, then the application is invalid. Presumably if they do not reject the notice at the time of application, it cannot be questioned afterwards. The Courts will always have the last word.

2.3.12 The Applicant's Interest

Article 22(1) of S.I. 600 of 2001 requires applications to state 'the legal interest held by the applicant'. This was interpreted until 1975 as meaning that an application could be made for lands in which the applicant had no interest, provided this was made clear, and as a result many planning applications were made, as fishing exercises, in respect of properties the owners of which were unaware of the existence of the application. This position was changed by the case of *Frescati Estates Ltd v Marie Walker* [1975] IR 177. In this case the defendant had applied for permission relating to land owned by Frescati Estates, in respect of which she had no legal interest. The Supreme Court held that this was not in accordance with the intention of the Acts and held that for an application to be valid, 'it must be made either by or with the approval of a person who is able to assert a sufficient legal estate or interest to enable him to carry out the proposed development'. This principle was upheld in *McCabe v Harding Investments Ltd* [1982] Supreme Court, 17th October, where it was held that an inaccurate statement that the applicants had a freehold interest in the property, whereas in fact they were entitled to a conveyance, did not invalidate the application. The information given was held not be misleading and that the actual interest held was sufficient to satisfy the requirements.

Similarly, in *Schwestermann v An Bord Pleanála* [1994] High Court, 29th October, a minor mistake in the name of the applicant company was held not to be a defect in the permission. However, it is prudent to be as accurate as possible. In *State (NCE) v Dublin County Council* [1979] High Court, 4th December, it was held the application by a subsidiary company in respect of land owned by the parent company was invalid, as the subsidiary company had no interest in the lands in question. It is always prudent to enquire from the client what the accurate position is, particularly in the case of large or complex organisations.

2.3.13 Details, etc, Required

The interpretation of this section of the regulations by differing planning authorities has been very diverse. Some planning authorities require very different information from others as an examination of planning application forms will show although the new legislation is more specific than heretofore. It has been already pointed out that there are eighty eight planning authorities in the country and this could result in eighty eight different forms. The process is difficult enough as it is. It is suggested that a standard application form be drafted by the Department of the Environment. This is done in the case of the site notice, an application form for a Commencement Notice and a Fire Safety Certificate under the Building Control Act so there would appear to be no reason why it should not be done in the case of a planning application. The RIAI has prepared a checklist of the various items which need to be considered when making a planning application. A copy of this is reproduced at par. 2.7. At the moment this runs to 121 items and the initial response by planning authorities to planning applications under the new regulations is to reject as invalid any application where one single item has not been correctly attended to. Practitioners will have to be extremely careful in making planning applications as their clients may not always apportion the blame appropriately.

i) General

All planning applications must contain the information required in Article 22 of S.I. 600 of 2001 (in addition to the other requirements dealt with in par. 2.3.3 and par. 2.3.4) which is:

a) the name and address of the applicant, and if the applicant is not the owner, the name and address of the owner; a new requirement is for the names of company directors to be given where the applicant is a company registered under the Companies Acts 1963 to 1999

b) whether the application is for permission, retention of development, an outline permission, or a permission consequent on the grant of an outline permission

c) the address, etc, of the land or structure concerned

d) the legal interest of the applicant and, if none, the name and address of the owner

e) the area of the land, the number of dwellings, and except in the case of dwellings, the floor area of the buildings

f) state if an integrated pollution control licence or a waste licence is required

g) state if the development involves a protected or a proposed protected structure

h) if the application involves a residential, or partially residential, development, how the applicant proposes to comply with Section 97 of the Act (Part V)

i   six copies of drawings are now required and Article 21(3) allows the planning authority to request further copies of drawings; the full details of drawing requirements are set out in the next part. A map showing the location of the site notice must be supplied

j)   where the application is for a material change of use, a statement as to the existing and proposed uses is required

k)   a copy of the newspaper notice and of the site notice

l)   state if the development requires a licence under the Environmental Protection Agency Act 1992 or if it is covered by a number of European Union Regulations concerning industrial hazards

Any planning application that requires an environmental impact assessment and is not accompanied by one will not be dealt with by the planning authority until the requirement is fulfilled (Article 25). See also Chapter 3.

ii) Drawings

All drawings must now be metric. The full details are set out in Articles 23 and 24 of the 2001 regulations. A summary would be (non-exhaustive): Location maps must be to a scale of 1:1000 in built-up areas and 1:2500 elsewhere, site plans to be 1:500, and plans, sections and elevations to be not less than 1:200 or such other scale to be agreed with the planning authority.

Further requirements for drawings in the case of an application for permission are:

a)   the site must be clearly defined in red and adjacent roads, buildings, septic tanks, trees, walls, etc, must be shown. Adjoining land under the control of the owner or applicant to be outlined in blue, and wayleaves to be shown in yellow

b)   alterations and extensions should be marked or coloured.

c)   'contiguous' buildings must be shown. The precise meaning or intent of this requirement may cause some problems,

d)   principal dimensions shall be shown on plans, elevations, etc, together with distances from boundaries,

e)   any map based on an Ordnance Survey map must show the O.S. number. Maps and plans must show a north point,

f)   protected structures, or proposed protected structures, may require further particulars such as larger scale drawings, photographs etc.

g)   all drawings must state the name and address of the person who prepared them, and

h)   the planning authority may request a model of the proposed development.

iii) Outline Permission

Very often all that is required by way of drawings in the case of an outline application is a location map and a site plan. The Regulations require 'such particulars as are necessary to enable the planning authority to make a decision in relation to the siting, layout or other proposals for development'. (Article 24 – S.I. 600 of 2001).

iv) Permission consequent on the grant of an Outline Permission

The detail required for such an application is the same as that required for a permission. Applications for permission may be made for parts of an outline permission.

v)   Permission for Retention of Development

This requires the same detail as for a permission and in the case of a retention of a use a statement as to the former use and the use proposed to be continued.

It is always best to ensure that sufficient information is supplied, as otherwise the 'further information' provisions set out in par. 2.3.15 may be applied. If the planning authority considers that the application does not conform with all the requirements they will declare the application as being invalid. This is dealt with in the next section.

2.3.14 Receipt of Planning Application

Article 26 of the 2001 regulations provides that a planning authority must consider the application received and that when they are satisfied that it conforms to the requirements they shall so notify the applicant. If, however, they are satisfied that it does not conform, they shall return the application and the fee, specifying why they consider the application is invalid. It is curious to see that they will also require the removal of the site notice. The decision to return the application must be entered on the register. Anyone who made a submission must be informed and any fee returned.

At the time of writing there is very considerable concern being expressed over the number of applications declared invalid. Some planning authorities returned every application received in the first month after the regulations came into effect. Quite a number were returned for minor infringements of the requirements concerning drawings. The reporting of an application being returned because a drawing did not show a north point may be apocryphal [Article 23(1)(h)] but it indicates that the public reaction to the initiation of the new regime is one of baf-flement. It is submitted that a planning authority has discretion in these matters (see the comments on the interpretation of statutory instruments in Chapter 1) and where it is clear to the authority that it has adequate information to consider the application it should do so. The regulations would, in the author's view, be regarded by the Courts as being directory only and would not be such as to inval-idate the application.

Article 28 of the 2001 regulation lists the various bodies which must be notified by a planning authority whenever a planning application affects certain specified areas of development. There are twenty such types of bodies or organisations list-ed. The body notified has a five week period in which to make submissions or observations. However, if the body concerned has not been notified, they may appeal the decision of the planning authority to An Bord Pleanála, after the deci-sion is made, otherwise they may only appeal where they have made a submis-sion within the five week period.

2.3.15 Further Information

If the planning authority is of the view that it needs more detail in order to deter-mine an application, it may request the applicant to submit further information (Article 33 – 2001 regulations). When such a request is made, a four week peri-od is allowed to the planning authority for making a decision, running from the date on which the authority receives this further information. The practice of ask-ing for further information in order to extend the decision period, where no real need for such a request existed, but merely to give the planning authority more time is not as widespread as heretofore, but it does frequently happen, and this is particularly irritating both for the proposer who will very often suffer inconven-ience and sometimes actual loss, and for the architect who is, naturally, suspect-ed by his client of not making a properly detailed submission in the first place. That there is still some reason for concern, however, is reinforced by the 2000 Planning Statistics issued by the Department of the Environment. It appears from these figures that nearly 25% of all planning applications are subject to further information requests.

The Strategic Review Committee, already referred to, in their report BUILDING OUR FUTURE TOGETHER, recommended that a planning authority be required to seek additional information within one month of the application being lodged. The reduction in the new legislation of the period allowed to the planning authority after the receipt of additional information from two months to four weeks acknowledges the validity of this recommendation.

When a request for additional information has been made, the planning authority is not permitted a second request except as 'may be reasonably necessary to clarify the matters dealt with in the applicant's response'. It would be good practice to check with the authority as to the sufficiency of the initial response, as otherwise the process could drag out for over six months, instead of an anticipated eight weeks. If no answer is received by the planning authority within six months of the request being made, the application shall be declared to have been withdrawn. Article 33 of the regulations is the section for the time scales involved.

2.3.16 Planning Guidelines

A very welcome, and recent, development is the issuing by the Dept of the Environment of Planning Guidelines. These are issued for areas where there have been difficulties, particularly in obtaining consistent advice or decisions from differing planning authorities. These include guidelines for tree preservation, wind farms, antennae support structures, residential density, retail planning, and childcare facilities. A guide relating to landscape and landscape assessment is being drafted.

2.4   Planning Decisions

2.4.1   Grants and refusals

When a planning authority has considered an application it can do one of three things:

i)   decide to grant a permission

ii)   decide to grant a permission with conditions, or

iii) refuse the application.

Whichever course the authority decides on, it must come to its decision within eight weeks of the date of application unless it requests further information (see 2.3.15 above) or unless the applicant agrees to extend the time under Section 34(9) of the 2000 Act. A period of eight weeks can vary significantly from the former two month period and practitioners should carefully consult their calendars in view of the strict interpretation of the legislation. It must be noted in this regard that while regulations may be sometimes regarded as being only directory, any provisions in the Acts regarding time must be strictly interpreted and the eight week period is stated in the Act [Section 34(8)(a)]. Another factor to be noted is that Section 251 of the 2000 Act provides that the period from 24th December to 1st January (both days inclusive) shall not count in any period set out in either the Act or the regulations.

The 2001 regulations (Article 31) require the authority to state on any decision notice the register reference number, the date of the decision, the subject matter of the application, the length of time during which the permission remains valid, the purposes for which a structure may be used (if appropriate) and any conditions which may be imposed. A new requirement in the 2001 regulations is that where a planning decision differs from any report submitted to the Manager, then the reasons for such a decision must form part of the application. Conditions are dealt with in 2.4.2. In the case of a refusal and in the case of conditions the reasons for the refusal or conditions must be given. A planning authority cannot refuse an application, or impose a condition because it fears that some unauthorised event might result. It cannot anticipate a future situation (*Kelly v An Bord Pleanála* [1992] High Court, 6th April).

If the decision is not appealed within four weeks of the date of the decision then the authority will issue a grant of permission 'as soon as may be' [Section 34(11)]. If a refusal is not appealed, no further action is necessary by the planning authority. Occasions have occurred where a permission has been granted by mistake after an appeal has been lodged. There does not seem to be any case deciding the issue, but opinion seems to agree that it is the appeal and not the grant of permission that is valid. Occasions have also occurred where a local authority has neglected to inform interested parties of a notification of a decision to grant permission, as they are required to under Article 31 of the 2001 Regulations. The High Court has held, by way of an application for *certiorari* and *mandamus* (*Dolan v Dublin Corporation* [1989] IR 124) that in such a circumstance the notification of decision was invalid and should be removed from the register even though no appeal had been received.

A radical innovation in the 2000 Act is Section 35 dealing with 'past failures to comply'. The core of the provision is that where the planning authority is satisfied that the applicant had not complied with a previous permission, it may refuse permission for the proposed development irrespective of any other considerations. The previous irregularity must have been substantial. It may have been with regard to possible constitutional challenges that the procedure set out in this section involves the High Court. If a planning authority decides to refuse permission under this section, it will apply to the High Court for an authorisation to refuse permission. In such a case the eight week period for a decision will run from the date of the High Court decision. The Court may grant or refuse the application or give any direction that it considers appropriate. There is no appeal to An Bord Pleanála from the High Court decision.

A potential problem in this provision was seen to be the difficulty of identifying the appropriate persons who might be involved. This would particularly apply to companies and this is presumably why Article 22 of the 2001 regulations requires a planning application to list the names of the directors of any company applying for a permission, together with the address and registration number of the company. Section 35 of the Act provides for applying the section to companies which are related to, or under the control of, companies which previously offended.

The requirement that the authority make a decision within eight weeks of the application requires further examination. The Act says that if no decision is communicated to the applicant within the appropriate period, then a decision to grant permission is regarded as having been given on the last day of the period. The eight week period begins on the day of the receipt by the authority of the application and the 2001 regulations (Article 26) require the authority to stamp the application documents with the date of receipt and to notify the applicant of this date. There has been some difficulty with regard to the exact limits of this eight week period. The period itself is clear enough. The Interpretation Act 1937 says at section 11(b): 'where a period of time is expressed to begin on, or be reckoned from a particular day, that day shall, unless the contrary intention appears, be deemed to be included in such period.' This has been clarified in the case of *McCann v An Bord Pleanála* [1996] IPELJ 3 186, where the Court held that a planning decision made on 7th June 1995 had to be appealed by 6th July 1995 as a month means a calendar month and cannot include two days of the same date. It is the matter of notification that has caused some problems.

One part of the problem is that the various Statutes set out different methods of notification, and the other part of the problem is that the Courts interpret these provisions in differing ways. Since the matter is of such vital importance it is proposed to deal with it in some detail. The Act at Section 250 lists five ways in which the planning authority may notify anyone:

a)   where it is addressed to him by name, by delivering it to him

b)   by leaving it at the address at which he ordinarily resides or, in a case in which an address for service had been furnished, at that address

c)   by sending it by post, in a prepaid registered letter addressed to him at the address at which he ordinarily resides or, in a case which an address for service has been furnished, at that address

d)   where the address at which he ordinarily resides cannot be ascertained by reasonable enquiry and the notice or copy is so required or authorised to be given or served in respect of any land or premises, by delivering it to some person over sixteen years of age, resident or employed on such land or premises or by affixing it in a conspicuous position on or near such land or premises

e) in the case of an enforcement notice, by delivering it to someone who is employed in the carrying out of the development to which the notice relates.

On the other hand, the 2000 Act sets out different ways in which an appeal may be sent to the Board. It does not include any such provision as (d) above on the reasonable grounds that the Board will be easily located.

Section 127(5) of the 2000 Act says at sub-section (5):

An appeal shall be made:

a) by sending the appeal by prepaid post to the Board, or

b   by leaving the appeal with an employee of the Board during office hours, or

c) by such other means as may be prescribed.

What gives rise to the difficulties is the differing interpretations as far as postal notice is concerned. The basic law covering this is section 18 of the Interpretation Act 1937:

'Where an Act of the Oireachtas or an Instrument made wholly or partly under any such Act authorises or requires a document to be served by post whether the word 'serve' or any of the words 'give', 'deliver', or 'send' or any other word is used, then unless a contrary intention appears, the service of such document may be effected by properly addressing, prepaying (where requisite), and posting a letter containing such document and in such case the service of such document shall, unless the contrary is proved be deemed to have been effected at the time at which such letter would be delivered in the ordinary course of post.'

The different interpretations of the Courts do not help. In *The State (Murphy) v Dublin County Council* [1970] IR 253 the Court observed: 'The planning authority was to be required to do its part within the appropriate period by dispatching notice of its decision, but the time of receipt of the notice seems not to be of importance.' An opposite view was taken in *Freeney v Bray Urban District Council* [1982] ILRM 29 where the Court was of the view that taking all the provisions of Section 7 of the 1963 Act together, the intention of the legislature was that planning applications were to be dealt with as matters of some urgency and the strict time limits must be observed, and the notice must be received in time. As the Freeney case is the later, it must be presumed to be the position with regard to planning notification.

The position with regard to appeals is now much the same. In *The State (Connolly) v The Minister for Local Government* [1968] High Court, 13th November an appeal was received after the appropriate period. The Court held that in such a case the appeal was valid if it was posted in time. 'All that is required is that the letter or document be posted in the time so limited.' However the Judge added: 'This approach and reasoning would not, of course, apply were it provided that the appeal should be received by the Minister within the appointed time.' This was precisely what section 17(1)(a) of the 1992 Act decreed: 'Subject to paragraph (b) of the provisions of Section 26(5) of the Act authorising appeals to be made before the expiration of the appropriate period within the meaning of that sub-section shall be construed as including a provision that an appeal received by the Board after the expiration of the appropriate period shall be invalid as not having being made in time.'

This is the direct opposite of section 18 of the Interpretation Act. In view of the stringency of the requirements of the appeal provisions of the 2000 Act where an appeal must contain the entire detailed case at first submission and in view of the provisions of section 127(1)(g) it means in effect that to be posted and to be certain of delivery an appeal must be completed within about three weeks after the decision by the local authority. In the case of large or complex projects this can hardly be described as reasonable and it would not be surprising if a legal challenge were made to these provisions particularly as a day or so can make no difference to what are purely matters of administrative convenience. Interestingly, Section 22(1) of the 1976 Act, now revoked, provided that if an appeal was received by post three days after the expiry of the period it would be regarded as having been made in time. There is a minor softening of the limits in section 141 of the 2000 Act providing that where the last day of an appeal period is a day on which the offices of the Board are closed, the next following day shall be the last day. The basic rule can be stated as being that it is the date of communication and not the date of the decision that is important.

The question of default permissions, which might arise as a result of disputes with regard to these time limits, is dealt with later at 2.4.8, and appeals generally are dealt with at 2.4.4.

There is provision in the Act for an extension of the eight week period. Section 34(9) of the Act says that if the applicant, before the end of the eight week period, gives his consent to the planning authority to extend the period then the agreed extended date will form the end of the appropriate period. This can often be a useful device where there is a genuine need for some further research or information by the planning authority and where the absence of such an extension of time might necessitate a refusal. It was established in *Flynn and O'Flaherty Properties v Dublin Corporation* [1996] High Court, 19th December, that it was valid to give more than one extension of the period. In that case four extensions of time were agreed.

There is provision in the Act and regulations for a minimum period for making decisions resulting from a notorious instance where a planning authority issued an approval the day after a revised newspaper advertisement was published. Article 30 of S.I. 600 of 2001 provides that five weeks must elapse from the date of application to the date of decision.

There is, also, a provision in the case of a transboundary EIS that no planning decision shall be made until all the necessary consultations have been completed. It is not expected that this regulation will have much effect on many applications

Finally in this section, it must be noted (and many planning decisions make such a statement) that planning permission of itself does not entitle the developer to proceed. All other relevant legislation, which might range from as far back as the Public Health (Ireland) Act 1878 to the Waste Management Act 1996 – and beyond – must be addressed before the planning permission is implemented. This was clearly pointed out in the case of *Cablelink Ltd v An Bord Pleanála* [1999] High Court, 23rd February where the Court upheld a decision of the Board to grant permission for a television deflector system even though the owner had no licence to operate it. The Court pointed out that this was a distinct and separate matter. The same comment, it is suggested would apply to the conditions which are attached to planning permissions requiring conformity with other legal codes such as the Building Regulations.

2.4.2 Reasons and Conditions

When coming to a decision a planning authority is required under Section 34(10)(a), both in the case of a decision to grant and a decision to refuse, to give reasons and considerations upon which the decision is based. The reasons attached to a refusal can be general or specific and, while they can be very wide ranging, they should normally relate to the development plan. The Courts have usually allowed a fair degree of latitude to planning authorities in this matter and in the case of *Maher v An Bord Pleanála* [1992] High Court, 10th April, a reason of diminution of the value of adjoining properties was accepted as valid.

The general power of a planning authority to attach conditions to a permission is contained in Section 34 of the 2000 Act. It would not be an exaggeration to say that the whole area of conditions has proved to be one of the most difficult and contentious areas of practical concern to applicants and their advisors. It is submitted that an application to a planning authority should be largely acceptable or not as the case may be, and that the imposition in some cases of more than 50 conditions indicates a lack of proper consultation between the parties. In October 1982, the Department of the Environment published Development Control – Advice and Guidelines, primarily for the benefit of planning authorities. This is a useful document and covers many aspects of the system. Many of the points made below are endorsed in this guide, particularly in relation to conditions. At par 5.6 of that document it suggests that all conditions should be necessary, relevant both to planning generally and to the application in particular, enforceable, precise and reasonable. At the time of writing, the Department of the Environment and Local Government has asked for submissions in relation to the issuing of an up-to-date edition of this guide.

The 1982 guide endorses the view that conditions should be kept to a minimum and that conditions relating to other legislation should never be included. Sometimes the reasons given are very unsatisfactory or imprecise. An example would be: 'The proper planning and development of the area' but there is very little that can be done to question this, even though the use of the phrase was viewed with disapproval by the Court in the 'Tara Radio Case' (see par. 2.4.5).

The planning authority may issue conditions in respect of eleven listed matters but it is accepted that conditions would not necessarily be restricted to those areas listed in the 2000 Act [Section 34(4)]. In any event the listed categories are very wide ranging.

A summary of the listed conditions follows and would deal with:

a)   Any land which is under the control of the applicant, and which is adjacent to the land which is the subject of the application, can be restricted by condition as far as its future development is concerned.

b)   The applicant can be required to carry out works including the provision of facilities which are not part of the application, but which the planning authority considers would be necessary for the completion of the proposal. The provision of a car park is a good example. The Supreme Court has held (*McDonagh v Galway Corporation* [1993] 17th May) that a planning authority was entitled to require a developer to provide more car parking than the development itself required on the grounds that the site was zoned for a public car park and, also, that such an undertaking was capable of providing a profit. This decision reversed a High Court ruling which was felt to be in more general accord with the overall intent of conditions.

c)   The problem of noise, both from within any proposed development, and the effect of outside noise on occupants of any proposed structure, may be controlled by condition. This sub-section, inserted by the 1976 Act, arose largely out of concern about aircraft noise in the vicinity of airports (see par. 3.6 on noise generally).

d)   The provision of open spaces can be controlled by conditions, but most applications will contain the open space provision of the appropriate development plan.

e)   The planting of trees, or other landscaping, may be required.

f)   A condition can be imposed which would require the completion of a devel-
g)   opment within two years. This type of condition is most often imposed in the
     case of housing developments to ensure that the proposer will complete all
     roads, footpaths, landscaping, etc. Adequate security to insure the compli-
     ance with this condition may be sought.

h)   Conditions covering the sequence and timing of works.

i)   The maintenance and management of the proposed property

j)   The maintenance, until taken in charge, of roads, open spaces, etc

k)   The collection and storage of recyclable materials

l)   The recovery and disposal of construction and demolition waste

m)   Related somewhat to b) is the provision that the planning authority may
     require, by way of condition, roads, car parks, sewers, etc, in excess of the
     immediate needs of the proposed development. The local authority must,
     however, either pay for these extra works or take them in charge.

n)   Limit the term of the permission. Normally, once a planning permission is
     implemented it is valid for ever, unless revoked, and this sub-clause can be
     used where the planning authority considers it appropriate to limit the length
     of time for which the development can exist. This limitation should not be
     confused with the length of time for which a permission remains valid before
     implementation. This is normally five years (see par. 2.4.5) but it appears
     from the wording of Section 34(4) – 'without prejudice to the generality of
     that sub-section' – that a planning authority could limit this period by way of
     condition.

o)   The numbering and naming of roads and buildings.

p)   Where a protected structure is removed or altered the recording by way of
     drawings or photographs of the structure, or the salvage or reinstatement of
     any particular item.

As far as conditions are now concerned it is important to point out that Section
34(2)(c) of the 2000 Act reserves absolutely to the Environmental Protection
Agency any decisions relating to emissions under the Environmental Protection
Agency Act 1992 or the Waste Management Act 1996.

Under the previous legislation, conditions were often imposed requiring mone-
tary contributions to the local authority to cover expenditure by the authority in
providing services which would facilitate the proposed development. These sums
of money varied substantially from one planning authority to another, and were
usually reduced on appeal by the Board. A number of disputes ended up in the
Courts, one in particular – *Bord na Mona v An Bord Pleanála and Galway County*

Council [1985] IR 205 providing a useful commentary on conditions generally. To regularise the situation, sections 48 and 49 set up a new system of contribution that may be required by way of condition.

In essence, the new system requires (Section 48) the planning authority to make a development contribution scheme for it functional area, or other schemes for particular areas. These schemes must be made within two years of the coming into force of the Act, i.e. by March 2004. The schemes may set out different contributions for different classes of development, and there is provision for exceptional circumstances. The planning authority must set out the basis for contributions for the different classes and must also relate these contributions to the actual costs that might be incurred. Contribution schemes are covered by the, now, usual requirements concerning public involvement. Any such scheme must be advertised, submissions sought, the Minister consulted and finally approved. The approval of the scheme must also be published.

Two very important new provisions regarding contributions are made in Section 48(10). Firstly, no appeal may be made against a condition imposing a contribution except on the grounds that the contribution scheme was not properly applied, and secondly, such an appeal will not delay the implementation of the development provided that there is no other appeal and also provided that the appellant provides security to the planning authority for the amount specified in the condition. It is very important to note [Section 48(13)(a)] that any such appeal will not, unlike other appeals, imperil the entire permission as the Board will be restricted to considering the condition itself. This provisions was originally suggested in the Strategic Review Committee report referred to in par. 1.6.

There are limitations on the extent of the scope of these contributions. If the works which the local authority proposes to carry out as a result of the condition are not commenced within five years after payment, or finished within seven years or are not proceeded with at all, the local authority must refund the contribution together with any interest. All contribution monies must be held by the local authority in a separate account.

Section 49 deals with public infrastructure projects and the manner of requiring contributions by way of condition for them. The provisions of Section 48 are generally repeated. The 'supplementary development contribution scheme', as it is called, must specify the projects proposed. Public infrastructure projects are defined generally as rail, light rail, public transport, car parks, new roads, sewers, drains, etc.

In general, conditions are subject to certain restrictions. In *Mixnam's Properties Ltd v Chertsey UDC* [1965] AC 735 four principles were set out:

1   Conditions cannot be imposed which would fundamentally affect general law. This is logical. It has been pointed out before that one piece of legislation cannot be used to impose the provisions of separate and distinct legislation.

2   Conditions must be restricted to the matters set out in the statute. Many local authorities still impose conditions which have nothing at all to do with planning laws. The commonest are those requiring applicants to obtain the fire officers approval to the proposal, or requiring compliance with (formerly) building bye-laws, and now Building Regulations, or with Health Acts, and so on. A recent planning decision required, before occupation, by way of condition, a certificate from 'a competent professional person with professional indemnity insurance' that the building conformed with the building regulations. These are all clearly invalid and the Minister for the Environment in his DEVELOPMENT CONTROL – ADVICE AND GUIDELINES (October 1982) at par 5.28 has specifically asked planning authorities not to include such conditions. The courts also agree. The case of *Smith v East Elloe RDC* [1956] AC 736 was quoted with approval in *Listowel v MacDonagh* [1968] IR 312: 'It is certainly an abuse of power to seek to exercise it when the statute relied upon does not truly confer it and the invalidity of the Act does not depend in anyway upon the question whether the person concerned knows or does not know that he is acting *ultra vires*. It is an abuse of power for a purpose different from that for which it is entrusted to the holder not less because he maybe acting ostensibly for the authorised purpose.'

This view has also been set out very clearly in the case of *Carty v Dublin County Council* [2000] 1 ILRM 64. Permission was obtained from An Bord Pleanála for a development that had been refused permission on grounds of inadequate drainage capacity by the planning authority. The same local authority, now acting in the role of sanitary authority, refused bye-law approval on the same grounds that they had originally used in refusing planning permission. The court held that they were perfectly entitled to do this on the grounds that the areas of planning and of bye-laws were controlled by different legislation. An interesting English case, *T & S Contractors v Architectural Design Consultants* [1992] 10-CLD-06-21 held that a building was an unauthorised development because it did not comply with the planning permission and the fact that the same local authority had approved the changed building under the building regulations was not relevant.

However, it has been argued that the inclusion in the Fourth Schedule of the 2000 Act at paragraph (f) – previously in the 1990 Act – of 'health and safety' being a ground to exclude compensation, somehow tied in building regulation matters to the planning code but this, it is submitted, is far-fetched. The practice of imposing these invalid conditions, however, persists.

3   Conditions must not be unreasonable. This is clearly set out in case law and

a condition 'must fairly and reasonably relate to the permitted development' (*Pyx Granite Co. Ltd v Ministry of Housing and Local Government* [1960] AC 260). In *Ashbourne Holdings Ltd v An Bord Pleanála* [2002] 1 ILRM 321, the court held that a condition in a decision regarding an application to develop a golf course at the Old Head, Kinsale, was unreasonable in that it would have frustrated the entire development. A condition cannot be imposed where the co-operation of a third party is required. This follows from a decision in *Killiney and Ballybrack Development Association v Minister for Local Government* [1978] Supreme Court, 24th April.

4   Conditions must be clear.

5   Validity: if conditions do not meet the criteria set out in 1 to 4 above, they may be invalid. As commented above, it seems to be accepted that conditions which require applicants to, for instance, 'comply with the requirement of the Fire Officer', or some other extraneous legislation, are invalid. Other clear breaches of the restrictions would be equally invalid, but the question then arises as to what to do in practice. One remedy would be to appeal to An Bord Pleanála to remove the offending condition. This, however, can be a risky route (see 8 below). Another remedy would be to apply to the Courts to have the condition struck out, but this is a lengthy and, therefore, costly route. Further, a developer rarely greets the news of an impending Court action with pleasure. The developer could always ignore the condition, carry out the works, and in effect defy the planning authority, but in these days of omnipresent opinions or certificates of compliance this seems a dangerous option.

The condition referred to in par. 2.2.2 where a planning authority required the applicant to agree the interior layout behind a shopfront for a distance of 6 metres was clearly invalid as being contrary to Section 4(1)(g) of the 1963 Act. The same decision attempted by condition to, in effect, redesign the shop front. The Department guidelines mentioned above advises that 'special care should be taken to secure that matters of personal preference or taste are not allowed to affect decisions on planning proposals, particularly where these are prepared by competent and qualified designers'. (par. 1.13). This can be particularly irritating when experienced and qualified architects are being dictated to by people who, however competent they may be in other areas, have no qualifications of any sort in the sphere of architectural design. Since the first edition of this book was published this practice has become very widespread and some planning authorities are, in effect, redesigning applications on the basis of their own subjective views or prejudices. It is to be hoped that, sooner or later, this practice will be tested in the Courts. It would seem, in any event, to be only fair that if the planning authority is having a substantial design input that they should also accept a concomitant measure of liability for the project.

The question then arises as to the status of a permission which has an invalid condition attached. Does this invalidate the entire permission? In *Bord na Mona v An Bord Pleanála and Galway County Council* [1984] High Court, 22nd November, it was held that a condition which was fundamental to the permission would invalidate the entire permission if the condition itself is invalid. This view was upheld in *The State (FPH Properties SA) v An Bord Pleanála* [1989] ILRM 98. Whether or not the condition is fundamental would be decided by the Courts on the facts in each case. Interestingly enough, the Court in this case held that the practical effect of the decision was that the entire permission was a nullity and the unfortunate plaintiff had to apply all over again. So the legal route is not recommended. It is interesting to note that in issuing permissions, the Board invariably removes the invalid conditions referring to fire officers, etc.

6   Conditions attached to outline permissions: Since the purpose of an outline application is to establish the parameters and limitations upon which the subsequent approval will be based, it is essential that any conditions setting such targets, or imposing such limitations, should be defined at the outline stage.

7   Conditions are sometimes attached to permissions which require matters 'to be agreed' between the applicant and the planning authority, or in default of agreement by the Board [Section 34(5)]. The former use of the word 'approval' was undesirable as it is now accepted that this can only mean that the formal process be applied and that notice, application and possible appeal are in fact intended. My own view is that the Board would be wrong to require a successful appellant to seek a further permission. The Board would, in effect, be giving permission to an applicant to apply for permission. The matter should be concluded by the Board. It is preferable that matters 'be agreed'. This process has been criticised on the grounds that such agreements, being between the applicant and the authority, deprive the public of any rights of objection, and such agreements should be restricted to matters which would not seriously affect third parties. (*Keleghan and Others v Dublin Corporation* 111 ILTR 144). A further case, *Houlihan v An Bord Pleanála* [1992] High Court, 4th October, again emphasised that a matter subsequently agreed between the applicant and either the planning authority or An Bord Pleanála must not be significant enough to deny or restrict third part rights of appeal. Two recent cases, *Boland v An Bord Pleanála* [1996] 3 IR 465 and *McNamara v An Bord Pleanála* [1996] 2 ILRM 339 dealt with the problems of conditions which required further matters to be 'agreed'. Certain tests were suggested in the Boland case such as the desirability of leaving technical matters, particularly when they are the responsibility of the planning authority to be agreed and also whether any member of the public could reasonably object to such a condition. The McNamara case, however, specifically approved the practice of requiring agreement between the appli-

cant and the planning authority provided that the matter was not substantive. Where the parties fail to agree on such matters they can be resolved by An Bord Pleanála. It has been decided however, that by agreeing to any matter which are referred to in a condition, the planning authority is not making a decision as defined in the Act (*O'Connor and Dublin Corporation v Borg Developments* [2000] High Court, 3rd October).

The concerns expressed in cases such as those mentioned above have led to the introduction of new safeguards in Articles 34 and 35 of the 2001 regulations. Article 34 is a restatement of the old Article 35 in the 1994 regulations providing for the submission of revised plans where the planning authority is disposed to grant a permission. The next Article, 35, sets out the details involved. Prescribed bodies and those who made submissions within five weeks after the date of the application must be notified and they may inspect or purchase the proposed revisions. Further submissions may be made within a time to be specified. No further fee is due provided that a fee was paid at the time of the original submission. The applicant is required to publish a notice indicating that revisions have been lodged. It is presumed that the planning authority has a further four weeks to consider the application after receipt of the revisions. The Board has also power, under section 142 of the 2000 Act, to invite modification and to require publication of new notices. The annual report of the Board contains a list of such decisions.

8   It was mentioned in 5 above that an appeal may be lodged against a condition. This is a risky route to take, as the legislation required the Board to consider an appeal as if the application for permission had been made to it in the first instance [2000 Act, Section 37(1)(b)]. The danger was that the entire permission might be overturned, and not merely the condition. Section 139 of the 2000 Act specifically authorises the Board to consider conditions separately, without looking at the full decision and without regarding the application as being *de novo*. But it is important to notice that the Board's power to review the entire proposal is not impaired. The report of the Comptroller and Auditor General (April 2002) on the workings of An Bord Pleanála reveals, alarmingly, that 20% of all such appeals against conditions result in the entire permission being overturned. As mentioned in par 2.4.2, an appeal against a contribution does not now either imperil the decision or delay the project. It would be a matter of judgement for practitioners to decide the safe course, taking into account the status of the application in relation to the relevant development plan. The Court in the case of *MCD Management Systems Ltd v Kildare County Council* [1995] 2 ILRM 532 made the interesting argument that where the Board decided to exercise its discretion under section 15 of the 1992 Act, it would not regard the application as being made to it in the first instance, and that only the documents submitted to the planning authority would be considered, and the appeal letter would not be taken into account.

A final matter to be considered in the area of conditions is where the planning authority requires a person 'interested in land' to enter into an agreement with them to regulate or restrict the use of land. This is set out in Section 47 of the 2000 Act (better known as Section 38 of the 1963 Act, which is similar). The object of the section is to limit the development of land, usually relating to family use, or sterilised land, and is a separate binding agreement not affected by a planning permission. Such agreement cannot be used to alter materially a development plan, and details of any such agreement must be entered on the register.

2.4.3 **Lists, Documents and the Register**

The Act and regulations require both the planning authority and An Bord Pleanála to maintain lists referring to aspects of the planning process for the information of the public.

As far as a planning authority is concerned, it is required under Article 23 of the 2001 regulations to provide a weekly list of planning applications, giving in considerable detail all relevant information in respect of the applications received the previous week. This list is to be made available at the offices of the authority and in every public library in the authority's area, and must also be available for purchase at a reasonable cost, or free if the authority decides.

Article 32 of the same regulations requires the planning authority to make available, on the same conditions, a list of all planning decisions. Article 72 requires An Bord Pleanála to keep lists of appeals and referrals on a weekly basis and to have these available at the offices of the Board. The lists will be available for four weeks and may be displayed electronically.

In addition to the lists referred in the above paragraph, documents are also to be made available. The regulations [Article 18(1)(e)] say that a planning application can be inspected, or purchased, at the office of the planning authority 'as soon as may be' after the application is lodged. The copyright difficulties have been commented on in par. 6.7(b). After the making of the decision the purchase and inspection of documents, according to Section 38(1) of the Act, is to be available within three working days after the planning decision. These documents include all reports, observations, etc, received by the authority. They are to be retained by the authority for inspection for not less than seven years after the decision, and after that in a local archive in accordance with the Local Government Act 1994.

As far as an appeal is concerned, An Bord Pleanála is required to send details of the appeal to the offices of the planning authority involved and to be available for inspection by the public until the appeal is determined (Article 68). Section 146 of the Act provides for the making available of appeal documents within three working days of the making of the appeal decision and also for the purchase of copies of these documents.The documents are to be available for public inspection for a period of five years following the appeal decision.

A feature of the administration of the planning system which has changed out of all recognition over the years is the recording of certain data in the register. Originally, in the 1963 Act, the register was intended to record, in the main, matters relating to the granting or revoking of permissions, compensation decisions and enforcement notices. The 2000 Act, at Section 7, lists 25 items that must be registered, ranging from planning applications to the operation of quarries and ending with a twenty sixth item: 'Any other matters as may be prescribed by the Minister.'

The importance of the register, and of accuracy in relation to entries, was emphasised in *Readymix (Eire) v Dublin County Council* [1974] Supreme Court, 30th July, where it was stated: 'A proper record of permission is therefore necessary. This is provided for by Section 8 (of the 1963 Act) which prescribes that a planning authority shall keep a register of all land in their area affected by the Act. This register is the statutorily designated source of authoritative information as to what is covered by a permission. The Act does not in terms make the register the conclusive or exclusive record of the nature and extent of a permission, but the scheme of the Act indicates that anybody who acts on the basis of the correctness of the particulars in the register is entitled to do so.'

2.4.4 Appeals

The appeal procedure first appeared in the 1963 Act, and has been modified several times since then, the last significant changes being contained in the 2000 Act. Formerly anyone could appeal. This unrestricted right of third party appeal was unique to Ireland, and not only led to, but encouraged malicious and blackmail appeals. Practitioners know how cynically this invitation to license was pursued. The provisions in previous legislation relating to 'frivolous and vexatious' appeals (section 14 of the 1992 Act) or powers relating to awarding costs against appellants (section 19 of the 1976 Act) seem rarely, if ever, to have been used. The April 2002 report on planning appeals by the Comptroller and Auditor General seems surprised that 'the Irish planning appeals system is unusual in Europe'. It noted that 1.3% of decisions in Northern Ireland were appealed, as compared to 7% in the Republic of Ireland. The report was also concerned that there seemed to be a disturbing difference in both the number of appeals and the appeal decisions in differing planning authority areas. For instance, in the five year period from 1995 to 1999, 58% of decisions to refuse permission in Dublin city were appealed, as opposed to 12% in Wexford. The outcome of these appeals was that in Dublin city 21% of the decisions were overturned as opposed to 10% ion Wexford. The report generally expressed concern over an apparent lack of uniformity in the system. The new legislation goes some distance towards correcting the abuses, but much scope for ingenious misuse of the system remains.

The main provision which has been introduced to curtail previous abuse is contained in Section 37 of the 2000 Act which restrict appellants to applicants and to those who made submissions or observations to the planning authority within five weeks of the lodging of the application. Presumably, any appeal lodged by those who made submissions will be restricted to the headings or points made in the submission. There are two exceptions to the rule. One [Section 37(4)(a)] allows any prescribed body which has not been properly notified of the application to appeal within the four week period. The second allows an adjoining land owner [Section 37(6)] to appeal within four weeks of the decision to the Board by way of an application for leave to appeal where the landowner can satisfy the Board that conditions attached to the permission will materially affect the original proposals and that these changes will affect either the landowners enjoyment of the land, or the value of the land. An error in drafting uses the phrase 'permission has been granted' in the Act instead of the intended 'decision has been taken to grant planning permission'. Obviously, no appeal of any sort can be made after a grant of permission, and it will be interesting to see what the courts, if asked, would have to say. The new provisions will at least flush out the last minute appellants but the blackmail appeals referred to in section 1.3.8(1)(a)(ii) will not diminish unless the powers of the Board as set out in section 145, and in particular in subsection (1)(b)(ii) where the Board can order compensation by way of such sum as the Board in its absolute discretion specifies are widely and rigorously used. To date no direction has ever been made by the Board requiring compensation to be paid.

When an appeal is made to the Board, the decision of the planning authority is set aside and the Board considers the application as if it had been made to the Board in the first instance – Section 37(1)(b) of the 2000 Act. A valid appeal annuls the decision of the Planning Authority.

The decision as to whether or not an appeal should be made is a matter for the judgement of the applicant, and his advisors. There are a number of factors to be considered, one of the more important being the chances of success. Figures released by the Comptroller and Auditor General show that only 18% of appeals against refusals succeeded, while only 5% of appeals against decisions to grant permission were confirmed without alteration, 67% were varied, and 28% overturned. Other factors to be considered would be the cost and time involved. It might be that further consultation with the planning authority could result in a revised application being successful, and this route should be examined.

The appeal process, and the nature and extent of the information to be presented to the Board, including the possibility of requiring the submission of an environmental impact statement, is now such that a planning consultant is often engaged, particularly in complex proposals. Such experts, in addition to their technical knowledge, can be very useful in assessing the most successful tactics and approaches.

Over the years, dissatisfaction had been expressed about the length of time taken by appeals and by the possible use of improper influence on decisions. Originally, appeals were determined by the Minister for the Environment. In the 1976 Act this function was transferred to An Bord Pleanála, and the 1983 Act further removed the Board from any possibility of political interference. The 1992 Act at last addressed the question of time. This was badly needed. At certain periods appeals had taken up to two years to determine, and while the average time had been greatly reduced, it was accepted that a specific time restraint, much as that imposed on planning authorities, would be of advantage. This point is dealt with later on.

The main features of the appeals system are:

i) Time for appeal

An appeal must now be lodged within four weeks of the date of the decision by the planning authority [2000 Act, Section 27(1)(d)]. Par. 2.4.1. deals with the law affecting time limits, and in summary it can be said that as far as appeals are concerned the appeal must be received by the Board within the appropriate period, no matter how delivered. This is very strictly interpreted by the courts (*Graves v An Bord Pleanála* [1997] IRISH TIMES, 18th August).

Under previous Acts, a third party was required to appeal within 21 days of the date of the decision. The applicant was given one month from the date on which he received the decision to appeal. This had the considerable advantage that an applicant knew whether or not an appeal had been lodged before he was required to appeal, and a decision as to appeal or not against a condition, for instance, could be made in the light of that knowledge.

Now this advantage has disappeared as third party appeals are invariably made at the last minute, although the new provisions restricting appeals will help. However, an applicant can withdraw an appeal at any time, and the loss of the maximum fee of 380 may not be too much of a penalty if the applicant wishes to proceed. If an appeal is withdrawn, provided no other appeals relating to that application have been received, then the planning authority will automatically issue the grant of permission. Submissions by those who are not parties to the appeal must be made within four weeks of the receipt of the appeal by the Board.

ii) Details required for a valid appeal

Up till the passing of the 1992 Act, there were a number of factors that contributed to the long delays involved in the appeal process. There were no specific requirements as to the amount of detail necessary for an appeal. Often, a general appeal was lodged with a statement that details would follow. Even though the 1977 Regulations at Article 36 (now revoked) required the notice of appeal to state the grounds the Courts had held in *The State (Genport Limited) v An Bord Pleanála* [1983] ILRM 12 that failure to state the grounds at the time of appeal did not invalidate the appeal. Section 127 of the 2000 Act makes it clear that the grounds are now mandatory at the time of lodgement. The section is worth quoting in full:

1   An appeal shall:

    a) be made in writing

    b) state the name and address of the appellant or the person making the referral and of the person, if any, acting on his or her behalf.

    c) state the subject matter of the appeal or referral

    d) state in full the grounds of appeal or referral and the reasons, considerations and arguments on which they are based

    e) in the case of an appeal under Section 37 by a person who made submissions or observations in accordance with the permission regulations, be accompanied by the acknowledgement by the planning authority of receipt of submissions or observations

    f) be accompanied by such fee (if any) as may be payable in respect of such appeal or referral in accordance with regulations made under section 144 of the Act of 2000 an

    g) be made within the period specified for making the appeal or referral

2   a) An appeal which does not comply with the requirements of subsection (1) shall be invalid.

    b) The requirements of subsection (1)(d) shall apply whether or not the appellant requests, or proposes to request, in accordance with section 134, an oral hearing of the appeal.

3   Without prejudice to section 131 or 134, an appellant shall not be entitled to elaborate in writing upon, or make further submission in writing in relation to, the grounds of appeal stated in the appeal or to submit further grounds of appeal and any such elaboration, submissions or further

grounds of appeal that is or are received by the Board shall not be considered by it.

4   a)   An appeal shall be accompanied by such documents, particulars or
other information relating to the appeal as the appellant considers
necessary or appropriate.

     b)   without prejudice to section 132. the Board shall not consider any
documents, particulars or other information submitted by an appellant other than the documents, particulars or other information which
accompanied the appeal.

5   An appeal or referral shall be made

     a)   by sending the appeal or referral by prepaid post to the Board, or

     b)   by leaving the appeal or referral with an employee of the Board at
the offices of the Board during office hours, (as determined by the
Board), or

     c)   by such other means as may be prescribed.

The procedures and requirements as set out above are a considerable improvement on the previous arrangements and must be rigidly observed. The references to sections 131, 132 and 134 are to those parts of the Act which allow
the Board to request further details from those who have made submissions.

Some concern has been expressed over the fact that the parties to an appeal
do not have the opportunity to comment on each others case, and the possibility of a constitutional challenge in this area is not impossible. It was, presumably, to deal with this eventuality that the provisions in the Act allowing
the Board to request further submissions from the parties are introduced by
the words 'Where the Board is of opinion that, in the particular circumstances
of an appeal or referral, it is appropriate in the interests of justice, etc.'
(Section 131)

iii) Time allowed for decisions

As stated in the introduction to this section, the original legislation did not set
any limit on the time taken by the Board to determine appeals. This was
clearly unsatisfactory particularly since, at worst, appeals could take up to
two years to be decided. Further, since time limits were imposed on the planning authority in the first place, there seemed no good reason why the appeal
process should not be similarly controlled.

This problem was finally addressed in the 1992 Act and is continued in the
2000 Act.

The most significant section of the Act as regards time is section 126. This requires the Board to have as its objective the determination of every appeal within eighteen weeks of the lodging of the appeal. This is not as clear cut a time table as the planning permission one, and there is no question of a default decision. The Board however, will be encouraged to adhere to this timetable by a provision in section 126(6) requiring the annual report of the Board to state the number of appeals that have been dealt with in the eighteen week period, and the number that have not.

The Act allows the Board to extend the eighteen week period if it seems appropriate, but the parties must be informed of the reasons why the appeal is being delayed, and the Board must set a date by which the appeal will be determined. It was hoped that this subsection would be sparingly used, but experience at the moment indicates that the majority of appeals are taking from six to nine months to determine. The degree of adherence by the Board to what can only be described as aspirational targets depends entirely on the state of the construction industry and of the resources available to the Board. A further sub-section, 124(4) allows the Minister not only to set different, and presumably longer, periods for particular classes of appeal, but also to alter the basic eighteen week period. This last provision was probably inserted to allow the timetable to be reviewed after it would have been in operation for some time.

Other relevant provisions relating to the process of appeal would include:

1   Any appeal documentation is to be available at the offices of the relevant planning authority until the appeal is withdrawn, dismissed or determined by the Board. This includes any direction given by the Board under section 139 relating to appeals against conditions (Article 68 – 2001 regulations).

2   When the planning authority receives notice of an appeal from the Board, it shall 'as soon as may be' notify any person who made a submission or observation. This notice shall state that the appeal is available for inspection or purchase at the authority's office and that submissions or observations may be made within an unspecified appropriate period (Article 69 – 2001 regulations).

3   Any party to an appeal, and any person who made an observation or submission shall be notified by the Board 'as soon as may be' after making the decision. The notice is to contain the usual expected information [sub-Articles 74(2)(a) to (k)]. The most significant of these is a new requirement that where a decision of the Board differs from a recommendation in any report to the Board, reasons must be given. This is very welcome, as over the years some unusual decisions were taken in some cases, where long detailed inspectors reports being overruled by a single

Board member with a laconic 'in the interests of proper planning and development' reason. Up until now about 10% of inspectors' recommendations have been reversed by the Board, although the development value of projects affected by these reversals could represent a much more significant figure. The law governing these situations is set out in *O'Keeffe v An Bord Pleanála* [1992] ILRM 237 ('The Radio Tara Case'). In the High Court the plaintiff submitted 'that in this particular case, where the inspector's recommendation contained at the conclusion of his report was plain and unambiguous and recommended the refusal of permission, and where in essence the conclusions thereby reached were endorsed by the expert seconded to the inspector for the purpose of the hearing of the appeal, that for the Board to refuse to accept that recommendation was an irrational decision....' and the trial Judge agreed, stating that it was 'so irrational and so in breach of common sense as to be a nullity'.

However, on appeal to the Supreme Court this decision was reversed. The Court agreed that if a decision was 'fundamentally at variance with reason and common sense' then it must be overturned. It went on to say that if there was evidence before the Board which would justify it coming to a reasonable decision, even if it disagreed with strong and clear arguments to the contrary, then the decision was valid. In a very interesting comment the Court said that the reason given that the proposal 'would not be contrary to the proper planning and development of the area' was an insufficient reason taken on its own. This reason, as worded above, is very often given in planning decisions and the Supreme Court's comments should be noted. In this particular case the Board had, in fact, added nine other conditions with reasons to the decision.

iv) Oral hearings

When the 1963 Act came into force on 1st October 1964, Section 82 provided for oral hearings, and while the Act had arrangements for a certain formality, the early oral hearings tended to be of an informal nature. Requests for oral hearings were almost automatically granted. Over the years, however, the oral hearing process became more formal and grew to resemble Court hearings, with solicitors, counsel, experts, and so on, to the stage where it was obvious that some constraints would have to be imposed. The present arrangements are set out in sections 134 and 135 of the 2000 Act and Articles 76, 77 and 78 of the 2001 regulations. Section 134 of the 2000 Act opens with the ominous words 'The Board may in its absolute discretion hold an oral hearing.' A request for an oral hearing must be made at the time of lodging an appeal. The Board would now normally agree to hold an oral hearing where the proposal was of such a nature, either in complexity or public interest, that an oral hearing would be the more equitable method of determining the matter. Even if no party requests an oral hearing, the Board has the power to order an oral hearing itself if it decides it to be the appropriate course.

Further very useful advice on the various aspects of oral hearings is contained in the chapter headed 'A Practical Guide' by Fergal MacCabe in the book IRISH PLANNING LAW AND PRACTICE by O'Sullivan and Shepherd.

Lately there appears to have been a trend in some decisions by An Bord Pleanála to look at some factors which have not always been regarded as being relevant to strictly planning matters. It seems that national, commercial and employment objectives and the physical impact of a development on a local basis are now regarded as pertinent. One of these decisions related to the Masonite Corporation factory near Carrick-on-Shannon where the Inspector's report was not accepted by the Board in the face of the considerations mentioned above. The importance to the national forestry industry of having a wood pulping station was made in submissions to the oral hearing and it would appear, therefore, that the Board felt that the national importance of the project counterbalanced the objections which the inspector had to the site. This practice was specifically authorised in *Keane v An Bord Pleanála* [1997] 1 ILRM 508. Practitioners advising on proposed developments should bear this trend in mind.

As a final comment, it must be pointed out that whereas the planning authority in coming to a decision is restricted to considering the proper planning and development of the area and in particular the development plan (Section 34(2)(a) of the 2000 Act), the Board is not so confined. Sub-Section 37(2)(b) of the same section allows the Board to consider the effect which any decision it might make would have on matters outside those concerning the relevant planning authority. The Masonite decision might well come under this power. The Board, however, cannot anticipate problems which might be caused by a planning decision. *Kelly v An Bord Pleanála* [1992] High Court, 6th April, held that fears that a grant of permission would facilitate breaches of the planning code was not a relevant consideration.

2.4.5 Judicial Review and Referral to Court

Readers will have realised by now that the route of application, decision and appeal is not necessarily the complete process as far as obtaining a final permission is concerned. The courts can be invoked to prevent unauthorised development (and this is dealt with in par 2.4.13 -Enforcement) and can also be called on in the matter of planning decisions. Because of the importance of planning decisions from a social, financial and environmental point of view, it is inevitable that many aspects of the process will end up in court. Originally the full, expensive and lengthy process of a High Court action was needed, and while Section 82 of the 1963 Act required that such action be taken within two months of the planning decision, either by the planning authority or the Board, the time scale for a High Court hearing could run into years. This could be followed by an appeal to the Supreme Court, and possibly to the European Court. Recent developments have helped to shorten the process. The 1992 Act required that questioning decisions must be by way of judicial review which is a comparatively quick process, and a recent court case has held that issues cannot be referred to the European Court once a final decision has been made in the national court (*McNamara v An Bord Pleanála* [1998] 2 ILRM 313.

As mentioned above, the 1992 Act, altered the position so that decisions can now only be questioned by way of judicial review. This provision is continued in the 2000 Act. The difference is that the earlier Acts allowed cases to be taken by way of what is called plenary summons, which sets in train the lengthy process of claims, defences, counterclaims, discovery, and several other processes, leading eventually to a full hearing with witnesses and experts. The process of judicial review deals with the matter quite speedily by way of affidavit, without examination of witnesses. This could formerly be done *ex parte* but must now be made on notice to the planning authority, the applicant or the Board. The High Court will only grant leave to apply for judicial review where the Court is satisfied that there are substantial grounds for contending that the decision is invalid or ought to be quashed [Section 50(4)(b)]. This view was confirmed by the Supreme Court in *Scott and Others v An Bord Pleanála* [1995] 1 ILRM 424. The application for judicial review must be made within eight weeks of the date of the decision in question and any applicant must have made a submission on the planning application to the planning authority within the five week period referred to in Article 29 of the 2001 regulations.

For the grounds to be substantial it has been held in *McNamara v An Bord Pleanála* [1995] 2 ILRM 125 that the ground must be reasonably arguable and weighty but that it is not necessary to evaluate each argument. Leave to apply was granted. However, when the High Court heard the McNamara judicial review [1996] 2 ILRM 339, it refused to alter the decision of An Bord Pleanála (see par. 2.4.2.). No appeal will be granted to the Supreme Court unless the High Court is satisfied that a point of law of exceptional public importance is involved, or unless there are constitutional implications. In the case of *KSK Enterprises Ltd v An Bord Pleanála* [1994] 2 ILRM 1, an appeal was allowed to the Supreme Court on these grounds. The case was, in essence, about the two month time limit (relevant at the time) allowed after the appeal decision and it was enforced very strictly. The Supreme Court has held in *Irish Asphalt Ltd v An Bord Pleanála* [1996] IPELJ 3 182, that it is at the absolute discretion of the High Court as to what constitutes a point of law of exceptional public importance or if there are constitutional issues involved. This decision should greatly reduce the number of Supreme Court appeals in the matter of judicial review.

The Courts have made it clear that judicial review proceedings should be a device of last resort and only to be used in significant cases. In the Lancefort case referred to later on the Supreme Court said 'The Courts are bound in their decisions to have serious regard to the fact that the Oireachtas has made plain its concern that, given the existence of an elaborate appeals procedure which can be invoked by any member of the public and the determination of the issue by an independent board of qualified persons, the judicial review procedure should not be availed of as a form of further appeal by persons who may well be dissatisfied with the ultimate decision on a planning application, but whose rights to be heard have been fully protected by the legislation.'

The Courts will not look at any planning argument when considering judicial review. In *Furlong v McConnell* [1989] IRISH TIMES, 4th December, the Court stated 'It was not the function of the High Court to determine what would constitute good planning for a particular environment. Such a function belonged properly to the planning authority.' The position was dealt with in more detail in *Tennyson v Dun Laoghaire Corporation* [1991] 2 IR 527: 'The Oireachtas has provided in the planning code a forum for the adjudication of appeals from decisions of planning authorities within the first category, i.e. those relating to planning matters *per se*. Such appeals are heard and determined by An Bord Pleanála which is a tribunal having the benefit of special expertise in that area. The Court is not an appropriate body to adjudicate in such matters and, in my view, ought not to interfere in disputes relating to purely planning matters. However, where the dispute raises an issue regarding a matter of law such as the interpretation of the wording of the development plan in the light of relevant statutory provisions and the primary objective of that document, then these are matters over which the Court has exclusive jurisdiction. An Bord Pleanála has not the authority to resolve disputes on matters of law.' This was put even more firmly in *Tesco Stores v Secretary of State for the Environment*, THE TIMES, 13th May 1995: 'A fundamental principal of British law was that the Courts were concerned only with the legality of the decision-making process and not with the merits of the decision. If there was one principal of planning law more firmly settled than any other, it was that matters of planning judgement were within the exclusive province of the local planning authority or the Secretary of State.' The only circumstances where the Courts would intervene would be if the decision were considered irrational. This was touched on before in the references to the overturning of inspectors reports by An Bord Pleanála in the case of *O'Keeffe v An Bord Pleanála* [1991] ILRM 237, where the Supreme Court took the view that a decision of the Board would not be overturned unless it was clearly irrational. That the decision was opposed to expert evidence was not sufficient. In *Gregory v Dun Laoghaire / Rathdown County Council* [1996] High Court, 16th July, an interpretation by the planning authority of a Bord Pleanála condition requiring revisions 'to be agreed' was held to be unreasonable and therefore *ultra vires*.

An aspect of judicial review proceedings which has caused some concern is the matter of costs. It would be usual in these cases to award costs against a party which failed in such proceedings but a few high profile cases have not followed this line. In the case of *Seery v An Bord Pleanála* [2001] High Court, 26th January part of the judgement read 'It would be commercial folly to embark upon the development envisaged by the planning permission sought to be impugned while these proceedings are pending. Of necessity the development must be put 'on hold' pending final determination of these proceedings. This may well result in loss and damage to the notice parties. It is then necessary to consider whether this application for judicial review has the necessary public nature which would justify the Court exercising its discretion in favour of the applicants in not seeking an undertaking as to damages ... As the existence of an application for judicial review is of the like effect in the present case to an interlocutory injunction, in considering an application for an undertaking as to damages upon leave to apply for judicial review being granted, the Court should apply the same principals and adopt the same approach as on an application for an interlocutory injunction and, therefore, should not have regard to the relevant strength of the cases of the relevant parties ... In these circumstances it is appropriate in the present case that I should require of the applicant and undertaking as to damages as a condition of their continuing the application for judicial review.' This seems to be a very practical judgement.

The matter of *locus standi* has arisen in a number of planning appeals. *Locus standi* is the right to be heard in Court based on whether or not the person concerned has sufficient interest to maintain such proceedings. The question was considered in detail by the Supreme Court in the case of *Lancefort Ltd v An Bord Pleanála* [1998] 2 ILRM 401. This case arose from the decision of An Bord Pleanála to grant permission for the building of the Westin Hotel in Dublin. Following the decision, a limited liability company called Lancefort was formed in order to bring judicial proceedings so as to annul the permission. The Court held that such a company, with no assets, and formed after the proceedings with regard to the appeal had concluded, had no such *locus standi*. The Court came to this conclusion, not solely on the basis of the company's formation but because the judicial review proceedings were based on matters not raised before the Board at the oral hearing. The Court went on to point out that companies such as Lancefort were not automatically refused *locus standi* and quoted with approval a statement in another such case (*Blessington Heritage Trust Ltd v Wicklow County Council* [1998] High Court, 21st January) to the effect that 'blanket refusal of *locus standi* to all such companies may tip the balance too far in favour of the large scale and well resourced developer'.

The question of a fair balance as between an applicant and an appellant was also considered in the case of *The Village Residents Association v An Bord Pleanála* [1999] High Court, 5th November where the court said: 'I have come to the conclusion that on the principals enunciated by Keane J. in his judgement in the Supreme Court appeal in *Lancefort Ltd v An Bord Pleanála* the applicant does have sufficient *locus standi*. Planning is a matter of great public importance and it is not just of interest to the particular parties involved in a particular planning permission. A liberal view should therefore be taken in relation to *locus standi*. On the other hand of course, having regard to the restricted statutory grounds on which judicial review can be sought and having regard to the well established general reluctance of Courts to interfere with decisions of statutory tribunals, a restrictive view must be applied to the determination of the actual judicial review itself.' This seems to be in line with the view of the Supreme Court in Lancefort. The revised provisions of the 2000 Act have sought to clarify this matter by requiring, at Section 50(4)(b), that any applicant in judicial review proceedings must have a 'substantial interest' in the subject matter of the review.

In the case of *Healy v Dublin County Council* [1993] High Court, 29th April, a complication was introduced into the area of judicial review. The Court held that an application for judicial review would not be entertained where the applicant had not challenged the decision of the planning authority by way of an appeal to An Bord Pleanála. A problem could follow from this procedure in that it has been pointed out that if An Bord Pleanála makes a decision before the judicial review proceedings have been heard, there is no decision left to review as Section 37 of the 2000 Act, says that a decision of the Board 'shall operate to annul' the decision of the planning authority as from the time when it was given. This position can be contrasted with the case of *Molloy and Walsh v Dublin County Council* [1989] ILRM 633, where the Court held that a default permission, which was the subject of an application for a declaration of permission, need not be appealed before a judicial review application on the grounds that the permission was valid even if by default.

Finally it should be stated that the whole area of judicial review is one where the practitioner should always advise his client to seek legal advice. For those interested in reading an up-to-date review of the position, an article by Eamon Galligan in IRISH PLANNING AND ENVIRONMENTAL LAW JOURNAL, Vol. 1, p.119 is to be recommended.

2.4.6   **Duration, Extension and Revocation of Permissions**

In the 1963 Act there was no time limit on the validity of permissions, and they remained in force indefinitely, or until revoked. Revocation, dealt with later, was rarely invoked. This was a very unsatisfactory situation as far as planning authorities were concerned for they had no idea when, if ever, any permission would be implemented and this made forward planning, and the preparation of future development plans very difficult. The 1976 Act, at Section 29, introduced the concept of time limits for planning permissions. This principle has been continued in Section 40 of the 2000 Act. The process is commonly referred to as 'withering' but as has been pointed out this is an odd word to use about an event which occurs suddenly.

The general rule is that planning permissions expire five years after they were granted. It is very important to note that an outline permission expires three years after it was granted (or after five years if approved by the planning authority) unless an application is made for a subsequent permission during that period. The subsequent permission has a five year life dating from the grant of that permission.

A planning authority may extend the period of validity when granting permission, (Section 41) and terms up to ten years are not unknown. These longer periods are granted in the case of large or complex developments, or in the case of, say, mining operations where a much longer time scale is anticipated. The planning authority has no power, however, to reduce the five year period. A planning authority may also extend a five year period which had been previously granted, but subject to strict requirements. These are set out in the 2000 Act in sections 42 and 43, and in Articles 40 to 47 of the 2001 regulations. The requirements can be summarised as follows:

i)   To extend the period beyond five years (or whatever period was originally granted) the applicant must show that the development commenced before the period expired, that substantial works have been completed, and must state the additional period of time required. Further details of the information required are set out in the regulations. The application cannot be made more than one year before the permission expires.

The question immediately arises as to what are 'substantial works'. It must always be decided on the facts in each case but it has been suggested that works which would show an intention to complete should be regarded as substantial. Extensive piling and drainage works would be so regarded. What is or is not substantial works is discussed in detail in *Frenchurch Properties Ltd v Wexford County Council* [1991] ILRM 769. Both that case, and the later case of *Littondale Ltd v Wicklow County Council* [1996] 2 ILRM 519, held that the decision as to whether 'substantial' works had been carried out was a matter for the planning authority and not for the Courts. The case of *Garden Village Construction Co. Ltd v Wicklow County Council* [1993] Supreme Court IPEL 1 188 dealt with an unusual case where approvals had been obtained for different areas of a housing layout which had been the subject of a single outline permission. The High Court has originally held that 'substantial' works carried out as part of one approval would enable the original outline permission to be extended in time in respect of a second approval granted under it, but the Supreme Court ruled that the approvals were totally separate and could not be regarded as being connected. This seems to be somewhat at odds with the same Court's decision in *McDonagh v Galway Corporation* [1993] 17th May, where two permission were considered together by the Court.

ii) To further extend the period beyond the original extension, the applicant must show that the development was delayed by circumstances beyond their control, and must give an estimate as to when the works will be completed. In this case, and in the case of an application for an initial extension, the extensions are granted by default if the planning authority does not decide the matter within eight weeks.

Revocation of a permission is covered by Section 44 of the 2000 Act. A planning authority may revoke, or modify, a permission but only where there has been a change in the development plan and these changed circumstances must be cited by the planning authority in their notice to the owner or occupier of the lands. Generally, the notice of revocation must be served before development commences, but works which have been completed cannot be affected. It is clear that the Courts will be very particular in seeing that revocation is properly done. In *Hughes v An Bord Pleanála* [2000] 1 ILRM 452 the Court pointed out that it was not sufficient that there had been a change of circumstances, as the then legislation required, but there must be good reasons in addition for revocation. In the case of *Eircell v Leitrim County Council* [1999] IRISH TIMES, 13th December, dealing with revocation, the Court stated: 'Furthermore, the authority, in making this decision, is obliged to act judicially and has a duty to ensure that fair proceedings are observed notwithstanding that this had not been specifically provided for in the Act. Notwithstanding the existence of an alternative remedy, namely an appeal from the authority's decision, the applicant was entitled to relief by way of judicial review as it was in the interest of justice that the public at large should know that the planning authority could not ride roughshod over principles of constitutional justice and fair procedures.'

Revocation, or modification, of a permission is a 'reserved function' as defined in the County Management Act, 1940. This means that the action can only be taken by the elected representatives of the planning authority and not by the manager.

2.4.7 Completion of Development

A question often asked is whether or not a development must be carried out in its entirety in order to be valid. Firstly it must be said that if the planning authority attaches a condition to the permission requiring all the works to be carried out, then the position is clear. This is often done by requiring the works to be carried out in accordance with the lodged drawings. Changes cannot be made during construction, even if the proposed changes would in a completed building be exempted development. This is confirmed in a Section 5 reference (see par 2.2.4) to An Bord Pleanála were it was held that Section 4(1)(g) which defines what alterations might be exempted development does not apply to alterations carried out during construction to an approved development (ref. 31.RF.0750). Equally clear is the position regarding permissions that relate to housing schemes, industrial estates, or any development that is obviously intended to be built, if circumstances require, on an incremental basis. Each completed unit in such developments has a valid permission. In the case of *Dwyer-Nolan Developments Ltd v Dublin County Council* [1986] High Court 21st April, an English case, *Lucas v Dorking and Horley District Council* was quoted as giving authority for the proposition that permission does not have to be implemented in its entirety in these situations unless the planning authority imposes a condition to that effect: 'Without, as I say, going into any detailed consideration of inconvenience, I think it is right to approach this problem on the basis of an assumption that Parliament cannot have intended to leave individual owners of separate plots comprised in the contemplated total housing scheme dependent on completion of the whole scheme by the original developer or by some purchaser from him so that they will be vulnerable, were the whole scheme no completed, separately to enforcement procedure which might deprive them of their houses and of the money which they would have invested in these houses whether or not they built them themselves.'

A number of cases have decided that generally speaking, and apart from the exceptions mentioned above, a permission must be implemented in its entirety. In *Horne v Freeney* [1982] High Court 7th July the Court held: 'I take the view that planning permission is indivisible; that it authorises the carrying out of the totality of the works for which approval has been granted and not some of them only. A developer cannot at his election implement a part only of the approved plans as no approval is given for the part as distinct from the whole.'

This view was quoted with approval in *Dwyer-Nolan Developments Ltd v Dublin County Council* [1986] High Court 21st April (referred to above) where it was held that it is not acceptable to take parts of different permissions relating to the same lands, and to combine them to form, in effect, a new composite development. To some extent this point was also debated in the case of *McDonagh v Galway Corporation* referred to in par. 2.4.2.

2.4.8 **Default Decisions**

The 2000 Act at Section 38(8)(f) says that if a planning authority does not give a decision in regard to an application for permission within the 'appropriate period' then the decision is regarded as having been given on the last day of that period. As set out above, the appropriate period would normally be eight weeks after receipt by the planning authority of the application, or four weeks after receipt of further information. Some points to note about default decisions are:

1   A default decision is still subject to appeal, although potential objectors might not be aware of what has occurred. As will be appreciated this will always be by a third party. A default decision is 'clean' in the sense that no conditions are attached to it, and the proposals as lodged constitute the permission.

2   A default permission cannot be obtained where the proposals would materially contravene a development plan or a Special Amenity Area Order. The cases of *P. & F. Sharpe Ltd v Dublin City and County Manager* [1988] Supreme Court, 14th December, *Dublin County Council v Michael Marren* [1984] High Court, 23rd July, and *Calor Teoranta v Sligo County Council* [1991] 2 IR 267, all deal with the subject of default decisions and material contravention. The attitude of the Courts is clearly set out in *McGovern v Dublin Corporation* [1999] 2 ILRM 314 where the judgement stated: 'The wording of the sub-section implies that a right of permission in default is restricted to an application which, in the course of events, is one that in principal is entitled to succeed. It would be unreal and potentially unjust to interpret the sub-section as applying to development which is not 'normally permissible' and where sanction is dependent on the planning authority being satisfied that the proposed development is consistent with the proper planning and development of the area in the special circumstances of the case. The proposed development was outside the scope of the development normally permitted under the relevant development plan and, further, on account of its scale, was outside the ambit of development 'open for consideration.' In the circumstances, the application for planning permission was not one for which default permission could be obtained.'

3   The Courts are generally unsympathetic to requests for default decisions and the judgement of McCarthy J. in *Creedon v Dublin Corporation* [1983] Supreme Court, 4th February is a good statement of the principles involved. 'It was never the intention of the legislature that mistakes by Housing or Planning Authorities – misconstructions of their powers, misconception of the facts or the like – would be used as a basis for abandoning the statutory procedures and seeking to use the courts as some form of licensing or enabling authority in a field in which the legislative and executive organs of government have prime responsibility.' The decision of Walsh J. in *The State (Abenglen Properties Ltd) v Dublin Corporation* [1982] ILRM 590 is equally clear on the reluctance of the Courts to grant default permissions. Strict adherence to the regulations will normally be looked for. While a less rigid view was taken in *Molloy and Walsh v Dublin County Council* [1989] ILRM 633, where the Court held that 'substantial' compliance with the regulations was sufficient, the case of *Murray v Wicklow County Council* [1996] IPELJ 180 reverted to the strict view and held that an applicant who had been less than meticulous himself could not benefit from a mistake made by the plan-

ning authority. The whole idea of default permissions was viewed with dis-approval in *Flynn and O'Flaherty Properties v Dublin Corporation* [1996] High Court, 19th December where the Court recommended that the proce-dure should be abolished.

4   Even if the planning authority makes a decision that is *ultra vires*, or beyond its powers, this decision is regarded as being valid as far as the other provi-sions of the Act are concerned, and no default permission will follow. This was confirmed in the *Abenglen* case mentioned above.

5   There is a minimum time for a planning decision, as well as a maximum time (see par. 2.4.1).

6   There seems to be some doubt as to whether or not a planning authority is required to issue a grant of permission in default cases. In PLANNING AND DEVELOPMENT LAW (Walsh and Keane) it says: 'However, once a decision, actual or notional, has been made, and the time limit for an appeal to the Board has expired, the planning authority is obliged to make the grant of per-mission itself. The appropriate procedure accordingly, for an applicant who claims to have obtained a permission by default to follow is to apply to the High Court for an order of *mandamus* requiring the authority to make the grant of permission.'

Contrast that with the view of Barrington J. in *The State (Pine Valley Developments Ltd) v Dublin County Council* [1982] ILRM 169: 'At the expira-tion of the relevant period a decision to grant the approval is to be regarded as having come into existence by operation of law.' This view was quoted by O'Hanlon J. in *Freeney v Bray Urban District Council* [1982] ILRM 29 when he added: 'Accordingly, no further act or decision on the part of the planning author-ity is then needed to entitle the applicant to proceed with his development, and it is, in my opinion, inappropriate to seek relief by way of *mandamus* against the authority to compel it to make or give a decision in favour of an applicant, when it is already deemed to have done so by act and operation of law.'

This latter view will cause some practical difficulties. Very many building devel-opments will require certificates of compliance with planning and other statutes for submission to funding institutions or for conveyancing purposes. In these cir-cumstances, the grant of permission document will be required, and it is suggest-ed very few planning authorities will voluntary agree to issue a 'default' permis-sion and will have to be required by the Courts to do so.

2.4.9   **Material Contravention**

In Section 2.3.1 the development plan was described, and it was pointed out that a planning authority must observe the provisions of that plan when considering a planning application. There is, however, an exception. Section 34(6) of the 2000 Act provides for the granting of permissions which contravene the development plan. It was pointed out before (par 1.3) that the functions of a local authority are separated into 'executive' functions which are those of the manager, and 'reserved' functions which apply to the elected representatives. Planning decisions are executive functions, although the adoption of the development plan on which they are based, is a reserved function. It is sometimes the case that the elected representatives are of the view that an application for permission should be granted even though it contravenes the development plan. The decision as to whether or not the proposal is a 'material' contravention is that of the manager. The Courts will not interfere in the Manager's decision unless it is clearly 'unreasonable' (*O'Keeffe v An Bord Pleanála* [1993] IR 39). This view was also taken in *Byrne v Wicklow County Council* [1994] High Court, 3rd November, where a manager's decision was held clearly to be one that the evidence before him entitled him to reach.

The Courts have, however, considered the meaning of material contravention. In *Healy v Dublin County Council* [1993] High Court, 29th April, the Court held that while the decision as to whether or not a contravention was material was primarily a matter for the planning authority, nevertheless the Courts had the capacity to determine such an issue. This is a rare example of a Court stating that it would decide planning matters and is not in general accord with the attitude of the Courts (see par. 2.4.5). A related case, *Blessington and District Community Council v Wicklow County Council* [1996] High Court, 19th July, held that demolishing a listed building was not necessarily a material contravention, though this is no longer the case under the 2000 Act legislation. The case of *Kennedy v South Dublin County Council* [1998] 5 IPELJ 31 produced an unusual situation where the Court decided that even if the planning authority was wrong in giving a permission for a development that was a material contravention, this was of no effect because an appeal annulled that decision. The question of what the situation would be if there was no appeal was not answered.

If the manager decides that the application, while being in contravention of the development plan is not materially so, the normal planning process applies. On the other hand if he decides that the contravention is material then the procedure set out in the 2000 Act must be followed and the members must pass a resolution to grant the permission. Originally the 1976 Act required only one third of the members of the planning authority to support such a resolution, but the perceived misuse of this power led to the introduction, in the Local Government Act 1991, of a requirement that three quarters of the members of the authority, irrespective of their attendance at the meeting, must vote in favour of the resolution. A newspaper notice must be published of the intention to grant such a permission, and four weeks are allowed for any objections or representations. If the resolution is then passed, the manager has no option but to grant the permission, even if his planning officials are satisfied that the permission is contrary to their advice.

It must be noted that the passing of a material contravention resolution must be followed by a planning application in the normal sense. The planning authority will then be required to grant the permission, but will still have the power to impose conditions. Even though a planning authority is normally precluded from granting a permission which is contrary to its development plan, An Bord Pleanála is not so strictly constrained (see par. 2.3.1). This power was specifically upheld in *Schwestermann v An Bord Pleanála* [1995] 3 IR 437. Lastly in this section, a planning authority has no power to carry out a development itself which is contrary to its own development plan. Such a proposal would remove the development from the exempted development classification. (Section 178).

2.4.10 Section 4 Orders

The City and County Management (Amendment) Act 1955 at Section 4 empowered the elected representatives to direct the manager to carry out his executive functions in a specific way and what were known simply as 'Section 4' orders were a feature of local planning politics. The 1955 Act has been revoked by the Local Government Act 2001 and the powers of direction are now contained in section 140 of that Act. It will be some time before the label 'Section 4' disappears and that title is used in this section in preference to the new section 140, but the comments equally apply. This section was primarily used by planning authorities with regard to the Manager's functions under the planning acts, and normally directed him to grant permissions against the advice of his officials. Some planning authorities used this power in such a widespread way that some restrictions had to be imposed. Section 2.4.9 deals with this matter in relation to material contraventions but the position is similar where the members of the planning authority require the manager to approve, refuse or impose conditions on an application where material contravention is not an issue and where the officials do not wish to follow the course favoured by the members of the planning authority. Section 44 of the Local Government Act 1991 provided that where 'Section 4' motions related to planning matters they must be signed by three members of the local authority electoral area concerned, and the motion must then be supported by at least three-quarters of the members of the entire authority. This requirement is repeated in Section 34(7) of the 2000 Act. In the case of Dublin Corporation this would be 39 members, an obviously difficult target. There has been a deal of legal argument over the effects and consequences of such Section 4 orders and the position now seems to be, after the case of *P. & F. Sharpe Ltd v Dublin City and County Manager* [1988] Supreme Court, 14th December, that:

1   The manager has no discretion as far as a 'Section 4' order in relation to a planning decision is concerned.

2   The elected members must act in the same way as the manager would when coming to a decision. They must act in a judicial manner, and must record the material considerations which persuaded them to overrule the advice of the authority's own planning staff.

The case of *Kenny Homes v Galway City and County Manager* [1995] 2 ILRM 586 is going to make Section 4 orders more difficult to impose as far as planning matters are concerned. The Court held that any Section 4 order to a manager must be framed in such a way as to come within the provisions of Section 26 of the 1963 Act (in force at that time), which deals with the granting of permissions. The members of the local authority must act in a judicial manner and must have regard to the imposition of any suitable conditions. The judge observed that he saw difficulty in reconciling the simplicity of any Section 4 order of the 1955 Act with the requirements of Section 26 of the Act.

In the case of a Section 4 order which the manager considers would materially contravene the authority's own development plan, he will make an order which will bring into effect the provisions of Section 34(6) of the 2000 Act which control material contravention (see 2.4.9).

2.4.11 Fees

Over the years since 1963 the cost of obtaining planning permissions has increased dramatically. The original Act contained no provisions for fees, and it was not until 1982 that the Act of that year, in section 10, empowered the Minister to make regulations concerning fees, and the first such fees were contained in S.I. 30 of 1983. The latest fees are contained in S.I. 600 of 2001. The conversion to euros of fees previously expressed in Irish pounds is covered by Local Government (Planning and Development) (Fees) Regulations – S.I. 525 of 2001.

The original statutory instrument contained no maximum fee provisions and this was clearly seen to be inhibiting development and investment. The maximum fee is now 38,000. An interesting innovation in S.I. 86 of 1994 was that any application for retention of a structure or for the continuance of a use would attract a fee of more than the standard fees and this is continued in S.I. 600 of 2001 with a maximum of 125,000.

There is provision in the regulations for:

a)   The Standard Fees. These are set out in the Ninth Schedule to the Regulations (S.I.600 of 2001). The ones with which most practitioners would be concerned are the amounts of 65 (or 195 for retention) of dwellings, 34 (or 102 for retention) for alterations and extensions to dwellings, and 3.60 per square metre (or 10.8 for retention) for other buildings. In the case of agricultural buildings, there are varying amounts for different uses. S.I. 149 of 2002 introduced a fee of 50 for 'fingerpost' signs in relation to accommodation etc.

b) Outline application. The fee is three quarters of the full amount specified (Article 160), subject to a maximum of 28,500 As mentioned earlier (2.3.2) the size of this maximum fee may act as a deterrent to the more widespread use of the outline permission.

c) Exemptions. Article 157 of S.I. 600 of 2001 provides that applications by voluntary organisations for development of a variety of social or religious purposes will attract no fee.

d) Reduced fees. In cases where the application is for a permission consequent on the grant of an outline permission, or for a permission to change a house type, or to modify a design, then the fee payable will be one-quarter of the full fee, but only if a fee had been previously paid. A minimum fee of 34 is payable in every case.

e) It should also be noted that applications to extend a planning permission beyond its normal five-year life (or whatever is the period) will attract a fee of 62 (Schedule 10). An appeal on a request for a declaration under Section 5 (disputes as to development) attracts a fee of 80. The planning authority can also refund three-quarters of a fee already paid where, generally, the application is much the same as a previous one (Article 162 – S.I. 600 of 2001) but the revised application must be made within one year of the determination or withdrawal of the first application..

f) Fees to the Board. The 2000 Act altered the status of fees payable to An Bord Pleanála. Previously these fees were set by the Department of the Environment but section 144 of the 2000 Act now allows the Board to set its own fees. Until this is done, Article 172 of the 2001 regulations specifies that the fees set out in S.I. 86 of 1994 will apply.

The fees in S.I. 86 of 1994 and confirmed in S.I. 525 of 2001 provide for a fee of 380 for an appeal relating to a commercial development, 150 for other appeals, and 45 for submissions by those who are not parties to the appeal. A request for an oral hearing requires a fee of 75. Practitioners must note that an appeal involving two or more houses is regarded as a commercial development. This was first defined in S.I. 338 of 1989 but the restriction is not stated in the latest statutory instrument. It would be helpful if this fact were included in future fee schedules.

The fees required for applications for fire safety certificates under the Building

Control Act 1992 are an entirely separate matter, although the proliferation of these fees and charges cannot do much to encourage investment in building, and would be much more equitable as a form of general rates.

2.4.12 Enforcement and Penalties

This section, and that dealing with compensation, enter the areas where the law is both complex and detailed, and practitioners should always recommend owners or occupiers, when faced with a situation that might result in either the compensation or the enforcement provisions being applied that formal legal advice be sought. This has been a very unsatisfactory part of the planning code since its inception, and has been subject to a considerable amount of doubt and uncertainty. Because the time limits on the serving of notices was rather confusing, it had become very difficult for owners or occupiers to know where they stood in relation to law. It was necessary in some instances to try and establish what was the precise use of premises as far back as 1st October 1964, and in the case of a possible intensification of use in apartment buildings, even before that. Various parts of the differing Acts and Regulations seemed to be unclear or contradictory and this was partly addressed in the 1992 Act. The 2000 Act has simplified the system. The basic offence is set out in Section 32 of the 2000 Act at subsection (2): 'A person shall not carry out any development in respect of which permission is required... and in accordance with a permission granted under this part of the Act' and confirmed in section 151: 'Any person who has carried out or is carrying out unauthorised development is guilty of an offence.'

It should be noted that the courts will allow a reasonable amount of deviation from exact compliance with a planning permission or with conditions attached to a planning permission. *Cork County Council v Cliftonhall* [2002] IPELJ 49. Planning authorities and the Board should, it is suggested, pay more attention to court decisions which would eliminate many of the unnecessary consequences of trying to enforce strictly the phrase 'The development is to be carried out in accordance with the documents lodged'.

Readers are referred to an article entitled 'Enforcement under the Planning and Development Act 2000' by Eamon Galligan in the IRISH PLANNING AND ENVIRONMENTAL LAW JOURNAL, Vol. 8, No. 1 for a detailed, but very clear, analysis of the provisions of Part VIII of the 2000 Act – Enforcement.

There are three main types of enforcement remedy in the 2000 Act. The first is criminal prosecution for unauthorised development, secondly the issue of enforcement notices to owners and occupiers and the prosecution for non-compliance with these notices, and thirdly the old Section 27 injunction procedure of the 1976 Act which is continued in the new legislation.

As was said above, the basic offence is the carrying out of unauthorised development, which development is defined in Section 2 of the Act. The offence is defined, in non-legal language, as not obtaining permission for works where such permission is required under the Act. The first step in the process is usually the issuing of a warning letter (section 152). A radical change in the enforcement mechanism is the provision that a planning authority must issue a warning notice where any person has made a representation to the authority regarding unauthorised development, provided that the authority is satisfied that the representation is neither vexatious nor frivolous, and that the matter is not of a trivial or minor nature. The authority may also, of course, issue such a warning letter when it is itself satisfied that unauthorised development is occurring or has occurred. The warning letter allows the person on whom the notice is served to make submissions to the authority within four weeks of service.

The next step is the issue of an enforcement notice (sections 153 and 154). Following investigation the planning authority may decide to issue an enforcement notice. A significant improvement on the old legislation, which provided for five types of enforcement notice for differing offences, is that there is now just one such notice. A planning authority should have as its objective the issuing of an enforcement notice within twelve weeks of the issue of a warning letter but this is not mandatory. An enforcement notice may, in any event, be issued even where no warning letter is served and particularly where the matter is urgent (section 155). Those who made representations in the matter must be notified of the authority's decision. The notice may be served on 'the person carrying out the development' and also if the authority considers it necessary, on the owner or occupier. This simplifies the process as previously it was sometimes difficult if not impossible to locate owners or occupiers.

The requirements of an enforcement notice can be drastic and can include the complete demolition of structures. Other provisions allow the authority itself to take the steps necessary, including demolition, to remedy the offence. All costs incurred become chargeable to the offender. After the expiry of the period stated in the notice, or as extended, if the requirements of the notice have not been met, an offence has occurred. The planning authority must enter details of the enforcement notice and of the reasons for issuing it, on the register. An enforcement notice ceases to have effect ten years after it is issued. The time limits for the issue of both warning letters and enforcement notices are seven years from the date of the commencement of a development where no permission existed, or seven years from the date of the expiry of a permission where a permission was granted. There is no time limit for the issue of proceedings regarding a condition attached to a planning permission concerning the use of land. Proceedings can be issued against individual directors or officers of any company concerned in offences (section 158).

Offences under the 2000 Act are indictable offences. An indictable offence is one where the accused is entitled as of right to trial by jury in the Circuit Court and the offence must be regarded as major. A summary offence is defined as one heard in the District Court without a jury and for which the maximum punishment is six months imprisonment and/or a fine. The offence must be regarded as minor. The District Court has power to deal with an indictable offence where the Director of Public Prosecutions consents and where the maximum punishment would be twelve months imprisonment and/or a fine. The differences between summary and indictable offences are important for two reasons. Firstly, an indictable offence must, with the exception stated above, be prosecuted by the Director of Public Prosecutions and the penalties can be very severe. Secondly, summary offences can be prosecuted by the planning authority concerned and the penalties are restricted.

The differences in the penalties that can be imposed are, indeed, dramatic. Indictable offences can attract fines of up to 12,697,380, and/or two years imprisonment. On the other hand, the maximum fine for summary conviction is 1,904 and/or six months imprisonment. A new, and appropriate provision, is that fines are to be paid to the planning authority involved rather than to the State. The Court is required, unless there are 'special and substantial' reasons for not doing so, to award costs to the planning authority where a prosecution succeeds. Perhaps not so welcome is the abandonment of the innocent until proved guilty principle as far as some offences are concerned. The burden of proof is reversed for offences under section 154. It will be up to the defendant to prove the existence of a planning permission [section 162(1)] and also to prove that the matter was not development [section 156(6)]. Finally, it will no longer be a defence to show that an application has been made for retention, or even been granted permission, since the initiation of the enforcement proceedings.

A long-standing feature of the planning code is the injunction procedure established under Section 27 of the 1976 Act. This section allowed any person, whether with an interest in the land or not, to apply to the High Court for an injunction to prevent any unauthorised development or use. The planning authority itself could also apply. There were a number of defects in the arrangements. The first was that the proceedings could only be taken in the High Court, and in practice this limited such applications to Dublin which could make the procedure very expensive for those living any considerable distance from Dublin. The second problem was that the injunction could only be obtained while an unauthorised development was being carried out, and thirdly, there was no time limit for seeking an injunction against an unauthorised use at any time after the use commenced.

The 1992 Act entirely revoked Section 27 of the 1976 Act, and by virtue of section 19(4)(g) inserted a completely new Section 27 which addressed the three matters referred to.

1   From the 19th October 1992, any person or the planning authority, could seek an injunction in the High Court, or the Circuit Court in respect of an unauthorised development or use.

2   The injunction could be sought after a development has been completed, and the Court could order the building to be demolished, or restored as the case requires.

3   The taking of an injunction, in the case of an unauthorised development, was limited to five years after the substantial completion of the development, and in the case of an unauthorised use, after the 1st January 1994, for five years after the commencement of the use.

The revised provisions of the 1992 Act have been continued in the 2000 Act at section 160. There are, however, three significant changes. Firstly, separate applications were previously required where no permission had been sought and where the permission was been departed from. These two situations are now 'unauthorised development' and regarded as the same. Secondly, anticipated breaches of the Act can be prevented. It had been held (*Mahon and Other v Trustees of the Irish Rugby Football Union* [1998] ILRM 284, that a Section 27 application cannot be made in respect of an anticipated breach of the Acts. The relief was only available when the breach actually occurred. Section 160 refers to unauthorised development which 'is likely to be carried out.' Thirdly, the jurisdiction of the Circuit Court is limited to dealing with applications where the rateable valuation of the land does not exceed 200. On an application by an interested party, the proceedings must be transferred to the High Court where this limit is exceeded but may, of course, remain in the Circuit Court jurisdiction by agreement. There is a time limit [section 160(6)] on the taking of proceedings of seven years from the start of the development or from the expiration of a permission authorising the development. A new, and potentially wide-ranging innovation (which is also contained in the time limits concerning enforcement notices) is the provision that there is no time bar regarding a condition to which the development is subject concerning the on-going use of land.

The High Court has wide discretion in dealing with Section 160 applications. In *Avenue Properties v Farrell Homes* [1982] ILRM 21 the Court held that while it was not necessary for the applicant to show that he had suffered any damage by the alleged breach, nevertheless the court ought to decide the issue on the basis of the public interest. In the *Avenue* case there had been significant variations from the planning permission granted but the Court refused the relief sought on, amongst others, the ground that no public amenity had been damaged. In this case the respondents obtained permission to retain the altered structure. This case was quoted with approval in *White v McInerney Construction* [1995] ILRM 374 when the Supreme Court restated the wide discretion allowed to the Courts under this Section.

A very important aspect of unauthorised development, apart from the penalties, is that the development itself will always remain unauthorised even after the expiry of the time limits for the issue of enforcement notices or the imposition of penalties. The result of this is to remove any such structure or use from the exempted development provisions in the 1994 Regulations, to remove the structure from the compensation provisions of the Acts and regulations, and finally to remove the protection of the Acts if the building is destroyed by fire or otherwise.

A very sensible suggestion is made in John Gore-Grimes' KEY ISSUES IN PLANNING AND ENVIRONMENTAL LAW that an amnesty, on the general lines of the bye-law amnesty (see par. 4.12), should be introduced into the planning code. He points out that such amnesties are common in other jurisdictions, and suggests a ten-year period as being appropriate. It would, he points out, simplify and speed up conveyancing.

2.4.13 Compensation

Together with enforcement, this has proved to be the most difficult sector of the planning code, as far as the application of the law to the general planning process is concerned. The concept of compensation was one of several provisions originally introduced to ensure, amongst other things, the constitutionality of the planning code. The Constitution in Article 40.3.2 says that the State will 'protect as best it may from unjust attack, and in the case of injustice done, vindicate the life, person, good name and property rights of every citizen.'

The case of *Central Dublin Development Association v The Attorney General* [1975] 109 ILTR 69 was the first attempt to question the constitutionality of the Act, and failed. One of the conclusions reached by the Court was that an unjust attack on property rights is invalid, unless compensation is provided. The judgement said: 'Town and regional planning is an attempt to reconcile the exercise of property rights with the demands of the common good and Part IV defends and vindicates as far as practicable the rights of the citizens and is not an unjust attack and their property rights.' The original compensation provisions were contained in Part IV of the 1963 Act.

Originally, as at present, there were a number of exceptions to the general rule, (and these were listed in Section 56 of the 1963 Act) but while planning authorities issued decisions which they felt would not attract compensation, the Courts were interpreting the Acts very liberally. One particular case, *Shortt v Dublin County Council* [1983] ILRM 377 allowed applicants the right to connect to existing sewerage systems or be paid compensation. Other cases allowed compensation claims arising from refusals on zoning grounds. These developments led to planning authorities granting permissions for alternative developments, as they could do under Section 57 of the 1963 Act even where the proposals breached the development plan. This practice, however, was stopped by the case of *Grange Developments Ltd v Dublin County Council* [1986] Supreme Court, 13th May, and planning authorities, who generally have very restricted funds, were placed in a very difficult position. However, the general arrangement for avoiding compensation by allowing an alternative development is still retained and, presumably, the altered wording will escape the restrictions imposed by the Grange case. Similarly, the *Shortt* case was dealt with by providing new grounds for refusing compensations.

The general rule is now set out in section 190 of the 2000 Act: 'If, on a claim made to the planning authority, it is shown that, as a result of a decision on an appeal under Part III involving a refusal of permission to develop land or a grant of permission to develop land subject to conditions, the value of an interest of any person existing in the land to which the decision relates at the time of the decision is reduced, that person shall, subject to the other provisions of this Chapter be entitled to be paid by the planning authority by way of compensation:

a)   such amount, representing the reduction in value as may be agreed,

b)   in the absence of agreement, the amount of such reduction in value, determined in accordance with the Second Schedule, and

c)   in the case of the occupier of the land, the damage (if any) to his or her trade, business or profession carried out on the land.

This restates section 11 of the 1990 Act, with the exception of the insertion of the words 'on an appeal' in the second line. This is, presumably, to ensure that an applicant for compensation has exhausted all the processes available before a claim is made. The schedules set out how the amount is to be calculated and also list the numerous restrictions on the granting of compensation. These are so widespread that a prudent planning authority ought to be able in every decision to avoid attracting any compensation. A new provision in section 191(2) excludes the paying of compensation where land is rezoned in a development plan. Another new provision allows for compensation following the making of an area of special planning control (section 198). Any claim relating to compensation must be made within six months of the decision giving rise to the claim The revocation of a permission may also attract compensation (section 195)

A number of cases, *Wood v Wicklow County Council* [1995] I ILRM 51 and *McKone Estates v Dublin County Council* [1995] 2 ILRM 285 have held that the provisions of the 1990 Act applied to any planning decision made after the coming into operation of that Act where the application was made before that date. This is now recognised as being correct in that Article 175 of the 2001 regulations provides that the 1994 regulations will continue to apply to any claim made before the coming into force of the 2001 regulations.

Four of the schedules attached to the Act are those of interest to anyone seeking compensation.

The schedules deal with:

1   Second Schedule: Rules for determining the amount of compensation. The detail is not a matter for readers of this book, but for the lawyers, account- ants and valuers. The basic rule, however, is that compensation will be the difference between the value of the land before the decision and the value of the land after the decision, both values being open market prices from a will- ing seller.

2   Third Schedule: This lists the developments where a refusal of permission will not attract compensation. The biggest change introduced in the 1990 Act, and continued in the 2000 Act, is that no compensation will now be payable for the refusal of permission which involves the material change of use of any land. This was the area which caused the biggest problems to planning authorities as far as compensation was concerned.

3   Fourth Schedule: This schedule lists the reasons which will exclude com- pensation when a refusal is issued. There are 20 reasons quoted, ranging from deficiency in sewerage or water facilities, to traffic, road layouts, special amenities, pollution, etc. New reasons introduced in the 2000 Act involve major accident hazards, risk of flooding, architectural conservation areas and landscape conservation areas and the linguistic and cultural heritage of the Gaeltacht.

4   Fifth Schedule: This lists the conditions which may be imposed on the grant- ing of permission, without attracting compensation. There are 34 in all. Some confirm that contributions required under Section 26 of the Act do not give rise to compensation. The others cover a very wide variety of subjects reflect- ing the entire range of conditions which might normally be imposed.

A number of Court cases have established that it is essential for the precise word- ing in the Act to be reproduced in the planning decision. In the case of *Dublin County Council v Eighty Five Developments Limited* [1992] ILRM 815 the Court quoted with approval the following extract from THE LAW OF LOCAL GOVERNMENT IN THE REPUBLIC OF IRELAND by Judge Keane: 'It is, accordingly, of the highest importance for planning authorities to ensure that, in such cases, the reasons for refusal follows precisely the words of the section. So far as the Board are concerned, it would seem reasonable that, in cases where they are satisfied that the application should be refused for non-compensatable reasons, they should ensure that the wording of the refusal does not confer a right of compen- sation where none was intended by the legislature.'

It is theoretically possible that the compensation provisions are now so limited that the original constitutional challenge made in the Central Dublin case might be tried again. In general, however, it must again be emphasised that this is a very specialist area, but practitioners should be aware of the general framework.

2.5 **Cases Referred To**   *par.*

Ashbourne Holdings v An Bord Pleanála [2002] 1 ILRM 321   2.4.2
Attorney-General v Calderdale Borough Council [1983] 46 P&CR 399   2.3.2
Attorney-General (McGarry) v Sligo County Council [1989] ILRM 768   2.3.1
Avenue Properties v Farrell Homes [1982] ILRM 21   2.4.12

Blessington and District Community Council v Wicklow County Council
    [1996] High Court, 19th July   2.4.8
Blessington Heritage Trust v Wicklow County Council
    [1998] High Court, 21st June   2.4.5
Boland v An Bord Pleanála [1995] Supreme Court, 12th March   2.4.2
Bord na Mona v An Bord Pleanála and Galway County Council
    [1984] High Court 22nd November   2.4.2
Burdle v Secretary of State for the Environment [1972] 3 AER 24   2.2.3(iv)
(Butler) Irish Rugby Football Union v Dublin Corporation
    [1999] 1 ILRM 481   2.2.3(iv)
Byrne v Fingal County Council [2002] 2 ILRM 321   2.3.1
Byrne and Others v The Commissioners of Public Works in Ireland
    [1993] ILRM 665   2.1.2
Byrne v Wicklow County Council [1994] High Court, 3rd November   2.4.8

Cablelink v An Bord Pleanála [1999] High Court, 23rd February   2.4.1
Cairnduff v O'Connell [1986] ILRM 465   2.2.2
Calor Teoranta v Sligo County Council [1991] 2 IR 267   2.4.8
Carroll, Colley v Brushfield Ltd [1992] High Court, 9th October   2.2.3(iv)
Carty v Dublin County Council [1991] High Court, 16th October   2.4.2
Central Dublin Development Association Ltd and Others
    v the Attorney General [1975]109 ILTR 69   2.3.1, 2.4.13
Chambers v An Bord Pleanála [1992] ILRM 296   2.3.3(d)
Commission v Ireland [1998] 3 CMLR 727   2.2.2
Cork County Council v Cliftonhall [2002] IPELJ 49   2.4.12
Creedon v Dublin Corporation [1983] Supreme Court, 4th February   2.4.8
Crodaun Homes Ltd v Kildare County Council [1983] ILRM 1.   2.3.11(c)
Cunningham v An Bord Pleanála [1990] High Court, 3rd May   2.3.11(c)

Dolan v Dublin Corporation [1989] IR 129   2.4.1
Dillon v Irish Cement [1986] 26th November   2.2.2

Tom Chawke Caravans v Limerick County Council
[1991] High Court, July   2.3.1
T & S Contractors Ltd v Architectural Design Associates
[1992] 10-CLD-06-21   2.4.5

Village Residents Assoc. v An Bord Pleanála [2000] 2 ILRM 59   2.3.1, 2.4.5

Webber v Ministry of Housing and Local Government
[1967] 3 AER 981   2.2.3(iv)
Westmeath County Council v Michael Quirke [1996] IPELJ 3 181   2.2.3(vi)
Westmeath County Council v Moriarty [1991] High Court, 30th July   2.2.2
White v McInerney Construction [1995] ILRM 374   2.4.12
Williams v Minister for Housing and Local Government
[1967] 65 LGR 495   2.2.3(iv)
Wood v Wicklow County Council [1995] 1 ILRM 51   2.4.13

2.6 Planning Checklist

query	*law*	*par.*

1   When is permission necessary?
    Almost always. The exemptions are:

a) for building works	2000 Act – Section 4	2.2.2
	S.I. 600 of 2001 – part 2	
	Second Schedule	
	– parts 1, 2, 3	
b) for changes of use	2000 Act – Section 3(3)	2.2.3
	S.I. 600 of 2001 – Article 10	
	Second Schedule – part 4	

2   What are the rules for making
    an application?

a) Notices required	S.I. 600 of 2001	2.3.3
	Articles 17 –20	
b) What interest is required	S.I. 600 of 2001 – Article 22	2.3.12
in the site?	Case law decisions	
c) What information must be	S.I. 600 of 2001	2.3.13
submitted?	– Articles 22-24	
d) Can further information be	S.I. 600 of 2001 – Article 33	2.3.15
required?		

3   When must I submit an EIS?   S.I. 600 of 2001   2.3.3
                                        2000 Act – part X – Article 93

4	What must the EIS contain?	S.I. 600 of 2001 – Article 94	2.3.3
5	How long will the application process take?	2000 Act – Section 34(8)	2.4.1
6	What conditions can be made?	2000 Act – Section 34(4)	2.4.2
7	What is the appeal procedure?	2000 Act – part VI – chapter III S.I. 600 of 2001 – part 7 – chapter 2	2.4.3
8	Can I go to court after an appeal?	2000 Act – Section 160	2.4.5
9	How long will the permission last?	2000Act – Sections 36, 40, 43	2.4.6
10	Can the permission be extended?	2000 Act – Section 42	2.4.6
11	Can the permission be revoked?	2000 Act – Section 44	2.4.6
12	Must I build the entire proposal?	Case law decisions	2.4.7
13	What happens if the planning authority does not decide in time?	2000 Act – Section 38(8)(f)	2.4.8
14	Can a permission be given for a material contravention	2000 Act – Section 34(6)	2.4.9
15	Can the planning authority overrule the manager?	2001 Local Government Act – Section 140	2.4.10
16	How much will it cost?	S.I. 600 of 2001 – part 12 and Ninth Schedule	2.4.11
17	What documents am I entitled to see in the Planning Office or An Bord Pleanála?	S.I. 600 of 2001 – Articles 18, 68	2.4.3
18	What are the penalties for infringing the planning code	2000 Act – Part VIII	2.4.13
19	Can I stop an unauthorised development?	2000 Act – Section 160	2.4.12
20	Can I get compensation if my proposals are refused?	2000 Act – part XII and schedules 2, 3, 4, 5 S.I. 600 of 200 – part 13	2.3.13

2.7 RIAI Planning Application Checklist

(facsimile of checklist overleaf)

RIAI

The Royal Institute of the Architects of Ireland

Issue 1   **May 2002**

METHODOLOGY WORKSHEET FOR THE PREPARATION OF PLANNING APPLICATIONS

This worksheet sets out the steps that the RIAI recommends be followed by architectural practices in the preparation of a Planning Application under the Planning and Development Regulations 2001-2002. Use of this document as a quality control and auditing tool should minimise the risk of having your Planning Application rejected as invalid by the Planning Authority. It is recommended that the worksheet be used by the Project Architect and that the documentation be verified against the worksheet by a separate, senior, member of staff prior to lodgement.

PROJECT DETAILS

Project No._____   Project Title:_____   Date Registered:_____

Project Address:_____

Client:_____   Project Description:_____

Partner in Charge:_____   Project Architect:_____   Validated by:_____

STEP 1 – RESEARCH & BACKGROUND INFORMATION

Reference*	Activity	N/A	Yes	No	Action
	Check zoning of site in current Development Plan				
	Is site affected by any road proposal?				
	Check routing of services (ESB, Gas, drainage, water, telecom, etc.)				
	Are there any rights of way or Wayleaves that affect the site?				Mark on location plan
	Is the site in an Architectural Conservation Area?				See Step 9 below
Sch.2	Is the proposed development exempted under **Section 4** of the Act? That is, is it a class of development listed as exempted in Schedule 2 of the Regulations?				If yes, no application needs to be made for permission.
5	Is there doubt about whether the development is or is not exempted development?				If yes, you may seek a Declaration under **Section 5** of the Act.
18(1)(d)(iii)	Is the building a Protected Structure, or a Proposed Protected Structure? If it is, then an application for Outline Permission cannot be sought.				If yes, state in notices, see next item and Step 9.
57	Has the owner sought a Declaration under **Section 57** of the Act?				If yes, have regard to its contents.
18(1)(d)(iv)	Will an Integrated Pollution Control or Waste Licence be required?				If yes, state in notices
18(1)(d)(v)	Is the site in a Strategic Development Zone?				If yes, state in notices
98	Will an EIS be necessary?				If yes, state in notices
37(5)(a)	Is there an Appeal pending for a similar development on the site?				If yes, await outcome
133	Is the building an "Establishment"?[1]				If yes, state in notices
Part V	Is this a residential development or mixed use containing residential?				If yes, comply with Part V of the Act

* References are to the Articles of the Planning and Development Regulations 2001; those in **bold** are to the Sections of the Planning and Development Act 2000

NOTE: All questions should be answered by ticking the relevant boxes. Tick N/A for cases where the question is not applicable.

STEP 2 –COMPLIANCE WITH PART V OF THE ACT – SOCIAL & AFFORDABLE HOUSING

Reference*	Activity	N/A	Yes	No	Action
96(1)	Is site zoned residential or mixed use including residential?				If yes, Part V applies
96(14)	Is the development exempt from Part V? That is, works to an existing house, for a reconstruction or conversion where >50% of external fabric is retained, or housing for letting by approved body under Housing Acts				If yes[2], proceed to Steps 3 to 8
97(3)	Is development eligible for a certificate of exemption from Part V? That is, is it for less than 4 houses, or on a site of less than 0.2 Ha?				If yes, apply for exemption certificate
48(1)(a)	Does the application for an Exemption Certificate state the name, address, phone number and e-mail of the applicant and agent (if any)?				
48(1)(b)	If the applicant is a company, are the names of the Directors given together with the address and registration number of the company?				
48(1)(c)	Does the application state the location, Townland or address of the development site?				
48(1)(d)	Does the application state the number of houses for which it is intended to apply for permission?				
48(1)(e)	Does the application state the area of the land in respect of which it is intended to apply for permission?				
48(2)	Is the application accompanied by a location map of sufficient size and detail to permit the identification of the site to which the application relates and are the boundaries of the site clearly marked?				Minimum scale of 1:1000 in urban areas and 1:2500 in rural areas.
97(5)	Prepare Statutory Declaration[3] to accompany application for exemption certificate.				
97(3)	Apply[4] for certificate of exemption. Include site location plan, Statutory Declaration and completed application form (where applicable)[5]. The Planning Authority must issue decision within 4 weeks[6]				Ensure that this application precedes lodgement of the Planning Application.
97(14)(a)	Was the application refused?				If yes, appeal to court is possible[7]

* References are to the Articles of the Planning and Development Regulations 2001; those in **bold** are to the Sections of the Planning and Development Act 2000

STEP 3 – ACTIONS TO UNDERTAKE BEFORE LODGEMENT OF PLANNING APPLICATION

Reference*	Activity	N/A	Yes	No	Action
17(1)(a)	Publish notice in a newspaper from the approved list[8] of the relevant Planning Authority in the 2 week period[9] before lodgement				Follow checklist at Step 4 to ensure contents comply
17(1)(b)	Erect the site notice(s) on the site in the 2 week[10] period before lodgement of the Application				Follow checklist at Step 5
97(3)	Apply for certificate of exemption under Part V (if applicable)				Refer to Step 2 above
22(1)	Prepare the contents of the application (drawings, application form, fee, specification etc.) as set out in Steps 6 to 9 below				
	It is recommended that you request from your client a letter describing his legal interest in the site. If the client is a company, then you should also request the names of the Directors and the registration number of the company.				

* References are to the Articles of the Planning and Development Regulations 2001; those in **bold** are to the Sections of the Planning and Development Act 2000

NOTE: All questions should be answered by ticking the relevant boxes. Tick N/A for cases where the question is not applicable.

STEP 4 – CHECKLIST FOR CONTENTS OF NEWSPAPER NOTICE

Reference*	Activity	N/A	Yes	No	Action
18(1)	Is notice headed with the name of the Planning Authority?			.	
18(1)(a)	Does the notice state the name of the applicant?				
18(1)(b)	Does the notice state the location, Townland or postal address of the development site?				
18(1)(c)	Does the notice state the type of application?[11]				Read endnote
18(1)(d)	Does the notice state the nature and extent of the proposed development?				
18(1)(d)(i)	For housing developments, is the number of houses (meaning the number of dwellings to be provided) stated?				
18(1)(d)(ii)	In the case of retention, does the notice state the nature of the proposed use of the structure?				
18(1)(d)(iii)	Where the structure is a Protected Structure, does the notice state this fact?				
18(1)(d)(iv)	Where the development comprises or is for the purposes of an activity requiring an integrated pollution control licence or a waste licence, does the notice state this fact?				
18(1)(d)(v)	Where the application relates to a development in a Strategic Development Zone, does the notice state this fact?				
18(1)(e)	Does the notice state that the application may be inspected or purchased at the offices of the Planning Authority?				
18(1)(e)	Does the notice state that an observation or submission can be made to the Planning Authority in writing on payment of the prescribed fee (currently €20) within 5 weeks of receipt of the application by the Planning Authority?				
98(a)	Where an EIS has been required to be prepared to accompany the application, is a statement of that fact included in the notice?				
98(b)	Where an EIS has been prepared, does the notice state that it may be inspected or purchased for a fee not exceeding the reasonable cost of copying?				

* References are to the Articles of the Planning and Development Regulations 2001; those in **bold** are to the Sections of the Planning and Development Act 2000

STEP 5 – CHECKLIST FOR CONTENTS OF SITE NOTICE

Reference*	Activity	N/A	Yes	No	Action
19(1)(a)	Is the notice set out substantially to the like effect as shown in Schedule 3 of the regulations?				
19(1)(b)	Is the notice printed in indelible ink on a white background, fixed to durable material and protected from the effects of bad weather?				
19(1)(C)	Is the notice fixed in a conspicuous place on or near the each entrance to the site or structure and easily legible by persons using the public road?				
	Is there independent documentary proof of the date on which the notice(s) was erected on site?				Arrange site notices to be erected by a signage company[12]

NOTE: All questions should be answered by ticking the relevant boxes. Tick N/A for cases where the question is not applicable.

Reference*	Activity	N/A	Yes	No	Action
19(3)	If the site is large, or has multiple entrances and/or public frontages, then several site notices should be erected on the site.				
Sch.3(1)	Is the notice headed with the name of the Planning Authority?				
Sch.3(2)	Does the notice state the name of the applicant?[13]				
Sch.3(3)	Does the notice state the type of application?[14]				
Sch.3(4)	Does the notice state the location, Townland or postal address of the development site?				
Sch.3(6)	Does the notice state the nature and extent of the proposed development?				
Sch.3(6)(a)	For housing developments, is the number of houses (meaning the number of dwellings to be provided) stated?				
Sch.3(6)(b)	In the case of retention, does the notice state the nature of the proposed use of the structure?				
Sch.3(6)(c)	Where the structure is a Protected Structure, does the notice state this fact?				
Sch.3(6)(d)	Where an EIS has been prepared in respect of the Planning Application, does the notice state this fact?				
Sch.3(6)(e)	Where the development comprises or is for the purposes of an activity requiring an integrated pollution control licence or a waste licence, does the notice state this fact?				
Sch.3(6)(f)	Where the application relates to a development in a Strategic Development Zone, does the notice state this fact?				
Sch.3(6)(g)	Where the application relates to development consisting of the provision of or modifications to an establishment, does the notice state this fact?				
Sch.3(7)	Does the notice state that the application may be inspected at the offices of the Planning Authority and are the address and public opening hours[15] of the Planning Authority given?				
Sch.3	Does the notice state that an observation or submission can be made to the Planning Authority in writing on payment of €20 (the current prescribed fee)?				
Sch.3(8)	Is the site notice signed by the applicant or his agent? If it is the agent, is his address also given?				
Sch.3(9)	Is the date that the site notice was erected on site given?				
19(4)	Is the notice required to be yellow? That is, has there been an application for a development of like description on the same site within the previous six months?				If yes, ensure that it is.

* References are to the Articles of the Planning and Development Regulations 2001; those in **bold** are to the Sections of the Planning and Development Act 2000

STEP 6 – PLANNING APPLICATION DOCUMENTATION

Article*	Activity	N/A	Yes	No	Action
	Is the application form being used a current form that takes into account the requirements of the Planning and Development Regulations 2001-2002 and is it completed fully?				If no, get one from the relevant Planning Authority
22(1)(b)(1)	Is the applicant's name, address, phone number and e-mail given in the application form?				

NOTE: All questions should be answered by ticking the relevant boxes. Tick N/A for cases where the question is not applicable.

Reference*	Activity	N/A	Yes	No	Action
22(1)(b)(iii)	If the applicant is a Company, have the names of ALL Directors been given together with the registration number and address of the company?				
22(1)(h)	If the development is for housing, is a statement of how compliance with Section 96(2) of the Act will be achieved included? Consultations in relation to this provision must take place prior to the lodgement of the application.				If no, prepare one in consultation with the Housing Supply Unit of the Planning Authority
22(2)(a)	Is the page of the newspaper containing the required notice included?				
22(2)(a)	Is one copy of the site notice (of the appropriate colour) included?				
22(2)(b)	Are there 6 copies[18] of all drawings included? (See Step 7 below for specific guidance on contents of the drawings)				
22(2)(d)	Is there a schedule listing all drawings, documents and particulars making up the application included?				
22(2)(e)	If the development is eligible for exemption from Part V, is the certificate or a copy of the application for a certificate enclosed?				
22(2)(f)	Is the appropriate fee enclosed?[17] Some calculations can be complex, if in doubt agree the calculation with the Planning Authority before lodgement.				
22(3)(b)(i)	If the application relates to a development consisting mainly of any material change of use, is there a statement of the existing uses and the proposed uses together with a description of the extent and nature of the proposed use?				

* References are to the Articles of the Planning and Development Regulations 2001; those in **bold** are to the Sections of the Planning and Development Act 2000

STEP 7 – PLANNING APPLICATION PLANS, DRAWINGS AND MAPS

Reference*	Activity	N/A	Yes	No	Action
23(2)	Is the application for works to a protected structure?				Step 9 also applies
24	Is the application for Outline Permission?				Go to Step 8
23(1)	Are all drawings to metric scale?				
22(3)(a)	Are there 6 copies of all drawings included?				
22(2)(b)	Is the location plan at 1:1000 for urban sites and 1:2500[18] for rural sites?				Read endnote
22(2)(b)	Is the location plan sufficiently clear so as to allow ready identification of the site to which the application relates?				
22(2)(b)	Is the site to which the development relates outlined in red, with adjacent land, that is in the control of the applicant but not part of the site to which the application relates delineated in blue and Wayleaves that affect the site delineated in yellow?				The site plan must also show the site boundary in red.[19]
22(2)(c)	Is the position of the site notice(s) clearly indicated?				
23(1)(a)	Is site or layout drawing to a scale of 1:500 or greater?				
23(1)(a)	Is the site boundary clearly delineated in red on the site plan?				
23(1)(a)	Does the site plan clearly show buildings, roads, boundaries, septic tanks and percolation areas, bored wells, significant tree stands and other features in the vicinity[20] of the site?				

NOTE: All questions should be answered by ticking the relevant boxes. Tick N/A for cases where the question is not applicable.

Reference*	Activity	N/A	Yes	No	Action
23(1)(b)	Are all drawings, other than the site location and layout plans, at a scale of 1:200 or greater?[21]				
23(1)(c)	Do the site layout and other plans show levels or contours relative to an Ordnance survey or temporary datum?				
23(1)(d)	Do the elevations show the main features of buildings that are contiguous to the proposed structure?[22]				
23(1)(e)	For extensions, alterations and reconstruction projects, are the proposed works clearly distinguished from the existing structure?[23]				
23(1)(f)	Are all plans, drawings etc clearly dimensioned, showing overall heights of structures and the distance to the site boundaries?[24]				
23(1)(G)	If the location or site plan is an Ordnance Survey extract or based on an Ordnance Survey drawings, is the OS sheet number indicated?				See Step 10 below for clarifications on using OSI maps
23(1)(h)	Do all plans show a north point?[25]				
23(1)(i)	Do all drawings show the name of the person who drew them?[26]				
23(4)	Has a scale model of the proposal been requested by the Planning Authority?				If yes, is it ready to go with the application?

* References are to the Articles of the Planning and Development Regulations 2001; those in **bold** are to the Sections of the Planning and Development Act 2000

STEP 8 – REQUIREMENTS FOR OUTLINE APPLICATION

Reference*	Activity	N/A	Yes	No	Action
21	An application for Outline Permission cannot be made in respect of (a) Retention of Development (b) Development consisting of works to a Protected Structure or a proposed Protected Structure (c) Development requiring an Integrated Pollution Control or Waste Licence and				
96(1)	(d) Development for which an EIS is required.				
22(2)	The Outline Application must be accompanied by the completed application form, the prescribed fee, the page of the newspaper containing the notice, a copy of the site notice, a certificate of exemption under **Section 97** (if applicable) and 6 copies of drawings and particulars as necessary to describe the development as in next item.				
24	Submit only such information as is necessary to allow the Planning Authority to decide on siting, layout and any other specific matters being applied for.[27]				

* References are to the Articles of the Planning and Development Regulations 2001; those in **bold** are to the Sections of the Planning and Development Act 2000

STEP 9 – ADDITIONAL REQUIREMENTS FOR PROTECTED STRUCTURES[28]

Reference*	Activity	N/A	Yes	No	Action
23(2)	Does the proposed development consist of works to a protected structure, a proposed protected structure or to the exterior of a structure located within an architectural conservation area, or an area designated as such in a draft development plan?				If yes, then the additional information set out in this Step must be provided.
23(2)	Is the application accompanied by such photographs, plans and other particulars as are necessary to show how the development would affect the character of the structure?[29]				

NOTE: All questions should be answered by ticking the relevant boxes. Tick N/A for cases where the question is not applicable.

Reference*	Activity	N/A	Yes	No	Action
23(2)	Are the locations and directions from which any appended photographs taken clearly indicated on the plans?				
23(2)	Is the structure of particular importance? If so, provide black and white large format photographs of the structure to act as a record of the building.[30]				
23(2)	Where the structure is in an Architectural Conservation Area and not itself a Protected Structure, you are only required to submit details of how the exterior is affected by the proposed development.				

* References are to the Articles of the Planning and Development Regulations 2001; those in **bold** are to the Sections of the Planning and Development Act 2000

STEP 10 – USING ORDNANCE SURVEY MAPS[31]

Reference*	Activity	N/A	Yes	No	Action
	Ensure that you are properly licensed to use the maps issued by OSI. This is achieved by the purchase of "Planning Packs" prepared by OSI or a recognised agent or by the purchase of a licence to copy OSI maps.				
	The OSI monitors the use of its maps through random examination of files held in Planning Department files available to the public for inspection.				
	You are not required by the regulations to use OSI maps for your location plans, but OSI is the only source of detailed maps for the entire country.				
	You may add information to an OSI map to illustrate your development, a north point and a title block to identify the project and the person who prepared the map. Such additions do not breach copyright.				
	If you have a licence you may draw information onto one map and then copy it yourself to make up the required 6 sets. Such copying must be authenticated by the licence holder's authorised stamp.				
	Licences are issued by OSI for a 12-month period and the cost varies depending on the number of persons who will use the licence, not on the number of copies made in the 12 month period.[32]				
	OSI can provide digital maps so that the information can be incorporated into your own AutoCAD work. Such use is arranged by specifically negotiated agreements.				

* References are to the Articles of the Planning and Development Regulations 2001; those in **bold** are to the Sections of the Planning and Development Act 2000

STEP 11 – APPLICATIONS IN RURAL AREAS REQUIRING ON-SITE EFFLUENT TREATMENT

Reference*	Activity	N/A	Yes	No	Action
	Is the site served by a public sewer?				If no, proceed with this Step
	Does the Planning Authority publish a prescribed form for a site suitability test?				If yes, use it
	Decide on type of effluent treatment system to be used and ensure that it is acceptable to the relevant Planning Authority.				

NOTE: All questions should be answered by ticking the relevant boxes. Tick N/A for cases where the question is not applicable.

Reference*	Activity	N/A	Yes	No	Action
	Arrange for the carrying out of the appropriate tests in accordance with the provisions of NSAI recommendation reference SR6:1991[33]				
	If the site is adjacent to or in the vicinity of any site listed in the Record of Monuments and Places[34], then the prior written consent of Duchas The Heritage Service is required to dig trial holes and percolation test holes.				
	The tests must be supervised and verified by a "suitably qualified person".[35]				
	A map showing the location of the trial holes should accompany the application and it should show the location of any wells, streams, water courses or ditches within 100m of the proposed site of the effluent treatment system and its percolation area.				

End of guidance

CONFIRMATIONS[36]

I **confirm** that this Methodology Worksheet was **used in the preparation of the planning application** referred to in the section entitled "Project Details" above and that each Step has been followed as set out. I **further state** that I have **checked the documentation** prepared using this Methodology Worksheet and I hereby confirm that it complies in full with the details marked at each Step.

Signed: _____   _____
Registered Member of the Royal Institute of the Architects of Ireland   RIAI Membership Stamp

The RIAI is the representative body for professionally qualified architects in Ireland and is a member of the Architects Council of Europe and the International Union of Architects

Advice Notes

[1] An "establishment" is defined by the Major Accidents Directive (Seveso II) and can be considered as any building or site where dangerous, toxic or explosive materials are handled, processed or stored. There are restrictions, given in Schedule 8, Table 2 of the Regulations, for the distance that certain buildings must be from the perimeter of sites containing establishments.

[2] In this case the development is entirely exempt from Part V and there is no need for an application for a certificate of exemption to be lodged.

[3] The Statutory Declaration must set out the ownership history of the site over the previous 5 years; it must identify any partners of the applicant in the development; it must declare any interest that the applicant or his partners have in any land within 400m of the subject site; and it must include a statement by the applicant that he is not aware of any reason that would lead the Planning Authority to refuse the application.

[4] It is not clear to whom an application should be addressed. If the planning department cannot advise you, then address the application to the County Manager.

[5] It appears that some Planning Authorities have developed a separate application form for this purpose.

[6] The Planning Authority may request further information and the 4 weeks until the decision is reached then runs from receipt of that information. The Planning Authority shall not grant an exemption certificate if:
  (a) An exemption certificate has been issued in respect of the same or similar development within the previous 5 years or
  (b) The applicant (or a person acting in concert with him) has permission for or has carried out a development on the site, or on land in the vicinity of the site, in the period of 5 years before the application date (but not before 1st November 2001), unless the aggregate of houses developed, with the two permissions, will be <4 or the overall site area is <0.2 Ha.

[7] The appeal must be made within 3 weeks of the decision and the court may dismiss the appeal, uphold the refusal or overturn the refusal.

[8] Each Planning Authority is now required to publish a list of approved newspapers, for their administrative area, in which it is acceptable to publish the required notice.

[9] Where the last day of the 2 week period is a Saturday, Sunday or Public Holiday, or a day on which the offices of the Planning Authority are closed, then the application will be valid if submitted on the next following day on which the offices are open.

[10] ibid.

[11] The relevant types are Permission for development, Permission for retention of development, Outline permission for development or Permission consequent on the grant of outline permission (in which case the reference number of the outline permission must be stated).

[12] It is strongly advised that you arrange for site notices to be erected by an independent company, so that if the notices are vandalised, you can show documentary proof of the date on which they were erected. If there is no notice on site on the day of inspection by the Planning Authority, your application will be invalid unless you can show such proof.

[13] This must not be the agent for the applicant.

[14] The relevant types are Permission for development, Permission for retention of development, Outline permission for development or Permission consequent on the grant of outline permission (in which case the reference number of the outline permission must be stated).

[15] The relevant hours are those during which a member of the public can view the file held at the enquiries desk of the Planning Authority.

[16] In the case of an application for a protected structure or a proposed protected structure, you may be required to submit up to four additional sets of drawings.

[17] The table of fees is published in Schedule 9 of the Regulations and is generally provided by each Planning Authority with the application form. As the fees are subject to change on an occasional basis, it is important to ensure that you are referring to the appropriate and up-to-date table.

[18] References to a scale of 1:1250 in SI 600 of 2001 have been superseded by SI 70 of 2002 which states that a scale of 1:2500 is to be substituted for all such references. The required scale for rural sites therefore becomes 1:2500.

[19] SI70 of 2002 changed references to scales and changed the requirements for delineating the site in red, blue and yellow from Article 23(1)(a) to Article 22(2)(b), thus meaning that the only coloured delineation required on the site plan is the site boundary.

[20] The meaning of "vicinity" in this context is not clear. The intention seems to be that any existing features on which the proposed development would have a direct impact should be shown on the site or layout drawing.

[21] If your scheme would be better described by a scale of less than 1:200, then you must agree the scales with the Planning Authority before you submit the planning application.

[22] No guidance is given as to the meaning of "contiguous", and the guidelines on the Regulations issued by the DoELG use the word "adjacent to" instead. Dictionary definitions imply that such buildings would be immediately beside the proposed development.

[23] The Regulations allow for the new works to be distinguished from the existing structures by marking (hatching) OR colouring.

[24] The intent here is to show single figures for critical dimensions. It is not considered acceptable that multiple dimensions have to be added together to determine an overall height or distance.

[25] The Regulations require that all plans and maps other than elevations and sections show the North point. This presents difficulties for housing estates – something that needs to be clarified by the DoELG. Note that each plan should have a North point, that is, where a drawing contains two plan drawings two North points are required.

[26] The initials of the person are not acceptable. It is recommended that the name of the project architect be the name shown on drawings, as he is the proper person to whom queries relating to the project should be addressed.

[27] Specifically, elevations, sections and detailed plans may not be necessary, but the impact of the proposal on adjacent buildings and landscapes must be adequately described.

[28] For works to Protected Structures you are strongly advised to familiarise yourself with the publication published jointly by t Department of Arts, Heritage, Gaeltacht and the Islands and Duchas The Heritage Service entitled "Architectural Heritage Protection - Draft Guidelines for Planning Authorities". This document sets down detailed guidance on how to document Protected Structures and comply with the requirements set down in the Planning and Development Act 2000.

[29] Any survey information should be drawn at 1:50 scale, with 1:20 scale drawings of spaces affected by the proposal also provided. If there are features of special interest (skirtings, architraves, panelling etc.) these should be draw at an appropriate scale so as to record them for future restoration work i.e. typically 1:2, but sometimes 1:1.

[30] To discover whether or not the structure on which you are working is worthy of such a detailed photographic record, you will have to consult the Conservation Officer of the Planning Authority in advance of the Planning Application submission.

[31] There are particular requirements that the Copyright Laws set down for the use of copyright material, and the maps published by OSI are one example of such material. These requirements relate to the use of the maps themselves and of tracings of the maps that extract specific information shown on the maps. Any doubts you have should be addressed to the OSI offices in Dublin. The notes set down in Step 10 are for general guidance only.

[32] Current (May 2002) costs for a 12-month licence are €380 for 1 person, €700 for 2-3 persons, €1,000 for 4-5 persons, €1,250 for 6-8 persons and by negotiation for larger numbers.

[33] The full title is "Septic Tank Systems: Recommendations for Domestic Effluent Treatment and Disposal from a single Dwelling House".

[34] This list was set up under Section 12 of the National Monuments (Amendment) Act 1994 and is issued by the National Monuments and Historic Properties Division of Duchas The Heritage Service.

[35] The persons qualified to carry out these tests are not set down in the Regulations, but Planning Authorities generally accept architects, engineers, experienced technicians and surveyors.

[36] It is strongly recommended that, where possible, two members of staff check the documentation. In this case, the first person should be responsible for the project; the second should be a Partner, Director or other senior member of staff, being a Member of the RIAI. It is this second person who should sign the confirmations section.

2.8 Definitions

The following list of definitions has been selected from those given in the 2000 Act and the 2001 Regulations. References to 'sections' relate to the Act, and references to 'articles' relate to the regulations. The prefix a) indicates that the definition is contained in Part I of the Act, b) that it is is in Part V of the Act, and c) that it is either in Part I or Part II of S.I. 600 of 2001.

b)   **'accommodation needs'** means the size of the accommodation required by an eligible person determined in accordance with the regulations made by the Minister under section 100(1)(a);

a)   **'advertisement'** means any word, letter, model, balloon, inflatable structure, kite, poster, notice, device or representation employed for the purpose of advertisement, announcement or direction;

a)   **'advertisement structure'** means any structure which is a hoarding, scaffold, framework, pole, standard, device or sign (whether illuminated or not) and which is used or intended for use for exhibiting advertisements or any attachment to a building or structure used for advertising purposes;

c)   **'aerodrome'** means any definite and limited area (including water) intended to be used, either wholly or in part, for or in connection with the landing or departure of aircraft;

b)   **'affordable housing'** means houses or land made available, in accordance with Section 96(9) or (10), for eligible purposes;

a)   **'agriculture'** includes horticulture, fruit growing, seed growing, dairy farming, the breeding and keeping of livestock (including any creature kept for the production of food, wool, skins or fur, or for the purpose of its use in the farming of land), the training of horses and the rearing of bloodstock, the use of land as grazing land, meadow land, osier land, market gardens and nursery grounds, and 'agricultural' shall be construed accordingly;

c)   **'airport'** means an area of land comprising an aerodrome and any buildings, roads and car parks connected to the aerodrome and used by the airport authority in connection with the operation thereof;

c)   **'airport operational building'** means a building other than a hotel, required in connection with the movement or maintenance of aircraft, or with the embarking, disembarking, loading, discharge or transport of passengers, livestock or goods at an airport;

a)   **'alteration'** includes

    a)   plastering or painting or the removal of plaster or stucco, or

    b)   the replacement of a door, window or roof

that materially alters the external appearance of a structure so as to render the appearance inconsistent with the character of the structure or neighbouring structures;

c)   **'amusement arcade'** means premises used for the playing of gaming machines, video games or other amusement machines;

a)   **'appeal'** means an appeal to the Board;

c)   **'approved newspaper'** means a newspaper approved by a planning authority for the purposes of the Regulations in accordance with Article 18;

a)   **'architectural conservation area'** shall be construed in accordance with Section 81(1);

a)   **'area of special planning control'** shall be construed in accordance with Section 85(8);

a)   **'attendant grounds'**, in relation to a structure, includes land lying outside the curtilage of the structure;

c)   **'betting office'** means premises for the time being registered in the register of bookmaking offices kept by the Revenue Commissioners under the Betting Act 1931 (no. 27 of 1931);

a)   **'the Birds Directive'** means Council Directive No. 79/409/EEC of 2nd April 1979(1) on the conservation of wild birds;

c)   **'bring facility'** means a facility of purpose-built receptacles in which segregated domestic wastes may be deposited by the public, provided in an area to which the public have access;

c)   **'built-up area'** means a city or town (where 'city' or 'town' have the meanings assigned by them by the Local Government Act, 2001) or an adjoining developed area;

c)   **'business premises'** means

    a)   any structure or other land (not being an excluded premises) which is normally used for the carrying on of any professional, commercial or industrial undertaking or any structure (not being an excluded premises) which is normally used for the provision therein of services to persons

b)   a hotel or public house

c)   any structure or other land used for the purposes of, or in connection with, the functions of a State authority;

c)   **'care'** means personal care, including help with physical, intellectual or social needs;

c)   **'childminding'** means the activity of minding no more than 6 children, including the children, if any, of the person minding, in the house of that person, for profit or gain;

a)   **'a dangerous substance'** has the meaning assigned to it by the Major Accidents Directive;

c)   **'day centre'** means non-residential remises used for social or recreational purposes or for the provision of care (including occupational training);

b)   **'eligible person'** means subject to subsection (3) and to the regulations, if any, made by the Minister under section 100(1)(b), a person who is in need of accommodation and whose income would not be adequate to meet the payments on a mortgage for the purchase of a house to meet his or her accommodation needs because the payments calculated over the course of a year would exceed 35 per cent of that person's annual income net of income tax and pay related social insurance;

c)   **'establishment'** means an establishment to which the Major Accident Regulations apply;

a)   **'European site'** means

a)   a site

   i)   notified for the purposes of Regulation 4 of the European Communities (Natural Habitats) Regulations, 1997 (S.I. No. 94 of 1997), subject to any amendments made to it by virtue of Regulation 5 of those regulations, or

   ii)   transmitted to the Commission in accordance with Regulation 5(4) of the said regulations, or

   iii) added by virtue of Regulation 6 of the said regulations to the list transmitted to the Commission in accordance with Regulation 5(4) of the said Regulations, but only until the adoption in respect of the site of a decision by the Commission under Article 21 of the Habitats Directive for the purposes of the third paragraph of Article 4(2) of that Directive,

b) a site adopted by the Commission as a site of Community importance for the purposes of Article 4(2) of the Habitats Directive in accordance with the procedure laid down in Article 21 of that Directive,

c) a special area of conservation within the meaning of the European Communities (Natural Habitats) Regulations, 1997,

d) an area classified pursuant to paragraph (1) or (2) of Article 4 of the Birds Directive;

c) **'excluded premises'** means

a) any premises used for purposes of a religious, educational, cultural, recreational or medical character

b) any guest house or other premises (not being a hotel) providing overnight guest accommodation, block of flats or apartments, club, boarding house or hostel

c) any structure which was designed for use as one or more dwellings, except such a structure which was used as business premises immediately before 1st October, 1964 or is so used with permission under the Act;

a) **'exhibit'**, in relation to an advertisement, includes affix, inscribe, print, paint, illuminate and otherwise delineate;

a) **'existing establishment'** has the meaning that it has in the Major Accidents Directive;

a) **'fence'** includes a hoarding or similar structure but excludes any bank, wall or other similar structure composed wholly or mainly of earth or stone;

c) **'fish counter'** means a device capable of mechanically or electrically enumerating fish as they pass a specific point or area;

c) **'gross floor space'** means the area ascertained by the internal measurement of the floor space on each floor of a building (including internal walls and partitions), disregarding any floor space provided for the parking of vehicles by persons occupying or using the building or buildings where such floor space is incidental to the primary purpose of the building;

a) **'habitable house'** means a house which

a) is used as a dwelling,

b)   is not in use but when last used was used, disregarding any unauthorised use, as a dwelling and is not derelict, or

c)   was provided for use as a dwelling, but has not been occupied;

c)   **'hazard'** means the intrinsic property of a dangerous substance or physical situation, with a potential for creating damage to human health or the environment;

a)   **'house'** means a building or part of a building which is being or has been occupied as a dwelling or was provided for use as a dwelling but has not been occupied, and, where appropriate, includes a building which was designed for use as 2 or more dwellings, or a flat, an apartment or other dwelling within such a building;

c)   **'house'** does not, as regards development of classes 1, 2, 3, 4, 6(b)(ii), 7 or 8 specified in column 1 of Part 1 of Schedule 2, or development to which Articles 10(4) or 10(5) refer, include a building designed for use or used as 2 or more dwellings or a flat, an apartment or other dwelling within such a building;

b)   **'housing strategy'** means a strategy included in a development plan in accordance with Section 94(1);

c)   **'illuminated'** in relation to any advertisement, sign or other advertisement structure means illuminated internally or externally by artificial lighting, directly or by reflection, for the purpose of advertisement, announcement or direction;

c)   **'industrial building'** means a structure (not being a shop, or a structure in or adjacent to and belonging to a quarry or mine) used for the carrying on of any industrial process;

c)   **'industrial process'** means any process which is carried on in the course of trade or business, other than agriculture, and which is

a)   for or incidental to the making of any article or part of an article, or

b)   for or incidental to the altering, repairing, ornamenting, finishing, cleaning, washing, packing, canning, adapting for sale, breaking up or demolition of any article, including the getting, dressing or treatment of minerals

and for the purposes of this paragraph, 'article' includes

i)   a vehicle, aircraft, ship or vessel, or

ii) a sound recording, film, broadcast, cable programme, publication and computer program or other original database;

c)   **'industrial undertaker'** means a person by whom an industrial process is carried on and 'industrial undertaking' shall be construed accordingly;

a)   **'land'** includes any structure and any land covered with water (whether inland or coastal);

c)   **'light industrial building'** means an industrial building in which the processes carried on or the plant or machinery installed are such as could be carried on or installed in any residential area without detriment to the amenity of that area by reason of noise, vibration, small, fumes, smoke, soot, ash, dust or grit;

a)   **'major accident'** has the meaning assigned to it by the Major Accident Directive;

c)   **'Major Accident Regulations'** means the European Communities (Control of Major Accident Hazards Involving Dangerous Substances) Regulations, 2000 (S.I. No. 476 of 2000);

b)   **'market value'** in relation to a house, means the price which the unencumbered fee simple of the house would fetch if sold on the open market;

c)   **'minerals'** means all minerals and substances in or under land of a kind ordinarily worked by underground or by surface working for the removal but does not include turf;

c)   **'mobile telephony'** means public mobile telephony;

b)   **'mortgage'** means a loan for the purchase of a house secured by mortgage in an amount not exceeding 90 per cent of the price of the house;

a)   **'new establishment'** has the meaning that it has in the Major Accidents Directive;

a)   **'occupier'**, in relation to a protected structure or a proposed protected structure, means

     a)   any person in or entitled to immediate use or enjoyment of the structure

     b)   any person entitled to occupy the structure, and

     c)   any other person having, for the time being, control of the structure;

a)   **'owner'**, in relation to land, means a person, other than a mortgagee not in possession, who, whether in his or her own right or as a trustee or agent for any other person, is entitled to receive the rack rent of the land or, where the land is not let at a rack rent, would be so entitled if it were so let;

c)   **'painting'** includes any application of colour;

c)   **'peat extraction'** includes any related drainage of bogland;

a)   **'proposed protected structure'** means a structure in respect of which a notice is issued under Section 12(3) or under Section 55 proposing to add the structure, or a specified part of it, to a record of protected structure, and, where that notice so indicates, includes any specified feature which is within the attendant grounds of the structure and which would not otherwise be included in this definition;

a)   **'protected structure'** means

   a)   a structure, or

   b)   a specified part of a structure

which is included in a record of protected structures, and, where that record so indicates, includes any specified feature which is within the attendant grounds of the structure and which would not otherwise be included in this definition;

a)   **'protection'**, in relation to a structure or part of a structure, includes conversation, preservation and improvement compatible with maintaining the character and interest of the structure or part;

c)   **'provision of an establishment'** means development as a result of which an area would become an establishment;

a)   **'public place'** means any street, road, seashore or any other place to which the public have access whether as of right or by permission and whether subject to or free of charge;

c)   **'repository'** means a structure (excluding any land occupied therewith) where storage is the principal use and where no business is transacted other than business incidental to such storage;

a)   **'risk'** has the meaning assigned to it by the Major Accidents Directive;

a)   **'seashore'** has the same meaning as in the Foreshore Act, 1933;

c)   **'shop'** means a structure for any or all of the following purposes, where the sale, display or service is principally to visiting members of the public

   a)   for the retail sale of goods

   b)   as a post office

c) for the sale of tickets or as a travel agency

d) for the sale of sandwiches or other food for consumption off the premises, where the sale of such food is subsidiary to the main retail use

e) for hairdressing

f) for the display of goods for sale

g) for the hiring out of domestic or personal goods or articles

h) as a launderette or dry cleaners

i) for the reception of goods to be washed, cleaned or repaired,

but does not include any use associated with the provision of funeral services or as a funeral home, or as a hotel, a restaurant or a public house, or for the sale of hot food for consumption off the premises, except under paragraph (d) above, or any use to which class 2 or 3 of Part 4 of Schedule 2 applies;

a) **'structure'** means any building, structure, excavation, or other thing constructed or made on, in or under any land, or any part of a structure so defined, and

    a) where the context so admits, includes the land on, in or under which the structure is situate, and

    b) in relation to a protected structure or proposed protected structure, includes
        i) the interior of the structure
        ii) the land lying within the curtilage of the structure
        iii) any other structures lying within that curtilage and their interiors, and
        iv) all fixtures and features which form part of the interior or exterior of any structure or structures referred to in sub-paragraph (i) or (iii);

a) **'substratum of land'** means any subsoil or anything beneath the surface of land required

    a) for the purposes of a tunnel or tunnelling or anything connected therewith, or

    b) for any other purpose connected with a scheme within the meaning of the Roads Act, 1993;

c) **'supermarket'** means a self-service shop selling mainly food;

c) **'telecommunications network'** means the whole of the telecommunications infrastructure and any associated physical infrastructure of any network operator;

c) **'telecommunications service'** means services which consist wholly or partly in the transmission or routing of signals on a telecommunications network or both transmission and routing;

a)   **'traveller'** means a traveller within the meaning of Section 2 of the Housing (Traveller Accommodation) Act, 1998;

a)   **'unauthorised development'** means, in relation to land, the carrying out of any unauthorised works (including the construction, erection or making of any unauthorised structure) or the making of any unauthorised use;

a)   **'unauthorised structure'** means a structure other than

    a)   a structure which was in existence on 1st October 1964, or

    b)   a structure, the construction, erection or making of which was the subject of a permission for development granted under Part IV of the Act of 1963 or deemed to be such under Section 92 of that Act or under Section 34 of this Act, being a permission which has not been revoked, or which exists as a result of the carrying out of exempted development (within the meaning of Section 4 of the Act of 1963 or Section 4 of this Act);

a)   **'unauthorised use'** means, in relation to land, use commenced on or after 1st October 1964, being a use which is a material change in use of any structure or other land and being developed other than

    a)   exempted development (within the meaning of Section 4 of the Act of 1963 or Section 4 of this Act), or

    b)   development which is the subject of a permission granted under Part IV of the Act of 1963 or under Section 34 of this Act, being a permission which has not been revoked, and which is carried out in compliance with that permission or any condition to which that permission is subject;

a)   **'unauthorised works'** means any works on, in, over or under land commenced on or after 1st October 1964, being development other than

    a)   exempted development (within the meaning of Section 4 of the Act of 1963 or Section 4 of this Act), or

    b)   development which is the subject of a permission granted under Part IV of the Act of 1963 or under Section 34 of this Act, being a permission which has not been revoked, and which is carried out in compliance with that permission or any condition to which that permission is subject;

a)   **'use'**, in relation to land, does not include the use of the land by the carrying out of any works thereon;

a)   **'warning letter'** means a notification in writing under section 152(1);

a)   **'waste licence'** means a waste licence under Part V, Waste Management Act 1996;

a) **'works'** includes any act or operation of construction, excavation, demolition, extension, alteration, repair or renewal and, in relation to a protected structure or proposed protected structure, includes any act or operation involving the application or removal of plaster, paint, wallpaper, tiles or other material to or from the surfaces of the interior or exterior of a structure;

c) **'wholesale warehouse'** means a structure where business, principally of a wholesale nature is transacted, and goods are stored or displayed.

Chapter 3 – **The Environment**

3.1 **Introduction**

A visitor to our world might be forgiven for thinking that the environment was invented in the last 20 years, but there are good reasons for the greater awareness of, and respect for, the natural environment. Until the advent of the industrial revolution in the 18th Century, the impact of man's works on nature generally was insignificant, and even after that date the effect was largely ignored. The social conscience of the day saw no problem in requiring the workers to live in polluted and crowded towns, while the upper strata of society enjoyed the clear air of the suburbs or country. But the steady raising of standards in the area of health and welfare, together with proliferation of man-made activities affecting the environment made some form of regulation inevitable.

This was effected in Ireland by two separate, though related, ways. The first is the concept of the environmental impact assessment, through the impact statement, and secondly the establishment of the Environmental Protection Agency. The area of environmental law is now very complex, and taken with the scope and detail of the Planning Acts and Regulations, presents the average practitioner with the dual problems of ascertaining the up-to-date position and then understanding it. As in many areas, specialists are now available, but as has been pointed out before in this guide, it is essential for anyone involved in the building process to be aware of the general requirements. This chapter will only deal with the basic position, which was changed by the introduction of the Planning and Development Act 2000. Until then, the matter of environmental impact statements and assessments was dealt with under S.I. 349 of 1989 – The European Communities (Environmental Impact Assessment) Regulations, which brought into effect the provisions of the Environmental Impact Assessment Directive – 85/337/EEC, later amended by Directive 97/11/EC. Environmental impact assessment, as it now effects the planning process, is regulated by Part X of the Planning and Development Act 2000 and Part 10 of S.I. 600 of 2001 – the Planning and Development Regulations.

Further details can be obtained by consulting either IRISH PLANNING LAW AND PRACTICE by O'Sullivan and Shepherd published by Butterworths, ENVIRONMENTAL AND PLANNING LAW by Dr Yvonne Scannell, or IRISH ENVIRONMENTAL LEGISLATION by Maguire, O'Reilly and Roche, both published by the Round Hall Press. As the various regulations produced in connection with environmental impact assessment have by now amended fourteen Acts of the Oireachtas, the area is a nightmare for architects, developers, and lawyers.

3.2 **The Legislation**

Environmental Impact Assessment Directive (85/337/EEC)
Environmental Protection Agency Act 1992

The number of statutory instruments issued under the Environmental Protection Agency Act 1992 is now very substantial. Some of these instruments are very detailed and the following summary is only intended as a guide to the main areas of the legislation.

There are three important groups of statutory instruments. The first is the 'Commencement' group (S.I. 82 of 1994, S.I. 57 of 1995 and S.I. 77 of 1996) which brings into effect, as far as Part IV of the 1992 Act is concerned, the activities mentioned in the First Schedule of the 1992 Act. The second group is the 'Established Activities' group (S.I. 83 of 1994, S.I. 58 of 1995, S.I. 204 of 1995, S.I. 78 of 1996 and S.I. 140 of 1997) and these list the dates on which licenses must be sought for established activities, which are in effect activities which were being carried on when the Minister specifies a certain date. The third group is the 'Licensing' group (S.I. 85 of 1994 and S.I. 240 of 1996 and they give the dates from which the activities listed in the First Schedule to the 1992 Act must have licenses.

S.I. 215 of 1992, Environmental Protection Agency (Selection Procedures) – This is the statutory instrument issued under the 1992 Act and deals with the selection procedures for the board of the Agency. All subsequent orders with the exception of S.I. 84 of 1994 which is issued under the Directive, are prefaced by the title Environmental Protection Agency and this description is omitted for simplicity in the following list.

S.I. 43 of 1993 (Advisory Committee) – This deals with the composition of the advisory committee set up to advise the Minister or the Agency under Section 27 and 28 of the 1992 Act with regard to the functions of the Agency.

S.I. 213 of 1993 (Establishment) – This order establishes the Environmental Protection Agency.

S.I. 215 of 1993 (Dissolution of An Foras Forbatha) – All the powers, functions and assets of An Foras are taken over by the Environmental Protection Agency under this Order.

S.I. 235 of 1993 (Commencement) – This order brings into effect Section 104 of the 1992 Act which gives the Agency power to deal with incidents of environmental pollution.

S.I. 82 of 1994 (Commencement) – This brings into effect Part IV of the 1992 Act with regard to paragraphs 1, 2, 4, 5, 7, 8, 10 and 11 of the First Schedule to the Act. This lists the activities to which Part IV (Integrated Pollution Control) will apply. This order affects: minerals; energy; mineral fibres; chemicals; food and drink; wood, paper, textiles and leather; cement; and waste.

S.I. 83 of 1994 (Established Activities) – This order, and subsequent similarly names orders, lists the dates on which specified existing activities shall come under the control of Section 82(2) of the 1992 Act and which will require a licence from that date onwards. Established Activities are commented on in par 3.4.2. This order schedules the manufacture of pesticides, pharmaceuticals or veterinary products and the incineration of hazardous waste. Care must be taken when consulting any of these orders to ascertain if the Order has been amended or revoked by subsequent orders.

S.I. 84 of 1994 (Environmental Impact Assessment) (Amendment) – This order amends sections 25, 26, 41 and 78 of the Local Government (Planning and Development) Act 1963 as respects licences, section 18 of the Local Government (Planning and Development) Act 1992 dealing with information requirements of An Bord Pleanála, revokes Regulations 12, 15, and 23 of S.I. 349 of 1989 dealing with amendments to the Public Health (Ireland) Act 1878, the Water Supplies Act 1942 and with State authorities duties under the regulations. It also amends Section 3, 83 and 87 of the 1992 Act dealing with environmental impact statements.

S.I. 85 of 1994 (Licensing) – These are the overall regulations dealing with the issue of integrated pollution control licences under Section 83 of the 1992 Act. It also lists the dates, both prescribed and for established activities in respect of classes 1, 2, 4, 5, 7, 8, 10 and 11 of the First Schedule to the 1992 Act.

S.I. 130 of 1994 (Fees) – This is the first order dealing with fees and covers any of the activities that had been scheduled up to that time (First Schedule, pars 1, 2, 4, 5, 5.6, 7, 8, 10 and 11).

S.I. 178 of 1994 (Commencement) – This order which brings into effect Section 18(1) of the Act repeals Section 51 of the Local Government (Planning and Development) Act 1963 dealing with noise, and also amends the Air Pollution Act, 1987.

S.I. 179 of 1994 (Noise) – This controls noise problems, originally dealt with in Section 51 of the Local Government (Planning and Development) Act 1963 and follows from S.I. 178 of 1994.

S.I. 204 of 1994 (Section 36(4)) – This deals with employment remuneration in the Agency.

S.I. 205 of 1994 (Declaration of Interests) – This provides for any declaration of interests of any employees of the Agency or others as required under Section 37 of the 1992 Act.

S.I. 206 of 1994 (Extension of Powers) – This order confers additional powers on the Agency as far as the provisions of the Local Government (Water Pollution) Act of 1977 and the amending Act of 1990, and of the Air Pollution Act 1987.

S.I. 345 of 1994 (Genetically Modified Organisms) – This brings into the scope of the Agency the dealing in micro-biological entities which have been altered in a way that does not occur naturally.

S.I. 419 of 1994 (Urban Waste Water Treatment) – This order prescribes requirements with regard to urban waste water treatment plants both generally and with regard to sensitive areas. The order identified ten water bodies as sensitive areas.

S.I. 57 of 1995 (Commencement) – This order brings in to effect paragraphs 3, 12 and 13 of the First Schedule to the 1992 Act, completing the list commenced in S.I. 82 of 1994 with the exception of paragraphs 6 and 9 dealt with in S.I. 77 of 1996. The areas dealt with are metals, surface coatings, engine testing, the manufacture of printed circuits, lime and coarse ceramics.

S.I. 58 of 1995 (Established Activities) – This order lists, for a very wide range of items, the dates from which the stated activities will require a licence. They include the incineration of waste and hospital waste, the manufacture of cement, paper and artificial fertilisers. It revises the dates originally given in S.I. 85 of 1994.

S.I. 60 of 1995 (Licensing fees) (Amendment) – This order extends the original list of fees set out in S.I. 130 of 1994 (First Schedule, pars 3, 12 and 13).

S.I. 76 of 1995 (Licensing) (Amendment) (No.2) – This order deals with the availability of documents in respect of licence applications.

S.I. 204 of 1995 (Established Activities) (No. 2) – This extends the previous lists requiring licences to include the manufacture of inorganic chemicals, glass and adhesives

S.I. 337 of 1995 (Commencement) – Brings into effect Sections 43 and 105 of the 1992 Act dealing with the establishment of regional units of the Agency and with the setting up of inquiries to deal with incidents of pollution.

S.I. 13 of 1996 (Commencement) – This order brings into effect Section 100 and

101 of the 1992 Act dealing with the Minister's powers under the Water Pollution Act 1977 and the Air Pollution Act 1987.

S.I. 77 of 1996 (Commencement) (No. 2) – This order completes the list of activities set out in the First Schedule of the 1992 Act and initiated by S.I. 82 of 1994 and S.I. 57 of 1995, by bringing into effect paragraphs 6(intensive agriculture) and 9(fossil fuels).

S.I. 78 of 1996 (Established Activities) – Further activities now requiring licences include the manufacture of glass, sugar, synthetic fibres, integrated circuits, boilers and electroplating; the slaughter of animals; the dying of fibres; and the working of leather.

S.I. 79 of 1996 (Licensing) – This order amends the introduction date for the activities specified in paragraphs 6 and 9 of the first schedule of the Act.

S.I. 126 of 1996 (Extension of Powers) – This Order provides further powers beyond those set out in S.I. 206 of 1994 with regard to the Local Government (Water Pollution) Act 1977 and the amending Act of 1990, and of the Air Pollution Act 1987.

S.I. 185 of 1996 (Freedom of Information) – This Instrument revokes S.I. 133 of 1993 and sets out the information which the public is entitled to as regards environmental matters.

S.I. 229 of 1996 (Advisory Committee) – This order expands the list of bodies set out in S.I. 43 of 1993 to advise the Minister of the Agency.

S.I. 239 of 1996 (Licensing fees) (Amendment) – This order deals with the fees required for further listed activities. (First Schedule, pars 6 and 9).

S.I. 240 of 1966 (Licensing) (Amendment) (No. 2) – This order lists revised dates in respect of all the activities set out in the First Schedule to the 1992 Act and revokes S.I. 59 of 1995 and S.I. 79 of 1996.

S.I. 132 of 1997 (Ozone) – This Instrument empowers the Agency to set up sites to measure ozone in the atmosphere as required by the Directive 92/72/EEC.

S.I. 140 of 1997 (Established Activities) – This latest list of dates by which certain activities will require a licence, brings, amongst others, such activities as the formulation of pesticides, storage of certain chemicals, manufacturers of wood pulp, treatment of wood, production of non-ferrous metals, rearing of poultry or pigs, manufacture of dairy products, matters dealing with gas or petroleum and brewing into the control system.

S.I. 374 of 1997 (Volatile Emissions) – This Instrument controls the storage and transport of petrol.

S.I. 460 of 1998 (Established Activities) – A further list of activities is scheduled such as asbestos, aluminium ore, ceramics, pig rearing, and the use of coal, gas or peat for energy production.

S.I. 93 of 1999 (Environmental Impact Assessment) – This order sets out various activities covered by differing pieces of legislation which will require and environmental impact assessment and also lists the information requirements. Those dealing with planning have been overtaken by S.I. 600 of 2001 but activities covered by the Foreshore Act 1933, the Harbours Act 1946 and the Roads Acts 1993 and 1998 remain.

S.I. 48 of 2000 (Advisory Committee) – Amends S.I. 229 of 1996.

S.I. 450 of 2000 (EIA Amendment) – This transfers to An Bord Pleanála from the Minister the duty of certifying with regard to an environmental impact assessment related to a local authority's own developments.

S.I. 538 of 2001 (EU Directive) – This order is now incorporated into S.I. 600 of 2001 and dealt with limits regarding turbary and afforestation.

3.3 The Environmental Protection Agency Act 1992

3.3.1 The Environmental Protection Agency

The primary piece of environmental legislation is the Environmental Protection Agency Act, 1992. This Act, which became law on 23rd April 1992, has two main arms. The first of these is 'to make further and better provision for the protection of the environment' and secondly to 'establish an Environmental Protection Agency.'

The first Act to show overall concern for the environment could be said to be the Public Health (Ireland) Act 1878, which provided the basis for, amongst other things, bye-law control of buildings. But there was no control over the other effects of building development, particularly in the industrial field. The position prior to the passing of the 1992 Act was that separate licences or permits were required for activities that might affect air, water, or other areas, adversely. The legislation was contained in different Acts and Regulations, such as the Fisheries Acts, 1959-1980 and the Local Government (Water and Pollution) Acts 1977-1990.

These licences were issued by the 33 major local authorities. There was bound to be inconsistency and unfairness in such an arrangement, and the integrated pollution control licence to be issued under the Environmental Protection Agency Act by one central agency was clearly an advance. The Agency is now fully operational and has been set out in par. 3.2 many statutory instruments have been issued dealing with all aspects of the licensing arrangements. It was decided in introducing the Environmental Protection Agency Act that a single licensing arrangement should be provided to cover air pollution, water pollution, waste disposal, and noise as might be generated by a very wide range of activities, listed in the First Schedule to the Act.

The Environmental Protection Agency Act is very long and involved and contains over one hundred sections. Section 72 deals with environmental impact assessment and should be read in conjunction with Part X of the Planning and Development Act 2000 and Part 10 of S.I. 600 of 2001 – the Planning and Development Regulations. As mentioned earlier, this section empowers the Environmental Protection Agency to issue guidelines with regard to the information to be contained in any environmental impact statement.

3.3.2 Integrated Pollution Control Licences

The main points of which any one proposing a development which might require an integrated pollution control licence should be aware are:

1 A licence will be required under the Act for any of the activities listed under thirteen headings in the first schedule to the Act i.e. the production of minerals and other materials, energy, metals, mineral fibres and glass, chemicals, intensive agriculture, food and drink, wood/paper/textiles and leather, fossil fuels, cement, waste, surface coatings and other activities.

   The Act applies to 'established activities' as set out in the various statutory instruments. An established activity is one where a valid planning permission exists, or one which was carried on during a period of twelve months before a day to be specified by the Minister. This latter category is unclear and likely to lead to difficulties. Does it refer to exempted developments or developments carried out before 1st October 1964? No doubt the High Court will ultimately inform us.

   It is important to remember that activities that are 'established' or are not scheduled in the Act will still require the separate air, water and waste licences as before. The penalties in the new Act are very severe and range up to a fine of €12.7m or 10 years imprisonment, or both, on indictment.

2 One of the more radical proposals in the Act is one that precludes the plan-

ning authority, or An Bord Pleanála, from considering any matters relating to environmental pollution if the application before it is also the subject of an application for a licence under the Environmental Protection Agency Act [Section 98(1)].

This is made very clear in the Planning and Development Act 2000 at Section 34(2)(c) where it is confirmed that the control of emissions is a function of the Environmental Protection Agency and not of the planning authority

3   The procedure for applying for a licence is straightforward and entails the following steps:

a)   The application is made to the Agency. At the same time the applicant must notify the local authority and anyone specified in the regulations. A newspaper notice and a site notice must also be published. Certain documents, as specified in S.I. 76 of 1995, must be made available to the public by the Agency.

b)   There is no time limit on the Agency as far as coming to a decision is concerned, but the Agency must notify the applicant, the planning authority and anyone who made submissions within two months of the application of its intention, whether or not to grant a licence.

c)   Any person may, within 21 days of the notification, object to the proposed granting of a licence. The applicant may object, presumably to a proposed refusal or to conditions, within 28 days of such notification. After that the decision will be made 'as expeditiously as may be'. The Agency may hold an oral hearing. If no objections are received the decision is to be made 'as soon as may be' whatever that means.

d)   If any decision is taken to challenge a decision of the Agency in the courts, either by way of judicial review or by any other legal proceedings, this must be done within two months of the agency's decision.

4   The Act provides (Section 80) that the Agency must have regard to a very large number of factors in coming to a decision. Basically this is to ensure that the Agency is satisfied that no significant pollution will occur. An intriguing factor to be considered is that of BATNEEC. This buzz-word acronym stands for 'Best Available Technology Not Entailing Excessive Cost', and means simply, that the economics of the proposed pollution prevention measures must be sensible, and must relate to the risk.

5   The Agency can impose conditions on a licence (Section 81). The section lists sixteen different types of condition including the payment of costs to the Agency for monitoring conditions.

6   Unlike a planning permission, which is attached to the property, a licence under this Act enures – that is, is available for – the activity licensed and all interested persons. Any change in ownership must be advised to the Agency.

7   There are provisions in the Act which allow for the review but not the revocation of licences, and also to enable the Agency to direct local authorities to perform certain statutory functions.

8   There are also, of course, fees and these range up to €22,855 for licences for pharmaceutical or veterinary products (S.I. 130 of 1994).

     In addition, costs can range up to €126,973 for legal and other professional advice.

A number of Statutory Instruments have been published in relation to several aspects of the operation of the Agency. Sections 21 and 24 of the Act provided for the appointment of a Director General and of other directors. S.I. 215 of 1992 contains further details in respect of these appointments. Sections 27 and 28 of the Act deal with the establishment of an Advisory Committee and S.I. 43 of 1993 lists the various organisations prescribed by the Minister as being involved or concerned with the environment. There are 35 such organisations listed in the regulations and the omission of the Royal Institute of the Architects of Ireland from such a list is very difficult to understand, particularly in view of the inclusion of a British organisation (the Royal Town Planning Institute) and also in view of the involvement of so many practising architects in environmental and planning matters, very often as lead consultants in major projects.

3.4   **Waste Management**

The Waste Management Act 1996
The Waste Management (Amendment) Act 2001

Directives – General directive regarding waste – 75/442/EEC amended by 91/156/EEC. A separate directive, 1999/31/EC deals with landfill waste

S.I. 192 of 1996 (Commencement)

S.I. 133 of 1997 (Licensing) – The details involved in the application and review of waste licences are contained in this order.

S.I. 137 of 1997 (Planning) – Under the Act, Local Authorities are required to make and publish a plan setting out their proposals for dealing with waste and this order sets out the regulations.

S.I. 183 of 1997 (Register) – Under the Act (Section 19) both the Agency and the Local Authority involved are required to keep a register of waste licences and this instrument sets out the details.

S.I. 242 of 1997 (Packaging) – This deals with the control of packaging waste.

S.I. 315 of 1997 (Farm Plastics) – This instrument sets out the procedures for the control of the disposal of farm plastics.

S.I. 64 of 1998 (Licencing) – Controls the issuing of licences by the Environmental Protection Agency in connection with the incineration of hazardous waste.

S.I. 166 of 1998 (EU Directive) – This order brings the Waste Management Act 1996 into line with the amendments in Directive 91/156/EEC.

S.I. 146 of 1998 (Sewage) – Regulates the operation of sewage plants.

S.I. 147 of 1998 (Hazardous Waste) – Deals with the supervision and control of shipments of hazardous waste in, into or out of the EC.

S.I. 148 of 1998 (Sewage in Agriculture) – This order regulates the use of sewage sludge in agriculture.

S.I. 149 of 1998 (Hazardous Waste) – Further regulations involving trans-frontier shipments of waste and the responsibilities of the Environmental Protection Agency and the relevant local authority.

S.I. 162 of 1998 (Licensing) – Further operating dates for licensing operations and fees.

S.I. 163 of 1998 (Hazardous Waste) – This order deals specifically with the disposal of asbestos waste, PCBs, batteries, waste oils and hazardous waste generally.

S.I. 164 of 1998 (Miscellaneous) – Dates are given in these relations by which the collection of waste oil will require a permit.

S.I. 165 of 1998 (Permits) – Permits can be granted by local authorities for specified waste disposal and recovery activities in lieu of a licence from the European Protection Agency.

S.I. 166 of 1998 (Amendment to Waste Management Act) – This instrument allows local authorities to issue permits for specified waste activities rather than the Environmental Protection Agency.

S.I. 382 of 1998 (Packaging) – This regulation amends S.I. 242 of 1997 regarding the packaging of waste.

S.I. 162 of 1998 (Licensing) – Gives more details of various licensing dates.

S.I. 73 of 2000 (Hazardous Waste) – Further amending regulations.

S.I. 185 of 2000 (Licensing) – This order revokes S.I. 133 of 1997 and amends S.I. 152 of 1998.

S.I. 341 of 2001 (Farm Plastics) – This revokes and replaces S.I. 315 of 1997.

S.I. 402 of 2001 (Collection Permit) – From 30/11/2001 waste collection on a commercial basis will require a permit from the local authority.

S.I. 540 of 2001 (Collection) – This order amends S.I. 402 of 2001 as regards the collection of animal slurry.

S.I. 605 of 2001 (Plastic bags) – This order provides the details of the plastic bag levy authorised by the Waste Management (Amendment) 2001.

S.I. 267 of 2001 (Sewage in Agriculture) – This order amends S.I. 148 of 1998 regarding amounts of sewage sludge that are permissible per hectare.

S.I. 86 of 2002 (Landfill Levy) – This specifies the amounts of the levy authorised by the Waste Management Act 2001.

S.I. 336 of 2002 (Licensing) – This order amends S.I. 185 of 2000 and provides for classification of landfill waste facilities by the Environmental Protection Agency and controls the type of waste allowed for each classification.

Associated with the Environmental Protection Agency Act and under the control of the Environmental Protection Agency is the matter of waste. Until now this had been regulated almost entirely by public health legislation and some diffuse European Union Directives. It is not an area where practitioners would be expected to be expert, but a general knowledge is advisable. The importance attached to this subject was indicated in the policy statement 'Changing Our Ways' issued by the Department of the Environment and Local Government in September 1998. This document highlighted the fact that in 1995 over 90% of all waste was disposed of by landfill, which is regarded as the least favoured option as far as waste disposal is concerned. The other options, such as energy recovery, recycling, reuse and minimisation will be promoted as official policy. The statement also pointed out that the 'polluter pays' policy, together with strict control an management of landfill sites under the new legislation, will encourage the development of strategies leading towards more desirable practices. A target has been set by the Department of achieving a 50% recycling figure for demolition and construction waste by 2003 and an 85% figure by 2013. The Forum for the Construction Industry has recommended the setting up of a National Construction and Demolition Waste Council to oversee and monitor the construction industry response.

It specifically impinges on the planning world in two areas. Firstly, Section 22 requires local authorities to prepare, and review every five years, a waste management plan which must have regard to the proper planning and development of the area, the development plan and special area amenity orders. Secondly, Section 54 deals with planning applications involving an activity which requires a waste licence. The planning authority or An Bord Pleanála may not deal with environmental pollution arising from such an activity. It is purely a matter for the Environmental Protection Agency [Section 54(3)].

There are now three main players. The Waste Management Act 1996 (brought into effect on 1st July 1996 by S.I. 192 of 1996 with the exception of Section 6(2) – revocation of Statutory Instruments, Section 32(2) – transfer of control of waste and Sections 57 and 58 – applications to the Court) gives the Minister wide residual powers, mainly that of issuing regulations, (Section 7) it gives the Environmental Protection Agency the central control of the arrangements, and it requires local authorities to collect household waste amongst other responsibilities (Section 33).

The 1996 Act was amended by the Waste Management (Amendment) Act 2001. One of the reasons that this Act was introduced was to deal with the Directive 1999/31/EC on landfill waste. An interesting feature of this act is that it removes control of making a waste management plan from the elected representatives and gives the power to the Manager. It can be presumed that the NIMBY attitude of virtually every local authority gave rise to this change. The act also gives authority for both the landfill and the plastic bag levies. The reluctance of may organisations to address realistically the problem of waste, taken with our rather odd planning process, has been a bar to progress and, at the time of writing, the Minister for the Environment and Local Government is preparing legislation so as to exclude the provision of incinerators and landfill sites from the normal planning process. The idea is that any proposal for such facilities would be submitted initially to An Bord Pleanála and not to the Local Authority on the very logical ground that 100% of all such proposals would end up with An Bord Pleanála in any event.

Waste is described in the Act as 'any substance or object belonging to a category of waste specified in the First Schedule or for the time being included in the European Waste Catalogue which the holder discards or intends or is required to discard, and anything which is discarded or otherwise dealt with as if it were waste shall be presumed to be waste until the contrary is proved'. It is a rather cumbersome definition but revolves around the concept of discarding. The First Schedule referred to separates wastes into recognisable categories. The Act also recognises 'hazardous' waste and provides for more strict regulations for such items.

The purpose of the Act is to prevent environmental pollution. Section 5 of the Act defines this as 'the holding, transport, recovery or disposal of waste in a manner which would, to a significant extent, endanger human health or harm the environment'. Anyone dealing with waste, other than local authorities, must obtain a permit from the local authority where they intend to collect waste, (Section 34) or be authorised by the Environmental Protection Agency where they intend to transport it (Section 36), or finally and most importantly, must obtain a licence from the Agency where they intend to dispose or recover waste (Sections 39 to 49). Before issuing the licence the Agency must consult with the relevant planning authority and can add conditions to licences to reflect the proper planning and development of the area. The regulation of land-fill sites is also part of the legislation. Under Section 62 of the Environmental Protection Agency Act the Agency is obliged to specify and publish criteria and procedures for the selection, management and termination of use of land-fill sites, and local authorities must have regard to these criteria. The Waste Management Act at Section (4)(2)(b) allows conditions to be attached to waste licenses to deal with post closure land-fill management. And there are, of course, fees (Section 50).

Penalties under the Act are very severe. They range up to a maximum fine of €12.7m or a term of imprisonment of up to ten years. An unusual feature is the specific provision whereby individuals such as directors or managers of companies who have personal responsibility for the actions of the company can be prosecuted as individuals. Either the local authority or the Agency can initiate prosecutions and there are the usual powers of inspection and monitoring.

Construction will be much affected by this new legislation and costs will be in incurred. The landfill levy, which will be at an initial rate of 15 per tonne will apply to construction waste with two exceptions in particular being of interest. Firstly, the dumping of non-hazardous waste from construction, or more likely demolition, activities consisting of concrete, bricks, tiles, etc, with a particle size of 150mm or less where the material is used for landfill site engineering, and secondly, the dumping of excavation material for the same purpose will also be exempt. The cost will obviously be passed on to the employer under the contract.

3.5 Environmental Freedom of Information

The European Communities Act 1972 (Access to Information on the Environment) Regulations – S.I. 125 of 1998.

A further area in the environmental sphere concerns the freedom of information. An EU directive 90/313/EEC adopted in June 1990 initiated this process. The basic proposal is that any member of the public, with or without an interest in the matter, is entitled to receive any information in the possession of Ministers, local authorities and state or semi-state companies that relates to the state of the environment, activities adversely affecting the environment or activities designed to protect the environment. This specifically environmental arrangement is unaffected by the Freedom of Information Act 1997 (see par. 6.7(f)). Regulations have been published to bring this directive into effect. Originally this was done in S.I. 133 of 1993 but this has now been revoked and replaced by S.I. 185 of 1996. They are published in particular under the powers conferred on the Minister under section 110 of the Environmental Protection Agency Act. The bodies affected are described as 'public authorities' and these are defined in the Act as:

• A Minister of the Government
• The Office of Public Works
• A Local Authority
• A Harbour Authority
• A Health Board
• Any other board established by statute
• A semi-state body

There are exceptions to the general rule that information be made available and these are:

i) information held in connection with, or for the purposes of, any judicial or legislative function. This, it appears, includes the deliberations of An Bord Pleanála acting in its appellate capacity and this restriction has given rise to criticism. This criticism is understandable as it is precisely in the area of planning appeals that the ultimate environmental decisions will be made. Whether the activities of the Environmental Protection Agency in the granting or refusing of an integrated pollution control licence will be protected remains to be seen.

ii) personal information held in relation to an individual who has not given his consent.

iii) material supplied to a public authority by a third party where there is no legal obligation to supply the material in the first place.

iv) where international relations, national defence or public security is concerned.

v)   matters which are sub-judice

vi) where the confidentiality of the proceedings of a public authority are concerned.

vii) where commercial, industrial or intellectual property confidentiality is concerned, or where the internal communications of a public authority are concerned, and

viii)where the information requested is too general or is considered unreasonable.

The Regulations also require the authority to answer such a request for information within two months and allows for a 'reasonable' charge to be made.

This list of exceptions is very widespread and it is not anticipated that there will be any real change in the range and scope of information that is currently available. An indication has been given that the Regulations may be reviewed after a fairly short period of operation.

3.6   **Noise**

A question often asked is whether noise is controlled by any legislation, and the answer is yes. Originally, this problem was addressed in the Local Government (Planning and Development) Act 1963 at Section 51 but this was repealed by the Environmental Protection Agency Act 1992 and replaced by sections 106, 107 and 108 of that Act. These sections allow the Minister to issue Regulations specifying limits for noise, allow the local authority or the Environmental Protection Agency, as appropriate, to prevent or limit noise and finally deals with noise as a nuisance. Noise caused by aircraft is excluded from the provisions of the Act but, on the other hand, the provisions of the Safety Health and Welfare at Work Act 1989 are not affected by these sections.

The Regulations covering prosecutions under these sections are contained in S.I. 179 of 1994 (Noise) which came into force on 1st July 1994. A local authority, the Environmental Protection Agency or a private individual can apply to the District Court for an order to reduce or limit noise which is 'so loud, so continuous, so repeated, of such duration or recurring at such times as to give reasonable cause for annoyance'. A condition in a planning permission can also require that measures be taken to reduce or prevent noise that might cause annoyance to persons in the neighbourhood [Planning and Development Act 2000, Section 34(4)(c)]

Sound is also covered by the Building Regulations. Part E of the First Schedule to S.I. 497 of 1997 deals with noise but only as it affects habitable rooms in dwellings. Noise caused by machinery is regulated by S.I. 632 of 2001 (Noise Emission by Equipment for Use Outdoors). This statutory instrument deals with noise levels from machinery and is based on over 20 EU Directives dealing with the subject. The regulations list 57 different types of equipment ranging from concrete mixers to lawnmowers and defines the maximum permitted sound level for each type of machine.

Noise in the workplace is governed by the Communities (Protection of Workers) (Exposure to Noise) Regulations – 1990 (S.I. 157 of 1990)

3.7 **Environmental Checklist**

query	*law*	*par.*
1 How does the Environmental Protection Agency Act affect planning applications?	Environmental Protection Agency Act 1992 – sections 72 and 98	3.3.1
2 For what projects do I need an Integrated Pollution Control Licence?	EPA Act 1992 – First Schedule Statutory Instruments listed	3.3.2
3 Can I do anything about noise?	EPA Act Sections 106-108 S.I. 179 of 1994 S.I. 632 of 2001 Building Regulations – part E	3.6

Chapter 4 – **The Building Regulations**

4.1 Introduction

Building Regulations are first referred to in Irish legislation in sections 86, 87 and 88 of the Local Government (Planning and Development) Act 1963. Although nearly thirty years were to pass before Building Regulations were actually introduced, there are some striking similarities between the provisions of the 1963 Act and the eventual legislation. The Fifth Schedule to the 1963 Act lists sixteen areas where Building Regulations may prescribe standards, and only three of them are not specifically addressed in the twelve parts of the 1991 Regulations, now revised as the 1997 Regulations. Interestingly, daylight is listed as a subject for which a standard may be set in the 1963 schedule but this is not provided for in the Regulations. It must, of course, be emphasised that the legislation covering Building Regulations is totally separate from the Planning legislation.

Further similarities exist in that there is provision in sections 87 and 88 for relaxation or dispensing with Regulations, and also a system of appeal. One of the more interesting survivors of the 1963 legislation is the definition of a material change of use. This definition was retained in principle in the 1990 Building Control Act and, as will be seen later, is one of the items which is giving rise to serious problems of interpretation and implementation.

This chapter will deal only with the legislation covering the Building Regulations, and the up-to-date application of the Regulations. The Regulations themselves will not be examined in detail. This is done in a splendid book by Eoin O'Cofaigh entitled THE REGULATIONS EXPLAINED and published in summer 1993 by the Royal Institute of the Architects of Ireland. This book is an essential reference work for anyone in practice in the building industry, either on the design or construction side.

The new regulations introduced in 1997 make considerable changes to many of the previous regulations and care must be taken to ensure that the up-to-date version is being used. The new building regulations also change some time honoured rules with regard to domestic buildings. The more noteworthy would be the use of upstairs windows as escape routes, the provision of smoke alarms powered from the mains, the dropping of the old 'permanent vent' requirement in bedrooms and the allowing of adjoining kitchens and bathrooms. Provision is also made for the introduction of a voluntary heat energy rating system in houses.

The history of construction regulation is long. Bye-laws were introduced into Ireland under the Public Health Act of 1878, but like the 1934 Planning Act, the Public Health Act was discretionary. It was up to each local authority to decide whether or not to make such bye-laws and, in the event, very few did. Cork City and County, Dublin City and County, and the Borough of Dun Laoghaire adopted bye-laws which covered general construction standards and some other local authorities introduced limited bye-laws for particular areas of construction. But the vast majority of local authorities, and there were over 30 in the country, saw no benefit in entering into this control system and decided, presumably consciously, to entrust the protection of the citizens under their jurisdiction to their rights in common and statute law. Up till now it has been a contentious, and profitless, subject of debate as to whether or not an additional layer of protection is obtained from bye-law or building control. Are buildings which were constructed up to 1990 on one side of the Dublin/Kildare county boundary noticeably better or worse than those built on the other side of this notional line? This debate became academic as the protection of the consumer grew in importance, and it was perceived that all citizens had to be protected from their own preferred indiscretions; in other words, nanny knows best.

The position with regard to building control might have remained very much as it was more or less indefinitely were it not for the fact that the fire safety aspect of buildings acted as a tail and wagged the Building Regulations dog. The inaction which followed the first statutory reference to Building Regulations in the 1963 Act continued until the Stardust tragedy of 1981. This appalling event led to a tribunal which reported very adversely on a number of aspects of the regulation of fire safety standards, and also on the absurd position where totally unqualified people are allowed to design buildings which are places of public resort and where fire danger is ever present.

A delaying factor in arriving at an answer to the problem of choosing suitable Building Regulations was because of difficulties with regard to control. The Department seemed to be unable to decide whether the responsibility of control should be carried by the local authorities or by those engaged directly in the building process. The local authorities did not want to take on board a further set of responsibilities, involving increased costs and possibly more importantly, increased exposure to liability. Various well-known cases in England had brought local authorities to the forefront as potential and substantial defendants. This has recently been modified there but the position in Ireland is still such as to leave local authorities very uneasy about accepting any responsibility for building works, which are a notorious source of litigation.

But there were equal difficulties in trying to impose the load onto the professionals or the contractors. The Department, then reluctant to recognise the need for proper qualification, was unable to agree with the various professional bodies as to who would or would not be a suitable certifier, and the further complication of trying to persuade anyone to certify the proper construction, as opposed to the proper design, of the project made progress even more unlikely.

The publication of the Building Control Bill in 1984 was the first indication of the way things were moving. This Bill was passed by Dáil Éireann on 13th

December 1989, by Seanad Éireann on 14th March 1990, and was signed into law by the President on the 21st March 1990. The responsibility for compliance with the law was firmly placed on the shoulders of the designers and the contractors. The Act is very much a piece of enabling legislation and most of the detail which concerns the architect was contained in the eleven Statutory Instruments made under it. These now have been consolidated into two statutory instruments. Some concern is expressed from time to time about the amount of legislation which occurs by way of Regulations issued under various Acts of the Oireachtas. Whereas any Act which is passed into law receives obvious scrutiny both in the Oireachtas and by the general public, Regulations on the other hand can very often appear without any noticeable publicity except for being listed in Iris Oifigeal and being placed on the table of the Dáil, and some enabling legislation, such as, for instance, the European Communities Act 1972, gives Ministers the power to amend basic legislation by way of Statutory Instrument. The Planning Acts have been dramatically altered in this way. This practice has recently been curtailed (see par. 1.3).

It is important to remember that the Building Control Act recognises, as far as is known, for the first time in building legislation, that there is a distinction between designing and building and that it would be reasonable to require architects or engineers to confirm that the building or other structure was designed in accordance with the Regulations, but that it would be the builder who would confirm that the building was built in accordance with the Regulations. Many clients and solicitors seem to think that the architect's responsibility for site works, either by way of inspection, supervision or observation should logically put the onus on the architect to certify that the building has been built in accordance with the Regulations. With the greatest of respect it must be pointed out that the building contract is between the building owner and the contractor and the responsibility to carry out this contract properly is that of the contractor and the contractor alone. This particular matter is addressed in the area of certificates or opinions of compliance which will be dealt with later on (par. 10.5).

4.2 The Legislation

The following is the legislation:

The Building Control Act 1990

The legislation can be divided into two main strands. The first relates to the Building Regulations themselves, and the second is the mechanism for ensuring that these Regulations will be observed. The Act also contains provisions for dispensation, relaxation, appeals, enforcement, penalties and transitional provisions.

These are all dealt with in the Statutory Instruments set out below.

The Statutory Instruments

S.I.304 of 1991 – This is the commencement order and brought certain sections of the Act into force on the 4th December 1991. The remaining sections came into force on 1st June 1992, as did the provisions of the two main statutory instruments, i.e. nos 305 and 306 of 1992, both subsequently revoked.

S.I. 113 of 1992 – This instrument listed the members of the Building Regulations Advisory Body set up under section 14 of the Act. This body is to advise the Minister with regard to the operation of the Building Regulations, and as is referred to later, has already submitted advice to the Minister with regard to difficulties which have arisen in dealing with the areas of material alterations and material changes of use. A series of subsequent instruments detail changes in the personnel of the Advisory Body. These are not listed here.

S.I. 496 of 1997: The Building Control Regulations – This instrument revoked S.I. 305 of 1991, S.I. 111, 112, and 182 of 1992 and S.I. 153 of 1994. It dealt with commencement notices, fire safety certificates, the register, fees and appeals. It came into force on 1st July 1998.

S.I. 497 of 1997: The Building Regulations – This instrument revoked S.I. 306 of 1991 and S.I. 154 of 1994. It contains the Building Regulations themselves. It also came into force on 1st July 1998

S.I. 10 of 2000: Building Control (Amendment) Regulations – This instrument amends S.I. 496 of 1994 by substituting the Organisation of Working Time Act 1997 for the Holidays (Employees) Act 1973 at Articles 5(6) and 28(3). More importantly, at Article 21, it requires a Building Control Authority to keep a register of commencement notices, fire safety certificates and relaxation and dispensation decisions. The third schedule sets out a new standard fire safety certificate application form.

S.I. 179 of 2000: Building Regulations (Amendment) Regulations – This instrument introduced the new Part M bringing dwellings commenced after the 1st January 2001 under those regulations.

S.I. 249 of 2000: Building Regulations (Amendment) (No. 2) Regulations – This alters Part D in respect of the height of letter plate apertures installed after the 1st January 2001.

S.I. 441 of 2000: Building Regulations (Amendment) (No. 3) Regulations – This extends exemption of electricity supply utilities to all such organisations under Class 9 exemption, Column 1, Article 8, third schedule.

S.I. 284 of 2002: Building Regulations (Amendment) Regulations – This sets higher standards for insulation in dwellings – Part L. It also extends the Building Regulations to any repair or renewal of an existing building 'likely to affect the structural integrity of the building or building element being renewed or repaired.' This does not apply in respect of such works to a protected structure or a proposed protected structure.

EC Directive

89/106/EEC (as amended by 93/68/EEC) – This is the construction products directive which is dealt with in par. 4.4.

S.I. 198 of 1992 – This instrument brings the Directive into effect.

It would be useful at this point to comment on two of the newer statutory instruments listed above. Firstly, S.I. 179 of 2000 extends the requirements of Part M to dwellings. They were previously exempt. It should be noted that the requirement in the 1994 Regulations to provide 'reasonable' access to all buildings covered by Part M has being changed to require 'adequate' access. Dictionary definitions generally define reasonable as being average or moderate, while adequate is normally defined as being sufficient.This is clearly a more rigid standard but, as before, compliance with the revised Technical Guidance Document should keep practitioners safe. The transitional arrangements are that the new statutory instrument shall not apply, firstly, to dwellings where a planning application was made before 31st December 2000 and where substantial works have been completed by 31st December 2003; secondly, the same dates apply to a notice involving dwellings under Part X of S.I. 86 of 1994 – Local Authority Development; and thirdly, to any building where a Fire Safety Certificate was granted before 1st January 2001 and where the works commence between 1st January 2001 and 31st December 2003.

The second statutory instrument S.I. 284 of 2002 imposes improved insulation standards in dwellings. As in the case of S.I. 179 of 2000, this will add substantially to building costs. The revised regulations apply at the moment only to dwellings, but it is intended to extend the new standards to factories, offices, shops and places of leisure by early 2003. Protected structures, or proposed protected structures, are not covered by the new measure. The transitional arrangements are that the new standards will apply to all new dwellings started after 1st January 2003, or to the replacement of doors, windows, or roof lights in existing dwellings after 1st July 2003.

Further, it is proposed at the time of writing to amend Part F (Ventilation) so as to improve standards of ventilation in bathrooms, kitchens and utility rooms in new dwellings commenced on or after 1st January 2003. A draft amendment and a draft revised Technical Guidance Document have been circulated for discussion purposes.

4.3 The Building Regulations

S.I. 497 of 1997 – The Building Regulations
S.I. 179 of 2000 – Amendments to Part M
S.I. 249 of 2000 – Amendments to Part D
S.I. 441 of 2000 – Amendment to electricity supply utilities exemption
S.I. 284 of 2002 – Amendments to Part L

The Building Regulations apply to 'works' which is defined as 'any act or operation in connection with the construction, extension, alteration, repair or renewal of a building'. It does not, therefore, apply to demolition. The Building Regulations are not contained in the Act, but in S.I. 497 of 1997 issued under the Act. Some confusion still seems to exist as to the basic legal position. A building which is covered by the Regulations must conform to what is contained in the Statutory Instruments. Whatever that says is the law. The old building bye-laws were prescriptive, that is, they set out specific rules. The new regulations are functional: they set standards.

For example the Regulation with regard to ventilation (Part F) says that 'adequate means of ventilation shall be provided for people in buildings' and any building that achieves that aim has conformed to the law. It is obvious that in the case of the more complex areas of the Regulations such as structure (Part A) and fire (Part B) some indication should be given as to what might be officially acceptable, and this is where the technical guidance documents come in. They are issued under Article 7 of S.I. 497 of 1997, which is the instrument that contains the Regulations. The article reads as follows:

7 (1) The Minister may publish, or arrange to have published on his behalf, documents to be known as 'technical guidance documents' for the purpose of providing guidance with respect to compliance with the requirements of any of the provisions of the Second Schedule.

(2) Subject to the provisions of sub-article (3), where works or a building to which these Regulations apply is or are designed and constructed in accordance with any guidance contained in a technical guidance document, this shall, prima facia, indicate compliance with the relevant requirements of these Regulations.

(3) The provision of any guidance contained in a technical guidance document published under sub-article (1) concerning the use of a particular material, method of construction or specification, shall not be construed as prohibiting compliance with a requirement of these Regulations by the use of any other suitable material, method of construction or specification.

Compliance with either the technical guidance documents or the construction products Directive will, therefore, under the provisions of Article 7 of S.I. 497 of 1997 be taken as complying with the Regulations. Because of this the technical guidance documents will be used by most practitioners for no argument can result, whereas the proposed use of some construction or design which is not so specified will require the designer, if the matter were challenged, to convince the building control authority that the proposals do conform and this might not always be easy. It is thought that one of the reasons why the technical guidance documents are regarded as being somehow of greater standing than the Regulations themselves is that the guidance documents are produced in a shiny coloured briefcase, containing expensive looking documents whereas the Regulations are distributed as ordinary A4 photocopies. So the appearance is misleading. There is a wide range of options available under most of the technical guidance documents. Indeed over 300 differing standards or codes of practice are specifically approved. It is advisable to ensure that the latest version of any standard or code is being used, but it is important to note that the edition quoted in the technical guidance documents will always be accepted as conforming to the requirements. However, there seems, so far, to be very little, if any, detailed examination of lodged drawings and specifications.

A welcome introduction in all the later technical guidance documents was a paragraph making clear that the Building Regulations related to new buildings or current extensions or alterations. It is specifically stated that they did not apply to buildings constructed prior to 1st June 1992. This should help architects being sued for professional negligence, usually involving alleged personal injury, by making clear that the Regulations should not be applied retrospectively.

It will be necessary to define what buildings are exempt from various provisions of the Acts or Regulations, but as the exemptions differ as regards the Regulations themselves and as regards the control mechanism it has been thought more useful to include a separate section on exemptions.

4.4 The Construction Products Directive

Part D of the Building Regulations refers to the Construction Products Directive and says that materials which comply with the Directive will conform with the

Regulations. This directive (ref: 89/106/EEC – amended by 93/68/EEC) came into effect on 1st January 1993 by virtue of S.I. 198 of 1992. It can be summarised as follows:

The full title of the Directive is given as being 'the approximation of laws, Regulations and administrative provisions of the Member States relating to construction products'. A construction product is defined as any product, other than a minor product, which is produced for incorporation in a permanent manner in construction works including both building and civil engineering works. The basic requirement of the Directive is that such products may only be placed on the market if they are fit for their intended use. This in turn is defined as meaning that the products shall have such characteristics that the works in which they are to be incorporated, assembled, applied or installed can satisfy certain essential requirements. These requirements are subject, in the case of Ireland, to the Building Regulations set out in S.I. 497 of 1997 and must, where appropriate, conform to the headings which follow. The detail relating to these headings is in Annex 1 of the Directive, reproduced as the Schedule to S.I. 198 of 1992. Account may be taken of economy, which means in effect that the requirements of the Directive may be reduced if the economics of the proposal would render strict adherence to the Directive unreasonable. The factors covered are:

1   Mechanical resistance and stability.
2   Safety in case of fire.
3   Hygiene, health and the environment
4   Safety in use.
5   Protection against noise.
6   Energy, economy and heat retention.

A product which meets these requirements may be marked with the EC mark (reproduced as 'CE') subject to certain confirming procedures set out in the Regulations to ensure that the appropriate technical specifications, either national or European, have been complied with. The detail is contained in S.I. 210 of 1994 – European Communities (Construction Products) (Amendment) Regulations.

The use of the phrase 'fit for their intended use' will bring a smile of anticipation to the lawyers' faces. The whole concept of fitness for purpose has led to many actions and to the introduction of the Sale of Goods and Supply of Services Act 1980. A lengthy commentary on this subject is given in THE RIAI CONTRACTS – A WORKING GUIDE, 4th edition (published by the Royal Institute of the Architects of Ireland) at pp 103-109.

A minor product, which is defined as being a product which plays a minor role with regard to safety and health, may be placed on the market but only after the manufacturer has certified that it complies with 'the acknowledged rule of technology'. This last phrase is defined as being a technical provision acknowledged by a majority of representative experts as reflecting the developed state of technical capability at a given time as regards products, processes and services.

There are powers of inspection and search under the Regulations and the building control authorities will be the bodies who will carry out these functions. The Building Regulations Advisory Body may be asked to advise the Minister when requested with regard to decisions prohibiting the placing of certain products on the market.

Penalties for infringement of the Regulations include a fine of up to €1,270 and six months imprisonment or both. Prosecutions may be taken by a building control authority and provision is also made for the forfeiture of products where an offence was committed. In certain criminal proceedings it will be a good defence for a person other than the manufacturer of the product, or his agent, to show that he took all reasonable steps to avoid the offence concerned.

4.5   Exemptions

The first problem for the Architect is to decide whether or not the various provisions of the Act and Statutory Instruments apply to any particular project. There are four categories of exemption.

A   The first and simplest exemption is contained in the Act itself at Section 3(13). Prisons, and places of detention are completely exempt both from the Building Regulations and the control procedures. These are the only building types that are specifically exempt. Also exempt from all the provisions of the Act are buildings that had obtained bye-law approval in those local authority areas that had such control, and, in addition, any building that had been commenced before 1st June 1992 was also exempt. There seems to be some confusion as to the position that arises where alterations are made to buildings which had obtained bye-law approval, particularly with regard to fit-outs. There seems little doubt that Section 22 (the transitional provisions) allows alterations to occur without having to have regard to the Building Regulations. Sub-section 22(2) is worth quoting in full:

2)   *Any bye-law to which subsection (1) relates and which is in force on the operative day shall continue to apply in relation to:*

    a)   any plans which, in accordance with such bye-laws, were deposited before the operative day

> b) *any works carried out in accordance with plans which were so deposited whether such works were carried out in accordance with those plans, with or without a departure or deviation from those plans*
>
> c) *any works carried out and completed before the operative day.*

In the opinion of the writer this can only mean that any alterations can be validly carried out, of whatever size or nature, provided that these alterations would have been in accordance with the bye-laws that were in force in the area at the time.

The powers of inspection granted under Section 11 obviously do not apply to prisons and places of detention, although buildings in the occupation of the Defence Forces and the Garda Síochána, while exempt from inspection, must comply with the Building Regulations themselves.

B Secondly, we then come to the exemptions from the Building Regulations and this is where care must be taken to distinguish between buildings which are exempt from the Building Regulations themselves and buildings which are exempt from the control mechanism, i.e. the commencement notice and the fire safety certificate. It should be noted that Part E (Sound) of the Building Regulations applies only to dwellings. Firstly, we can look at the buildings which are exempt from the Building Regulations themselves. These are set out in Article 8 of the Statutory Instrument S.I. 497 of 1997 and this says that works in connection with a building referred to in the Third Schedule or a building referred to in the Third Schedule shall be exempt. It is worth setting out the Third Schedule in full. It will be seen that as far as dwellings are concerned, the planning regulation exemptions are largely followed as far as garages, conservatories, porches, are concerned.

C Thirdly, there are the buildings which are exempt from the control Regulations but not the Building Regulations. These are set out in Article 6 of S.I. of 1997 and consist of:

a) buildings designed and constructed, or altered by a building control authority in its own functional area. Clearly it would have been meaningless to require a local authority to give itself a commencement notice or to require it to apply to itself for a fire safety certificate.

b) buildings for the Garda Síochána or the Defence Forces.

c) a courthouse.

d) buildings occupied by the President, Taoiseach, Dáil, Senate, and various Government Departments.

e) buildings involving national security.

f)   the material change of use of any of the foregoing classes provided the building is still within the listed classes.

D   The fourth and final category are the exemptions from the requirement to issue a commencement notice or to apply for a fire safety certificate. This is where the first difficulty arises, for the exemptions which apply to development under the Planning Acts differ from those exemptions which apply to the need to issue a commencement notice, and these in turn differ from the exemptions which apply to the need to seek a Fire Safety Certificate, though all three are inter-related.

The exemptions from the need to issue a commencement notice are contained in Article 7 of the Building Control Regulations (S.I. 496 of 1997). This article says that such a notice will be required for the erection of a building, the alteration or extension of a building, or a material change of use of a building, provided that the Building Regulations will apply to the works. It further says that the notice is not required if the proposed works are exempted development under the Planning Acts. However, if a fire safety certificate is required for the works, then a commencement notice is required, even if the works would be otherwise exempt. It should be noted, however, that there is a requirement to issue a commencement notice in respect of material alterations to a shop, office or industrial building even if no fire safety certificate application is required. We shall see later on what works require to seek a fire safety certificate. It can be envisaged, for instance, that a major refurbishment of the interior of a building might be exempted development as far as the Planning Acts are concerned, but would certainly require a fire safety certificate and therefore a commencement notice is also required.

We can take it then that the Building Regulations and the Control Regulations will apply to most buildings or alterations that architects will deal with, and also to works in connection with services, fittings and equipment. These last words are not defined in the Regulations but are identified as being works which would be covered by Part G (Hygiene), H (Drainage and Waste Disposal), or J (Heat Producing Appliances) of the Building Regulations.

The position can be summed up by asking two questions:

1   Is planning permission required?

2   Is a fire safety certificate required?

If the answer to either of those questions is 'yes', then a commencement notice is required. However, even if a fire safety certificate is not required a commencement notice is required in the case of material alterations to shops, offices or industrial buildings.

THIRD SCHEDULE – Exempted Buildings

description of development   *conditions and limitations*

building related to dwellings

CLASS 1
A single-storey building used as a domestic garage.

1   The building shall be detached from any other building.

2   The building shall have a floor area not exceeding 25 square metres.

3   The building shall have a height not exceeding 3 metres, or, in the case of a building with a pitched roof, not exceeding 4 metres.

CLASS 2
A single-storey building (not being a building described in Class 1) ancillary to a dwelling (such as a summer house, poultry-house, aviary, conservatory, coal shed, garden tool shed or bicycle shed).

1   The building shall be detached from any other building.

2   The building shall have a floor area not exceeding 25 square metres.

3   The building shall have a height not exceeding 3 metres, or in the case of a building with a pitched roof, not exceeding 4 metres.

4   The building shall be used exclusively for recreational or storage purposes or the keeping of plants, birds or animals for domestic purposes and shall not be used for the purposes of any trade or business or for human habitation.

CLASS 3
A single-storey extension to an existing dwelling which is an ancillary to the dwelling and consists of a conservatory, porch, carport or covered area.

1   The building shall have a floor area not exceeding 25 square metres (or in the case of a porch, 2 square metres).

2   The building shall have a height not exceeding 3 metres, or in the case of a building with a pitched room, not exceeding 4 metres.

description of development *conditions and limitations*

buildings related to agriculture

CLASS 4
A single-storey glasshouse (not being a building described in Class 2)

1   The building shall be detached from any other building.

2   Not less than three quarters of the total external area of the building shall be comprised of glass (including glazing bars).

3   The building shall be used solely for agriculture.

CLASS 5
A single-storey building which is used exclusively for the storage of materials or product, for the accommodation of plant or machinery or in connection with the housing, care or management of livestock.

1   The building shall be detached from any other building.

2   The building shall have a floor area not exceeding 300 square metres.

3   The building is used solely for agriculture.

4   The only persons habitually employed in the building shall be engaged solely in the care, supervision, regulation, maintenance, storage or removal of the materials, products, plant, machinery or livestock in the building.

miscellaneous

CLASS 6
A building erected in connection with any mine or quarry other than a house or a building used as offices, laboratories or showrooms.

CLASS 7
A building the construction of which is subject to the Explosives Act, 1875.

description of development   *conditions and limitations*

miscellaneous

CLASS 8
A building subject to the National
Monuments Acts 1930 to 1994.

CLASS 9
A building constructed for an used by
the Electricity Supply Board as a gener-
ating, transmission or distribution station.

CLASS 10
A temporary dwelling as defined in the
local Government (Sanitary Services)
Act, 1948 (No. 3 of 1948).

CLASS 11
A temporary building used only in connection with the sale or letting of buildings or building plots in course of development.

1 The building shall be detached
   from any other building.

2 The building shall be erected on
   or in close proximity to the development.

CLASS 12
A temporary building, which is used
only in connection with and during the
construction alteration, extension or
repair of any building or other work.

CLASS 13
A building or a temporary nature erected on a site for a period not exceeding
28 consecutive days or 60 days in any
period of 12 months.

CLASS 14
A lighthouse or similar structure which
is an aid to navigation or water.

4.6   **Alterations and Changes of Use**

There are two areas of legislation which are giving rise to difficulty as far as practitioners, and indeed some Building Control Authorities, are concerned, and these are the provisions dealing with alterations to buildings, and those dealing with changes of use.

A   Material Alterations

These are defined in Article 11 of S.I. 497 of 1997 as being an alteration where the work, or any part of the work, carried out by itself would be subject to the requirements of Part A (structure) or Part B (fire) of the Building Regulations. The article also says that the Regulations shall apply 'to every part of an existing building as affected by a material alteration or extension but only to the extent of prohibiting any material alteration or extension which would cause a new or greater contravention in the existing building of any provision of these Regulations'. Repairs and renewals of a minor nature are exempt. 'Repair or renewal' has now been defined in Article 5(4) of S.I. 497 of 1997 as meaning works of maintenance or restoration of a routine nature relating to (a) the keeping of a building in good condition or working order, or (b) the return of the fabric of a building to its original condition. The word 'minor' is not defined but there appears to be an acceptance that it applies to the provision or alteration of fixtures and fittings whereas works would apply to the building itself.

This gives rise to the difficulty that as the requirements of Parts A and B extend to almost every part of any building, such as doors, wall linings, stairs, handrails, etc, works which might normally be regarded as minor become subject to all the Regulations and control procedures. It is felt that this will simply discourage repairs and maintenance, and this was hardly the intention of the legislation. In any event, some old buildings can simply not be brought up to the standards set out in the various codes referred to in the technical guidance documents. All of these codes refer to new building works, and it is becoming obvious that some guidance will have to be given in regard to the standards that will be applied to older buildings. As a general rule it can be taken that any new works themselves carried out must conform to the regulations, and the overall status of the building with regard to the regulations must not be made any worse.

The new Technical Guidance Documents issued in December 1997 provided some comfort in dealing with existing buildings:

'In the case of material alterations or changes of use to existing buildings, the adoption without modification of the guidance in this document may not, in all circumstances, be appropriate. In particular, the adherence to guidance, including codes, standards or technical specifications, intended for application to new work may be unduly restrictive or impracticable. Buildings of architectural or historical interest are especially likely to give rise to such circumstances. In these situations, alternative approaches based on the principles contained in the document may be more relevant and should be considered.'

It remains to be seen if the various Building Control Authorities are sufficiently flexible to allow the system to work efficiently and reasonably.

B Material Changes of Use

In addition to the problems arising under material alterations, some difficulty has been experienced by architects in establishing what exactly is a 'material change of use'. Firstly, the Act itself in Section 3(3) says that a material change of use occurs when:

1   an existing building becomes a dwelling

2   an existing dwelling is sub-divided, and

3   when the use of a building becomes changed so that it comes within the provisions of the Building Regulations.

The definitions of 'Material Changes of Use' are contained in Article 13 of S.I. 497 of 1997 and Article 5 of S.I. 496 of 1997. They are identical as far as the categories included are concerned. It now appears that almost any change of use will be a material change of use. It is provided that where any building not so previously used becomes a hostel, hotel, guesthouse, institution, place of assembly, office, factory, shop, shopping centre or an industrial building, then a material change of use has occurred. The previous provision that the Regulations would then apply as if it were a new building has been dropped.

It must be noted that Parts D (materials and workmanship), E (sound), K (stairways, ramps and guards) and M (access for disabled people) do not apply to material changes of use themselves, but they do apply to any works carried out on foot of the change. A very welcome introduction in S.I. 154 of 1994 (now revoked) and retained in S.I. 497 of 1997 is the exclusion of Part A3 from material changes of use to existing buildings. This deals with disproportionate collapse and was causing great difficulty with regard to inner city buildings of five or more storeys.

Care must be taken to distinguish between the material changes of use that can occur under the Building Regulations from changes of use that are listed under the Planning Acts. In the case for example where a place of public resort is changed in use to a storage use, the Building Regulations might or might not apply, but the Planning Acts would require that planning permission be obtained for that change of use. Conversely, a change of use within a class of use in the Planning Acts, say from a day nursery to a convalescent home would be exempted development but would almost certainly come within the scope of the Building Regulations. Each case must be judged on the facts and an informal approach to the building control authority might be of benefit in establishing if any precedents exist or if any guidance can be given. It was suggested in par. 2.2.3 that a common list of defined uses be issued that would apply both to the planning acts, regulations and to development plans. This list could also cover the building regulations and so provide a practical and useful help to both the authorities themselves and to practitioners.

4.7   **The Control Mechanism**

The Act had originally envisaged a number of differing certificates, only one of which survived through to the eventual control procedure. It had been intended that a certificate of compliance would be submitted to the building control authority before work commenced, and that a certificate of approval would be issued by the authority when the work had been completed. These two certificates were not incorporated in the eventual system. The fire safety certificate was included in the Act and still remains.

The Building Control Regulations
(S.I. 496 of 1997)

There are two control documents:

a) The Commencement Notice

The need to submit a commencement notice is covered by Article 7 of Part II of S.I. 496 of 1997. It is required for any works to which the Building Regulations apply, unless the proposal is exempted development under the planning acts, and where there is no need to obtain a fire safety certificate. A commencement notice is required, however, for any material alteration of a shop, office or industrial building even where no fire safety certificate is required.

For those building works that need a commencement notice, the basic requirement is that this notice must be submitted not less than 14 days or more than 28 days before the commencement of the works. It should be submitted by 'the person who intends to carry out the works'. In practice this will tend to be the architect, although in some circumstances it might be more convenient for the contractor to submit it. The Building Control Authority must acknowledge receipt of the commencement notice and enter it on the register.

There has been some discussion as to when is the point at which the commencement notice should be sent. It appears to be accepted that the works 'commence' when the first operations which involve the Building Regulations is the appropriate time, and this could most likely be site preparation works (Part C). The position with regard to a project which is commenced and then postponed is not clear. Is a new commencement notice required when the project is restarted? Some Building Control Authorities will not accept a commencement notice as being valid unless details of the Fire Safety Certificate are submitted with the commencement notice. The legislation does not appear to validate these actions. The only indicator that there might be some justification for such actions is a requirement on the standard commencement notice form that the number of the Fire Safety Certificate be quoted. There are, of course, projects where a Fire Safety Certificate will not be required but where a commencement notice will.

The commencement notice was required by Article 7(d) of S.I. 305 of 1991 to give the name and address of the person from whom 'plans, documents and information as may be necessary to show that the building or works will comply with the requirements of the Building Regulations' may be obtained. This caused a lot of difficulty as it was clearly impossible for a designer to undertake that such compliance would occur. Article 7 of S.I. 153 of 1994 addressed this problem by inserting the phrase 'if built in accordance with the design' into the relevant section and this change is retained in S.I. 496 of 1997. The Building Control Act mentions, for the first time I believe in Irish legislation, the distinction between design and construction (Section 3(1)(a)), so it is appropriate to separate the design and construction responsibility in the commencement notice. There is now a standard form of commencement notice and a fee is now required (par 4.10).

b) **The Fire Safety Certificate**

The next matter that must be addressed is that of fire safety certificates. The exemptions to this requirement, as mentioned before, differ from the exemptions with regard to commencement notices. The main difference is that exempted development under the Planning Acts, while generally exempt from the commencement notice procedure, is normally covered by the requirement to obtain a fire safety certificate. On the other hand, individual houses, while requiring the issue of a commencement notice do not require a fire safety certificate; neither do extensions to individual houses. In view of the fact that most people in this country who die in fires do so in houses, this seems an odd exemption but there must be some administrative reason why this exemption was allowed. It is again emphasised that these buildings must conform to the Regulations themselves. Single-storey buildings used for agricultural purposes are also exempt from the requirement to obtain a Fire Safety Certificate.

An important exemption is that of works carried out in compliance with a notice served under the Fire Services Act 1981. This had been causing considerable problems involving a potential farcical situation of building owners having to apply, in effect, to a fire officer for approval under Part III of the Building Regulations for works which the same fire officer had required under the Fire Services Act.

Finally in the new exemptions are the extension of any building up to an area of 25 square metres, and material alterations in a shop, office or industrial building where no additional floors or sub-division is envisaged. The subdivision must involve physical works and not mere subtenanting arrangements.

Generally, apart from houses, a fire safety certificate is required in respect of all new buildings, material alterations, extensions and material changes of use for buildings covered by the Building Regulations. The procedure is now somewhat similar from that of the commencement notice.

The application must be made on the prescribed form which is contained in S.I. 10 of 2000 – Building Control (Amendment) Regulations, and sufficient information by way of plans and specifications must be lodged with the application to show that the proposed works will comply with Part B of the Building Regulations. An application for a fire safety certificate which does not conform with the requirements will be rejected as invalid.

A fee is required to be paid and these are set out in S.I. 496 of 1997, Part V. The fee is calculated on a floor area basis. The legislation mirrors that of the Planning Acts in that a decision must be made within two months, unless this period is extended by agreement (Section 6(5) of the Act); the building control authority may approve the applications, approve it with conditions, or reject it. A building control authority is required to keep a register of all valid applications, together with the decision made by them or the Board.

A right of appeal lies to An Bord Pleanála either against conditions or a rejection, and it is comforting to see that the timetable which is set out for appeals under the Planning Acts will be applied to appeals under the Building Control Act. There is, mercifully, no right of third party appeal. An interesting development is that, while there is no provision for oral hearings, the Board can convene meetings of the parties if it feels that this may help the appeal process.

Some of the questions that have arisen in the minds of architects who will be dealing with fire safety certificates are firstly, what happens when the default mechanism applies; secondly, what happens in the case of large developments where ultimate uses may not be determined at the application stage; thirdly, can certificates be obtained retrospectively; fourthly, do minor revisions during construction require new applications, and lastly, what is the status of the Fire Services Act, 1981 now that Building Regulations are in force. There may, indeed, be other questions that may arise, and it must be said that at the moment many of the views being expressed as to the day-to-day workings of the Regulations can be no more than inspired guesswork and only experience of the system and no doubt some expensive High Court cases, will provide permanent answers.

But to return to the questions posed. If the building control authority does not decide on an application within two months then the building owner can proceed to build in the absence of a fire safety certificate. What is very important to remember, however, is that all the provisions of the Building Regulations must still be complied with and the powers of the building control authority with regard to enforcement and inspection still remain.

In the case of large developments, such as shopping centres, where the ultimate uses are not known at the outset, it seems to be accepted that further applications will be required as the precise uses are established. The adoption of codes such as BS 5588, Part 10, is useful in this case. It may be possible when the initial application is being made to specify the fire resistance and/or the surface spread of flame of materials and finishes that would be generally acceptable.

The question of retrospective applications was raised at a very early stage of the debate on the Regulations and as yet no definitive position has emerged. There is no provision in any of the legislation for such applications but neither are they specifically excluded. The regulations state that a fire safety certificate is required before work starts. There are many circumstances in which this will not happen, in some cases quite innocently, and it seems iniquitous that a building owner cannot 'correct' the situation by applying subsequently. This would seem all the more reasonable since a fire safety certificate applies only to the 'design' of a building and is unrelated to the actual construction, although the certificate only remains valid if the building is constructed in accordance with the drawings as approved. Such a facility exists in the operation of Building Regulations in the UK and the provision for 'retention' under the Irish Planning Acts could also be regarded as a precedent. The Department in its Guidance to Building Control Authorities makes it quite clear that retrospective applications could be valid. This being so, it seems reasonable, to make specific provision for retrospective applications in the Regulations. It is, of course, recognised that there can be occasions when it will not be possible to verify materials in an existing structure thereby rendering the issue of a retrospective certificate very difficult if not impossible. No doubt each building control authority will adopt what they consider a reasonable policy towards this area, but owners and architects must remember that even in the case of an honest but mistaken view that no certificate is required, it is an offence to undertake any building work where such a certificate was in fact required.

Minor revisions during the course of the building works, and these are almost inevitable, should not necessarily lead to new applications. The test should be to see if the revision is still within the standards as set out in Part B of the Regulations (particularly as set out in the technical guidance documents) and where this test is passed, it can safely be assumed that no new application would be necessary. The more general a specification is the easier it will be to alter the works without endangering the validity of an existing certificate.

Lastly in this section, is the question of the status of the Fire Services Act, 1981. This, you will remember, is the Statute which was passed shortly after the Stardust disaster, and it gave very wide powers to fire authorities. It is on the basis of this Act that fire officers have up till now required buildings to contain specified features. Fire authorities are now synonymous with building control authorities. The issue of a fire safety certificate will, certainly in the case of a new building, preclude the authority from imposing further requirements under the Fire Services Act, as the fire authority is specifically restricted in Part B to considering an application for a fire safety certificate. But it must be remembered that apart from the physical building aspects of fire safety, there are also areas such as fire safety management which might be subsequently addressed by the building control authority under the Fire Services Act.

Another possible problem is that of extensions to existing buildings. An application might well be received by the building control authority for a fire safety certificate in respect of an extension to say, a hotel, and it may be that the extension would satisfy the Regulations. However, an examination of the drawings might reveal to the building control authority, acting in its role as fire authority, serious deficiencies in the existing building as regards fire safety and they might consider it necessary to invoke the provisions of the Fire Services Act.

An Enforcement Notice requiring works to an existing building may be issued under the Fire Services Act by the Fire Officer. As has been pointed out before, these works would now be exempt as far as Part III of the Building Control Regulations is concerned.

4.8 Dispensation and Relaxation

Section 4 of the Building Control Act contains the provisions for dispensation or relaxation. At the time that Act was drafted, it was anticipated that the Building Regulations might be in the form of the revised draft Building Regulations which were originally published in 1981, but in the event the Regulations as they finally appeared were so concise that any relaxation or dispensation is almost impossible. Take for instance Part F, which says: 'Adequate means of ventilation shall be provided for people in buildings.' Remember that the technical guidance documents are not the Building Regulations. The Building Regulations are the items set out in S.I. 497 of 1997and nothing else. They are the law. It would be difficult to imagine a situation where an application could be made to allow inadequate means of ventilation for people in buildings. It can be taken that the relaxation and dispensation provisions will not trouble us very much, although it is possible that sympathetic use might well be made of them in the difficult cases of material alterations.

There is a recommended standard form for applying for a relaxation or dispensation and this is contained in the fourth schedule to S.I. 497 of 1997. The standard fee for such an application is €125 for dwellings and €250 for other buildings. A list of all dispensations and relaxations must be entered on the register required under S.I. 10 of 2000.

4.9 Appeals

An appeal may be made to An Bord Pleanála under Section 7(1)(a) or 7(1)(b) of the Building Control Act. The first sub-section deals with appeals against dispensations or relaxations referred to above, and the second deals with appeals against a decision made in respect of a fire safety certificate application. There is no right of third party appeal.

The Regulations governing appeals with regard to the Building Regulations are set out in S.I. of 496 1997 (Part VI). In a number of respects the procedures are similar to those which govern appeals under the Planning Acts. The appeal must be made within one month of the Building Control Authority decision; the full grounds of appeal must accompany the appeal application, and no further submissions are permitted; the Building Control Authority must send its observations on the appeal to the Board within one month of being notified of the appeal; and the Board may, if it considers it appropriate request further submissions, or even convene a meeting of the parties.

The Board is required to have as its objective the determination of all appeals within four months, and where this is not possible, must so inform the parties and also must specify the date before which the appeal will be determined.

4.10 Fees

When the building regulations were first introduced in 1992, the required fees were set out in S.I. 112 of 1992 and S.I. 182 of 1992, both now revoked. Fees were required for a dispensation or relaxation, for a fire safety certificate, for an appeal and for copies of documents.

Apart from substantially increasing the amounts involved to 2.90 per square metre in the case of a fire safety certificate application, an additional fee was introduced in S.I. 496 of 1997, Part V. This was for a commencement notice and was set at 30 or 30 per building in the case of housing schemes. There is a maximum fee of 12,500 for a fire safety certificate application and €3,800 for a commencement notice.

There is power to refund fees and certain charities are exempt. The fees are set out in full in the Part V of S.I. 496 of 1997.

4.11 Enforcement and Penalties

There is what might be described as a two tier system of legal control over the working of the Building Control Act. The first tier concerns the Enforcement Notice Procedure, and this is set out in Section 8, 9, and 10 of the Act. The second tier is dealt with at the end of this section.

An enforcement notice may be served either on the owner, or the contractor and will be served when either the design or construction of the building does not comply with the Building Regulations. The building control authority must be satisfied that it would not have issued a dispensation or relaxation in the particular case. The enforcement notice will specify what works are required to remedy the breach.

It is comforting to see that some Building Control Authorities are vigilant in the carrying out of their powers in this area, and a number of successful prosecutions have taken place. On the other hand, in those areas of the country where there was previously no bye-law control there is an almost total absence of inspection and unless some improvement in policing occurs the system will be widely ignored.

There is a time limit on the service of an enforcement notice. It must be served within five years of the completion of the works, or of the material change of use involved. If the notice is not complied with, or is not appealed to the District Court, the building control authority may carry out the required works themselves, and recover the costs from the owner. To enable them to carry out this function, section 11 of the Act empowers the building control authority to enter and inspect the premises. This does not apply to prisons or places of detention, or to premises in the occupation of the Defence Forces or the Garda Síochána.

The owner, or whoever is served the notice, may apply to the District Court, on a number of grounds such as unreasonable expense, for the notice to be annulled or modified.

The penalties for infringements of the Act are also of a two-tier nature. If the contravention is relevant to Section 3(5), which is the sub-section which requires the Building Regulations to be observed, or sub-section 8(6) which deals with the options open to anyone served with an enforcement notice, then the maximum penalties are €1,000 and/or six months imprisonment, or a fine of €12,500 and/or two years imprisonment on indictment. If the offence relates to any other section of the Act, then the charge is limited to a summary offence only, carrying the €1,000/six months penalty. In both cases, a fine of €190 per day is scheduled for continuing offenses.

The second tier of control in the Building Control Act is set out in section 12. If the building control authority considers that building works, or a material change of use, might endanger health and safety, and also that immediate steps are needed, the authority may apply to the High Court for an order which will remedy the position. This would usually require the cessation of works, or of the use concerned, and provision for making the structure safe. This power of the Court can be applied even if permission has been obtained under, say, the Planning Acts for such use.

4.12 **Transitional Provisions**

Many of the transitional provisions will, by now, be largely academic. The Building Control Act, 1990, contained provisions to deal with building proposals that had been lodged for bye-law approval before 1st June 1992. In effect, any scheme lodged for bye-law approval, or any works carried out on foot of a bye-law approval, before the 1st June 1992 are not covered by any of the provisions of the Building Regulations. Section 22(2) of the Act, which is reproduced in full in par. 4.5 dealing with exemptions provided that in works carried out in accordance with plans lodged for bye-law approval, the bye-laws would continue to apply (in other words the Building Regulations shall not apply) even if such works are carried out 'with or without a departure or a deviation from those plans'. The first sentence of sub-section 22(2) says that 'any bye-law which is in force on the operative day shall continue to apply' to these works. It would seem to be a logical conclusion, then, that a scheme which had obtained bye-law approval, may be altered in any way provided that it would, presumably in the architect's opinion, have complied with the bye-laws. This view is not universally accepted but it is hard to see what else the words used can mean.

A point to watch is that a bye-law approval may be limited in time by a local authority (Section 15 of the Public Health (Amendment) Act 1907). There is nothing to prevent a local authority revoking a bye-law approval if it feels that the system is being abused.

There is an amnesty under sub-section 22(7) as far as buildings which do not comply with the bye-laws is concerned. Unless the building control authority served notice on the owner of a building that did not comply with the bye-laws or for which bye-law approval had not been sought, by 13th December 1989 then the building will be deemed to have obtained bye-law approval.

There are transitional provisions in S.I. 496 of 1997 and S.I. 497 of 1997. Generally the new regulations came into force on 1st July 1998. Until then S.I. 305 of 1991 (as amended by S.I. 153 of 1994) and S.I. 306 of 1991 (as amended by S.I. 154 of 1994) remained in force. It should be noted, however, that the new regulations will not apply to works where a fire safety certificate has already been granted and the proposed works are carried out between 1st July 1998 and 31st December 2002.

Finally under the transitional provisions, Section 23 deals with the Local Government (Multi-Storey Buildings) Act 1988. Section 4 of that Act required that multi-storey buildings which were not completed before the coming into effect the Act must have a certificate from an engineer before being occupied that it is, in effect, safe. The Building Control Act, Section 23(1) removes such buildings from the multi-storey Act since they will now be covered by the Building

Regulations. It must be noted that any multi-storey building that obtained bye-law approval, and which is commenced after 1st June 1992, is still covered by the multi-storey Act.

4.13 Building Regulations Checklist

query		law	par.
1	What are the regulations?	S.I. 497 of 1997 S.I. 179 of 2000 S.I. 249 of 2000 S.I. 441 of 2000 S.I. 284 of 2002	4.3
2	How are the bye-laws affected?	1990 Act – Section 22	4.12
3	Are there exemptions?	1990 Act – Section 3(13) S.I. 496 of 1997 – Article 7 S.I. 497 of 1997 – Article 8	4.5
4	What about alterations, additions, changes of use or repairs ?	1990 Act – Section 3(1)(b), (d) S.I. 497 of 1997 – Article 5(4) S.I. 497 of 1997 – Article 11	4.6
5	Are services, fittings and equipment affected?	1990 Act – Section 3(c) S.I. 497 of 1997 – Article 12	4.5
6	What fees are necessary?	1990 Act – Sections 4, 6, 7, 18 S.I. 496 of 1997 – part V	4.10
7	Can a dispensation or relaxation be obtained?	1990 Act – Sections 4, 6, 7 S.I. 497 of 1997 – Article 8	4.8
8	What is the status of the Technical Guidance Document?	S.I. 497 of 1997 – Article 7	4.3
9	What are the requirements of the Construction Products Directive?	89/106/EEC S.I. 198 of 1992	4.4
10	What notices are required?	1990 Act – Section 6(2) S.I. 496 of 1997 – parts II, III	4.7

11 When must the notices be sent?	S.I. 496 of 1997 – Articles 8, 12	4.7
12 Is there a time limit on the response?	1990 Act – Section 6(5)	4.7
13 Is there an appeal process?	1990 Act – Section 7	4.9
14 Can a fire safety certificate be obtained retrospectively?		4.7
15 Can a fire safety certificate be obtained to include later fit-outs?		4.7
16 What is the status of the Fire Services Act 1981	S.I. 496 of 1997 – Article 11	4.7
17 How are the regulations enforced?	1990 Act – Sections 8, 9, 10, 11, 12	4.10
19 What penalties can be imposed?	1990 Act – Section 17	4.10

Chapter 5 – **Safety at Work**

5.1 **Introduction**

Most of the present requirements regarding safety on building sites already existed in previous legislation and codes and the most significant effect of the legislation introduced in 1995 was to tie clients and designers explicitly into the matter of safety on construction sites. It had been argued that the need for this new legislation arose from recent trends involving the fragmentation of sites and the proliferation of sub-contractors making control more difficult. While this may be, it is clear that the regulations added to the increasing burden of administrative bureaucracy which attends construction. The third edition of this book suggested that it would also be likely to provide fertile ground for those who are engaged in litigation in respect of personal injuries. It is less certain that it would do much to reduce accidents on building sites. Notwithstanding that, there is now a duty on Clients and Architects to do what they reasonably can to reduce accidents without assuming the role, duties and responsibilities of the contractor.

This legislation had been creeping up on us for some time. In 1975 regulations were issued called the Construction (Safety, Health and Welfare) Regulations to deal with general safety matters on building sites, but did not involve clients or designers. In 1989 the Safety, Health and Welfare at Work Act was passed and this is still in force. It referred to safety at work generally not only in construction but for all employers and employees including non-employees using any premises.

Then in 1992 came the notorious EU Directive 92/57, 'Safety on Sites' with its absurd and unverified opening paragraph that 'Whereas unsatisfactory architectural and/or organisational options or poor planning of the works at the project preparation stage have played a role in more than half of the occupational accidents occurring on construction sites in the Community' and going on to erect an edifice on these unsound foundations, which is not a prudent thing to do. No evidence was ever produced for this piece of nonsense, though it has been established that the alleged factual report FROM DRAWING BOARD TO BUILDING SITE, published by the Commission, is a complete fabrication. Furthermore, no engineer or architect was included in the group that drafted the Directive and the statistics used for the odd statement related to fatal accidents only, which form a tiny proportion of all building accidents. The Safety on Sites Directive (92/57/EEC) is made under the Framework Directive (89/391/EEC). The Framework Directive is confined to the relationship between employers and employees only. It has been argued that in seeking to include clients and designers, the Safety on Sites Directive goes outside the scope of the Framework Directive and is therefore *ultra vires*. A similar argument can be made in respect of the relationship between the new regulations and the Safety, Health and Welfare at Work Act 1989. However the Directive was adopted eagerly by our legislators and was followed by the Safety, Health and Welfare at Work (General Application) Regulations

1993 (S.I. 44 of 1993). These are referred to as the Principal Regulations in the Statutory Instrument (No.41 of 2001).

Construction was specifically addressed in the next relevant piece of legislation, S.I. 138 of 1995, the Safety, Health and Welfare at Work (Construction) Regulations, which has now been revoked and replaced by the Safety Health and Welfare at Work (Construction) Regulations – S.I. 481 of 2001. Vigorous representation by the RIAI and the ACEI, resulted in a watering down of one of the main defects of the EU directive, which had required a greater involvement by designers in the construction phase of the project. At the time of the writing of the second edition of this book in 1994, the proposed regulations were much more onerous. Even as it is, two serious defects remain. Firstly, it is a basic principle of good safety management that decisions and control of safety should be made as near as possible to the workplace itself. The effect of moving responsibility to clients and designers is in direct contravention of this principle. Secondly, it confuses the issue of responsibility and serves partially to separate the management of safety from the execution of the work.

When these regulations were being framed the RIAI and the ACEI pointed out that the legislation was based on a number of serious misconceptions. Firstly, that all buildings are designed by architects or engineers. Random sampling by the RIAI of planning applications would indicate that less than half of all buildings, and possibly only 20% of houses are designed by properly qualified architects. Secondly, that architects and engineers control the building site. This is not so. The contractor has absolute and sole control of the site. Thirdly, that architects and engineers supervise the works. Again this is not so. The duty of the designer to ensure that the client receives the building he has contracted for does not supplant the primary duty of the contractor, as one of the contracting parties, to carry out his contract. Fourthly and finally, that designers can somehow design buildings so that they can be safely built. It is the building process itself allied with the carelessness of the average person that makes building dangerous and the amount of construction safety that can be built in is very limited. Par 5.7 deals with the aspect of design responsibility in safety legislation.

If architects have been less than enthusiastic about this legislation it is not, as has been unhelpfully suggested, that they are indifferent to safety standards but because they are satisfied that the provisions are seriously flawed and they doubt if the regrettable accident statistics will be significantly altered. Accidents are basically caused by human nature. That will not change. This was well summed up in the Association of Consulting Engineers of Ireland's GUIDANCE FOR MEMBERS – DESIGNING FOR SAFETY IN CONSTRUCTION, issued in 2002: 'While designers generally have a reasonable understanding of construction methods, they do not require expertise in regard to the particular means, methods and procedures of construction that the builder must possess. Nor does the designer determine or control either the resources to be made available by the builder or the management, planning, supervision etc, of the construction site itself. It is important therefore to acknowledge the limitation of what a designer can bring to bear when seeking to identify and assess risks that can be avoided or mitigated at design stage.'

5.2 The Legislation

Safety in Industry Act 1980
Safety, Health and Welfare at Work Act 1989

S.I. 44 of 1993	Safety Health and Welfare at Work (General Application) Regulations
S.I. 357 of 1995	Safety Health and Welfare at Work (Repeals and Revocation)
S.I. 358 of 1995	Safety Health and Welfare at Work (Miscellaneous Welfare Provisions)
S.I. 481 of 2001	Safety Health and Welfare at Work (Construction) Regulations
S.I. 188 of 2001	Safety Health and Welfare at Work (General Application) (Amendment) Regulations – this instrument deals with work equipment and the duties of the employer in this regard. It will not much affect the practitioner.

EU Directive – 89/391/EEC – Framework Directive
EU Directive – 92/57/EEC – Safety on Sites

In 1989 the Safety, Health and Welfare at Work Act was passed. It referred to safety at work generally not only in construction but contained specific reference to design. Section 11 stated that 'It shall be the duty of any person who designs (or constructs) places of work to design (or construct) them so that they are, as far as is reasonably practicable, safe and without risk to health.' This was a fairly general requirement and caused little problems for architects in that the non-specific nature of the law did not impinge on detail design.

There has, naturally, been some dispute as to what 'reasonably practicable' means. It was suggested in IRISH LAW OF TORTS (McMahon & Binchy) 2nd edition, p.119, that the phrase is probably close in meaning to the employer's common law duty of reasonable care. However, in the case of *Boyle v Marathon Petroleum (Ireland) Ltd* [1999] Supreme Court, 12th January, the Court implied that a stricter interpretation was appropriate: 'I have no doubt that onus of proof does rest on the defendants to show that what they did was reasonably practicable. I am also of the opinion that the duty is more extensive than the common law duty, which devolves on employers to exercise reasonable care in various respects as regards their employees. It is an obligation to take all practicable steps. That seems to me to involve more than that they should respond that they, as employers did all that was reasonably to be expected of them in a particular situation. An employer might sometimes be able to say that what he did by way of exercising reasonable care was done in the 'agony of the moment', for example, but that might not be enough to discharge his statutory duty under the section in question.'

A previous English case, *Edwards v National Coal Board* [1949] AER 743 held that 'Reasonably practicable is a narrower term than physically possible, and seems to me to imply that a computation must be made by the owner in which the quantum of risk is placed on one scale and the sacrifice involved in the measures necessary for averting the risk (whether in money, time or trouble) is placed in the other, and that, if it be shown that there is a gross disproportion between them – the risk being insignificant in relation to the sacrifice – the defendants discharge the onus on them.'

A more recent English case, *Regina v Balfour Beatty* [1999] Appeal Court, held that 'the employer's general duties under the Health and Safety at Work Act are qualified by taking steps so far as is reasonably practicable. Thus the law requires employers to do what good management and common sense require them to do anyway, i.e. look at what the risks are and take sensible measures to tackle them. Failure to perform general duties under the Act are particularly serious as those duties are the foundations for protecting health and safety.'

These cases seem to set a fairly consistent standard, but some warning notes must be sounded. The use of the phrase 'reasonably practicable' has be criticised by the European Commission as being potentially in breach of EU Directives. It has been pointed out that the 'reasonably practicable' phrase in the Health Safety and Welfare at Work Act 1989 has not been used in the ensuing regulations. In the case of *Everitt v Thorsman (Ireland) Ltd* [1999] High Court, 23rd June, the Court held that the duty to provide safe equipment under S.I. 44 of 1993 (General Application) Regulations was almost absolute: 'While there is not blameworthiness in any meaningful sense of the word on the part of the employers in this case, these Regulations do exist for sound policy reasons at least, namely, to ensure that an employee who suffers an injury at work through no fault of his own by using defective equipment should not be left without remedy.' This last case dealt with effective equipment but it can be anticipated, following the line of reasoning in recent cases that in future the Courts will tend to impose an absolute duty of care where construction accidents are concerned.

A further aspect of the Health, Welfare and Safety at Work Act 1989, that does affect almost everyone connected with the construction industry is the requirement in section 12 that all employers prepare a safety statement which 'shall specify the manner in which the safety, health and welfare of persons employed by an employer shall be secured at work'. This section also provides that the annual report of a company as detailed by the Companies Act 1963 shall evaluate how this policy statement was fulfilled. This safety statement is not to be confused with either the safety file or the safety plan which are required under S.I. 481 of 2001 and which are described in par 5.3.

Two main sets of regulations were introduced under the powers given to the Minister in the 1989 Act. The first of these, the 'Principal Regulations', S.I. 44 of 1993 require, as a general principle, 'the avoidance of risks' and dealt with safety at work generally. Some of the more specific requirements are:

a)   more specific standards for work places including provision for rest rooms and facilities for pregnant women and disabled employees

b)   a requirement to notify the Health and Safety Authority of all accidents

c)   the elimination of manual handling wherever possible

d)   the analysing of Visual Display Unit work stations to assess risks to health and safety, including eyesight

e)   the use personal protective equipment only where there is no other way of avoiding a risk

f)   the provision of adequate, first aid arrangements in all places of work.

The most significant piece of legislation as far as practitioners are concerned is, of course, the second of these regulations, S.I. 481 of 2001, the Safety, Health and Welfare at Work (Construction) Regulations. The regulations themselves are dealt with in detail in par. 5.3. The statutory instrument revokes S.I. 138 of 1995 but is not radically different. The most significant change from the previous regulations is the introduction of the FÁS Safe Pass scheme (8th Schedule) and the FÁS Construction Skills Certificate scheme (9th Schedule). The first of these is a scheme to issue cards to those who have attended the FÁS safety awareness programme and the second refers to the FÁS scheme which will issue certificates to those who have passed the relevant FÁS course. There are fourteen different tasks scheduled ranging from scaffolding to built-up roofing. Both the Project Supervisor Construction Stage and the contractor are jointly responsible for ensuring that all appropriate persons on site have the necessary cards to indicate that they have the proper training.

A question was raised as to whether it would be necessary for architects and other professionals on site to have a FÁS Safe Pass card. The regulations refer to persons who are 'at work' on a construction site (Articles 6 and 9)but more specifically in Article 129(4) which states that the 8th schedule is applicable to craft and general construction workers as well as to persons undertaking on-site security work. This would seem to exclude professionals but it might be prudent to check with professional indemnity insurers to be sure that no third party liability might arise from the absence of such a card.

Taking the two enabling pieces of legislation together, it is clear that the 1989 Act and Directive 89/391 establish the mutual obligations of employer and employee and do not differ in any material respect as to this object. The 1989 Act places a non-delegable duty on an employer to provide a safe system of work (recently reaffirmed by the Supreme Court in *Connolly v Dundalk UDC* [1992] 18th November). The Framework Directive likewise places non-delegable obligations on employers to provide a safe system of work. The principal of non-delegability of the employers obligation is central to the interpretation of the duties on the client and the project supervisors imposed by the 2001 Regulations. Project Supervisors will be discussed in pars. 5.5 and 5.6.

It follows that the Building or Civil Engineering Contractor is the Employer for the purposes of the statutory scheme: and that Regulations S.I. 481 of 2001 are to be read in the context that the Employer's obligation to provide a safe system of work cannot be in any way reduced or limited, and all ancillary provisions which relate to the Client and the Project Supervisor are separate to and in aid of, rather than in any measure in substitution of, this obligation.

Further Statutory Instruments issued under the Act are S.I. 357 of 1995, the Safety Health and Welfare at Work (Repeals and Revocations) Order 1995 and S.I. 358 of 1995, the Safety Health and Welfare at Work (Miscellaneous Provisions) regulations 1995. The first of these sets out in detail which Acts have been repealed and which Statutory Instruments have been revoked. Legislation affected by this Statutory Instrument would have dealt with matters now covered by the new safety and health legislation. Most prominent of these would be the Factories Act 1955 and the Safety in Industry Act 1980 which are partly repealed, and the Office Premises Act 1958 which is entirely repealed. The second statutory instrument requires places of work, in effect, to be clean, have adequate seating, be provided with drinking water and to have facilities for meals.

5.3 **The Regulations (S.I. 481 of 2001)**

The Regulations have a wide general application and also some implications which may not be immediately obvious. They came into force generally on 1st January 2002. All the provisions are now in force except those referring to the FÁS Safe Pass Scheme [Article 6(5)and (6)] and the FÁS Construction Skills Certificate Scheme [Article 9(3) and (4)]which come into force on 1st June 2003.

The revoked regulations were originally introduced on 6th June 1995. In March 1996 the Royal Institute of the Architects of Ireland introduced a 'Guide to the Implementation of the Safety Health and Welfare at Work (Construction) Regulations 1995', together with a set of standard forms dealing with all aspects of the regulations. It is strongly recommended, particularly by RIAI Insurances Services Ltd, that these standard forms be used wherever possible. These guidelines would still be relevant. Guidelines to the regulations were published in 1997 by the Health and Safety Authority but these unfortunately left unanswered some of the more difficult questions which had arisen. Some of the problems arise from a complex series of interdependent and sometimes poorly drafted definitions. For instance, the main duties as far as clients are concerned apply in respect of 'projects' which are defined as 'any development which includes or is intended to include construction work'. In turn 'construction work' means the carrying out of any building, civil engineering or engineering construction work and includes any of the following. (This list is a summary of the full definition given in the Statutory Instrument):

a) the construction, alteration, fitting out, commissioning, renovation, repair, upkeep, redecoration or other maintenance, etc, of a structure

b) the preparation for an intended structure, including site clearance, exploration, investigation and excavation, etc

c) the assembly of prefabricated elements to form a structure, etc

d) the removal of a structure or part of a structure, etc

e) the installation, commissioning, maintenance, repair or removal of mechanical, electrical, gas systems, etc.

The word 'structure' which occurs in most of the definitions of 'construction work' is defined as:

a) any building, railway line or siding, tramway line, dock, harbour, inland navigation, tunnel, bridge, viaduct, waterworks, reservoir, pipeline (whatever it contains or is intended to contain), underground or overground cables, aquaduct, sewer, sewage works, gas-holder, road, airfield, sea defence works, river works, drainage works, earthworks, lagoon, dam, wall, caisson, mast, tower, pylon, underground tank, earth retaining structure, or any structure designed to preserve or alter any natural feature, and any other structure similar to the foregoing

b) any formwork, falsework, scaffold or other structure designed or used to provide support or means of access during construction work

c) any fixed plant in respect of work which is installation, commissioning, decommissioning or dismantling and where any such work involves a risk of falling more than two metres.

All of this means that the scope of the regulations extends far beyond that envisaged by the Directive or of many items which would not have been traditionally regarded as 'construction'. It can, in some circumstances, be construed to include activities as diverse as erecting a television aerial, installing fixed manufacturing plant, installing a telephone or a computer system. It will have consequences in areas of activity which have nothing to do with construction. Within the construction field, it is clear that it will apply to almost any building or maintenance works including mechanical and electrical services. One example of how difficult it is to decide what is to be included or not would relate to maintenance. Maintenance is specifically included in the definition of construction works, but does replacing one door lock constitute a project? Almost certainly not. But replacing, say, five hundred locks in a prison would almost certainly constitute a project. Again, cleaning the glass on the front door of an office block would hardly be a project, but cleaning all the windows of the building would be. Who is to decide where the line is to be drawn? The official guidelines give no answers. Oddly enough the definition of the word 'client' in the regulations will exclude some straightforward construction work.

In the regulations, a 'client' is defined as 'any person, engaged in trade, business or other undertaking, who commissions or procures the carrying out of a project for the purpose of such trade, business or undertaking'. What this means, in effect, is that domestic work is virtually excluded except in the case of speculative house building. If Mrs Murphy wants to repair the roof of her own house, this is exempt. In short, everything apart from domestic work, no matter how small, will be covered by the requirements of the legislation. But if Mrs Murphy runs the post office from her house and wants to repair the roof, then the work is not exempt.

The duties of designers, contractors and others are set out separately. These are not dependent on the definition of the client which means that their duties and responsibilities apply to all projects, including domestic work, even though no project supervisors will be appointed.

It is important to note that in the regulations, a contractor means a main contractor, a nominated sub-contractor, a domestic sub-contractor or a self-employed person. Thus a project with a main contractor who engages a self-employed labourer is a project with 'more than one contractor' and this is relevant in relation to the keeping of the safety file which is referred to later.

The regulations contain a number of key elements which are the core of the new safety management system. Before proceeding to deal with the duties of the various participants, it is appropriate to be aware of and understand what these elements are:

a) Commencement Notice

Before work starts on site, a notification is required to be sent to the Health and Safety Authority by the Project Supervisor Construction Stage in respect of all projects (other than privately commissioned domestic construction) which are planned to last more than 30 days or on which the volume of work is scheduled to exceed 500 man days. A problem arises in regard to whether the project will in fact be covered by the Regulations. An Architect will not, in many circumstances, be in a position to know whether or not a project will last for more than 30 days or whether or not it will involve 500 man days. As this is one of the two criteria required for the preparation of a safety plan (the other being work with a particular risk) there will be uncertainty on this matter until the Contractor is appointed and, indeed, as the work proceeds. The notice is to contain particulars of the project as set out in the First Schedule of the Regulations. A copy of this notice is required to be displayed on site.

b) Safety Documents

There are three 'Safety' documents referred to in the overall legislative framework. The 1989 Act requires all employers to produce a 'Safety Statement'. Section 12 of that Act specifies what this statement must contain and it can be generally described as an overall description of the steps taken by the employer to further safety. A company which is an employer is required by the Companies Acts to evaluate the statement annually. The safety statement is company related. A safety plan is site specific and a safety file is building related. It is important to point out though that this safety statement is not part of the regulation package. There are two Safety Documents in the Regulations. They can be described as the 'before' – the Safety Plan – and the 'after' – the Safety File. The Safety and Health Plan, to give it its full title, is not defined in the Regulations but is referred to in the Directive as 'setting out the rules for the construction site'. It would include amongst other things:

• the setting out of the site, the location of cranes, storage areas, site huts
• the programming of the activities
• the control of sub-contractors and self-employed workers
• traffic routes and traffic control
• the arrangement of the temporary works, scaffolding
• the provision of canteens, rest rooms, etc
• the possible existence of particular risks.

A Safety Plan is required for all projects which require a commencement notice or which involve 'a particular risk' as set out in the Section Schedule to the Regulations. Where a Safety Plan is required it must be prepared before the commencement of the works on site and it is required to be updated as the work proceeds. It is the responsibility of the Project Supervisor Construction Stage to prepare this document, although it will be necessary for the Project Supervisor Design Stage to provide any relevant information which is available as soon as the Project Supervisor Construction Stage is appointed.

The second safety document referred to in the Regulations is the Safety File which again is not defined. It is, however, referred to as 'a file appropriate to the characteristics of the project containing relevant health and safety information to be taken into account during any subsequent construction work'. It is, in effect, an owners manual and would contain:

- as-built drawings of the building and services
- information on any known hazardous materials
- instructions for routine maintenance
- maintenance manuals for plant and services.

Again, not all projects require a Safety File. It must be prepared by the Project Supervisor Construction Stage where more than one contractor is engaged on the project Where it is required it must be given to the client at the completion of the project who is responsible for retaining it and passing it on to a subsequent purchaser or tenant. There is a gap in the regulations in that there is no requirement on this purchaser or tenant to make it available to their successors. Equally odd is the provision that a Safety File is not required to be prepared where there is only one contractor involved in the project. This, because of the definition of 'contractor ' referred to earlier, means that almost all projects will require one. However, it is not necessary for a person building a house for his private use to prepare a Safety File. There will therefore be a significant number of properties for which, quite legitimately, no Safety File will exist and there will be conveyancing problems in many circumstances.

Another unresolved problem relates to speculative housing developments. This would be, without any doubt, a 'project' under the regulations and the client would be responsible for ensuring that project supervisor (construction phase) would prepare a safety file. Should every house purchaser receive a copy? If the development company is wound up who 'keeps' the file? Should the local authority that takes charge of the roads and open spaces get the file? Nobody knows. The Health and Safety Authority guidelines point out that anybody who buys a house for their own habitation does not qualify as a client and that there is no obligation to pass on the safety file. It is, however, recommended that this be done.

It is interesting, in addition, to see that the Department of the Environment in issuing guidance notes to local authorities on the implementation of the regulations (Circular BC1/97) says that the original file, and presumably copies of it, should be transferred to future purchasers of houses in a local authority housing scheme.

The State is proposing a standard form for the appointment of project supervisors (design stage) which incorporates the following piece of legal nonsense in connection with the provision of professional indemnity insurance to cover the duties involved: 'This provision is without prejudice to the client's assertion that he has no liability under the regulations or at all from the moment he appoints the project supervisor for the design stage.' Government departments should know that the law applies to everyone. The appointment form incorporates the following statement: 'The project supervisor for the design stage shall confirm that the tender and contract documents comply in all respects with the requirements of the regulations.' This is not a duty of the project supervisor for the design stage and should not, in any circumstances, be agreed to.

5.4   The Client's Duties

The Client has two main duties and the Architect, or Engineer must advise the Client as to his responsibilities. The first is to appoint a project supervisor for the design stage and a project supervisor for the construction stage and, secondly, to keep the safety file for use on any subsequent work to the building or, if the client's legal interest in the building is passed onto a purchaser or tenant, to pass the safety file on to that person.

The regulations say that: 'It is the duty of every client to appoint, in respect of every project, a Project Supervisor for Design Stage and a Project Supervisor for Construction Stage.' 'Project Supervisor means a competent person or organisation appointed under regulation 3(1) and responsible for carrying out the appropriate duties specified in these Regulations.'

A significant point to note is that the person must be competent. Competence is not defined in the Act or Regulations, but is normally reckoned to result from training and experience. An English case, *Brazier v Skipton Rock Company* [1962] 1 WLR 491, says that a competent person is 'not the most competent man available nor one so competent that he never makes a mistake, but one who on fair assessment of the requirements of the task, the factors involved, the problems to be studied and the degree of risk of danger implicit, can be fairly as well as reasonably regarded by the manager, and is in fact regarded at the time by the manager, as competent to perform such an inspection.' The Institutions representing the design professionals may well be in a position to vouch for the competence of their members in respect of the specific duties which they would assume as project supervisors for design stage. It is not clear, however, how clients can be sure of the competence of contractors or other appointees given that they, the client, are being asked to make a judgement on competence in an area where they themselves are not competent and where there may be little in the nature of formal qualifications.

It is to be expected that architects or engineers acting on behalf of their clients would enquire as to the competence of the project supervisor for construction stage and that contractors would have available such evidence of competence as would reassure a client in this regard insofar as the client or his professional advisor is able to assess such evidence. One of the RIAI standard forms is a questionnaire for contractors which would enable the client to be advised as to the competence of any particular contractor.

A significant risk for clients may arise from a failure to appoint project supervisors through ignorance of their duties or a misinterpretation of what constitutes a 'project'. No guidance is given as to what constitutes an appointment. It would be prudent for clients to write formally to the appointed persons and to obtain an acknowledgement. In summary, the main points for clients to note is that they would make sure they appoint project supervisors where they are required to do so and that they have taken reasonable steps to see they are competent.

According to the regulations, provided they are competent, anyone can be appointed as Project Supervisor for Design Stage or Project Supervisor for Construction Stage. This, however, is not what the Directive says and there must be some doubt about the validity of appointing those who do not comply with the Directive's requirements. These are [Article 2(c)] that the project supervisors must be 'any natural or legal person responsible for the design and/or execution and/or supervision of the execution of a project'. A Court might well hold that anyone not coming within that definition would not be competent. In the case of organisations which provide in-house design services while also acting as the Client, it would be logical for the Client to act as Project Supervisor for the Design Stage but not for the Construction stage. The same person can act as Project Supervisor for both stages and can be the client, a member of the design team, the contractor or some other person. In the normal course of events, the Project Supervisor for Design Stage should be appointed at the commencement of that stage. In the case of the Project Supervisor for Construction Stage, it is necessary to make that appointment before the construction work starts so that the duties which are required to be carried out prior to construction can be completed.

It is expected that generally Architects or Engineers (probably the lead designers on a project) will act as Project Supervisors for Design Stage and that Contractors will act as Project Supervisors at Construction stage on projects where they are engaged. Where there is no designer, as in the case of design/build, it is expected that the contractor will be the Project Supervisor for both design and construction stages. The regulations allow the Project Supervisor to appoint Safety Co-ordinators. These are, in fact, assistants, and no responsibility is removed from the Project Supervisor by their appointment. Architects acting as Project Supervisor Design Stage should point out, where necessary, that variations occurring after construction starts are not the responsibility of the Project Supervisor Design Stage. This was confirmed in a District Court case, which although not a Court of precedent, is worth noting.

It has been pointed out that there are no transitional provisions in the 2001 regulations and that this could, in theory, affect the validity of appointments made under the 1995 regulations in respect of projects which would span both statutory instruments.

It is important, at this stage, that any person or organisation proposing to act as project supervisor for the design stage should inform their insurers. It is not anticipated that any additional premium will result. RIAI Insurance Services advise that the standard forms produced by the RIAI should be used whenever possible. It is interesting to note that there appears to be, so far, no noticeable increase in the number of claims in the UK against architects for either negligence or personal injury even though their regulations are more onerous. It is anticipated however that there will be an increase in the number of defendants and, unfortunately, the doctrine of joint and several responsibility will mean, in some cases, the Architect being pursued for the full amount of the claim even where he is only marginally responsible.

All of this would mean that professional indemnity insurance cover will have to be carefully examined to see if sufficient allowance is now made for awards for personal injuries which will in all likelihood now form part of these claims, remembering that Irish courts have tended to be more generous than their UK or Continental counterparts in awarding damages for personal injuries, and the kind of €500,000 or even €1.5m cover maintained by many public liability policies would need to be mirrored in the Architect's policies. Architects should enquire from their insurers as to the advisability of having a separate personal injuries policy relating only to their work as project supervisors should they decide to do such work. Some architectural practices have decided in principal not to accept such appointments and to advise their clients to appoint specialist firms for safety advice.

This part of the Regulations applies to all projects on which construction commenced on or after 6th March 1996.

5.5 Duties of Project Supervisor for the Design Stage

The main duties of the Project Supervisor for Design stage are to:

1   Take account, during the design of a project and when estimating the time required for the project, of the general principles of prevention as set out in the First Schedule to S.I. 44 of 1993.

2   Take account of any relevant safety file which may have been prepared in respect of the building. A project Supervisor for Design Stage should ask the client if there is a safety file for the building and should examine it for any obvious risks such as the presence of any hazardous materials or buried cables which would affect the proposed works. Such information as may come to light should be made known to relevant designers and be taken into account in the preparation of the design.

3   Take account of any Health and Safety Plan prepared for the project. This requirement may arise in refurbishment work or circumstances where on a long or multi-phase contract, design stage is proceeding after the safety plan has been developed by the Project Supervisor for Construction stage, and its requirements impinge on the design in some respect.

4   Co-ordinate the work of other persons engaged in work related to the design or the project where required. The design of a building or other project may include design input from specialist consultants, contractors or sub-contractors. It is the duty of the Project Supervisor for Design Stage to ensure that such persons are aware of their duties and to seek confirmations that they will comply with them in the course of their design. As these are all specialists, it would not be reasonable to expect the lead designer to be able to judge the work of these specialists, but it would be reasonable in some circumstances to ask for evidence of competence.

5   Provide the Project Supervisor for Construction Stage with any available information which needs to be included in the Safety File. In general, this would include such things as copies of working drawings, specifications, product maintenance leaflets or other information which is available and which would be relevant to the Safety File.

6   For projects which require a Health and Safety Plan, prepare on a preliminary basis, a safety and health plan for the purpose of providing information to the Project Supervisor for Construction Stage which gives:

   a)   A general description of the project;

   b)   Where required, the time-scale within which it is intended to complete the project. The inclusion of this clause arises from a claim by the contractors that clients did not always allow enough time to carry out projects and that this could be the cause of accidents. There is no evidence to suggest that a job built quickly is any more likely to result in accidents than one which is completed at a more leisurely pace. The pressure which may be put on workers is as much a function of the numbers employed, the methods used, the availability of equipment and the co-ordination of activities as the overall time allowed for the works. Notwithstanding this, it is clear that Project Supervisors for Design, if specifying a time for the project, should be satisfied that it is reasonable in the context of site safety;

c) Information on any other contracts or activities which will be taking place on the site at the same time as the contract;

d) Specifies any particular risks (as set out in the Second Schedule) which are expected to arise on the project.

A problem arises as to whether the project is covered by the Regulations. An Architect will not, in many circumstances, be in a position to know whether or not a project will last for more than 30 days or whether it will involve more that 500 man days. As this is one of the two criteria required for the preparation of a safety plan (the other being work with particular risk), there will be uncertainty on this matter until the contractor is appointed and, indeed, as the work proceeds.

However, the Project Supervisor Design Stage should never include any indication of safety measures to be adopted during construction. This is neither within the control nor competence of any architect. Very important in this regard is the matter of civil liability. Any detailed health and safety plan, drawing up at design stage and included in the tender documents would almost certainly embroil the client and the design architect in litigation in the event of any subsequent accident on the site.

5.6   Duties of Project Supervisor for Construction Stage

The main contractor is the person with the competence to undertake these duties and, at the same time, has control of the works, including sub-contractors and self-employed persons. It is anticipated therefore, that the main contractor will, in most circumstances, be the person most appropriate to be appointed by the client as the Project Supervisor for Construction stage. The Contractor always was in absolute charge of the site, and this situation should never have been qualified. Because of this, the provisions of this section are only dealt with in a general way. The view of the RIAI is that Architects are not competent, except where they have received special training or have had practical experience, to carry out these duties. Insurance advisors indicate that if an architect decides to act as the project supervisor for the construction phase, this is a material fact and the insurers must be notified. If the insurers are satisfied that the Architect involved has had adequate training and, in addition, considerable site experience, they would provide cover but an additional premium would be charged. The insurance market view is that something in the region of 20 years acting as a site manager for a major contracting organisation would be the level of experience sought.

It has been suggested that at this stage, when the client is making the appointment of the contractor as the Project Supervisor for the Construction Stage that this should be by way of a collateral agreement to the main building contract. This is to separate the building contract, with its special relationship between Employer, Contractor and Architect from the provisions of the Regulations dealing with the project supervisor construction stage where the Architect is not involved. The main contractor will offer in consideration of accepting his tender to enter into a collateral agreement, with the consent of his insurers, to provide the client with the services of a project supervisor for the Construction Stage and to indemnify the client from the consequences of any failure on his part in carrying out this duty.

The duties of the Project Supervisor for the Construction Stage can be summarised as follows:

- develop a Safety and Health plan for all projects which require a commencement notice or involve a particular risk as defined in the second schedule, before construction commences, and to update and revise this plan as necessary

- submit a commencement notice to the Health and Safety Authority.

The following duties apply where there is more than one contractor on the site:

- prepare the Safety File for the building and pass it on to the client on completion of the works

- co-ordinate the implementation of the general requirements in relation to technical, organisational or programming of the works

- co-ordinate the implementation of requirements to manage the site properly as set out in the First Schedule in S.I. 44 of 1993, and the Third Schedule of these Regulations (S.I. 481 of 2001)

- follow the provisions of the Safety and Health plan

- keep records in relation to safety matters

- co-ordinate measures to permit only authorised persons to enter the site.

5.7 **Duties of Designers**

There will be projects, as defined in the regulations, where the designer (either Architect or Engineer) will not be acting as the Project Supervisor for the Design Stage. It seems to the writer that architects should, if at all possible, avoid any involvement as Project Supervisor Design Stage. There may in addition be projects where there is a design input from specialist sub-contractors and indeed from the main contractor including such items as the design of temporary works.

In the six years that have elapsed since this legislation was introduced there have been, from the practitioners point of view, some disturbing developments. Obviously, the most serious is the possible involvement of the professionals in any criminal prosecutions. As far as the writer is aware, no designer or the Project Supervisor Design Stage has been successfully prosecuted for breaches of the legislation but it could happen. The recent decision by the Health and Safety Authority to carry out inspections of designer's offices is an indication of the way the official mind is heading. It is submitted that the amount of safety that can be designed into a building is limited.

The guide referred to earlier issued by the Association of Consulting Engineers of Ireland entitled 'Designing for Safety in Construction' contains many useful comments on the application of the legislation as far as designers are concerned. It points out that the primary duty of designers is to take account of the general principles of prevention as specified in the first schedule of the principle regulations and that these principles are not necessary relevant to what a designer can do. However, the guide does exhort designers to assess the design as it develops and to reduce any risks that might obviously result from specific design decisions. While pointing out that there is no statutory duty on designers to carry out formal risk assessments, the Guide details a method proposed by the Health and Safety Executive in the United Kingdom, in which risk (R) is defined as a product of probability (P) and severity (S), that is, $R = P \times S$. There are three grades of probability and three grades of severity giving a range of assessments from 1 to 9 on a matrix layout. The Guide, in a paragraph very sensibly entitled 'Realistic Limitations' points out that the opportunity for restricting hazards at a design stage is very limited(par. 5.1).

In such cases the Regulations set out the duties of these designers and they can be summarised as follows:

- to take account of the general principles of prevention as specified in the first schedule of the Principal Regulations (S.I. 44 of 1993) which are all of a general nature

- take account of any safety and health plan or of any safety file prepared for the project

- co-operate with the Project Supervisors for either phase and provide any necessary information to enable them to comply with the Regulations

- take into account the directions received from the Project Supervisors as far as the Design or Construction Stage is concerned, as appropriate

- to co-ordinate arrangements for the FÁS Safe Pass scheme and the FÁS Construction Skills Certificate scheme.

5.8   Liability, Enforcement and Penalties

The consequences of breaching the Act or the Regulations can be either civil or criminal. Section 60 of the Act is worded rather tortuously but, in summary, subsection 2 provides that breaches of the regulations are actionable *per se* in the civil courts. The fear of the architectural and engineering professions with regard to the widening of their liability in carrying out their duties was graphically demonstrated in a scenario suggested by the eminent construction lawyer, Timothy Bouchier-Hayes. Suppose a tenant fits out an office block and an employee of a domestic sub-contractor is injured. Who might be sued? The answer is the landlord, the tenant, the fit-out contractor, the domestic sub-contractor, the architect, the project supervisor for the construction stage fit-out, the project supervisor for the design stage fit out and the project supervisor for the construction stage of the original project. From the plaintiff's point of view it would be best to sue them all under the unjust provisions of our joint and several liability laws.

Enforcement and the criminal aspects of offences against the Act are contained in Parts V and VIII of the 1989 Act. It is anticipated that the enforcing agency will normally be the National Authority for Occupational Safety and Health although the Act does allow other bodies, such as local authorities, to act in this role. Inspectors will be appointed by the enforcing agency, and they have the usual wide powers of entry and inspection that occur in this type of legislation, including being assisted by the Gardaí. Medical inspectors may be appointed as necessary.

The inspector may issue an improvement notice, which will require remedial action and can also issue, in more serious cases, a prohibition notice requiring certain practices to cease. Ultimately, the authority may apply to the High Court for an order restricting or closing a place of work. A fairly harsh provision in the Act (Section 50) assumed that the accused was guilty until proved innocent. According to that Section it was up to the accused to prove that it was not reasonably practicable to do more than what was actually done (see par. 5.2).

Summary offences may be prosecuted by the authority or, if appropriate, by another enforcing agency. The District Court will hear the case and the penalty, on summary conviction, shall be a maximum fine of £1,000.

A conviction on indictment has no limit to a fine and in addition a term of imprisonment may be imposed. If an offence is committed in contravention of a prohibition notice, or if certain information obtained under the Act is disclosed, and for some other offences (see Section 49) then the Court is empowered on conviction on indictment to impose a prison sentence.

5.9 Cases Referred To   *par.*

Boyle v Marathon Petroleum (Ireland) Ltd
    [1999] Supreme Court, 12th January   5.2
Brazier v Skipton Rock Company [1962] 1 WLR 491   5.4
Connolly v Dundalk UDC [1992] Supreme Court, 18th November   5.2
Edwards v National Coal Board [1949] AER 743   5.2
Everitt v Thorsman (Ireland) Ltd [1999] High Court, 23rd June 5.2
Regina v Balfour Beatty [1999] Appeal Cases   5.2

5.10 Health and Safety Checklist

query	*law*	*par.*
1 When did the regulations come into effect?	S.I. 138 of 1995 – Article 1 (revoked by S.I. 481 of 2001)	5.3
2 What are the regulations?	S.I. 481 of 2001	5.3
3 How should I advise my client?		5.4
4 What building projects are covered?	S.I. 481 of 2001 – Article 2	5.3
5 What notices are required?	S.I. 481 of 2001 – Articles 7(2), 8 First Schedule	5.3
6 What are the duties of the project supervisors	S.I. 481 of 2001 – Articles 4, 6	5.5/6

7   What is a Safety Statement?   Safety Health and Welfare   5.3
                                       at Work Act 1989 – section 12

8   What is a Safety Plan?   S.I. 481 of 2001 – Article 4(1)   5.3

9   What is a Safety File?   S.I. 481 of 2001 – Article 6(2)   5.3

10 Are there any fees?   not yet

11 What penalties can be imposed?   Safety Health and Welfare   5.8
                                       at Work Act 1989 – part V

12 Will it affect sales of buildings? S.I. 481 of 2001 – Article 3.5   5.3

Chapter 6 – **General Building Legislation**

In addition to the specific legislation that addresses the construction process, that is the various Planning Acts and Regulations, and the Building Control Act and Regulations, there are a number of statutes which bear on building standards for particular uses and types of buildings and of which the practitioner must be aware. In most cases the requirements of these Acts or instruments would automatically be complied with if the primary building Acts mentioned above are observed, but there are some areas which would escape. There are, of course, many other statutes where buildings, their uses, their value and their ownership are covered but knowledge of the ones dealt with in this chapter should be sufficient for the average practitioner in his day to day work. The Principal Acts and Regulations are:

6.1 Shops (Conditions of Employment) Act 1938

This Act sets out the general working conditions which must be observed, primarily as regards working hours, holidays, wages, etc, but there are a number of sections which deal with the premises itself. They are listed below, and the references in brackets after each item refers to the section in the Building Regulations which deals with that area.

a)   sufficient ventilation (Part F) and temperature; the temperature required in buildings is not dealt with in the Building Regulations

b)   sufficient sanitary conveniences and washing facilities (Part G)

c)   sufficient lighting. There are no lighting standards, either natural or artificial, set out in the Regulations

d)   facilities for taking meals

e)   seats are to be provided for female employees (1 seat per 3 females)

6.2 Local Government (Sanitary Services) Act 1964

This is the Act under which a local authority has very wide-ranging powers to deal with dangerous structures. The vital point of this measure is that 'if any building or part of a building that, in the opinion of the sanitary authority, is or is likely to be dangerous to persons or property' then the authority can invoke the Act. The important phase is 'in the opinion of the sanitary authority'. The Act empowers the authority after giving notice to carry out any works to prevent the building being dangerous, or to order the owner to carry out the works. In both cases the owner must pay for the work. An owner can appeal to the District Court against the authority's decision, but the Courts are always very reluctant to refuse to accept an opinion from a sanitary authority in such a technical area. The Planning and Development Act 2000 requires the authority to consider the protected status of the structure before issuing a notice. Section 59(1) of the 2000 Act allows the authority to issue a notice requiring the owner to carry out certain works to maintain and protect the structure.

The authority can use force to enter a premises where an owner refuses to co-operate, and remove persons and property. It can also seek the assistance of a member of An Garda Síochána in carrying out this work. The Act also contains fairly standard compensation and compulsory acquisition powers.

In the past, owners of properties that were either subject to preservation or protection under local authority development plans have sometimes been accused of deliberately allowing properties to become run down so that the local authority would require their demolition and thereby render the provisions of any development plan irrelevant. It is one of the defects of the planning code that a building can be declared as a listed building without on the one hand providing any encouragement or inducement to an owner to protect it, or on the other hand, without providing the local authority with sufficient powers to compel the owner to protect and maintain the property.

6.3   **Housing Act 1966**

The building world has long been conversant with the Housing Act 1969, which controlled the demolition of habitable dwellings and which has now been repealed. The Housing Act 1966 is a comprehensive measure dealing with matters which need not concern us here except for sections 63-70 which relates to physical standards in housing.

This measure deals with overcrowding. This is judged to have occurred when a) any two persons being over ten years of age and of opposite sexes, not being husband and wife, must sleep in the same room, and b) where 400 cubic feet of air space is not available for each sleeping person.

The housing authority can require particulars from owners and occupiers of the number of occupants of any house, together with details of the number and size of rooms. They can also limit the number of people that may live in any house. If they are of the opinion that the house is unfit for human habitation they may serve a notice to that effect on the owner, requiring certain works to be carried out, or, indeed, the vacation and demolition of the house.

Other sections of the Act allow the authority to make bye-laws for rented houses which would deal with drainage, lighting and ventilation. The Building Regulations would now automatically provide for these standards in new housing, with the possible exception of lighting, but does not, of course deal with such defects in existing buildings.

6.4 Urban Renewal Act 1986 (partially repealed) Dublin Docklands Development Authority Act 1997 Urban Renewal Act 1998

The Urban Renewal Act is the Act that introduced the concept of the designated area. The Act provided that where the Minister is satisfied that there is a real need to promote urban renewal in certain areas, he may designate it so that it will enjoy certain financial advantages relating to taxation and rates. The Act itself prescribed the Custom House Docks area in Dublin to be such an area and set up the Custom House Docks Development Authority to carry out the development. One of the more controversial proposals in the Act was that the Custom House Docks Development Authority would not be required to obtain planning permission for any development it carried out. It would only have to 'consult' with Dublin Corporation. The Urban Renewal (Amendment) Act 1987 extended the Custom House Docks Development area.

In 1997 the Dublin Docklands Development Authority Act was published 'to make provision for the renewal of the Dublin Docklands area'. This Act repealed Part 111 of the 1986 Act dealing with the Custom House Docks Authority and repealed all of the amending Act of 1987. The area initially scheduled was a very large tract of land covering 1,300 acres on both sides of the river from Butt Bridge to the East Link Bridge. The Custom House Dock Development Authority was taken over by the new authority. The position with regard to development remains much the same. The authority is empowered to issue a certificate stating that the proposed works are exempted development as far as the Local Government (Planning and Development) Act 1963 is concerned. A difference between the present position and that which existed under the Custom House Docks Authority is that there is now provision for the attachment of conditions to the certificate. An intriguing query to which no answer has been obtained is whether or not the refusal of a certificate by the authority is a statement that the proposed works are not exempted development and if this would mean that the Principal Act would then apply

The Urban Renewal Act provided that the Minister could, by regulation, designate any area which, in his opinion, would benefit from such designation and to date a very considerable number of such orders have been made. Some concern had been expressed since the coming into operation of the Act in 1986 both with regard to the method of selection of areas for designation and also to the quality of the developments themselves. It was felt that both the social results and the architectural quality of many schemes left a lot to be desired. To remedy this the Department of the Environment and Local Government published in November 1997 A GUIDE TO URBAN RENEWAL. The main feature of this document was the introduction of the Integrated Area Plan. This concept of the integrated area plan was incorporated into law in the Urban Renewal Act 1998. The Planning and Development Act 2000 requires that a planning authority 'must take into account' integrated area plans when a development plan is being prepared. These will be prepared by local authorities and will identify areas that will benefit from desig-nation although the final decisions as regards designation will remain in the hands of both the Minister for the Environment and Local Government and the Minister for Finance.

There are, in addition, a considerable number of Statutory Instruments dealing with the financial implications and qualifying dates of the Urban Renewal Act and some of these have been issued under differing pieces of legislation such as the various Finance Acts. The subjects include rates remissions, general financial provisions and the establishment of the Custom House Dock Development Authority. Typical ones would be S.I. 343 of 1992 dealing with rates remissions and S.I. 441 of 1992 transferring property from Dublin Corporation to the Custom House Docks Development Authority. The following list deals only with those orders which designate certain areas:

S.I. 206 of 1987	This order extended the Custom House Dock area in Dublin which has originally been scheduled in the Urban Renewal Act. The area was again extended by S.I. 180 of 1994.
S.I. 105 of 1988	This provides for a further extension of the Custom House Dock area.
S.I. 238 of 1986	Dublin quays and north inner city, Cork, Limerick and Galway
S.I. 92 of 1988	Arklow, Castlebar, Dublin, Dundalk, Kilkenny, Letterkenny, Limerick, Tralee, Tullamore, Sligo and Waterford
S.I. 287 of 1988	Tallaght
S.I. 204 of 1990	Central Dublin, Cork, Galway, Limerick and Waterford
S.I. 289 of 1990	Ballina, Bray, Carlow, Clonmel, Drogheda, Ennis, Longford and Portlaoise
S.I. 156 of 1991	Temple Bar, Dublin
S.I. 342 of 1992	Tallaght
S.I. 228 of 1993	Ballymun
S.I. 361 of 1994	Tralee
S.I. 362 of 1994	Cork
S.I. 363 of 1994	Wexford

S.I. 364 of 1994	Limerick
S.I. 365 of 1994	Sligo
S.I. 367 of 1994	Wicklow
S.I. 368 of 1994	Roscommon
S.I. 369 of 1994	Galway
S.I. 370 of 1994	Waterford
S.I. 371 of 1994	Tullamore
S.I. 372 of 1994	Athlone
S.I. 373 of 1994	Ballinasloe
S.I. 374 of 1994	Bray
S.I. 375 of 1994	Clonmel
S.I. 376 of 1994	Dundalk
S.I. 377 of 1994	Enniscorthy
S.I. 378 of 1994	Dungarvan
S.I. 379 of 1994	Kilkenny
S.I. 380 of 1994	Killarney
S.I. 381 of 1994	Letterkenny
S.I. 382 of 1994	Longford
S.I. 383 of 1994	Mallow
S.I. 384 of 1994	Monaghan
S.I. 385 of 1994	Navan
S.I. 386 of 1994	Nenagh
S.I. 387 of 1994	Mullingar
S.I. 388 of 1994	Newbridge
S.I. 389 of 1994	Portlaoise
S.I. 390 of 1994	Carlow
S.I. 407 of 1994	Dublin
S.I. 422 of 1994	Athlone
S.I. 247 of 1995	Bray, Clonmel, Cork, Dublin, Sligo, Tralee and Waterford
S.I. 248 of 1995	Cobh
S.I. 366 of 1995	Temple Bar, Dublin

Three statutory instruments were issued dealing with the alteration of previously designated areas. These are S.I. 70 of 1997 (Ballinasloe); S.I. 336 of 1997 (Iveagh Markets area of Dublin); and S.I. 337 of 1997 (Dungarvan).

6.5 Derelict Sites Act 1990

This Act, which revokes the Derelict Sites Act 1961, is an attempt to deal with a problem which had affected urban areas for many years, and where property owners were either unable or unwilling to develop sites which had lain vacant for some time.

A derelict site is defined as any land 'which detracts, or is likely to detract, to a material degree from the amenity, character or appearance in the neighbourhood of the land in question because of:

a)   The existence on the land in question of structures which are in a ruinous, derelict or dangerous condition, or

b)   The neglected, unsightly or objectionable condition of the land or any structure on the land in question, or

c)   The presence, deposit or collection on the land in question of any litter, rubbish, debris or waste, except where the presence, deposit or collection of such litter, rubbish, debris or waste results from the exercise of a right conferred by statute or common law.'

The Act requires a local authority to keep a register of all sites which they consider to be derelict, but they are required to give notice and consider the owner's representations before registering the site. The Act empowers the local authority to give notice and specify measures to be taken to prevent sites from becoming derelict. If the owner does not conform, the authority can carry out the works and charge the owner with the cost. The carrying out of any such works is exempted development under the Planning Acts. The local authority, in the case of a protected structure, must have regard to that fact in drawing up any notices.

The local authority can, in addition, compulsorily acquire derelict sites, and the Act contains the usual provisions for notice, objection, ministerial consent and compensation. The Act also contains the standard sections dealing with offences, inspection, etc.

A further provision empowers the local authority to levy an annual charge on derelict sites. This levy can be up to 3% of the market value of the site for the first year, and up to 10% of the market value for subsequent years. The levy, and the areas that it relates to, are described in sections 21 and 23 of the Act.

This Act is obviously of particular concern to landowners who are not in a position to develop sites which they may own, and where they are awaiting an upturn in market conditions. Anyone advising such owners should bring this Act to their attention.

A number of Statutory Instruments have been issued in respect of the Derelict Sites Act and they are as follows:

S.I. 192 of 1990 (Derelict Sites Regulations) – This instrument amends the provisions in the Act relating to the register of derelict sites, deals with applications to the Minister to consent to the compulsory purchase of such sites, and sets out the form of notices required under the Act.

S.I. 286 of 1991 Derelict Sites (Commencement of Derelict Sites Levy) – This states that the levy described in the Act is to commence in the year 1992.

S.I. 362 of 1991 (Urban Areas) – Under the Act at Section 21 the Minister may by regulation prescribe any area to be urban land (Section 23). This instrument lists such areas in Limerick, Kerry, Kilkenny and South Tipperary.

S.I. 364 of 1992 (Urban Areas) – This lists urban areas for Clare, Dublin, North Tipperary and West Meath

S.I. 408 of 1992 (Urban Areas) – This lists urban areas for Carlow, Cork, Kilkenny, Laois, Mayo, Offaly and Waterford.

S.I. 392 of 1993 (Urban Areas) – This lists urban areas of Cavan and Louth.

S.I. 440 OF 2000 (Urban Areas) – The extends the urban areas provisions to parts of Tipperary North Riding, Louth, Meath, Clare and Dun Laoghaire / Rathdown.

S.I. 445 of 2000 (Derelict Sites) Regulations – Previous powers vested in the Minister are transferred to An Bord Pleanála.

S.I. 578 of 2001 – Areas of Clare and Laois are listed.

6.6   Local Government (Multi-Storey Buildings) Act 1988

In 1987 a gas explosion damaged an apartment building in Dublin, and a progressive collapse of the structure occurred. It was much the same in principle, but thankfully much smaller in scale, than the famous Ronan Point collapse in London of 1968. Following this 1987 incident, the Multi-Storey Buildings Act was introduced.

This Act required every local authority to prepare a register of multi-storey buildings. The Act defined a multi-storey building as one of 5 or more storeys, a basement being regarded as a storey. The owner of every building on the register was required to produce a certificate, signed by a competent person, that their building was built in accordance with various specified standards or codes, and further, that the occupiers were reasonably protected from risk. There was considerable argument between the local authorities and the engineering institutions before agreement was reached on the form and content of the certificates required.

Section 4 of this Act is affected by the Building Control Act, 1990. Section 23 of the 1990 Act says that Section 4 of the Multi-Storey Buildings Act will not apply to buildings which are in effect, covered by the Building Regulations, but specifies that multi-storey buildings which are covered by the transitional bye-law provisions of the 1990 Act are affected. Section 4 of the 1988 Act required that multi-storey buildings which were not completed before the coming into effect of that Act must obtain an appropriate certificate before being occupied.

6.7   Miscellaneous

a) Road Closures

It sometimes happens, particularly in large urban projects, that either the developer or the local authority or both would wish to close a road that no longer serves or would serve, after the completion of the development, any useful purpose, or any road which would seriously impede an otherwise desirable development. In these cases the local authority may apply to the Minister to make an order declaring the road closed. This power of the Minister does not apply to main roads, but since the Minister has the power to decide by order what is, or is not, a main road, this is not normally a problem.

The procedure would be that the local authority would publish a newspaper notice describing the road to be closed. Not less than one month after this notice appears the local authority may apply to the Minister to make an order closing the road. The Minister must hold a local public enquiry within one month of the advertisement appearing to hear any representations or objections. When the order is made the local authority is not empowered to spend any further money on the road.

While the closure of any road as described above (and the process is regulated by the Roads Act 1993 – Section 12) does not affect its status as a right of way, the local authority acting as the planning authority can make an order which requires to be approved by the Minister under Section 73 of the Roads Act 1993 which will extinguish the right of way. Again, a public enquiry must be held before the order is made. The whole process may seem cumbersome but rights of way have always been very jealously guarded and the various steps described above ensure that the public good is carefully watched.

Where it is desired to close a road temporarily for construction purposes, the local authority, acting as the roads authority is empowered to do this under

Article 12 of S.I. 119 of 1994 (Roads Regulations) as provided for in Section 75 of the Roads Act 1993.

b) Copyright

Enquiries are often made with regard to the position of an architect's design as far as copyright is concerned. In PATENTS, TRADE MARKS, COPYRIGHT AND INDUSTRIAL DESIGN by White and Jacob, published by Sweet & Maxwell, the purpose of copyright is well described: 'The primary function of copyright law is to protect from annexation by other people the fruits of a man's work, labour, skill or taste.'

Copyright was originally controlled by the Copyright Act 1963. This, the Copyright (Amendment) Act 1987 and the Intellectual Property (Miscellaneous Provisions) Act 1998 were all repealed by the Copyright and Related Rights Acts 2000. This new Act might in turn have to be amended by an EU Directive on Copyright which is imminent but for the moment, the new act is the current law. The sections dealing with architectural design in the new Act are virtually identical with the provisions of the 1963 Act.

An architect's copyright of his design lasts for the architect's lifetime and for a period of seventy years after his death (the term of years was extended by S.I. 158 of 1995 from the original fifty year period as a result of a European Union Directive). The first owner of the copyright is the author who, in the case of a building is the architect, or in the case of an employee, the architect's employer. This ownership can be assigned by agreement. It is not enough for the architect to prove that he has designed the building in question in order for him to be protected by copyright. The architect must be able to prove that his particular design is unusual or original to such an extent that it is unlikely that any other architect would have come to the same design solution. This is difficult to establish in practice. Many designs produced by architects are generic. This can apply to all classes of buildings but most of the disputes that arise in this particular field deal with houses. If an architect can show that the design derived from a well known example of the house type, then similarity to other designs also so derived would not constitute infringement of copyright.

The provision in the Planning and Development Act 2000 that members of the public can buy the architect's drawings which were submitted with the planning application obviously raises a copyright problem. This is dealt with briefly in par. 2.4.3. The copying of the drawings does not breach the copyright, but using the drawings for building purposes does. At the moment, the RIAI is endeavouring to persuade the Department of the Environment and

Local Government to introduce further regulations requiring anyone taking copies of drawings to produce proof of identity, and also to provide that a record of any such transaction is kept on the public file. An interesting aspect of the new Act is the broadening of moral rights for copyright owners. These new rights include a right of the owner of a copyright to object to derogatory treatment of a work. The concept of one architect taking proceedings against another architect for wrongly altering or extending an original work has its amusing side.

A question often asked is whether a person is entitled to build from a set of drawings which were prepared only for planning purposes without the payment of a further fee to the architect. The answer is yes. This point was specifically decided in *Blair v Osborne and Tomkins* [1970] 10 BLR 96 where an architect who had obtained planning permission and had been paid, tried unsuccessfully to obtain damages for infringement of copyright. Having paid for the design stage the client would be entitled to have the working drawings prepared by another architect and no further duty or responsibility would devolve onto the original architect for that portion of the work. This was confirmed in an Irish case, *Burke v Earlsfort Centre Ltd* [1981] High Court, 24th February, which held, generally, once the appropriate fee had been paid that copyright had passed to the client. However, if the fee for the original sketch plan was very small, it has been held that there is no right or licence implied for the client to proceed to build without payment of a further fee: *Stovin-Bradford v Volpoint Properties* [1971] 10 BLR 105. A largely similar case, *Hunter v Fitzroy Robinson and Others* [1977] 10 BLR 81, held that where the architect has been paid a substantial fee there was an implied licence for purchasers of the drawings to proceed without payment any further fee. The original architect would, however, be liable for any damages that might result from an infringement of the planning code resulting from his drawings in the unlikely event of a planning authority not adverting to the infringement at the application stage. A planning authority is not empowered to overrule its own development plan.

A point to be watched in this area is the possible use of drawings which were originally prepared for planning application purposes being used for fire safety certificate applications without the original architect being aware of this. All drawings for planning application purposes should state clearly that the drawings were prepared for that purpose and for that purpose alone.

The client would not be entitled to build more than once from the same design without payment of an additional fee unless this was agreed at the appointment stage. This point could be important in house design particularly but could also arise in the case of office parks, industrial estates or any other project where repetition is possible.

If copyright can be established the only remedy available to the architect after construction has commenced is damages. An injunction to prevent construction starting could be sought if the architect was aware that his design was being copied. This area is covered by the Copyright and Related Rights Act 2000. The architect's claim for damages would relate to the size of his design fee, and it is somewhat disturbing for architects to note that in this regard White and Jacob, referred to above, says 'architects work for modest scale fees'.

c) Easements

Architects, and other practitioners, will from time to time have to deal with restrictions or rights affecting property which are called easements. The most common are rights of way, right to water, right to support and right of light. Easements were defined in the Prescription Act (Ireland) 1859 and this has been summarised as being 'a right or privilege enjoyed by an owner of land in or over land which belongs to another owner, under which the latter is obliged to submit to a specified use of his land in a particular way.'

i)   Rights of way are not normally of much concern to the practitioner but the basic position is useful to know. A right of way is either private or public. A private right of way normally arises by way of continuous use for twenty years. A public right of way is a highway. If a local authority wishes to incorporate a public right of way in its development plan it must give notice of this intention to the owner, who has a right of appeal to the Circuit Court. This is provided for in section 14 of the Planning and Development Act 2000. Sections 206, 207 and 208 of the 2000 Act deal with the creation of public rights of way, either by agreement or compulsorily, and also with the maintenance of these rights of way.

ii) The easement of a right to support is often encountered in urban developments and is, quite simply, the right not to have support removed by a neighbour. This is commented on in par 6.7(h).

iii) The easement most often encountered by architects and others is the right to light, and this is a difficult and contentious subject. There is a Rights of Light Act (1959) in Britain, but in this jurisdiction the criteria have been laid down by case law. A right of light is defined in RIGHTS OF LIGHT – THE MODERN LAW, by Bickford-Smith and Francis (published by Jordans, 2000) as: 'A right of light is one which carries with it the entitlement to receive natural illumination from the sky through defined apertures in a building to enable use of the interior areas receiving light through such apertures for ordinary purposes for which the building is or may normally be expected to be put.'

There is a common misconception that the amount of light in question must not be diminished but this is not so. There must be a substantial deprivation of light so as to prevent the carrying out of the use of the premises which previously existed. In the case of a house this must be so as to render the house 'uncomfortable'. The nature of a business being carried out is affected by the sensitivity of the reduction.

The Bickford Smith book, referred to above, says: 'The test, accordingly, as to whether an actionable nuisance by interference with light has been caused, is not by reference to the amount of light originally received through the aperture before the obstruction complained of, but whether the amount of light received after the obstruction is in place will enable the building (or that portion of it which receives light through the aperture) to continue to be enjoyed for ordinary purposes.' This is expanded later on in the book: 'The extent of light acquired may depend on the building. In *Allen v Greenwood* [1979] 2 AER 819, it was held that in the case of a right to light acquired by prescription, the extent of light acquired under Section 3 of the Prescription Act 1832 was to be measured according to the nature of the building and the purposes for which it was normally used. In that case, the building was a greenhouse, and it was held that the extent of light acquired by prescription was the right to that degree of light and the benefits of light including the rays of the sun required to grow plants in the greenhouse, and not just the amount of light required for illumination.'

The case of *Colls v Home and Colonial Stores* [1904] AC 179 is still regarded as a bench mark: 'generally speaking an owner of ancient lights is entitled to sufficient light according to the ordinary notions of mankind for the comfortable use and enjoyment of his house as a dwelling house, if it is a dwelling house, or for the beneficial use and occupation of the house if it is a warehouse, a shop or other place of business.'

There is a common assumption that the 45° rule still applies. This relied on the old concept that if a building did not obtrude on a line drawn at 45° from the lowest window cill then no infringement had occurred. As far back as 1935 this rule was held to be no longer valid. (*Fishenden v Higgs and Hill* [1935] LT 153 128).

In recent years, however, the concept of the 'sky-factor' has been introduced and has prevailed in a number of cases although no reported cases seemed to be available. This idea, which is described in detail in British Standard 8206; Part 2; 1992, is an attempt to define by mathematical calculation the before and after effects of a proposed construction. There is further guidance available in the Building Research Establishment Digests 309 and 310. The book referred to above, RIGHTS OF LIGHT – THE MODERN LAW, gives a full account of how to measure and value any loss of light.

The best advice in the case of any possible difficulty concerning an easement is to talk to the adjoining owner or his advisors as the earliest opportunity if there is any reason to believe that an infringement of the easement might occur.

d) Barbed Wire Act 1893

This curious piece of legislation was brought to my attention by a colleague practising in Co Kildare and is introduced here to illustrate the never-ending corpus of law that the practitioner can be snagged on. As a result of a planning application for some stables, a request for additional information was received from the planning authority pointing out that some barbed wire in the vicinity of the stables was to be removed immediately. Leaving aside the fact that such a notice was invalid in that it was issued under the Planning Acts, the Barbed Wire Act requires that it be removed within one month and not immediately. The primary provision of the Act is that any barbed wire adjoining a highway must be removed if it is causing a nuisance.

e) Organisation of Working Time Act 1997

This particular Act, is based on the EU Directive on the Organisation of Working Time (93/104/EC). It is going to cause problems in sectors which are affected by booms and slumps and in sectors which are affected by the availability of daylight. The construction sector is affected by both of these factors.

In brief the Act proposes to restrict the normal working week to 48 hours with provision to allow this period to be averaged over four months. Although the Directive allows this to be averaged over twelve months in certain circumstances, all representations to the Department of Enterprise and Employment to allow the construction sector to avail of this concession have been rebuffed.

Other provisions in the bill provide for a holiday entitlement of twenty days, a minimum rest period of eleven hours in any twenty four hour period, a fifteen minute rest break when four and a half hours have been worked, a minimum uninterrupted twenty four hour rest period per week, and a maximum of eight hours night work in any twenty four hour period. Provision is also made for holidays etc.

f) Freedom of Information Act 1997

This Act was published in August 1997. To quote the Act itself, it is 'An Act to enable members of the public access, to the greatest possible extent consistent with the public interest and the right to privacy, to information in the possession of public bodies...' The Act comes into effect generally on the 21st April 1998 and as far as local authorities and health boards are concerned on the 1st October 1998. The Act mirrors, in many ways, the provisions in the freedom of information on the environment requirements set out in par. 3.5., but it is a separate piece of legislation affecting information held by public bodies.

The basic right of access is contained in Section 6(1) of the Act: 'Subject to the provisions of this Act, every person has a right to and shall, on request therefore, be offered access to any record held by a public body and the right so conferred is referred to in this Act as the right of access.' Public bodies are defined in the First Schedule of the Act and include all Government departments, State or semi-State bodies, the Garda Síochána, local authorities and health boards. Regulations are published from time to time extending the scope of the Act to other public bodies and the list is now very extensive.

The procedure is that a request is made to the head of the public body in writing and the request is to be acknowledged within two weeks. The head in question must answer the request within four weeks and may grant or refuse the request or grant it in part. The head may extend the period allowed by a further four weeks if the information requested is considered to relate to a large number of records. There are powers of review by the body itself, and the right of what is, in effect, an appeal to the Information Commissioner established under the Act. There is, ultimately, the right of appeal to the High Court. Practitioners should note that when they are retained as consultants by public bodies their own files become part of those that are open to public examination.

There is a long section dealing with fees, which are required to be charged by the body in question. The fee must relate to the cost of the search and the cost of copying any records. There are provisions for reducing or waiving the fee if the information would relate to a matter of national importance, and for the paying of a deposit where the fee is estimated to be more than €40

However, the most interesting section of any such Act is the exclusions. The first are personnel records relating to individuals who are members of the staff of public bodies, where the records were created more than three years before the commencement of the Act and where the record is not capable of being used against the interests of the person in question. The head of a body may refuse to provide records on substantial administrative grounds. The main exemption, however, is records relating to government business and decisions, and to records leading to decisions of public bodies. Restrictions also apply to records dealing with Parliamentary and Court matters, where law enforcement or public safety are concerned, or where security, defence or international relations are concerned. Finally, records dealing with information received in confidence, commercially sensitive information or personal information may also be withheld. In all of these cases the decision is initially taken by the head of the body and is, as stated above, subject to appeal.

A section of the Act (32) provides that the head of a body may refuse to supply records if the disclosure is prohibited by any other enactment. But there is a very long list of exceptions to that prohibition and the ones of interest to the building practitioner would be Section 28 of the Local Government (Planning and Development) Act 1963 dealing with information obtainable from An Bord Pleanála, Section 45 of the Safety, Health and Welfare at Work Act 1989 dealing with restrictions on disclosure and Section 39 of the Environmental Protection Agency Act 1992 again dealing with restrictions relating to the Director or staff of the environmental protection agency.

A very useful provision in the Act is the requirement (Section 15) for every public body to issue a reference book containing a general description of the body, its functions, operations and staff, together with the arrangements made by that body to provide access to its records.

g) Prompt Payment of Accounts Act 1997
The European Communities (Late Payment in Commercial Transactions) Regulations – S1 388 of 2002

It is to be hoped that this Act, which came into force on 2nd January 1998, and the Regulations, which came into force on the 7th August 2002, will be of benefit to all of those who have suffered at the hands of certain government departments, state and semi-state bodies and local authorities over the years. The legislation provides that all public bodies must pay either on the date agreed in any contract or within 30 days after the receipt of the invoice or of the goods, which ever is the latest. Failure to do this will result in interest being due at a rate of 7% over the rate applied by the European Central Bank to its most recent refinancing operation before 1st January and 1st July in any year. The interest penalty cannot be waived.

The world being what it is, there will still be public bodies who will attempt to continue their regrettable attitude to professional fees in particular. To try to limit such activities, the legislation now incorporates provisions whereby a representative body, such as the Construction Industry Federation, or a small or medium-sized firm, as defined in the Commission Recommendation 96/280/EC, can either apply to the Circuit Court for an order prohibiting 'grossly unfair or unenforceable terms', or may apply for the appointment of an arbitrator.

While at the moment the legislation only applies to the public sector, it is understood that a long-term proposal would be to extend the legislation to the private sector.

h) Party Walls and the Dublin Corporation Act 1890

Party walls can be a difficult area and the first thing to establish is whether any wall which is in potential dispute is a party wall. It is defined in PARTY WALLS by Bickford Smith and Sydenham (published by Jordans, 1997) as either (a) an external wall of a single building which sits astride a boundary. Footings projecting into a neighbouring property does not make it a party wall, or (b) walls attached to buildings on both sides, i.e. terraced houses. These walls do not have to be astride a boundary. What matters is that they separate buildings belonging to different owners.

It is difficult to set out precise guidelines as most of the reference books and precedents refer to the London legislation (The London Building Acts (Amendment) Act 1939). This was repealed in the UK by the Party Wall etc, Act 1996 but, naturally, nearly all the case law refers to the London Acts.

There are three general principles which practitioners should bear in mind when dealing with party walls. The first is that any work to a party wall should be agreed with the adjoining owner. If agreement cannot be reached it is suggested that the provisions of Section 2 of the 1996 UK Act dealing with owners' rights would probably be accepted in this jurisdiction as being reasonable. Secondly, a party wall after a period of twenty years, gives a right of support. Thirdly, there is a right of protection from the weather. Any wall which has given support or shelter for more than twenty years should be regarded as having conferred rights on adjoining owners although the famous Lord Denning in *Phipps v Pears* [1964] 2 AER 35, said that 'every man is entitled to pull down his own house if he likes ... there was no easement known to law as an easement to be protected from the weather.' The Courts in this jurisdiction do not agree. In *Todd v Cinelli and Others* [1999] High Court, 12th April, The Court held that demolition of one half of a semi-detached pair of houses did indeed infringe an easement and that exposure to weather would eventually lead to weakening of the easement of support.

While this case did not deal with a party wall dispute the same principle would apply.

It has often been remarked that while London had detailed and well known party wall legislation there did not seem to be any corresponding provisions in this jurisdiction but this is not so as the Dublin Corporation Act 1890 deals in considerable length with party walls. This Act, it must be emphasised, would apply only in the areas which were part of the Dublin Corporation area of 1890, and would not apply, for instance, to the former areas of Rathmines UDC, Pembroke UDC etc.

Sections 11 to 28 inclusive set out the various provisions with Section 12 in particular dealing with the rights of building owners in relation to party struc-tures. The basic right is one to repair and make good including pulling down and rebuilding any defective party structure. A specific provision is that a building owner has the right to pull down and rebuild any party structure that is not in conformity with the Bye-laws which were in existence at the time.

There are rights of adjoining owners which are set out and these would main-ly have to do with the receiving of notice and the paying of costs in propor-tion to the work being done. There is a form of dispute resolution whereby the owners on either side of the party structure would appoint an agreed architect or, failing that, appoint an architect for each party, the two appoint-ed architects then appointing a third.

Those portions of the Act which are still in force are set out in full THE LAW OF LOCAL GOVERNMENT IN THE REPUBLIC OF IRELAND by Judge Ronan Keane, published by the Law Society.

6.8   Cases Referred To   *par.*

Blair v Osborne and Tomkins [1970] 10 BLR 96	6.7(b)
Burke v Earlsfort Centre [1981] High Court, 24th February	6.7(b)
Colls v Home and Colonial Stores [1904] AC 179	6.7(c)
Fishenden v Higgs and Hill [1935] LT 153 128	6.7(c)
Hunter v Fitzroy Robinson and Others [1977] 10 BLR 21	6.7(b)
Phipps v Pears [1964] 2 AER 35	6.7(h)
Stovin-Bradford v Volpoint Properties [1971] 10 BLR 105	6.7(b)
Todd v Cinelli and Others [1999] High Court, 12th April	6.7(h)

Chapter 7 – **The Building Contract**

7.1 The RIAI Forms

The standard forms of contract, which are published by the RIAI, are four in number. The basic, and original, form is described as the RIAI form. It is issued by the Royal Institute of the Architects of Ireland in agreement with the Construction Industry Federation and the Society of Chartered Surveyors. It is suitable for all the range of building contracts, but is now primarily used for substantial contracts in the private sector. The latest edition was published in 2002. The second form is described as the GDLA form. These initials stand for Government Departments and Local Authorities. This form is based on the RIAI form and is similar in most respects. It is intended for use by Government Departments, Local Authorities, and by other bodies 'the placing of whose contracts is subject to approval by a Government Department or Local Authority when the work is to be paid for wholly or partly from Exchequer Funds' – GDLA form. The GDLA form is published by the RIAI, after consultation with the Construction Industry Federation and the Royal Institution of Chartered Surveyors, but only after approval by the Department of Finance. The first edition, which is still current, though with some amendments, was published on 1st March 1982. (at that date the name of the Royal Institution of Chartered Surveyors had not been changed to the Society of Chartered Surveyors).

Both the RIAI and GDLA forms are available in two different coloured versions, depending on whether or not a Bill of Quantities is one of the contract documents. The third form is that known as SF 88, which are the initials referring to Shorter Form, and which is intended for small or simple contracts. The first edition was published on 1st November 1988, and was updated in 1999.

The RIAI also published in early 1997 a 'plain language' contract which contains all the provisions of the older standard form but written in simpler language and with a more logical sequence of clauses.

The Forum for the Construction Industry, in its report BUILDING OUR FUTURE TOGETHER, recommended that national forms of contract should be drafted for main contracts, nominated sub-contracts and domestic sub-contracts for building, housing, and civil engineering works. Standard wordings and forms are also to be developed for collateral agreements, bonds and insurances. By mid 2002 the civil engineering contract had been completed and the building contract was well under way.

7.2 Standard Forms

The history of the standard form in Ireland is obscure. There is a reference in

1857 to the use of a standard form in relation to the 'Phibsboro Church Case'. At around the same time, a standard form was being developed in Britain, probably as a result of the rebuilding contract involving the Houses of Parliament. The original contract for that project was for £700,000 and was to take six years. In the event, the works cost £2,000,000 and took thirteen years to build. The ensuing disagreements seemed to focus the minds of those concerned in the construction field, and by 1870 the Builders Society and the RIBA had produced a standard form for use in the London area. In Ireland, by 1899, the RIAI had come to a decision to produce a standard form, but differences with the Dublin Master Builders Association led to many delays, and it was not until 1910 that the first RIAI standard form was published, in agreement with the Master Builders. Meanwhile, in Britain, a revision of the standard form in 1909 saw the introduction of the nominated sub-contractor, while by 1922 the Quantity Surveyors Association had produced the first Standard Method of Measurement. The Joint Contracts Tribunal was established in the 1930s and has been subsequently responsible for the revisions in 1939, 1952, 1963, and culminating in the present 1980 edition. Later versions of the JCT contract deal with contractors' design (1981) and management contracting (1987).

The development in Ireland was much the same. The RIAI first edition of 1910 seems to have been in general use up to around 1939, and at that time a revised draft of a new edition was circulated. An extremely long and unseemly row then broke out between the Federation of Building Contractors and Allied Employers of Ireland (now the Construction Industry Federation) and the RIAI. Without going into the details of the dispute it can be said that it derived from the mutual suspicion of the two bodies, the architects seeing the contractors as being only concerned with obtaining more favourable terms to themselves, and the contractors seeing the architects as being little more than the lapdogs of the employers. It was not until 1950 that matters were finally resolved, when a new agreed edition of the RIAI form was published. At the same time, to smooth the path to further revisions, a Liaison Committee was set up to interpret and review the standard form. This committee is representative of the RIAI, the CIF, the Society of Chartered Surveyors and the Association of Consulting Engineers of Ireland. Some uncertainty has been caused by the direct intervention of the Forum into the drafting process, and also by decisions of the Government Contracts Committee concerning changes in the GDLA form. No doubt the position will be regularised in time.

The advantage of using a standard form is that the provisions contained in it should be well understood and case law should have by now interpreted nearly all the difficult areas. While this is largely true, cases sometimes come before the Courts as to the meaning of various clauses. A problem with standard forms is that those awarded the task of revising them very often use previous versions as drafts and this can result in some rather confused words: 'There is no wholly satisfactory interpretation or explanation of the third Part of the clause, and one must choose between two almost equally unsatisfactory conclusions. In a case like this, where a clause in common use has simply been copied, one cannot try to find what the parties intended. They almost certainly never thought about things happening as they did.' *Compania Naviera Aeolus v Union of India* [1962]3 AER 670. However, the temptation to change a standard form often results in even greater confusion, as the changing of one clause can affect others in the same contract form, or even in subsidiary sub-contract forms, and this is frequently overlooked by those making the changes. The results of such changes can be seen in the cases of *H. A. O'Neil v John Sisk and Son* [1984] Supreme Court, 28th July and that of *Irishenco v Dublin County Council* [1984] High Court, 21st March 1963. This latter case is particularly interesting as far as standard forms are concerned, because the Court held that it was entitled to look at a clause that had been struck out, as well as looking at the one that replaced it, when trying to interpret the intentions of the parties.

The development of the standard form has led to the importation of the doctrine of '*contra preferentem*' into the construction industry. This doctrine provides that the least favourable interpretation of a document should be adopted against the person who has published or provided the document, on the grounds that he had the benefit of framing the document, as opposed to the other party who had to take it or leave it – *a prendre ou a laisser.* This factor is reflected in the differences between the RIAI and the GDLA standard forms. The GDLA form,deriving as it does from the Government, tends to favour the employer in all those cases where the two forms differ. The use of a standard form will bind the parties to that contract very precisely and the Courts will not look for implied terms or unusual meanings: 'The basic principle is that the Court does not make a contract for the parties. The Court will not even improve the contract which the parties have made for themselves however desirable the improvement might be. The Courts function is to interpret and apply the Contract which the parties have made for themselves. If the express terms are perfectly clear and free from ambiguity there is no choice to be made between different possible meanings; the clear terms must be applied even if the Court thinks that some other terms would have been more suitable. An unexpressed term can be implied if and only if the Court finds that the parties must have intended that term to form part of their contract; it is not enough for the Court to find that such a term would have been adopted by the parties as reasonable men if it has been suggested to them, it must have been a term that went without saying, a term necessary to give business efficacy to the contract, a term which, though tacit, formed part of the contract which the parties made for themselves.' *Trollope and Colls Ltd v North West Metropolitan Regional Hospital Board* [1973] 9 BLR 60.

7.3   The Parties (and others) to the Contract

There are five persons involved in the contract, described here in alphabetical order. Firstly, The architect, though not a party to the contract, has very wide powers under it and in effect controls it. He would normally be a member of the Royal Institute of the Architects of Ireland, though Ireland unlike many other countries, does not legally require a practising architect to be properly qualified. However, merely by describing himself as an architect, a person holds out that he has the appropriate skills and can be sued for negligence if he does not provide the appropriate standard of skill, whether he is qualified or not. An architect has been defined by Myles na gCopaleen as 'simply a chap who puts up artificial shelters'.

The next person is the contractor. He would normally be a member of the Construction Industry Federation, but not necessarily so for the carrying on of his business. He is a party to the contract. His duties are well described in Clause 1 of the SF 88 form: 'The contractor shall carry out and complete the works in a good and workmanlike manner.' He is closely associated with the fourth person, the sub-contractor. Thirdly we have the employer, who is the other party to the contract. The main requirement of the employer is that he would have enough money to pay all concerned in the process. 'The employer shall pay or allow to the contractor such sums of money as shall from time to time become due...' (SF 88 – Clause 2). Fourthly we have the nominated sub-contractor (and the nominated supplier) who has a contract with the contractor which is separate from the main contract and who normally would not have a contract with the employer, unless what is called a collateral warranty is signed. The subject of collateral warranties is dealt with in Chapter 10. Lastly we have the quantity surveyor who, like the architect, is named in the RIAI and GDLA forms but who again like the architect is not a party to the contract. He would normally be a member of the Society of Chartered Surveyors. His responsibility is to assist the architect in performing his duties under the contract in the area of cost and value.

7.4   Formation of the Contract

There have been many definitions of a legal contract, and possibly an equal number of criticisms of these definitions. A contract is primarily an agreement, and while all contracts are agreements, not all agreements are contracts. An agreement to meet someone is not a contract. The three basic requirements of all contracts are well known, those of offer, acceptance and consideration. The contractor 'offers' by way of tender to construct the building in question for a certain sum of money – the 'consideration'. The employer 'accepts' the offer, usually by way of letter and ultimately by signing the Articles of Agreement. There are few difficulties in the construction field with these three requirements, but some points should be noted.

The acceptance of the offer cannot qualify the original subject of the contract, that is, the employer cannot, in his acceptance, make any changes that would affect the contract. Equally, the contractor in making the offer, should not attempt to alter the original terms. If he wishes to vary any items, or make alternative proposals, this should always be done by way of supplemental prices or conditions, so that the original terms of the contract are identifiable. This is important because the law regards it as fundamental that any parties to a contract must be certain as to the details and intention of the contract.

Consideration causes few problems for while it would be possible to enter into a building contract where the contractor would perform the works for a consideration other than money, such as say part ownership of the building, this is very rare. In the case of *O'Neill v Murphy and Others* [1936]70 ILTR 57, the architect was offered prayers instead of fees. The Court held that prayers were not a sufficient consideration in law. This was a Northern Irish case. Contract law over the years has dealt with many cases in the fields of offer, acceptance and consideration and, like nearly all aspects of law, differing and contradictory results have occurred but practitioners in building can rely on the words of Professor Harrison over fifty years ago: 'Consideration, offer and acceptance are an indivisible trinity, facets of one identical notion which is that of bargain.' [1938] 54 LQR 233.

In addition to the three requirements mentioned above there are other aspects of a contract which are necessary to be present in order to ensure validity. The first, and possibly most important, is certainty. This means that both parties must be of one mind, and must intend the same outcome. The architect, despite his wide powers under the contract, cannot order a variation of the kind that would not have been contemplated by the contractor when making his tender bid. Secondly, there must be what is called the necessary formality, which in some contracts require that they be in writing. Generally speaking contracts need not be in writing, but the futility of trying to prove the contents of an oral contract will be obvious, and all building contracts should be confirmed in writing no matter how minor or insignificant. A contract that must be in writing is a contract for the sale of land, and this is required by the Statute of Frauds 1695 which was introduced in Ireland shortly after equivalent legislation in England. The political and social uncertainty in England at the time, and in particular the Penal Laws in Ireland, led to the introduction of this Statute which had as one of its objects 'the prevention of many fraudulent practices which are commonly endeavoured to be upheld by perjury and subornation of perjury'. Those in touch with the law to-day will observe that little has changed.

Finally, it is necessary that the parties to the contract have the capacity to enter into a contract, i.e. they must not be under age; the contract must not be for an illegal objective, or be tainted by illegality by, for instance, building in contravention of the Planning Acts or the Building Regulations and lastly, the object of the contract must be capable of performance.

It would be appropriate to mention letters of intent. It is common practice for some projects to start on this basis, and indeed for some of them to be completed without any form of contract ever having been signed. This can cause great difficulties and it is suggested that if a letter of intent is issued several basic points be included. A Court will often infer the existence of a contract in the absence of a concluded agreement but it would be prudent for the letter of intent to refer to the proposed contract form, the tender sum, the basis of payment, and the time for completion. It would also be sensible to suggest a limit to the amount that might be paid under a letter of intent.

7.5 Determination of the Contract

Having seen how a contract is entered into, it is logical now to see how a contract can be ended. The normal, and non- contentious, way of ending a contract is when the parties have performed, or carried out, the contract. In a building contract this will happen when the architect issues the final certificate but the parties will have on-going responsibilities for a number of years afterwards. This length of time depends on whether the contract is a 'simple' contract or is a contract 'under seal'. The Articles of Agreement allow for either. It is the normal practice for the State, government departments, large companies, etc, to sign under seal, i.e. to affix an official seal to the contract agreement. Contracts not under seal are 'simple contracts'. The distinction can be important. The Statute of Limitations 1957 sets out the time within which an action must be brought after the date of the occurrence of the act which gave rise to the cause of action. In a simple contract this is six years, but in the case of a contract under seal it is twelve years. It would tend to be in the interest of the employer to conclude a contract under seal as this would give him a longer period within which to commence any action for defects, but this distinction has become somewhat academic because of the development of the law of tort in the field of building (see par 9.3).

The standard forms of contract provide for circumstances which would entitle one party to the contract to, in effect, end it. The process is called 'determining the employment of the contractor' and it is defined in that way because the contract itself is not ended, but the employment of the contractor is ended. The contract must remain in being so as to give effect to the provisions which deal with the tidying up process after determination. The circumstances which allow the employer to determine the employment of the contractor are contained in RIAI and GDLA Clauses 33, and SF 88 Clause 21, and the comparable provisions which allow the contractor to determine his own employment are contained in RIAI and GDLA Clauses 34 and SF 88 Clause 22.

In ordinary law, however, there are a number of circumstances which could give rise to the ending of the contractual relationship. These would be if a contract is either void, voidable, or unenforcable. In the first case if a contract is void there is in law no contract at all. A contract may be void as far as the majority of build-, ing contracts would be concerned because of either 'mistake' or illegality'. As far as mistake is concerned it must be a basic and fundamental mistake such as to destroy the certainty requirement of the contract referred to earlier. The word 'misapprehension' might give a better idea of the situation required to render a contract void, but it must be a misapprehension as to the fundamental nature of the contract and not merely to some aspect of interpretation or performance. As far as illegality is concerned, this would normally affect a building contract where either planning permission had not been obtained or where the Building Regulations had not been observed but the deliberate contravention of any statute would be sufficient to render the contract void.

If a contract is voidable it means that one of the parties to the contract may treat it as being at an end, though he may continue if he wishes. In building contracts most of the voidable situations arise because of misrepresentation. This misrepresentation must have induced the innocent party to enter into the contract, and it must also be positive, and a fact. Failure to disclose a fact might not be a sufficient ground to render a contract voidable, and misrepresentation of an opinion would be no ground. If the innocent party continues to perform his part of the contract after becoming aware of the misrepresentation he loses his right to rescind the contract. In the case of a voidable contract, the innocent party is entitled to treat the contract as being at an end, and to obtain damages. This right is in addition to any rights to damages which are mentioned in the contract forms and explains why the contract forms refer to 'without prejudice to any other rights or remedies' (Clause 33 – RIAI and GDLA).

An 'unenforcable' contract is one where some statute, such as the Statute of Frauds 1695, has not been complied with. This particular contract results in a situation where a positive action, such as claiming damages, cannot be taken but where a passive action, such as making a defence, can be relied on. An unenforcable contract has been defined as 'a shield, not a sword'. (Contract F.R. Davies, p.81.)

The standard work on building contracts is Hudson's BUILDING AND ENGINEERING CONTRACTS, 11th edition, edited by Duncan Wallace. Another very useful work is KEATING ON BUILDING CONTRACTS, 5th edition. Both of these books are published by Sweet & Maxwell.

7.6   The RIAI Contracts – A Working Guide

The following sections of this chapter deal with the more important areas of the contract itself. For a full examination of the contract forms see THE RIAI CONTRACTS – A WORKING GUIDE published by the RIAI. That book deals with the three forms on a clause by clause basis, together with an examination of the sub-contract forms and the standard forms for collateral warranty. It necessarily follows that the brief description of the more important aspects of the contract in the present book is not exhaustive and reference should be made to the Working Guide where any contractual problem arises. It should be noted that KEATING ON BUILDING CONTRACTS, 1991 edition, p.319, says: 'An architect should, it is thought, have a general knowledge of the law as applied to the more important clauses, at least, of standard forms of building contract, particularly if he is to act as architect under such a contract.'

The contract can be regarded as dealing primarily with the three variable items in the contract, that is, the works, the time, and the contract sum. Strictly speaking the contract sum is not varied but is either added to or subtracted from. Normally a contract is not variable, but the nature of building is such that provision must be made for the changes which will inevitably occur. Other parts of the contract deal with more general areas such as determination, arbitration, sub-contracting, etc, and brief notes are given for these topics.

7.7   The Works

The Articles of Agreement which are set out at the beginning of the contract document is the actual contract. The clauses which follow are the conditions which apply. In the Articles the proposed building is described as 'The Works' and this description is applied throughout the document. The works can be varied during the course of the contract, and these variations will almost certainly affect the cost and the time. The primary source of these variations is clause 2.

This clause requires the contractor to 'carry out, and complete the works in accordance with the contract documents'. This is his primary duty. The contract documents are defined in the Articles of Agreement. However, the clause goes on to say that the architect may issue further drawings or details, and these are referred to as Architect's Instructions. The architect may issue these instructions under nine stated headings, the two most important being:

a)   the modification of the works, known as variations, and

e)   the removal of work not in accordance with the contract documents.

While the contract uses the phrase 'in his absolute discretion' with regard to the architects power to issue instructions, this is not the case and the architect, as agent for the employer, can only issue instructions which might have been contemplated by the parties to the contract. Since the architect is the agent of the employer he must confine his activities to those which would be considered as normal practice for an agent.

Only the architect can issue instructions and a contractor carrying out works ordered by someone other than the architect risks not being paid for these items.

The power in sub-clause 2(e) to order the removal of any works which are 'in his opinion' not in accordance with the contract relies on subjective judgement in many cases and common sense is called for here. The architect's decision is final, although the contractor can seek arbitration if payment is refused for any work so rejected. It must always be remembered that the responsibility of producing the works in accordance with the contract is that of the contractor alone. He is required to do this under Clause 2 and the architect has neither the power nor the authority to allow otherwise. Some confusion exists with regard to the architects role as far as inspection, supervision, observation or monitoring is concerned and the difficulty of settling on one word to describe the architects function is revealing. The architect's power and duty, to inspect or supervise, or observe is not referred to in the longer forms (although it is both implied and inferred), but it does form part of the RIAI Conditions of Appointment). 'The architect shall visit the site at intervals appropriate to the stage of construction to inspect the progress and quality of the work and to determine on behalf of the employer that the work is being executed generally in accordance with the contract. Frequent or constant inspection of the work is not the responsibility of the architect. Where such frequent or constant inspection is considered necessary separate arrangements will be agree between the architect and the client.'

The whole area of the architect's responsibility as regards inspection is one that requires continuing vigilance by the architect. The employment of site staff does not relieve the architect of any responsibility. It has been said that act of inspection can be delegated but that the responsibility of inspection can not. In other words, site staff can do the inspecting and will report to the architect, but it is always a matter for the architect whether or not he will accept these reports without a personal check for himself.

Clause 3 of the contract refers to the two differing versions of each contract form, i.e. with or without quantities. The wording of both versions is identical with the 'quantities' version pointed on yellow paper and the 'without quantities' form printed on blue paper. The basic difference is that where quantities form part of the contract, any difference between the quantities set out in the bill of quantities and the actual quantities used in the works will be taken into account when payment is being made. Where quantities do not form part of the contract, any resulting variations in the quantities will not be allowed as far as payment is concerned. In such cases the quantities in the bill are only provided as a guide, though it is now unusual to provide a bill of quantities without making it a contract document.

In some cases portion of the works will be omitted for one reason or another. Clause 14 (13 in the GDLA form) provides that in such cases the contractor will be allowed a sum to compensate him for any loss which might result, provided that the omission is 'extensive'. In addition, the contractor is allowed 10% of the cost of any omitted work when final measurement is completed, but PC sums are not taken into account. In the GDLA form, the overall credit on the contract must exceed 20% before the 10% is allowed.

7.8 **The Time**

The appendix to the contract forms will contain the 'date for possession' and the 'date for completion'. The contract form also provides that 'liquidated and ascertained' damages can be deducted from the contract if the contractor does not complete on time. Clause 28 deals with the dates for possession and completion, clause 29 deals with damages for non-completion, and clause 30 deals with extensions of time.

The date for possession will be fixed by the employer and any delay in providing possession of the site to the contractor will automatically extend the date for completion, sometimes by a period greater than that of the actual delay depending on the time of year and other factors. The date for completion will either have been agreed by the parties, proposed by the contractor, or set by the contract documents.

The damages that can be recovered by the employer, if the contractor finishes late, will be set out in the contract. The amount must relate to the loss that might result and arbitrary or penal amounts will not be confirmed by the Courts. The employer will be entitled to these damages and these damages only whether his actual loss is smaller or greater than the specified damages.

The architect will certify when, in his opinion, the works should have been completed, and any damages which are due will be calculated from this date until the date when the architect certifies that the works are 'practically complete'. This event occurs when, in the architect's opinion, the building is available for use. The damages are deducted by the employer from the money which has been certified by the architect.

If the works are, for any reason, delayed by an act of the employer, the architect must again certify what the delay is and the contractor shall be entitled to any damages which he may have suffered. In this case the damages are not pre-determined but should reflect the actual loss.

The time for completion will be extended by the architect if any one of ten (eleven in the case of the GDLA) events occurs. The most usual claims for an extension of time arise because of unusually inclement weather, by reason of architect's instructions or because materials were not available. The full list of events that can lead to a claim for an extension of time is set out in clause 30. The architect must always specify which event has caused the delay, as the consequences can vary. If an extension of time is granted under any heading, the contractor escapes the consequences of damages for non-completion. In addition, if the delay is granted because of late possession of the site, because of architects instructions, or late instructions, because of delay by other contractors retained by the employer, or because of any action by the employer, then the contractor is entitled in addition to be paid for any loss or expense arising from the delay.

7.9   **The Contract Sum**

There are quite a number of clauses that deal with the contract sum, and how it can be added to, or subtracted from. The first two are clauses 4 and 6. Clause 4 provides that any extra cost arising from any government action would be allowed. A change in the rate of VAT would be an obvious example. Clause 6 provides that the cost of any fees charged by local or other authorities would be paid to the contractor.

When the architect issues an instruction under clause 2 it will very often result in a variation. If this occurs, the cost of the variation will be calculated in accordance with clause 13. On most large contracts, a quantity surveyor will be retained, who will value the variations, and recommend payment. The quantity surveyor, though mentioned in the contract, has no power or authority and the ultimate responsibility for the correctness of any payment rests with the architect. The variations will be calculated either on the rates in the bill of quantities, or on rates which will be related to the rates in the bill or on day work prices.

Clause 18 and 19 deal with two other areas where the contract sum can be affected. These are provisional sums and prime cost sums. Neither term is defined in the contract but the accepted difference is that a provisional sum is included to cover unforeseen work such as the possibility of dry rot, whereas a prime cost sum is included to cover work which is foreseen, but where the actual cost is unknown at the signing of the contract. An example would be the cost of heating or electrical services. In the case of either a provisional sum or a prime cost sum the architect would estimate the probable cost of these parts of the work and would include sums of money in the specification or the bill of quantities. The actual cost of the work is paid to the contractor and the difference, if any, between that cost and the amount in the contract documents is either added to or subtracted from the contract sum.

Clause 35 deals with the conditions and procedures that affect the issue of certificates for payment. The contractor will apply to the architect at the intervals set out in the contract for payment. There is a general view that the issue of a certificate is a condition precedent to payment by the Employer. This was so held in *Dunlop and Rankin v Hendall Street Structures* [1957] 3 AER 344 which predated the issue of the standard UK form, JCT 80, which now includes this provision. However, if the employer interferes with the Architect's authority and instructs him not to issue a certificate, the contractor can sue in its absence (*Hickman v Roberts* [1913] AC 229). If a quantity surveyor is retained, the contractor will apply to him, and in turn the quantity surveyor will send a recommendation for payment to the architect. Normally the architect will accept the surveyor's figures but this does not relieve the architect of the full responsibility for the correctness of the amount. The architect will deduct from the amount recommended the value of any defective work and the percentage stated in the contract for retention. The contract will state both the percentage rate and the maximum amount of the retention fund, and when the limit of the fund has been reached, the full amounts of recommendations will be paid. Architects should be aware that the Courts regard a certificate issued by an architect as being in the nature of a negotiable instrument, that is a document where payment is due on presentation. If the architect has over-certified, the Courts will still order payment, and the employer will then have to recover from the architect. This is discussed in greater detail in the chapter on liability (Chapter 9).

Certificates can include payment for materials not yet fixed in the building and sub-clause 35(c) sets out the conditions under which such payments may be made. The final certificate is also dealt with in clause 35. In theory the issue of the final certificate is the completion of the contract which was entered into when the parties signed the Articles of Agreement. Their liability to one another under the contract would continue for six years in the case of a simple contract, and for twelve years in the case of a contract signed under seal. The problems which seemed difficult to resolve in arriving at the issue of a final certificate has led to the suggestion that an architect should have authority to issue a final certificate but could also reduce the amount certified to compensate the employer for defects which the contractor had not remedied. Nothing has yet come of this proposal although the retention bond provisions of the latest forms of contract address this difficulty.

Finally in the matter of the contract sum, the contract document, at clause 36, deals with the subject of wage and price variations. During the course of a long contract both wages and the cost of materials might increase substantially and this clause provides the framework for calculating these increases. This procedure is so complicated that a special supplement to be contract has had to be issued to control it. For many years a proposal to introduce a simple form of indexing cost increases has been argued, but this method never became part of the contract. It often occurs, particularly in times of recession and low inflation, that contracts are signed on a fixed price basis, with the contractor accepting the inflatory risk and clause 36 being deleted.

7.10 Sub-contractors and Sub-letting

A very considerable amount of the work in any building contract is sub-let. Up to, say the middle of the nineteenth century the building contractor would have employed directly all those engaged in the building works. A building might be very large and extensive but it would be a basically simple and straightforward matter as far as the construction process would be concerned. The primary trades of mason, bricklayer, joiner, carpenter, plasterer and painter would deal with the majority of the works with such assistance from general labourers as might be required. But as buildings grew more complicated, and as central heating, plumbing, electrical works, and lifts came on the scene, the general contractor found that he could no longer carry out all these works directly, and that it was necessary for him to go to specialist firms who would deal with these parts of the works. Nowadays, the list of specialist firms has expanded to include sub-contractors that deal with piling, structural steel, precast concrete, special roofing and floors, curtain walling, air-conditioning, etc.

A further complication arises because many of these nominated sub-contractors provide a considerable design input into their own specialist works, and this design responsibility has to be properly allocated.

In this chapter the phrase 'main contractor' is used for clarity, although the description does not occur in the contract but it does occur in the forms used for the sub-contract itself.

The employment of these specialist firms as sub- contractors caused no difficulty as long as they were sub- contractors in the normal sense and where it was clearly understood that they had no contractual relationship with the employer. However, contractual changes and developments in the law led to the rather involved position that exists to-day. The most significant of these developments was the idea of nomination or selection of the sub-contractor by the architect.

This practice arose from the wish of the architect to have a measure of control over the sub-contractors who might be selected to carry out parts of the works particularly in regard to quality of work and the cost of the work. The architect would usually require the contractor to obtain prices from a number of sub-contractors who would be selected by the architect, and if a satisfactory price were received, the particular sub-contractor would be nominated by the architect and the contractor would be instructed to enter into a contract with the selected sub-contractor.

But a difficulty arises if this nominated sub-contractor defaults in any way. The employer has no privity of contract with the sub-contractor, that is he has no contractual relationship with him, so it is essential that the employer be protected if such a default occurs, and that the employer be entitled to recover any loss from the contractor. This should cause no problem as far as the contractor is concerned, because in the first place the contractor is entitled to object to any nomination, and secondly, he can recover any loss which he suffers against the employer, from the sub-contractor. Contracts which are not very clear on these points could result in the situation where the employer could not recover his loss from either the contractor, or the sub-contractor.

As far as the practitioner is concerned there are two main areas of difficulty. The first concerns renomination of a sub-contractor. If the original sub-contractor defaults, the Courts have held that the architect must re-nominate on behalf of the employer. In these cases the contractor must accept the responsibility for any delay caused by the renomination but any extra costs that may arise shall be borne by the employer.

The second area of difficulty arises where the nominated sub-contractor has a design input as far as his part of the work is concerned. This is now a widespread practice. The accepted law is that the contractor has no responsibility for the consequences of any such design fault but does remain responsible for the standard of the sub-contractor's work.

Clause 16 of the contract, which deals with nominated sub-contractors, also sets out the payment arrangement. Normally the architect will endorse any certificate for payment with the amounts contained for the nominated sub-contractors. Before issuing a subsequent certificate the architect may request the contractor to show proof that he has paid any specified amounts to the nominated sub-contractors and if no such payments have been made the employer may, but is not obliged to, pay these amounts directly to the sub-contractor. The situation changes where a collateral warranty has been signed between the employer and the sub-contractor. Collateral warranties are dealt with in detail later on in this chapter (par 7.12) but the essence of the warranty as far as the contract is concerned is that in return for an undertaking by the employer to pay the sub-contractor directly in case of default by the contractor, the sub-contractor undertakes to be directly responsible to the employer for the quality of his work. This type of collateral warranty should not be confused with those arranged between professionals, building owners and financial institutions, and which are dealt with in chapter 10.

It should be noted that the GDLA contract differs from the RIAI form in two important aspects of sub-contracting. Firstly, there is no provision for a collateral warranty, though this does not prevent the parties from signing one if they so wish, and secondly, the architect is not obliged to re-nominate in the case of a defaulting sub-contractor except in the case of bankruptcy.

There are standard forms of sub-contract for completion by the contractor and the sub-contractor issued by the Construction Industry Federation and dealing in separate forms with the RIAI and GDLA contract forms.

7.11 Insurance

1 Contract Requirements

There are seven clauses (nos. 21 to 27) dealing with insurance in the standard forms and they are viewed with some apprehension by many of those involved in the construction industry, and while this view may be partly justified, the overall concept can be quite easily grasped, once the various sections of insurance cover are separately understood. Insurance itself is a very old concept originating in the western world sometime in the fifteenth century. In the Oxford Dictionary the word 'insurance' is dated as having first appeared in 1553. Various changes and events in society provoked the development of the various branches of insurance. One of the best known of these events, the Great Fire of London, was responsible for the rapid spread of fire insurance in the later part of the seventeenth century.

The first appearance of the word 'premium' is given in the Oxford Dictionary as the year 1666, which is the date of the Great Fire. Initially, the words 'insurance' and 'assurance' were used interchangeably, but a distinction eventually emerged so that 'insurance' was taken out to provide for an event which 'might' occur such as a fire, and hence 'fire insurance', whereas, 'assurance' was taken out for an event which must occur, such as death, and hence 'life assurance'. The first reference to insurance in the RIAI standard forms occurs in the 1910 edition at Clause 22.

Insurance has been defined as 'the equitable financial contribution of many for the benefit of an individual who has suffered loss' This definition is taken from CONSTRUCTION INSURANCE AND THE IRISH CONDITIONS OF CONTRACT by Dr Nael Bunni, published by the Association of Consulting Engineers of Ireland. This book can be recommended for those who would like to read a full exposition of insurance as it relates to the construction industry. The provisions of the RIAI forms are examined in a very clear and useful paper by Max Abrahamson,'Notes on the Insurance Clauses', issued by the Liaison Committee. The paper refers to the 1975 and 1977 editions but these are largely similar to the latest edition as far as the insurance clauses are concerned. Naturally, the standard forms will only deal with insurance as it affects the contract itself. The responsibility for insuring is generally placed on the contractor. This has been criticised, and it is argued that the ultimate benefit of these clauses is to the employer. 'In the absence of clear words a contractual requirement for insurance is unlikely to be construed as requiring more than insurance of the interest of the person taking out the insurance' HUDSON, p.311. Some contractors endeavour to have all the insurance clauses struck out and a specially drafted one inserted. This might not be a bad way to approach the whole problem in view of some of the problems which exist, but on the other hand, as has being pointed out before standard forms have their uses.

There are three basic insurance requirements:

a) The contractor or the employer must insure against any loss to property [clause 21(B)]. This reference to property does not include the works themselves but relates to other property such as adjoining buildings. The damage must be caused by the contractor's negligence. If this is not the case the employer becomes responsible unless non-negligence insurance is taken out (see 6.11 b).

b) The contractor or the employer must insure against any injury to persons [Clause 21(B)]. The public liability policy referred to in Clause 21(B) of the contract will cover injury to persons who are not employees of the contractor and the responsibility for such injuries is that of the contractor unless the injuries are caused solely by the negligence of the employer. The amount suggested for this insurance in the forms (€254,000 in the RIAI form and €317,435 in the GDLA form) is inadequate and should be at least €1,270,000.

The contractor will normally have an employer's liability policy and is required under clause 21(B) to have this in place.

c) The contractor must insure the works themselves (Clause 22). This insurance must be kept in force until the architect has issued the Certificate of Practical Completion (Clause 31) at which point the responsibility for insuring the works themselves passes to the employer. Damage to the works can occur in many ways such as fire, floods, winds, subsidence, defective workmanship or materials, negligent use of machinery, theft, etc. This list is not meant to be comprehensive, but the normal arrangement would be that all risks are covered, except for those allowed under Clause 23(d) to be excluded.

The Appendix requires two items to be specified as far as cost is concerned. The first is a sum for the professional fees that would result from the necessity to renew or repair any part of the works. The figure of 12.5% suggested if no other figure is given, is to cover the cost of architectural, engineering and surveying services. The other figure given in the Appendix is the cost of clearing the site, if this is required, after any damage has been caused. This sum would be agreed between the architect (and the quantity surveyor if one is retained) and the contractor.

It is important to be aware of the fact that the GDLA Contract recognises that the State sometimes bears its own risk and does not always carry commercial insurance. In the note to Clause 23(f) of the GDLA form it refers to the situation that arises 'if the employer does not intend to carry out the work himself without insurance'.

The insurance position changes completely in the case of alterations or additions to existing buildings. In these situations the risk of damage to the existing structures is solely that of the employer even if the damage is caused by the negligence of the contractor. The other insurances, that is public liability and employer's liability will still be required to be taken out by the contractor.

Before dealing with the individual clauses in the contract forms it is important to emphasise the architect's overall responsibility with regard to insurance. It was stated earlier that while the architect is not expected to have any general legal knowledge, he is assumed to have a working knowledge of the contract and of the usual consequences of any contract provision as well as having a reasonable working knowledge of the law relating to his own job as an architect. This assumption would apply to the insurance clauses, but it is submitted that no architect in practice would be expected to have the specialised knowledge that would be required to advise an employer in respect of the insurance provisions, apart from advising the employer as to the overall type of insurance required. Obviously, the architect would point out to the employer that the basic rule is that new buildings are generally the contractor's responsibility to insure, and that existing structures are the responsibility of the employer (Clause 26) but even here the two may overlap, as in the case of new additions to existing structures.

The architect should also be aware of the meaning of the basic terms used in insurance. The architect will also need to be advised of the details of the insurance policies held by the contractor as these may be of a general nature and not confined to any one project.

As a general rule, the architect should ensure that the insurers acting for the contractor and the insurers acting for the employer are in contact either directly or through brokers, so as to ensure that there are no gaps in the cover, and to make sure that the insurers to both parties to the contract are aware at all times during the course of the contract what the position is in regard to any factor which might affect the insurance provisions. The case of *Pozzolanic Lytag v Bryan Hobson Associates* [1999]16–CLD–06-25, held that a consultant, in this case an engineer, cannot simply act as a 'postbox' as far as advising the employer on insurance matters is concerned. If the consultant is not expert enough to advise the employer, the consultant must so notify the employer or must seek expert advice. This is much the same judgement that was given in *Quinn v Quality Homes* [1976/77] ILRM 314 discussed in par. 9.2.1.

Finally the architect must at all times remember that a contract of insurance is one of 'the utmost good faith', *uberrimae fidei*. This means that the parties seeking insurance must reveal to the insurers every relevant fact, and if this is not done, the insurer can repudiate the policy. This was graphically illustrated in, amongst others, the case of *Chariot Inns v Assicurazioni Generali SPA* ILRM [1981] 173. In this case very extensive damage was caused by fire to the Chariot Inn, Ranelagh, Dublin and the fire insurance claim was successfully repudiated by the insurers on the grounds that it had not been disclosed to them that a director of Chariot Inns had made a successful fire claim, on behalf of another company of which he was also a director, two years previously. An even more extreme example is the case of *Keenan v Shield Insurance Co. Ltd* [1985] IR 89. In this case the insurer was allowed to avoid a claim of £16,000 for fire damage to a house because the house owner had omitted to disclose a claim of only £53.00 in the proposal form the previous year.

There are, in addition, certain areas of risk which the Contract does not deal with. The following notes are a very brief summary of the three main types of insurance which are not dealt with in the standard forms.

2   Non-negligence Insurance

The risks which the contractor is required to insure against as far as damage to property is concerned, must be those relating to the contractor's own negligence [Clause 21(a)(i)]. Circumstances can arise, however, where damage will be caused even if the contractor is not negligent. The most obvious case would be where a new building is being erected between two older buildings, or where piling is being carried out near existing buildings. In these cases, even where the contractor takes all care, damage to other property can result, and Clause 21(a)(i) will not apply. This particular problem was highlighted in the case of *Gold v Patman and Fotheringham* [1958] 1 WLR, 697, where piling damaged an adjoining building. There were other insurance principles involved which are not relevant here, but the Court held that the employer, and not the contractor, was liable as no negligence had been displayed by the contractor or (as was the case here) the sub-contractor. This case is viewed as having led the development of non-negligence insurance to the stage which it has reached to-day, where it is an almost standard requirement on contracts where any such non-negligence damage can be anticipated. The JCT/RIBA (1980 edition) contract form contains provision for such insurance at Clause 21.2. It is important to remember that non-negligence insurance is issued for the protection of the employer. The contractor is named in the policy as it is necessary for him to provide certain information, and a contract of insurance is, as has been pointed out, a contract of the utmost good faith (uberrimae fidei). Non-negligence insurance takes some time to arrange as the insurers normally require their own consulting engineer to inspect the site or affected buildings before they will issue a policy. The arrangements for this type of cover must be put in hand as soon as possible to avoid delay.

3 Professional Indemnity Insurance

As mentioned in par 7.10 (Nominated Sub-Contractors), there is often a considerable design input from sub-contractors and to a lesser extent from contractors. Under Clause 25 (Damage due to Design) this damage from design must be made good by the contractor at his own expense, though not if the damage is caused by faulty design on the part of a nominated sub-contractor. Since the contractor is entitled under the exclusions allowed by Clause 23 at (e) and (g) to exclude damage due to design from his insurance policies, there is a gap in the cover which would be available under the insurance policies. This gap could be closed in either of two ways. Firstly, it could be closed by both the contractor and the nominated sub- contractor taking out professional indemnity insurance if it is thought appropriate, but they cannot be forced to do so under the standard contract forms. Secondly, the contractor could agree not to exclude the risk from the All Risks Insurance (commonly referred to as the C.A.R. – Contractors All Risks). It must be remembered, however, that damage due to design can affect areas outside the C.A.R. policy, such as damage to persons or other property and these risks should be kept in mind. Damage due to design on the part of the professional team is not relevant to the contract, and would be matter for the contracts drawn up between the employer and the architect, and any other professional advisers who might be involved. This aspect of professional indemnity insurance is dealt with in par. 9.2.1.

4   Decennial Insurance

This is a type of insurance that is being used more commonly, and it provides cover for the employer for a period of ten years against any damage resulting from defective design, materials, workmanship or construction. It is a comprehensive umbrella, and is consequently very expensive but the very simplicity of the arrangement, from the employer's point of view, in providing him with one overall protection from damage from almost any building defect, irrespective of the origin of the defect, is very attractive: Normal wear and tear would, of course, be excluded from such a policy. This subject is dealt with in more detail in chapter 10.

7.12   Collateral Agreements or Warranties

It will be recalled that in par 7.10 (Nominated Sub-Contractors) reference was made to the absence of any formal contractual relationship between the employer and any of the nominated sub-contractors. In some aspects this was useful as far as the employer was concerned. It meant that the employer had to deal with, and pay, only the one party, and that all the subsidiary contractors were dealt with, and paid by the contractor. But there were disadvantages, and these were, chiefly, that the employer had no direct rights against any sub- contractor for defective materials, workmanship or where defective design was concerned. As far as the nominated sub-contractors were concerned, the main defect in the contract arrangement was that, in the absence of any contractual relationship he had no right to claim against the employer if the contractor became bankrupt. It was obvious, therefore, that some contractual relationship between the employer and the nominated sub-contractor would be an advantage to both parties. This relationship is provided by the collateral agreement.

A collateral agreement or warranty is a contract. It is governed by the same contract law as any other contract. It is called 'collateral' – literally, 'by the side of' – because it lies alongside another contract, called the principal contract, in this case the RIAI form. It is necessary because in contract law, the only parties who can get the benefit of, or be held responsible, are the parties to the contract, and a nominated sub-contractor is not a party to the contract. The collateral agreement is sometimes referred to as a collateral warranty, because the sub-contractor warrants or undertakes to perform his work in a manner set out in the agreement.

The agreement referred to in Clause 37 as being a standard form is dated the 1st November 1988 and is published by the three parties mentioned in the clause. The relevant portion as far as the basic agreement is concerned is as follows, giving firstly the sub-contractors obligations.

A   (1) The sub-contractor warrants that he has exercised and will exercise all reasonable skill and care in:

   a)   the design of the sub-contract works in so far as the sub-contract works have been or will be designed by the sub-contractor; and

   b)   the selection of materials and goods for the sub- contract works in so far as such materials and goods have been or will be selected by the sub-contractor; and

   c)   the satisfaction of any performance specification or requirement in so far as such performance specification is included or referred to in the tender of the sub-contractor as part of the description of the sub-contract works.

The case of *Norta Wallpapers (Ireland) Ltd v John Sisk and Sons (Dublin) Ltd* [1978] 14 BLR 49 decided that the contractor was responsible to the employer for any defective materials or workmanship, so that sub-clauses (b) and (c) do not confer additional benefits on the employer., apart from the right of a direct claim against the sub-contractor in the case of default on the part of the contractor. Sub-Clause (a) however covers the gap which occurred after the Norta case, which decided, in addition, that the contractor had no liability for the design of a nominated sub-contractor where no opportunity was given to the contractor to examine the proposals. Sub-Clause (a) by giving direct responsibility to the sub-contractor in regard to the employer, ensures that the employer is adequately protected. In return for providing these undertakings the employer is required to pay the sub-contractor, both as far as the interim and final certificates are concerned, if the contractor defaults.

The collateral agreement goes on to provide that the sub-contractor will pay compensation to the employer in the event of a determination of the sub-contract, including any additional costs in re-nomination, and also provides that the tender of the sub-contractor shall not contain any exclusions or limits to his liability to the contractor. A problem, of course, arises if the employment of the sub-contractor is determined by reason of bankruptcy. In that case, there will be no point in seeking compensation, and this is why it is important for the architect to ensure that the collateral warranty is bonded, or guaranteed.

A bond is an undertaking by a financial institution, often an insurance company, to reimburse the employer for any loss or damage which results from breach of contract. The most frequent occasion when a bond is called in is in the case of bankruptcy. A bond can only exist where a contract exists, and this is why a collateral agreement is a pre-requisite to the obtaining of a bond. The amount of the bond will be agreed between the employer and the financial institution (generally referred to as 'The Bondsman').

The main contract itself is very often bonded, and in the case of large contracts, invariably so. The GDLA form refers to the Contract Guarantee Bond in Clause 28(a) where the production of the bond may be a precondition for possession of the site

The bond used to be for the full contract amount, but nowadays the bond will only be required to cover from 10% to 25% of the contract sum. It is important to remember that the purpose of the bond is to reimburse the employer, and that the Bondsman is under no obligation to complete the contract.

The question of collateral warranties taken out by members of the professional team, usually the architect, and not by the contractor is more controversial and is discussed in chapter 9.

7.13 Architect's Responsibilities and Duties under the Contract

The following is a list of the architect's stated responsibilities and duties set out on a clause by clause basis. The clause headings are generally taken from the RIAI form but there are a few differences between it and the GDLA form. The architect should be aware that even where his duties might not be itemised or specified, they could be understood or implied and a careful reading of the contract form is recommended.

Clause 1 – Definitions

1   Ensure that the Designated Date is set out in the appendix.

Clause 2 – Scope of contract

1   Issue instructions as required.

2   Ensure that valuation under Clause 13 is carried out without 'undue delay.'

3   Ascertain any loss or expense involved following compliance with instructions.

Additional responsibilities under GDLA

1   Ensure that proper notice is received of any claim for loss or expense.

2   Consult with the Quantity Surveyor on matters of cost adjustment.

Clause 3 – Drawings and Bill of Quantities

1   Decide on the necessity or otherwise of the contractors claims for remeasurement.

2   Retain custody of the Contract Documents (in the case of GDLA, only if they are not retained by the employer).

3   Furnish copies of drawings, specifications, instructions, to the contractor.

4   Return documents to the contractor (not in GDLA).

5   Ensure confidentiality of the Bill of Quantities or Schedule of Rates.

Clause 4 – Variations arising from legislative enactments

1   Certify any increase or decrease in the contract sum.

Clause 5 – Contractor to provide everything necessary

1   Decide on any matter raised by the contractor.

Clause 6 – Local and other authorities notices and fees

1   Certify any costs due to the Contractor.

Clause 7 – Setting out of works

1   Provide the information to set out the works.

2   Direct the contractor as to the rectifying of errors.

Clause 8 – Materials and workmanship to conform to description

1   Obtain vouchers, if required, confirming the correctness of materials.

2   Order any necessary tests of workmanship or materials.

3   Adjust the contract sum if required to allow for the costs of tests.

Clause 9 – Work to be opened up

1   Order work to be opened up if he is satisfied that there are good grounds for so doing.

2   Inspect work 'opened up' within a reasonable time.

Clause 12 – Clerk of works

1   Recommend the appointment of a Clerk of Works (or others).

2   Direct the Clerk of Works as to his duties.

3   Notify the contractor of any proposed appointment (not in GDLA).

4   Consider any objections from the contractor to an appointment (not in GDLA).

Clause 13 – Ascertainment of prices for variations

1   Acknowledge and confirm (if appropriate) the contractor's confirmation of a variation within five working days.

2   Measure and value (or instruct the Quantity Surveyor) without undue delay and variation.

3   Advise the contractor if measuring and valuing is being undertaken.

4   Provide the contractor (and in the case of GDLA the employer and the relevant Government Department if they request) with a copy of the Bill of Variations.

5   Decide under rule (a) if omissions vary subsequent works.

6   Decide if day work prices are appropriate (rule b).

7   Check on the providing of 'day work sheets'.

8   (GDLA only) Ascertain after consultation with the employer a reasonable sum for omitted work.

9   (GDLA only) Ascertain 10% of the value of the omitted work provided the credit exceeds 20% of the Contract Sum.

Clause 14 – (RIAI) Omission

1   Ascertain a reasonable sum for omitted work.

2   Ascertain 10% value of the omitted work.

Clause 14 (GDLA) – Vesting of materials and plant

1   Give consent, if appropriate, to the removal of materials, etc

2   Decide on the time to be allowed to the contractor to remove plant, etc, after completion.

Clause 15 – Assignment or sub-letting

1   Consider any request from the contractor or employer for assignment (RIAI only) or sub-letting.

Clause 16 – Nominated sub-contractors

1   Nominate any necessary sub-contractors.

2   Consider any reasonable objection by the contractor to such nomination.

3   Endorse the certificates to the contractor with any necessary list of payments due to nominated sub- contractors.

4   Obtain from the contractor any necessary proof of payment to nominated sub-contractors.

5   Certify, if appropriate, final payment to a nominated sub-contractor.

6   Re-nominate if necessary in case of default on the part of the original nominated sub-contractor (not in GDLA).

Clause 17 – Nominated suppliers

1   Select and nominate required suppliers.

Clause 18 – Provisional sums

1   Issue directions with regard to the expenditure of provisional sums.

Clause 19 – Prime cost sums

1   Make directions with regard to payments to nominated sub-contractor or nominated suppliers.

Clause 22 – All risks insurance

1   Ensure that the items relating to professional fees and site clearance are set out in the appendix.

2   Certify any monies due for making good damage to the works under the all risks policy.

Clause 23 – Contractor's insurance policies

1   To make certain that the necessary cover is in place if the employer proposes to take possession of any part of the works (RIAI). To draw the employer's attention to the necessity to obtain such cover (GDLA) if he proposes to insure.

Clause 26 – Responsibility for existing structures

1   Ensure that Clause 26 is struck out where appropriate.

Clause 28 – Dates for possession and completion

a)   RIAI

1   Ascertain and certify any loss due to late possession

b) GDLA

    2   Deal with any delay for late possession under Clause 30.

    3   Notify the employer and contractor of the issue of the notice of practical completion.

    4   Notify the employer of the change in insurance responsibilities.

    5   Instruct, if appropriate, the contractor to delay finishing works.

Clause 29 – Damages for non-completion RIAI and GDLA

1   Ensure that the dates for Possession and Completion are set in the appendix.

2   Certify that the building ought to have been complete on the date in the Appendix.

3   Ascertain any delay caused by the employer and (in the case of the RIAI form) certify the delay.

Additional Responsibilities under GDLA

1   Consult with the employer before ascertaining any delay.

2   Decide if the contractor has taken all reasonable steps to minimise any loss.

Clause 30 – Delay and extension of time

1   Make a fair and reasonable extension of time (certify in GDLA)

2   Note if any delay occurs under sub-clause (d)

Clause 31 – Practical completion and defects liability

1   Certify that the works are practically complete.

2   Issue instructions to the contractor to make good defects.

Clause 32 – Partial or phased possession

1   Issue a certificate describing the 'relevant part' and the 'relevant percentage'.

2   Issue a certificate of practical completion for the relevant part.

3   Issue a certificate of making good the defects for the relevant part.

Clause 33 – Determination of contract by employer

1   Decide if the contractor is in default, and issue the necessary notice.

2   Decide if any necessary assignments have been made.

3   Direct the removal of any necessary temporary buildings, plant, materials, etc

4   Certify the cost (or saving) or the determination to the employer.

5   Decide if site protection is necessary.

6   (GDLA only) Decide if registered employment agreements are being observed.

Clause 35 – Certificates and payments

1   Advise on guarantee account.

2   Issue interim certificates at appropriate intervals and deduct the appropriate retention.

3   Explain any differences, if so requested, between the contractor's statement and the issued certificate.

4   Conform to the contractual requirements with regard to the certification of materials.

5   Release one moiety of the retention fund on practical completion. Deal with retention bond matters.

6   Arrange, if requested, a joint account for the retention fund and administer that account (not in GDLA).

7   Give notice of, and issue, a final certificate.

Clause 36 – Wage and price variations

1   Certify, if satisfied, any monies due under this clause.

Clause 37 – Collateral agreements

1   Advise the contractor as to the desirability of obtaining a collateral agreement.

Clause 39 (GDLA only) – Fair wages clause

1   Decide on any question re the observance of this clause.

7.14   Cases Referred To   *par.*

Chariot Inns v Assicurazioni Generali SPA [1981] ILRM 173   7.11(a)
Compania Naviera Aeolus v Union of India [1962] 3 AER 670   7.2
Dunlop and Rankin v Hendall Street Structure [1957] 3 AER 344   7.9
Gold v Patnam and Fotheringham [1958] 1 WLR 697   7.11(b)
Hickman v Roberts [1913] AC 229   7.9

Chapter 8 – **Dispute Resolution**

8.1 Introduction

In the introduction to this book, the role of Courts acting in their criminal division has been described. A very large number of disputes arising from the design and construction process result in civil actions and a brief outline of the Civil Courts is given below. This chapter, in addition to dealing with litigation, also describes the process of arbitration and the developing fields of conciliation and adjudication. The question that must be asked when any dispute arises is which is the appropriate method for resolving that particular dispute. Subject to the consent of all the parties any dispute can be settled in any manner and in any forum chosen by the parties themselves. They can agree to toss a coin if they wish.

8.2 Litigation

The Civil Courts consist of a hierarchy of four steps. The basic Civil Court is the District Court. The limit of damages in this Court is 6,349, and while it has jurisdiction over a wide range of matters, defamation is not within its jurisdiction. An appeal from decisions of the District Court lies to the Circuit Court. Where an important point of law is involved, the District Court can ask the High Court to decide the matter by way of a 'case stated'. There is also a geographical limit on proceedings, in that the dispute must arise in the area where the Court sits. As the lowest of the Civil Courts, the District Court is extremely busy and deals with a very large number of cases.

There is also the Small Claims Court, which deals with disputes up to a value of 1,270 and relating to faulty goods, bad workmanship, minor damage to property and the non-return of rent deposits. The Court cannot deal with debts, personal injuries, hire purchase disputes or leasing agreements. There are no lawyers involved and the proceedings are fairly informal. A right of appeal lies from a decision of the Small Claims Court to the Circuit Court.

The Circuit Court is the next of the Civil Courts and deals with cases of first instance and appeals from the District Court. It has total civil jurisdiction, but is limited in the amount of damages it may award to 38,092 unless the parties agree to extend the limit. It has exclusive jurisdiction in dealing with liquor licences, malicious damage claims and certain landlord and tenant actions. Under section 19(4)(g) of the Local Government (Planning and Development) Act 1992 it can grant an injunction, An appeal from the Circuit Court lies to the High Court.

The High Court is the highest Court of first instance and has unlimited civil jurisdiction. It is the only Court that can grant orders of *parameters* or *certiorari*, and is the only Civil Court where the Judge, in certain cases, sits with a jury. An appeal from the High Court lies to the Supreme Court.

At the apex of the hierarchy of Courts is the Supreme Court. The Supreme Court hears appeals from the High Court, and by way of case stated from the Circuit Court. It is the final forum for all constitutional matters.

Many of the civil actions that arise in the construction field relate to allegations of defects in buildings, disputes over accounts, or professional negligence actions. The civil process has become, certainly at the higher levels, a very tedious and expensive route to follow with considerable advantages to the reluctant litigant. A defendant who wishes to postpone the evil day can be very successful in causing delays as the Courts are, naturally, very reluctant to impose sanctions which might be afterwards used as arguments in an appeal on the grounds that reasonable time or opportunity was not given. This defect is also present in arbitration proceedings.

A civil action is initiated by the aggrieved party, the plaintiff, by way of civil process in the District Court, civil bill in the Circuit Court and plenary, summons or special summons in the High Court.

8.3   Conciliation and Adjudication

Conciliation

In recent years there has been a spreading dissatisfaction with the process of litigation and with arbitration which is the form of dispute resolution most familiar to the construction industry. This is not the fault of the concept of arbitration itself but rather with the way it has developed into a mirror image of litigation. This has led to forms of alternative dispute resolution sometimes called mediation but more usually described in contract documents as conciliation. These descriptions cover what is now universally described as Alternative Dispute Resolution, or ADR. It is primarily an alternative to litigation and arbitration. When it is considered that there are over 10,000 cases listed every year in the High Court, that it takes two years on average for a case to come to hearing, and that the cost, of experts, witnesses, solicitors and counsel can run to 25,000 per day it is suggested that there must be a better way, particularly to resolve disputes of a specialist nature, such as insurances, property or construction disputes. The answer should be arbitration, but not only do all the costs mentioned before arise in an arbitration, the parties in dispute also have to pay for the hire of the room and for the arbitrator's fees, in addition to all the other costs. Another defect in both litigation and arbitration, and as far as some commercial areas are concerned, more of a disadvantage is the length of time taken. All of us are aware of commercial disputes that go on in various stages of litigation for five or even ten years, and arbitration can be as bad, indeed worse, as the arbitrators powers to deal with the relevant litigant are not as comprehensive as the Courts. *Jarndyce v Jarndyce* is not dead yet.

Originally mediation was used to describe a process where a mediator would try to convince the disputing parties to agree on some compromise which they would reach themselves. The mediator would not suggest a solution. On the other hand, a conciliator would try and convince the parties that a solution suggested by him would be fair and reasonable. These distinctions seem to be disappearing and the word conciliation is now used in most contracts.

Many engineering contracts had conciliation procedures, in addition to arbitration clauses, and these were invariably non-binding. The latest contract issued by the Institute of Engineers of Ireland contains a mandatory conciliation clause, but while recourse to conciliation was obligatory, acceptance of the recommendation was not. The standard RIAI form followed suit in 1996 and that contract document now requires the parties to conciliate in advance of arbitration. The person conducting the process is now usually called the conciliator. The engineer himself in those engineering contracts such as the New Engineering Contract (issued by the Institution of Civil Engineers) acts as the conciliator.

The basis of conciliation is aimed at correcting perceptions, reducing misunderstandings, and improving communication, so that rational bargaining can proceed. If the parties cannot agree to a solution, the conciliator will make a nonbinding recommendation. This is often very useful as either party will be aware of what an independent person views as a reasonable solution of the dispute and this fact will greatly reduce the temptation to go further along the expensive arbitration route.

Conciliation has been defined as the intervention into a dispute, or negotiation, by an acceptable, impartial, and neutral third party who has no authoritative decision making power in order to assist disputing parties in voluntarily reaching their own mutually acceptable settlement of issues in dispute. The two most important parts of that definition is that the process is voluntary, and that the conciliator has no power to impose a solution, even though he makes a recommendation.

The voluntary aspect might seem a disadvantage in that the parties cannot be forced to take part, but that in itself carries a psychological advantage. If a party, without any contractual requirement, agrees to meet the other party to a dispute, the seeds of settlement are already sown and a disposition towards agreement exists.

There is no adversarial content to the process and this helps to ease the parties towards a settlement. In this way many business relationships can be preserved, and in certain areas of business in a small society like Ireland, this can be very important when firms or individuals tend to work with one another on many occasions.

While the process is voluntary and can be broken off at any time it is important to have some basic rules agreed which lay down the terms which will be in force for as long as the conciliation proceeds and standard conciliation procedures are now issued with the RIAI form. Parties to a conciliation pay their own costs, which in comparison to either litigation or arbitration will be very modest. It has been estimated that the costs in a conciliation will average around 10% of costs in the more formal processes. Obviously where the process is part of a contractual framework the costs will be minimal.

The writer's view is that lawyers should not be present at a conciliation meeting. Parties should, of course, consult their legal advisors when the dispute arises initially, but the very nature of the adversarial framework in which lawyers are both trained and practice, is such as to make the informal and frank discussions which occur at these meetings seem dangerous and damaging to attending lawyers. With the best will in the world progress will be inhibited.

The agreement to a conciliation will contain a confidentiality clause, and will also make clear that no documents, or any evidence and facts, will be discoverable in subsequent proceedings if the conciliation fails.

The length of time taken to complete a conciliation can vary. The process very seldom lasts for more than two days, as it becomes obvious at an early stage whether or not a settlement is probable and a realistic mediator will stop the proceedings when he is satisfied that the process will not work. At the conclusion however, a degree of legal formality arises. The heads of agreement will be converted into a full agreement which will be signed by the parties and at this stage becomes an enforceable contract. It is important to have the agreement properly drafted as it could well be that, unlike documents produced during a conciliation, the agreement would be discoverable to a third party.

Of course conciliation is not always the most suitable method of proceeding. It may well be that it would be necessary to establish some form of precedent, and define a point of law, and clearly this must be done in Court. It must also be remembered that conciliation will, on occasion, fail and the dispute will then proceed to litigation or arbitration or indeed might revert to those processes because there is nothing to prevent parties to a dispute trying to conciliate even though they have already commenced formal proceedings.

Adjudication

A form of dispute resolution that has developed rapidly, particularly in Britain, is adjudication. The concept arose from the disadvantage inherent in most forms of dispute resolution whereby any process used tended to occur at, or towards, the conclusion of the project in question largely because of the length of time required to complete the pleadings. It was perceived that a method which could resolve disputes rapidly during the course of a contract would be beneficial. Such a process was initiated in Britain in the Housing Grants, Construction and Regeneration Act 1996. Under this Act, a party to a contract could at any time request adjudication of a dispute. This would be held very quickly and the adjudicator would give a decision which would be immediately binding on the parties so that work would not be delayed and vital cash flows would not be interrupted. However, at the conclusion of the contract either party, if dissatisfied with the adjudicator's decision could proceed to arbitration and the normal process of that system would than commence. However, experience to date has shown that the vast majority of adjudication decisions are accepted by both parties.

The overall objective of the procedure was set out by the Court in the case of *Macob Civil Engineering v Morrison Construction* [1999] BLR 93: 'The intention of Parliament in enacting the Act was plain. It was to introduce a speedy mechanism for settling disputes in construction contracts on a provisional interim basis, and requiring the decisions of adjudicators to be enforced pending the final determination of disputes by arbitration, litigation or agreement. The timetable for adjudications is very tight. Many would say unreasonably tight, and likely to result in an injustice. Parliament must be taken to have been aware of this. So far as procedure is concerned the adjudicator is given a fairly free hand. He may, therefore, conduct an entirely inquisitorial process, or he may, as in the present case, invite representations from the parties. Crucially, Parliament has made it clear that decisions of adjudicators are binding and are to be complied with until the dispute is finally resolved.'

Initially adjudication gave rise to many legal disputes and the Courts were quite busy trying to interpret the intent of the legislation. The idea of adjudication did not seem all that attractive. Recently the number of cases seems to be diminishing and there is a general acceptance of the system in Britain. This is summed up in an article in the Society of Construction Law Journal of December 2001: 'It is clear that the process of adjudication has got off to a very good start. The signs are that it has gained the confidence of the construction industry and the decisions of the Courts have been entirely in keeping with the underlying thinking and the overt purposes of the process. There is no doubt that the construction industry will benefit greatly, if for no other reason than that there will continue to be a significant reduction in expensive and time-consuming litigation or arbitration.'

In the nature of things, adjudication might well appear in this jurisdiction. The conciliation procedures of the Institute of Engineers of Ireland already have what is, in effect, an adjudication procedure available to disputing parties where the conciliator's recommendation becomes immediately binding, although ultimately liable to arbitration proceedings.

8.4 Arbitration

a) General

All of the standard forms of contract issued both by the RIAI (in conjunction with the SCS and the CIF) and the Institution of Engineers of Ireland require the parties to the contract to arbitrate, if conciliation fails, and under the Arbitration Act, 1980, such a clause precludes the parties proceeding to litigation. For this reason, a detailed description of arbitration is given.

The essence of arbitration as it affects the building industry is that the parties decide to refer any disputes which may arise to a tribunal of their own choosing, rather than to the Courts. But having done so, under any agreement that invokes the Arbitration Acts, the Courts are awarded ultimate control of the arbitration process. The Acts in question are the Arbitration Act, 1954, the Arbitration Act 1980 and the Arbitration(International Commercial) Act 1998. The development of arbitration proceeds from the idea that certain technical areas, such as insurances, marine law, building, etc, would be better served if some method of resolving disputes could be found which would be under the control of a person having expertise in that particular field. In this way engineers came to arbitrate in engineering disputes, architects in building disputes, and so on. The acceptance by the Courts of the resolution of technical disputes by those qualified in those areas was well put by a former Chief Justice in an address to the Chartered Institute of Arbitrators: 'Anybody who would remove from me the diligent, and I hope, patient consideration of damp-proof courses, the depth of foundations, Armstrong junctions, and, I regret to say, even the quality of door-knobs on built-in wardrobes is my friend, not my enemy.' It is not necessary that these arbitrators would have a legal background (though many do possess formal legal qualification), but they would be expected to be conversant with the law of arbitration. Whereas an arbitrator can be dismissed for 'misconduct' or have his award 'set aside' ignorance of the law is not normally a sufficient ground for this. Where the parties are concerned about matters of law, or where the arbitrator himself seeks advice, he can under Section 35 of the 1954 Act ask the High Court to 'state a case', that is, say what the law is in regard to the question posed.

Those interested in reading more about the arbitration process would be recommended JAGO V SWILLERTON AND TOOMER, by H.B. Cresswell (Orion Books, 1984), which is a fictional account of an arbitration written in a most entertaining way and containing, within the rather hilarious story, all the basic information about arbitration law and procedures.

b) Why arbitrate?

Originally, the arbitration process was said to have three advantages over Court actions. Firstly, it would be cheaper. The concern of the legislature in Britain over costs in arbitration can be seen in Section 1 of the Housing Grants, Construction and Regeneration Act 1996 where it says when dealing with arbitration:' The provisions of this Part are founded on the following principles, and shall be construed accordingly (a) the object of arbitration is to obtain the fair resolution of disputes by an impartial tribunal without unnecessary delay or expense, 'and again at Section 33(1): 'The tribunal shall adopt procedures suitable to the circumstances of the particular case avoiding unnecessary delay or expense, etc, (author's italics). Secondly, it would be quicker. Thirdly, it would be confidential. The first two listed advantages, cost and speed, are obviously linked, but it must be said that arbitration seems to be moving closer all the time to the norms which prevail in the Courts as far as these two areas are concerned. The main blame for this can be laid both at the door of the 'reluctant litigant' mentioned before and at the tendency of an arbitration to mirror a Court hearing with the full panoply of solicitors, barristers, witnesses and experts. The requirements of natural justice and the anxiety of an arbitrator to avoid any action which might justify the overturning of his award makes the conduct of the reluctant litigant usually successful. The ultimate sanction of a Court in this position would be to dismiss the action for want of prosecution. This remedy is not available to arbitrators in Ireland, though in Britain, through an amendment to the 1950 Arbitration Act this remedy is allowed. In Ireland the position would still be that held in *Bremer Fulkan Schiffbau und Maschienfabrick v South India Shipping Corporation* [1981] 1 AER 289 where it was held that an arbitrator had no power to strike out an arbitration for want of prosecution. Lord Searman said: 'The nearest he could get to a dismissal on grounds of delay would have been to fix a day for hearing and make an award on the merits based on whatever evidential material was then available to him.'

This was precisely the procedure adopted by the arbitrator in an arbitration which was reviewed in *Grangeford Structures Ltd (In Liquidation) v S H Ltd* [1990] ILRM 277. In this case the respondent was guilty of what the arbitrator considered were unreasonable delays and eventually set a date for the hearing of the arbitration. When the hearing opened the respondent's solicitor requested an adjournment on the grounds that he wished to submit a counterclaim. When the adjournment was refused by the arbitrator, the respondent's solicitor withdrew, and the arbitrator proceeded to hear evidence from the claimant. When the arbitrator made his award, the respondent sought to have his decision set aside by the High Court on the grounds of misconduct. This was refused, and when the case was appealed to the Supreme Court, it was held that in the face of unreasonable delays an arbitrator is entitled to proceed to hear evidence in the absence of one party and that his award is valid.

Much the same type of situation, involving a reluctant litigant, was seen in the case of *McCarrick v the Gaiety (Sligo) Ltd* [2001] High Court, 2nd April. Here an arbitrator decided, after been unable to obtain a response, unusually enough from the claimant, issued an award based on the respondent's submissions. However, unlike Grangeford, the Court remitted the award to the arbitrator on the grounds that the arbitrator might have been hasty but made it clear that this route was not to be lightly taken by awarding the costs of the application to the respondent. Notwithstanding the McCarrick case it is still the position that an arbitrator who has clearly no option but to proceed *ex parte* would be entitled to do so on the grounds set out in the Grangeford case.

An arbitration is, and must always be, a recognised legal procedure and the arbitrator has the backing of the High Court as far as his powers are concerned, but it is up to an arbitrator to ensure that procedures are in keeping with the scope of the arbitration and, by ensuring that evidence is relevant and concise, can minimise expense and delay. The arbitrator can warn a party which is being overzealous and detailed in evidence that he might take note of such behaviour in awarding costs.

The third advantage stated above, that of confidentiality, is of benefit. No person will be admitted to an arbitration hearing who is neither a party, a witness, or a legal representative and notetakers or reporters are only present when requested by the parties or the arbitrator. In this way, no publicity results and this may be desired by the parties.

c) Appointment

The arbitrator is appointed by the parties to the contract. Where the president of a learned body such as the Incorporated Law Society or the Royal Institute of the Architects of Ireland is involved, he nominates a person to be arbitrator, but the appointment is still made by the parties. One of the perceived disadvantages of arbitration is that a dispute in a building matter can often involve the architect, and other professional advisors to the employer, as well as the contractor. Under the terms of the most building contracts the parties to that contract are obliged to arbitrate, but there is no process by which the architect, or others, can be made join the proceedings. In a Court action the Court has the power to join third parties to an action, but the lack of this power to the arbitrator often means that the employer has to proceed on two separate, and often, consecutive actions as he will sometimes be unable to proceed against third parties until an arbitrator has made an award and the employer is aware of the amount of damage suffered. The agreement to arbitrate must be in writing in order to exclude the Courts. This was so held in *Sweeney v Mulcahy* [1993] ILRM 289. It was, nevertheless, held in *Lynch Roofing Systems v Bennett and Son* [1998]High Court, 26th June, that where each party would be expected to know that the custom in the construction industry would be to arbitrate rather than litigate, the Court would not need evidence in writing of an arbitration agreement. The decision in Sweeney would, however, be the norm.

An arbitration agreement should be clear as to the extent of the dispute and as to the arbitrator's jurisdiction. An arbitrator has no statutory right to determine his own jurisdiction: 'It is clearly appropriate for the Court to intervene since only when it has declared that the relevant contract is a construction contract will an effective adjudication be possible. This particularly so given that there is no statutory power given to an adjudicator, if appointed, to resolve disputes about his jurisdiction.' *Palmers Ltd v ABB Power Construction* [2000]17-CLD-O7-05.

In a contract that has an arbitration clause, and if that clause states that the arbitration will be governed by the Arbitration Acts, then the Courts cannot hear any dispute under that contract except in the case of disputes referred to the Small Claims Court – Section 18 of the Arbitration (International Commercial) Act 1998. Under the 1954 Act, in section 12(1) it provided that the Court 'may make an order staying the proceedings'. In the 1980 Act (Section 5) this was changed to 'shall make an order staying the proceedings'. It is important, however, that a party to an arbitration does not appear to acquiesce in the action of the other party if a Court proceeding is initiated. The Act requires that any party seeking to have Court proceedings stayed must make an application to that effect before delivering any pleadings, e.g. lodging a defence. The Courts themselves are reluctant to become involved in the arbitration process. In *Keenan v Shield Insurance Co Ltd* [1988] IR 89 it was commented: 'Arbitration is a significant feature of modern commercial life. It ill becomes the Courts to show any readiness to interfere with such a procedure; if policy considerations are appropriate, as I believe they are in a matter of this kind then every such consideration points to the desirability of making an arbitration award final in every sense of the term.'

An arbitration agreement used to be thought to survive even after a contract had been repudiated. It is assumed that the determination of the employment of the contractor under the RIAI contract form does not affect the validity of the arbitration clause. That is why the determination referred to is that of the employment of the contractor and not of the contract. In *Doyle v Irish National Insurance Company* [1998] High Court, 30th January, the Court held that the arbitration clause subsisted even after a purported repudiation of the contract. However, in *Superwood Holdings v Sun Alliance* [1995] 3 IR 303, an opposite view was taken. The position, which is now unclear, could well affect the arbitrator's jurisdiction referred to above.

d) Award

The arbitrator's decision is final, and there is no appeal. This is an aspect of arbitration that is disliked by some, although it does have the advantage of completing the legal process at an early stage. The 1954 Act at Section 27 says 'Unless a contrary is expressed therein, every arbitration agreement shall, where such provision is applicable to the reference be deemed to contain a provision that the award to be made by the arbitrator or umpire shall be final and binding on the parties and persons claiming under them respectively.' The only way in which the arbitrator's award can be upset is by an application to the High Court to have the Award 'set aside'. This may be done where the Court decides what the arbitrator has 'misconducted' himself. This term is mainly used to cover cases where there has been a breach of natural justice, and does not refer to moral turpitude.

Another example of the view taken by the Courts in supporting the finality of an arbitrator's decision can be seen in cases dealing with errors made by an arbitrator. The Courts are always reluctant to overturn arbitrators' awards unless there are compelling reasons. In the case of *Doyle v Kildare County Council and Shackleton* [1996] IRISH TIMES, 5th February, the Supreme Court reversed a decision of the High Court which had set aside an arbitrator's award. The decision of the Supreme Court was based on the view that, even though the arbitrator had clearly been inconsistent in calculating land values, no fundamental error of law appeared on the face of the award.

Another good example of the support by the Courts of arbitration as a form of dispute resolution can be seen in the case of *Sheehan v FBD Insurance* [1998] IRISH TIMES, 8th June, where the Court decision was: 'The Court has a common law jurisdiction to set aside an award of an arbitrator where an error of law appears on its face. Such an error must be so fundamental that the Court cannot stand aside and allow it to remain unchallenged. However, if a specific question of law is referred to an arbitrator for decision the award will not be set aside merely because the decision on the question of law is an erroneous one.'

While awards have been set aside on other grounds, or have been 'remitted' or sent back by the Court to the arbitrator for further consideration, it is only proposed to deal with the natural justice aspect here, as an architect who is advising his client cannot be expected to have more than a basic knowledge of this part of the contract.

The arbitrator should always be evenhanded. He should never take any action without informing both parties; he should always ensure that documents are circulated to both parties. 'When once they enter on an arbitration, arbitrators must not be guilty of any Act which can possibly be construed as indicative of partiality or unfairness. It is not a question of the effect which misconduct on their part had in fact upon the result of the proceedings, but of what effect it might possibly have produced. It is not enough to show that, even if there was misconduct on their part, the award was unaffected by it, and was in reality just, arbitrators must not do anything which is not in itself fair and impartial' re Brien and Brien [1910]2 IR 84. Human nature being what it is, arbitrators behave like everyone else from time to time, and it has been held that an arbitrator becoming 'completely intoxicated' at a dinner after the hearing was not misconducting himself (re Hopper) [1967] 36 LJQB 97) but that an arbitrator who charged excessive fees had (re Pebble and Robinson [1892] 2QB 602). A request for interim fees, even when made as a condition for proceeding further, has been held not to be misconduct. *Turner v Stevenage Borough Council* [1998] 15-CLD-05-18.

e) Reasoned award

Another aspect of arbitration which is disliked by many who get involved is that an arbitrator is not obliged to give reasons for his decisions, unless he has agreed to this in his terms of appointment. The Arbitration Act 1979 in the UK requires arbitrators to state reasons if asked. There are differing views as to whether or not an arbitrator should give or be made to give reasons, those approving saying that parties to an arbitration should have the right to know why they won or lost, and those disapproving saying that giving reasons will only enable dissatisfied parties to go to Court over the result. Some provisions of the UK 1979 Act attempt to curtail this.

In general, it is the practice in Ireland for an arbitrator to give no reasons for his award. In the case of *Vogelaar v Callaghan* [1996] 2 ILRM 226 the Court upheld the validity of the practice of an arbitrator not giving a reason. The Court further pointed out that if an arbitrator is asked to state a case or give reasons then he can but is not obliged to, but for an arbitrator to state, before any directions are given, that it is not his practice to give reasoned awards was not appropriate. This particular case see-sawed from the Arbitrator, to the High Court, to the Supreme Court and back to the Arbitrator over a dispute concerning costs and the status of an offer.

In confirming that arbitrators are not required to give reasons (*Manning v Shackleton* [1997] 2 ILRM 26) the Court quoted with approval the comments of McCarthy J. in *Keenan v Shield Insurance* [1988] IR 89: 'It ill becomes the Court to show any readiness to interfere in such a process; if policy considerations are appropriate as I believe they are in a matter of this kind, then every such consideration points to the desirability of making an arbitration award final in every sense of the term.'

f) Arbitrator's powers

An arbitrator has power to 'open up, review and revise any opinion, decision requisition or notice'. This is extremely wide power which the Courts have not taken to themselves and a justification for it was given in a passage in *Northern Regional Health Authority v Derek Crouch Construction Co Ltd* [1984] 26 BLR 1: (The case, naturally, referred to a JCT/RIBA contract, but the wording is generally similar to the RIAI/GDLA forms).

'Under the JCT contracts the architect, who is the agent of the building owner is a key figure in deciding such matters as what extensions of time should be granted for the performance of the contract, whether and to what extent contractors and sub-contractors are responsible for delay, how much each should be paid and when they should be paid and whether and when the works have been competed. These are very personal decisions and, within limits, different architects might reach different conclusions. Despite the fact that the architect is subject to a duty to act fairly, these powers might be regarded as draconian and unacceptable if they were not subject to review and revision by a more independent individual. That process is provided for by the arbitration clause. It is, however, a rather special clause. Arbitration is usually no more and no less than litigation in the private sector. The arbitrator is called upon to find the facts, apply the law and grant relief to one or other or both of the parties. Under a JCT arbitration clause (clause 35) the arbitrator has these powers but he also has power to 'open up, review and revise any certificates, opinions, decision, requirement or notice'. This goes further than merely entitling him to treat the architect's certificates, opinions, decisions, requirements and notices as inconclusive in determining the rights of the parties. It enables, and in appropriate cases requires him to vary them and so create new rights, obligations and liabilities in the parties. This is not a power which is normally possessed by any Court and again it has a strong element of personal judgement by an individual nominated in accordance with the agreement of the parties.'

In *Beaufort Developments v Gilbert Ash* [1998]88 BLR 1, this decision was reversed but the judgement in Crouch is given above as the phrase still exists in the RIAI forms of contract. No case has as yet dealt with this matter in this jurisdiction and it would be unwise to guess what might happen if the question arose. It seems to the writer that the power to review decisions of the architect is a power that improves the usefulness of arbitration as a dispute resolution mechanism. If the Courts in this jurisdiction were to follow Beaufort, a perceived advantage of arbitration would disappear.

g) Liability

Finally, it might be appropriate to comment on the arbitrator's position as regards liability for his actions. In the UK under the Arbitration Act 1996, Section 29, an arbitrator is granted immunity for his professional conduct except for proven bad faith. There is no such provision in the Irish legislation. The standard reference work, RUSSELL ON ARBITRATION, 21st edition, published by Sweet & Maxwell, gives further detail. In this jurisdiction, ARBITRATION LAW AND PROCEDURE by Dr Michael Forde, published by the Round Hall Press expresses the general view that an arbitrator is immune. The Rules of the Superior Courts, at Order 56, specifies that an arbitrator can only be a defendant where an application is made either to remove him, or is made to direct the arbitrator to state a case. Order 56 specifies that an arbitrator cannot be joined as defendant in proceedings, either to remit, set aside or enforce his award. This was confirmed in the case of *Bord na Mona v John Sisk and Son* [1990] High Court, 31st May.

8.5   Cases Referred To   *par.*

Chapter 9 – **Responsibility and Liability**

9.1 Introduction

This chapter is addressed primarily to architects, but also to any others who are trying to find their way through the labyrinth of statute and regulation which now enmeshes the world of construction. Just as in the case of a building project the professionals, the contractors and some other parties, are all working in a close relationship, so the consequences of their various actions are also intertwined and it is not possible, nor even desirable, to try and separate the responsibilities and liabilities of the various parties. In this chapter there are references to Hudson's BUILDING AND ENGINEERING CONTRACTS. The latest (11th) edition was published in 1995, and is a valuable source book and contains some very useful guidance and advice. It is published by Sweet & Maxwell. Another very useful book is KEATING ON BUILDING CONTRACTS (5th ed.), published also by Sweet & Maxwell.

9.2 The Architect's Responsibility

9.2.1 General

The extent to which the architect should be aware of the law and of the legal consequences of his various actions is fairly well defined. An architect should have a sound working knowledge of the general law as regards planning, building regulations, and building contracts, but he is not of course expected to be able to offer a service which would be more properly the role of a solicitor with regard to advice in purely legal matters. In *B. L. Holdings v Wood* [1978] 10 BLR 48 it was held that an architect is required to know enough law to be able to protect his client against bad advice from a planning authority: 'It may be thought by some to be 'hard' to require of an architect that he know more law than the planning authority or at least have sufficient awareness of what may be bad law enunciated by such an authority as to make him advise his clients to check up on it.' An architect should always advise the employer when he feels that formal legal advice should be sought. Equally an architect should be aware that *ignorantia juris neminer excusat* – ignorance of the law is no excuse.

It can be seen, therefore, that the architect's responsibility and liability is not a fixed or certain thing, nor indeed are the consultants, or even the contractor, in any better position. The quantity surveyor, and the engineers, will be bound by the standards set out above with regard to the architect. The expectation of skill will be the same. However, the architect must be careful as far as the selection and appointment of other consultants is concerned. The architect should always ensure that the appointments of these consultants are made directly by the employer and that any professional advice from them is conveyed to the employer in such a way a to make the employer fully aware of the view of all the consultants concerned. In *Quinn v Quality Homes (Ltd)* [1976/77] ILRM 314 it was pointed out that the architect could not act merely as a postman, and pass on the employer the advice of other consultants without any comment. He had a duty to point out to the employer what his views were on the advice being offered, even if it were only to say that he was relying entirely on the consultant's advice. This was confirmed in almost identical language in the case of *Pozzolanic Lytag v Bryan Hobson Associates* [1999] 16-CLD-06-25. A very interesting English case (*Chesam Properties v Bucknall Austin* [1997] 82 BLR 92) held that, on the facts, an architect had a duty to report to the client if he was of the opinion that the service being provided by other consultants was not satisfactory.

Finally in this section, the Supreme Court held in *Glencar Exploration v Mayo County Council* [2002]1 ILRM 481, that defendants in negligence cases should not be presumed to have duties of care generally. Until that case, if the plaintiff could show that the harm alleged was reasonably foreseeable, it was presumed that the defendant owed the plaintiff a duty of care. Now it will have to be proved that the imposition of a duty of care is fair and reasonable.

9.2.2 Standard of Skill and Professional Indemnity Insurance

The words duty, power and responsibility are used very widely in relation to the position of the parties to a contract. The meaning of these words should be understood. They are discussed in some detail in the case of *Dutton v Bogner Regis UDC* [1971] 3BLR 11. This is a case well worth reading in full as it gives a very comprehensive overview of the whole field of liability. Its decisions have been changed over the years but the background is well described and written very lucidly by Lord Denning. A power confers on someone the authority to decide or control specified matters. A duty arises in the carrying out of the power to see that it is exercised properly, and a responsibility evolves from the consequences of both the power and the duty. It would be difficult to improve on Hudson, p.284 for a definition of the architect's duty which he says, is to secure:

i)   a design which is skilful, effective to achieve his purpose within any financial limitations he may impose or make known and comprehensive, in the sense that no necessary or foreseeable work is omitted

ii) the obtaining of a competitive price for the work from a competent contractor, and the placing of the contract accordingly in terms which afford reasonable protection to the employer's interest both in regard to price and the quality of the work

iii) efficient supervision to ensure that the works as carried out conform in detail to the design, and

iv) efficient administration of the contract so as to achieve speedy and econom-
ical completion of the project.

While this extract covers the general areas for which the architect will be responsible, it is important to examine the precise level of skill that the architect will be
expected to achieve. If the architect fails to meet these goals he could well be
judged to have been negligent. What then is negligence? It is generally accepted
that negligence is acting in a careless way so that foreseeable injury or damage
results. For an action in negligence to be sustained against a professional it is necessary to prove three things: firstly that the professional owed a duty of care to
the injured party; secondly, that the duty must be breached, and thirdly, damage
must result.

It is accepted that the architect's duty is to use reasonable skill and care in the
course of his employment. This was laid down for professionals generally in a
well known medical case, *Bolam v Friern Hospital Management Committee*
[1957] 1 WLR 528, and expanded on in the case of *Chien Keow v Government of
Malaysia* [1967] 1 WLR 813: 'Where you get a situation which involves the use
of some special skill or competence, then the test as to whether there has been
negligence or not is not the test of the man on top of the Clapham Omnibus,
because he has not got this special skill. The test is the standard of the ordinary
skilled man exercising and professing to have that special skill; it is well established law that it is sufficient if he exercises the ordinary skill of an ordinary competent man exercising that particular art.' A later case, *Wimpey Construction UK
Ltd v D V Poole* [1948] Lloyd's Rep 499, confirmed the Bolam test and added,
very interestingly, that even if the employer had paid for someone with specially
high skills the basic negligence test did not alter. The Bolam test was approved in
Ireland in the case of *Ward v McMaster and Others* [1989] ILRM 400, which concerned a house valuation. There is, however, an important exception. What was
known as 'the State of the Art' defence was quite widespread in professional negligence actions and meant, in brief, that what was considered acceptable on a general scale by a profession would not be held to be negligent. This was upheld in
the case of *Flanagan v Griffith* [1981] High Court, 25th January, when the Court
held that 'an architect cannot be liable in negligence for forming a judgement
which conforms with the considered judgement of men prominent in his profession'. This is still the position in Britain. It was recently held (*Freyssinet v Byrne
Brothers* [1996] 15 CLD 09 30) that a firm of engineers was not negligent if 'they
had acted in accordance with practice accepted as proper by a reasonable body of
like professionals skilled in that particular role and expertise'. This is not the
position in Ireland as a result of what is now known as the rule in *Roche v Peilow*
[1986] ILRM 189 which was first set out in *O'Donovan v Cork County Council*
[1967] IR 173:' If there is a common practice which has inherent defects, which
ought to be obvious to any person giving the matter due consideration, the fact
that it is shown to have been widely and generally adopted over a period of time

does not make the practice any the less negligent. Neglect of duty does not cease by repetition to be neglect of duty.'

It has been held in Britain that in an action for negligence against a professional, the evidence must be given by a similarly qualified person: 'In my judgement, it is clear, that a Court should be slow to find a professionally qualified man guilty of a breach of his duty of skill and care towards a client without evidence from those within the same profession as to the standard expected on the facts of the case and the failure of the professionally qualified man to measure up to that standard.' *Sansom v Metcalfe* [1998] 15-CLD-02-15. It has also been held that the fact that an expert witness was much more highly qualified than the defendant was not relevant. *Hammersmith Hospitals v Troup Bywaters and Anders* [2000] 17-CLD-06-31.

The architect's design must be skilful, but he will not be expected to guarantee that the result will be reasonably fit for the purpose for which the building is designed. The distinction may be a fine one but it exists. The law does not imply a warranty that a professional man will achieve a desired result, but it does assume that he will use reasonable care. In *Greaves v Baynham Meikle* [1975] 4 BLR 56 it was said: 'A surgeon does not warrant that he will cure the patient. Nor does the solicitor warrant that he will win the case.' The concept of 'Fitness for purpose' is borrowed from the Sale of Goods Act 1893, which Act is concerned with 'products'. The reason why this concept is mentioned here is because it is suggested in a report on defective premises, published by the Law Reform Commission in 1982, that all buildings should measure up to this requirement. The layman might be pardoned for thinking that every building should, as a matter of course, be fit for its particular intended purpose but this in a strict legal sense is a concept demanding a higher acceptance of design responsibility for the building and an assurance against defect in any circumstance. The important point is that a building is not a product and the same rules should not apply. In a paper to a joint RIAI/SCS Conference in 1987, John O'Connor put it very well: 'Building is an attempt to place an untested, hand-crafted cube made of materials which expand, contract, shrink, creep and warp unilaterally on to foundations laid in a mosaic of erratic geological conditions owing its nature to the caprice of the ancient ice. It can never be the tested product of the laboratory and legislation governing defective products should have no application in building.'

If, however, it can be shown that it was the common intention that a building should be fit for a particular purpose, then the architect would be liable for this higher duty. Obviously a house must be fit for human habitation and the architect will be responsible for this (*Hancock v B.W. Brazier (Anerley Ltd)* [1966] 1 WLR 1317) but each building must be judged on the basis of the parties intentions. It has been held that in a design-build contract, or 'turnkey' arrangement there can be an implied fitness for purpose requirement. The case in question, *Viking Grain*

Storage v T. H. White [1985] 33 BLR 10, had unusual contract documentation but the danger is there in such arrangements.

The prudent professional will, of course, obtain insurance against claims for professional negligence. Even the smallest practice should insure. Time and again claims are being made as a result of seemingly innocuous work, such as the issue of opinions on compliance and it transpires that the unfortunate practitioner is not covered. Mistakes can turn out to be very expensive and the €1,500 or so that it costs at the moment to obtain insurance for a small practice is money very well spent. The legal dangers that professionals are exposed to in criminal prosecutions in the area of health and safety have been commented on in par. 5.7. While it is possible to insure against costs in such a contingency, any fine imposed by a Court cannot be covered by professional indemnity insurance and the amount, if convicted on indictment is unlimited.

Insurance generally is dealt with in par. 7.11 and most of the comments relating to building contract insurance would be valid as far as professional negligence is concerned. There are some important differences. The insurance cover available is that in force when the claim is made and not when the unfortunate event occurred. In addition, policies are annually renewable and cover cannot be obtained for longer periods. Most important for the professional is to ensure that any activity that the practice engages in (such as project management or health and safety measures) is covered as well as mainstream activities, and also to be diligent in informing the insurers immediately of any event which might give rise to a claim. RIAI Insurance Services offer advice on the appropriate levels of insurance.

9.2.3 **Certificates**

The architect's responsibility for the accuracy of any certificate is considerable. It has been held that 'The final certificate is conclusive evidence that the works have been carried out in accordance with the contract and to the reasonable satisfaction of the architect.' *Oxford University v Architects Design Partnership* [1999] 16-CLD-03-01. The finality of an architect's certificate has been emphasised in HUDSON: 'If the effect of the contract is to confer finality upon a certificate, it has been held that a certificate validly issued cannot, in the absence of a contractual provision to the contrary, or agreement or waiver by the parties be withdrawn in order to correct mistakes of fact or value on it. Having issued the certificate, the certifier has in theory discharged his function, and unless an arbitration or other clause empowers him to decide a dispute arising on a certificate, or to amend it, he has no jurisdiction to alter it or issue another.' 11th edition, p.839. In the Beaufort case referred to in par. 8.4, the arbitrator's right to review certificates was questioned by the Courts. Courts generally have held the view that an architect's certificate is almost a negotiable instrument and invariably will order that the certificate be honoured and that the client proceed, if necessary, against the architect to recover any money incorrectly certified. It used to be thought, as a result of *Chambers v Goldthorpe* [1901] 1 KB 624, that where an architect was bound to act impartially as between the parties to the contract, he was in the position of an arbitrator, and he had a quasi-judicial role. In these circumstances he would not be liable for an action in negligence in the exercise of that particular function. Over the years however, this position changed. In 1927 the case of *Wisbech U.D.C. v Ward*, 2 K B 556, decided that while the architect might be protected as far as a final certificate was concerned, this was not the case where interim certificates were issued. The matter of interim certificates was also examined in the case of *Townsend v Stone Toms* [1984] 27 BLR 26 where it was held that an architect was negligent in certifying defective work in an interim certificate, even where it would be possible to adjust the amount certified at the issue of the final certificate.

The case that settled the architect's overall liability for certification was *Sutcliffe v Thackrah* [1974] 25 BLR 147. The House of Lords held that in certifying, an architect was not acting in any arbitral or judicial capacity, and was liable for any negligence in certifying. To 'certify', after all, means that the certifier is 'certain'. It is vital for the architect to be aware of the fact that he is only to certify for work which has been properly done, and that he will be liable if he acts otherwise. It would be clear though that defects which he could not have observed, or any fraudulent concealment, would not form the basis of any negligence claim. It has been held, and architects should be aware of the fact, that an architect has a duty to notify the quantity surveyor in advance of any work which was not properly executed so that the quantity surveyor can exclude it from his valuation (*Sutcliffe v Chippendale and Edmondson* [1971] 18 BLR 149).

The conclusiveness of an interim certificate has been the subject of many Court decisions over the years and it might be useful to refer to the general position, as reference is constantly being made to this problem. What was called the 'rule' in *Dawnays Ltd v F.G. Minter Ltd* [1971] 1 BLR 19 held that an employer was not entitled to deduct money from an interim certificate because of defective work or over-valuation, even where there was a wide-ranging arbitration clause. It was decided that the employer must wait until the conclusion of the arbitration itself. Lord Denning made a much quoted statement: 'An interim certificate is to be regarded virtually as cash, like a bill of exchange. It must be honoured. Payment must not be withheld on account of crossed claims, whether good or bad, except insofar as the contract specifically provides.

However, the case of *Gilbert-Ash (Northern) Ltd v Modern Engineering (Bristol) Ltd* [1974] 1 BLR 75 abolished this rule, holding that an employer could deduct such monies. The position might well be academic, as the contractor can seek

arbitration during the course of the contract on the question of an interim certificate, but if he does not do so, it appears that the employer is entitled to withhold
the money. These matters were considered in a number of Irish cases. In *John Sisk
and Son Ltd v Lawter Products B.V.* [1976] High Court, 15th November, the 'old'
view was taken that the employer was not entitled to deduct anything from the
certificate. A different view was taken in *P.J. Hegarty and Sons Ltd v Royal Liver
Friendly Society* [1985] High Court, 11th October. It was held that an employer
was entitled to deduct monies and that 'an amount included in a certificate
(whether interim or final) does not constitute a debt of a particular character and
enjoys no special immunity from any cross-claim or right of set-off to which the
debtor may be entitled'. One of the main reasons given by the Court for this decision was the right of the parties to go to arbitration at any time on the question of
certificates. This view, however, was not followed in *Rohan Construction Ltd v
Antigen Ltd* [1989] ILRM 783. This case, which can now be taken as the law in
Ireland, held that a right of set-off was clearly inconsistent with the terms of the
RIAI Form, although it is allowable in the GDLA form. The Court also held that
judgement for payment of an interim certificate should be given even if the parties intend to go to arbitration. What Denning said in Dawnays still applies. The
wording of the contract can be the key to set-off rights, and this was recently the
argument in the case of *R M Douglas Construction Ltd v Bass Leisure Ltd* [1991]
7 CLJ 114 where set-off was allowed because the wording of the contract form
did not specifically exclude it. This could, presumably, now be argued against the
decision in the Rohan Case.

9.2.4 Supervision

It will be recalled that HUDSON says that an architect should provide 'efficient
supervision'. There is an on-going debate about the appropriate word.
'Supervision' was widely used but is now being replaced by words like 'inspection' as in the RIAI Architect's Appointment, and in the shorter form of the RIAI
Contract (SF88). It was felt that the use of the word supervision imposed an unreal level of responsibility on the architect and diluted the primary responsibility of
the contractor to build correctly. This is an area where there seems to be considerable doubt as to what is appropriate, building owners tending towards requiring
a substantial level of supervision. The RIAI Architect's Appointment (par. 1.7)
leaves the level to the architect's discretion.

It has been held that an architect is entitled to use his judgement as to how frequently he inspects. The decision in *East Ham Corporation v Bernard Sunley*
[1966] AC 406 has been much quoted and is worth repeating: 'As is well known,
the architect is not permanently on the site but appears at intervals, it may be of
a week or a fortnight, and he has, of course, to inspect the progress of the work.
When he arrives on the site there may be very many important matters with which

he has to deal: the work may be getting behind-hand through labour troubles; some of the suppliers of materials or the sub-contractors may be lagging; there may be physical trouble on the site itself, such as, finding an unexpected amount of underground water. All these are matters which may call for important decisions by the architect. He may in such circumstances think that he knows the builder sufficiently well and can rely upon him to carry out a good job; that it is more important that he should deal with urgent matters on the site than that he should make a minute inspection on the site to see that the builder is complying with the specifications laid down by him... It by no means follows that, in failing to discover a defect which a reasonable examination would have disclosed, in fact the architect was necessarily thereby in breach of his duty to the building owner so as to be liable in an action for negligence. It may well be that the omission of the architect to find the defect was due to no more than error of judgement, or was a deliberately calculated risk which, in all the circumstances of the case, was reasonable and proper.' This overall view was quoted with approval by the Judge in *Corfield v Grant* [1992] 59 BLR 102: 'What is adequate by way of supervision and other work is not in the end to be tested by the number of hours worked on site or elsewhere, but by asking whether it was enough. At some stages of some jobs exclusive attention maybe required to the job in question (either in the office or on site): at other stages of the same jobs, or during most of the duration of other jobs, it will be quite sufficient to give attention to the job only from time to time. The proof of the pudding is in the eating. Was the attention given enough for this particular job?' This view was confirmed in the case of *Dept of National Heritage v Steenson Varming Mulcahy* [1999] 16-CLD-05-18, where the Court firmly held that the level of supervision was dependent on the circumstances of each project.

9.3 The Relationship between the Parties

But what of the inter-relationship between all those involved. At one time, the various parties, employer, architect, contractor, sub-contractor, supplier etc, all had a contractual relationship, and a contractual relationship only, with some or most of the other parties. The architect had a contract with the employer but had no other legal relationship with the employer, and had no legal relationship of any sort with the contractor. Similarly the sub-contractor had a contractual relationship with the contractor but no relationship with anyone else. There was a clear and distinct division in law between contract, and particularly, tort.

A contract was a voluntary obligation, freely entered into. Tort was an involuntary relationship which arose from events not generally intended. A tort has been defined as a civil wrong, the remedy for which is damages. Injuries received in a motor accident would come under this heading. For any party to become involved with another party in tort, there are three basic requirements. Firstly, one party must owe a duty to the other party, such as to drive carefully or, in any event, not negligently. Secondly, this duty must be breached, and, thirdly, the innocent party must suffer some damage. It is the interaction between tort and contract, initiated by the Courts, over the last thirty years in particular that have resulted in the rather unsatisfactory and uncertain position that exists to-day. If the architect, or the engineer, or contractor were liable in tort, as well as in contract, then he might be liable to a wide range of persons, and over a very long period of time. If he were liable only in contract he would be liable only to the other party to the contract and for a period of six (or sometimes twelve) years.

It is worthwhile going into the development of this area of law because of its importance and also because of the way in which it can change from case to case. A knowledge of the history of the development of case law makes it easier to appreciate the points involved. It is generally thought that the boundaries between contract and tort only began to unravel in this century, but as far back as 1370 the case of *Walson v Marshall* dealt with the overlapping areas on contract and tort. The real expansion of tort was, of course, the 'snail in the bottle' case of *Donohue v Stevenson* [1932] AC 562 where it was held that a person whose actions injured another person was liable in tort if it could be reasonably contemplated that such a result would occur as had happened. This, however, did not affect architects in their relationship with the employer, and as recently as 1970 HUDSON could state with authority (p.123): 'But the duty owed by an architect or engineer to his employer arises in contract and not in tort.' HUDSON based this view on, amongst other, the then recent case of *Bagot v Stevens Scanlon and Co* [1964] 2BLR 67. The relevant part of the judgement read: 'It seems to me that, in this case, the relationship which created the duty on the part of the architects towards their clients to exercise reasonable skill and care arose out of the contract and not otherwise. The complaint that is made against them is of a failure to do the very thing which they contracted to do. That was the relationship which gave rise to the duty which was broken. It was a contractual relationship, a contractual duty, and any action brought for failure to comply with that duty is in my view, an action founded on contract. It is also, in my view, and action founded on contract alone.' This was clearly a very definite position.

But in the case of *Esso Petroleum v Mardon* [1976] 2 BLR 82 the following comment was made: 'A professional man may give advice under a contract for reward; or without a contract in pursuance of a voluntary assumption of responsibility, gratuitously without reward. In either case he is under one and the same duty to use reasonable care. In the one case it is by reason of a duty imposed by law. For a breach of that duty he is liable in damage, and those damages should be, and are, the same whether he is sued in contract or in tort.' This particular view was then followed in a whole series of cases, and it was well established and accepted that both tort and contract could be relied upon when proceedings were being contemplated against consultants.

Recently, however, this view has been questioned more and more in Britain and other common law countries, and the principle of combined liability in both contract and tort is now in considerable doubt in those countries. In *Sealand of the Pacific v McHaffie* [1974] 2 BLR 74 it was held that 'duty and liability ought to be discovered in the contract. If additional duties and liabilities are to be attached it will have the effect of changing the bargain made by the parties' More emphatically in *Tai Hing Cotton Mill Ltd v Liu Chong Hing* [1986] AC 80 the Privy Council did 'not believe that there was anything to the advantage of the law's development in searching for a liability in tort where the parties are in a contractual relationship'. One Judge said: 'But as far as I know it has never been the law that the plaintiff who has the chance of suing in contract or tort can fail in contract yet nevertheless succeed in tort; and, if it ever was the law it has ceased to be the law since *Tai Hing Cotton Mill v Liu Chong Hill.*' *National Bank of Greece v Pinios Shipping* [1989] 3 WLR 195. Again, in *Edgeworth Construction Ltd v N D Lea and Associates Ltd* [1991] 7 CLJ 238 it was held that a consulting engineer had no duty towards a contractor for inaccuracies in contract documents but only owed such a duty towards his client, with whom he was in a contractual relationship. This trend was reversed in the latest case that seems to have considered the matter in principal is *Arbuthnott v Feltrim and Fagan* [1994] 69 BLR 26. In this case the House of Lords had no doubts: 'Unless the contract precludes him from doing so, the plaintiff who has available concurrent remedies in contract and tort, may choose that remedy which appears to him to be most advantageous.' It was pointed out in *Holt v Payne Skillington and de Groot Collis* [1995] 77 BLR 51 that the duty under tort could be wider than the duty under contract, depending on the facts and circumstances in each case.

There is a typically informative and entertaining comment in the judgement of the late and much lamented Judge McCarthy of the Supreme Court in the case of *Ward v McMaster* [1989] ILRM 400 when he was dealing with these various developments: 'With the able assistance of counsel, we have travelled well charted legal seas seeking, for my part, to find a well marked haven, whether it be in Australia, Canada, Northern Ireland or England. Certainly, the judicial complements manning the several ports are not marked by unanimity.' He goes on to say with regard to an argument as to the different standings of the various cases that 'such a proposition, however, suffers from a temporal defect – that rights should be determined by an accident of birth'. If a Judge of the Supreme Court has difficulty with the subject the practitioner can be excused a certain amount of confusion.

However these cases separating tort and contract were unfortunately not followed in Ireland, and it can be taken that the established law here, following the case of *Finlay v Murtagh* [1979] IR 249 which was a case involving alleged negligence against a solicitor, is that a professional man owes a duty both in contract and tort to his clients. This was confirmed in the case of *Kennedy and Others v Allied Irish*

Bank [1996] Supreme Court, 29th October where the court held: 'Where a duty of care exists, whether such duty is tortious or created by contract, the claimant is entitled to take advantage of the remedy which is most advantageous to him subject only to ascertaining whether the tortious duty is so inconsistent with the applicable contract that, in accordance with ordinary principle, the parties must be taken to have agreed that the tortious remedy is to be limited or excluded.'

It would, of course, be possible for a professional to insist in his terms of engagement that no liability would result in tort but it is difficult to see a client accepting this. It was, none-the-less, proposed by the Judge in Conway and *Another v Crowe Kelsey and Partners* [1994] 11-CLD-03-01, where he held fast to the traditional view that a professional was liable in tort as well as contract unless he stipulated otherwise. It is to be hoped that this position might eventually change because the consequences of the double jeopardy of tort and contract can place an extremely heavy burden on the practitioner. The same case confirmed the now accepted view that the Statute of Limitations begins to run from the date on which the damage was suffered (see par. 9.5).

9.4 The Widening of Liability

9.4.1 Economic Loss

Back in the 1960s even if the architect owed a duty in tort and in contract it was still considered that he owed that duty only to the employer, but this view was in turn upset, particularly by the case of *Hedley Byrne v Heller* [1964] AC 465. This held that a negligent misstatement which resulted in financial loss gave rise to actions by persons who had no contractual relationship with the person who made the misstatement, provided that they were persons who, it might have been anticipated, would rely on that statement. The overall scope of *Hedley Byrne v Heller* applies to architects and other professionals. This widened the field of liability considerably, and brought into the architects area people such as borrowers from financial institutions like building societies, or tenants of buildings, and so on. Until that point it was the position that pure economic loss was not recoverable in tort and that there must have been physical damage present to sustain a claim. It was felt that economic loss was the domain of contract alone. However the case of *Junior Books v The Veitchi Co* [1982] 21 BLR 66 amongst others allowed the recovery of pure economic loss but this position was reversed by the decision in *D & F Estates v Church Commissioners* [1988] 41 BLR 1 which held that recovery for pure economic loss, as opposed to damage to property, was solely a matter for contract and not for tort.

A further twist in the economic loss saga is the case of *Invercargill City Council v Hamlin* [1996] THE TIMES, 15th January. In this case the Privy Council was considering a decision of the Court of Appeal of New Zealand and agreed that the New Zealand Court was correct in awarding economic loss against a local authority for defects in a building that had been examined by the authority, despite the decisions taken in the *D & F Estates* and *Murphy* cases (see par. 9.4.2 for details of the *Murphy* case).The basis of the decision was a difference in practice in New Zealand where more reliance was placed on local authority building inspections. And as recently as November 1996, Murphy was further complicated by the cases of *Rowlands and Wilson v Caradon District Council* (14-CLD-02-13) where the exception to the 'no economic loss' principle was questioned.

The distinction that case law made between economic loss occurring as a result of an negligent act or as a result of a negligent statement was so fine as to be almost perverse. If a defective drawing was an act then no economic loss is recoverable, but if a defective drawing was a statement comparable to, say, an auditor's statement then economic loss was recoverable. Is a drawing an act or a statement? While it has been held that an architect's drawing is not a 'negligent misstatement' ('It would be artificial to treat the submission of drawings and designs by an architect to his client as some form of implied statement as to the technical adequacy of the proposed building' – *Lancashire and Cheshire v Howard and Seddon* [1991] 65 BLR 21), the opposite view is taken in *Edgeworth Construction Ltd v N D Lea* [1993] 66 BLR 56. The Arbuthnott case mentioned before also dealt with economic loss and the Court comment was fairly strong: 'In recent years there have been several cases which deal with situations where no physical damage has resulted from the carelessness in question, but where the claimant has sustained financial loss or expense. To my mind the law draws no fundamental difference between such cases and those where there is damage to persons or property.'

Happily, and in contrast, the position in Ireland is now fairly clear, though subject to the comments in the next paragraph. The cases of *Ward v McMaster* [1989] ILRM 400 and *Sweeney v Duggan* [1991] 2 IR 274 were both approved in the recent case of *McShane Fruit v Johnston Haulage* [1997] 1 ILRM 86. Three rules have been established:

a) A sufficient relationship of proximity must exist between the alleged wrongdoer and the person who has suffered damage. A misleading advertisement which anyone can read is not sufficient to establish this link (*Bank of Ireland v Smith* [1966] IR 646) whereas a statement made directly to one person is specific enough to establish the link (*McAnerney v Hanrahan* [1994] 1 ILRM 210).

b) It must be in the reasonable contemplation of the alleged wrongdoer that carelessness on his part will be likely to cause damage to the other party.

c) The quality of the damage does not arise. It can be damage to property, to the person, financial or economic.

The position with regard to economic loss was, however, questioned by the Chief Justice in the case of *Glencar Exploration v Mayo County Council* [2002]1 ILRM 481. The case was primarily about the powers and duties of a local authority in relation to its own development plan but a question arose as to whether pure economic loss was recoverable. 'There remains the question of economic loss. The reason why damages for such loss – as distinct from compensation for injury to persons or damage to property – are normally not recoverable in tort is best illustrated by an example. If A sells B an article which turns out to be defective, B can normally sue A for damages for breach of contract. However, if the article comes into the possession of C, with whom A has no contract, C cannot in general sue A for the defects in the chattel, unless he has suffered personal injury or damage to property within the *Donoghue v Stephenson* principle. That would be so even where the defect was latent and did not come to light until the article came into C's possession. To hold otherwise would be to expose the original seller to actions from an infinite range of persons with whom he never had any relationship in contract or its equivalent.

That does not mean that economic loss is always irrecoverable in actions in tort. As already noted, economic loss is recoverable in actions for negligent misstatement. In Siney, economic loss was held to be recoverable in a case where the damages represented the cost of remedying defects in a building let by the local authority under their statutory powers. Such damages were also held to be recoverable in *Ward v McMaster*, the loss being represented by the cost of remedying defects for which the builder and the local authority were held to be responsible. In both cases, the loss was held to be recoverable following the approach adopted by the House of Lords in Anns. While the same tribunal subsequently overruled its earlier conclusion to that effect in *Murphy v Brentwood District Council* [1991] 1 AC 398, we were not invited in the present case to overrule our earlier decisions in Siney and *Ward v McMaster*. I would expressly reserve for another occasion the question as to whether economic loss is recoverable in actions for negligence other than actions for negligent misstatement and those falling within the categories identified in *Junior Books Ltd v Veitchi Co. Ltd* should be followed in this jurisdiction.'

9.4.2 Local Authorities

But not only were architects and other professionals under pressure from these developments, so also were some statutory bodies. The liability of local authorities for decisions taken by them in furtherance of their statutory powers and duties has been the subject of many legal decisions, and the position has very recently been completely altered. The famous case of *Dutton v Bognor Regis UDC* [1972] 3 BLR 13 can be taken as the starting point as far a modern developments go. The case decided that a local authority in carrying out its functions (in this case the passing by a building inspector of foundations which turned out to be defective) had a duty not only to the building owner but to subsequent parties who might reasonably have been foreseen as being affected by the council's actions. This duty was not to be negligent. Dutton also held that a council would be liable for physical damage to the property whether it endangered others or not but not liable for pure financial loss.

The case of *Anns v Merton* [1978] 5 BLR 1 brought the matter further. It decided that a local authority was not obliged to inspect every building as far as building bye-laws were concerned but that they must properly exercise their discretion in deciding what to inspect, and that if they did inspect, it must not be negligent. The case further held that no cause of action arose until such time as the defects which had appeared would constitute 'imminent danger to the health and safety of persons occupying the building'.

Finally in this section is the rather extraordinary case of *Murphy v Brentwood District Council* [1990] 50 BLR 1. Ever since the Dutton case it had been accepted, and case after case confirmed it, that local authorities (and builders) were liable for damage to property if caused by their negligence. The Murphy case decided that this only applied to ensure that no physical injury occurred either to occupiers or to any other property, and that damage to the property in question did not create a liability except for the injuries mentioned above. In other words, Dutton, Anns, and all the other cases were wrong. A footnote with regard to the unfairness of the law would be that the unfortunate Mr Murphy, despite winning in the High Court and Court of Appeal, and despite the House of Lords rulings in Anns and other cases, had to pay all the costs because the House of Lords changed the law. The New Zealand case mentioned above (Invercargill) has taken a different view again, but which route the Irish Courts might take is not yet clear.

The Murphy decision creates the extraordinary position that if, say, a ceiling is dangerous and the owner repairs it he has no claim against anybody whereas if he ignores it and it falls and injures somebody he has a claim. Max Abrahamson has pointed out that the Dutch boy should not have kept his finger in the dyke because as long as he did nobody could claim damages for the defective dyke.

In Ireland the case of *Siney v Dublin Corporation* [1980] IR 400 also dealt with the obligations of local authorities. The case did not deal with building bye-laws but was concerned with the Corporation's duty to provide housing under the requirements of the Housing Act 1966. A tenant sued the Corporation on the grounds that the house which had been let to him by the Corporation was not fit for human habitation. The Supreme Court examined the distinction between the duties and the powers which arose under statute as far as a local authority was concerned. It had always been accepted that breach of a duty would result in liability whereas breach of a power might not, and the Court confirmed that failure to exercise a power could not automatically guarantee immunity to a local authority. The Court's decision was in line with *Anns v Merton* and it remains to be seen what effect *Murphy v Brentwood* will have on future decisions. The Court specifically approved of *Anns v Merton*. A later case (*Sunderland v Louth County Council* [1990] ILRM seemed to be a warning that the Courts might not be as ready in the future to recompense for pure economic loss, but this line of argument has now been largely abandoned (see par. 9.4.1). Other cases such as *Convery v Dublin County Council* [1996] Supreme Court, 12th November held that local authorities acting as either planning authorities or roads authorities did not have a sufficient proximity of relationship with aggrieved individuals to create a duty of care.

9.5   **The Statute of Limitations**

The tort versus contract argument raised further issues but the real problem, as far as the construction industry was concerned, lay in the field of limitation. If a person was liable only in contract, that liability ended six years after the contract had been performed (or twelve years in the case of a contract under seal). But the length of liability in tort was uncertain. A number of cases (including the Anns case mentioned above) began to move the period until *Sparham-Souter v Town and Country Developments* [1976] 3 BLR 70 decided that the statute of limitations only began to run when the plaintiff knew of the defects or 'with reasonable diligence could have discovered them'. This extended the time indefinitely and led an exasperated commentator in the Building Law Reports to observe: 'The six year period (for limitation) begins to run afresh for all eternity with every new purchaser ... Is this really what Parliament intended.' At this time the exposure of professionals in the construction industry was extreme, both as far as the spread of liability in time and to various parties. The pendulum then began to move very slowly back.

In *Pirelli General Cable Works v Oscar Faber* [1982] 21 BLR 99 it was held that the time began to run when the damage occurred, whether it was observed or not. This case was not followed in Ireland in *Morgan v Park Developments* [1983] ILRM 156 when the old view was taken that time began to run when the defects were observed, on the grounds that otherwise 'it may have the effect of depriving an injured party of a right of action before he knows he has one'. The New Zealand case (Invercargill) mentioned in par. 9.4 also dealt with the limitation issue. When considering the case, the Privy Council declined to follow the Pirelli decision, leaving room for considerable uncertainty. However, the next case as far as this jurisdiction is concerned is *Hegarty v O'Loughran* [1990] ILRM 403 which is of considerable importance to practitioners as it concerned professional negligence relating in this instance to the field of medicine.

It is worthwhile examining this case in some detail as the appearance of defects in buildings occur on a varying time scale ranging from one day to up to fifty years afterwards, and any case or precedent which might indicate to a practitioner or contractor when his liability might end would be very welcome. The Statute of Limitations 1957 says at section 11(2)(b):

'An action claiming damages for negligence, nuisance or breach of duty (whether the duty exists by virtue of a contract or of a provision made by or under a statute or independently of any contract or any such provision) where the damages claimed by the plaintiff for negligence, nuisance or breach of duty consist of or include damages in respect of personal injuries to any person shall not be brought after the expiration of three years from the date on which the cause of action accrued.'

The Supreme Court considered three possible interpretations of this section:

1   The cause of action would be deemed to have accrued when the wrongful act was committed

2   The cause of action would be deemed to have accrued at the time when the personal injury, allegedly arising from the wrongful act, manifested itself, or,

3   The cause of action would be deemed to have accrued only when the injured party not only has suffered the committing of a wrongful act but has also suffered damage (personal injury) and could, by the exercise of reasonable diligence, have discovered that such personal injury was caused by the wrongful act complained of (i.e. objective discoverability).

The Court held that the first possibility was the correct one. The various judgements make it clearer: 'The time limit commenced to run at a time when a provable personal injury, capable of attracting compensation, occurred to the plaintiff which was the completion of the tort alleged to be committed against her.' Another judgement said: 'The period of limitation therefore begins to run from the date on which the cause of action accrued, i.e. when a complete and available cause of action first comes into existence. When a wrongful act is actionable *per se* without proof of damage as in for example, libel, assault or trespass to land or goods the statute runs from the time at which the act was committed. Where, however, when the wrong is not actionable without actual damage, as in the case of negligence, the cause of action is not complete and the period of limitation cannot begin to run until that damage happens or occurs.' And finally: 'The fundamental principal is that words in a statute must be given their ordinary meaning and I am unable to conclude that a cause of action occurs on the date of discovery of its existence rather than on the date on which, if it had been discovered, proceedings could lawfully have been instituted. I recognise the unfairness, the harshness and the obscurantism that underlies this rule but it is there and will remain there unless qualified by the legislature or invalidated root and branch by this Court.' The Court recognised that it was very difficult to strike a balance between the position of a plaintiff who might lose the right to take an action because of the passage of time in circumstances not due to his own fault against the position of a person being called on to defend an action many years after the event when his recollection, the availability of witnesses and documentary evidence might have disappeared, but the Court was satisfied that the 1957 Act was reasonable. The perceived unfairness of the Hegarty case gave rise to an amendment to the 1957 Act but only as far as personal injuries were concerned. The 1991 Amendment added the words 'or the date of the knowledge (if later) of the person injured' to the phrase 'shall not be brought after the expiration of three years from the date on which the cause of action accrued'.

Much the same arguments regarding the balance of fairness arose in the case of *Touhy v Courtney* [1994] 2 ILRM 503. This was another professional negligence case, this time involving solicitors but is of even more interest in that it was not concerned with personal injury but with the conduct of professional duties and would, therefore, be more relevant to practitioners in the construction field. The Court took the same view as was taken in *Hegarty v O'Loughran*, and this was that the cause of action accrued when the act complained of had occurred and not when the damage was discovered.

The 'six-year rule' can now be taken as being the law in this jurisdiction at the moment and it is a cause of considerable comfort to practitioners. The last word should be left to the Supreme Court: 'The counter balance to the objectives of the Statute of Limitations 1957 is the necessity for the State, as far as is practicable or as best it may, to ensure that the time limits do not unreasonably or unjustly impose hardship ... Viewed objectively, the limitation period of six years was a substantial period.' Arbitrators should be aware that Section 75 of the Statute of Limitations 1957 provides that any limitations defined in the statute apply to arbitrations just as much as to Court cases.

The whole question of limitations was reviewed by the Law Reform Commission in a report of March 2001. This report dealt with all aspects of limitations other than those involving personal injury and paid special attention to construction disputes. The report said 'Both because of the frequency of the disputes arising in the construction industry and because of the difficulties in insuring against latent defects, a fixed and easily ascertainable period of liability is essential.'

The report also addressed the contract and/or tort problem referred to in par. 9.3.

The recommendation of the Law Reform Commission was that any subsequent legislation should be as follows:

An action claiming damage in respect of loss or damage (other than personal injury) caused by a breach of duty whether the duty exists in tort, contract, statute, or independent of any such provision, shall not be brought after the later of either the expiration of:

a) six years from the date on which the cause of action accrued or

b) three years from the date on which the person first knew or in the circumstances ought reasonably to have known:
   i) that the loss for which the person seeks a remedy had occurred;
   ii) that the damage was attributable to the conduct of the defendant; and
   iii) that the loss, assuming liability on the part of the defendant, warrants bringing proceedings.

Notwithstanding subsections (1) and (2), a construction claim cannot be brought more than 10 years after the date of issue of the certificate of practical completion in respect of the construction operation or, the date of purported completion of the construction operation in cases where no certificate of practical completion is issued.

The long-stop proposal is particularly welcome and it is hoped will become the law. It will be a great comfort to all concerned in a project to know that no liability can continue after ten years from the date of the completion of the building. It is suggested in the report that this period might be extended to twelve years in the case of contracts under seal.

A further problem dealt with in the report is the difficulty of the position of a purchaser of a building which eventually develops defects. The simple historic view of 'caveat emptor' had long since been abandoned in the case of the purchase of property and the Law Reform Commission recommended that any statute of limitations legislation should provide that the time would run from when the defect was discoverable either by the present, or the previous, owner.

As has been seen, liability for personal injury has a different time scale but can be tied to a building defect. The normal time within which to make a claim for personal injury would be three years from the date of the injury. This of course means that a defective building or structure which injures somebody even 30 years after construction would still give rise to an action. This was the position in *Cowan v Faghaule and Others* [1991] High Court 24th January, where a defective wall which had been built in Croke Park in 1958 fell and injured a spectator in 1985. The original contractors were still liable.

The saga of all these cases can sometimes confuse the position as it relates to Ireland. Readers will probably be aware that English legal precedents are not binding on the Irish Courts but they are 'persuasive' and are being constantly pleaded. Some of the later ones referred to are not embodied in Irish decisions. The position as it appears to be at the moment is:

i)   Professionals are liable in both contract and tort (*Finlay v Murtagh*).

ii) The Statute of Limitations runs from the latest time that damage could have occurred, whether discovered or not. (*Hegarty v O'Loughran and Tuohy v Courtney*).

iii) Local authorities and contractors are liable if defects constitute imminent danger to health and safety of those occupying the building (*Anns v Merton as approved in Siney v Dublin Corporation*).

iv) Economic loss is no different to any other form of loss (*McShane v Johnston*). The comments on economic loss made in *Glencar Exploration v Mayo County Council* referred to par. 9.4.1 should be noted.

9.6   EU Proposals on Liability

The overall position with regard to liability for construction professionals could change drastically under legislation being considered by the European Union. One of the objectives of the Treaty of Rome, amended by the Single European Act, 1987, is to ensure the free movement of goods, services persons, and capital, together with the guarantee of free and fair competition. To this end, a draft directive was issued on 9th November 1990 with regard to liability for the Supply of Services which was to cover financial, transport, management, tourist, legal, and many other services. It was understood that construction services would be excluded but that did not occur. The proposals were radical and included:

1   A reversal of the onus of proof, placing the burden on the designer or contractor to prove that no fault of his caused the damage, in other words, guilty until proved innocent if the injured party can prove damage and cause.

2   An endorsement of the principle of joint and several liability, that is, if the damage is caused by a number of parties, the injured party can recover from all or any of them depending on their resources.

3   A ban on the exclusion of liability, or even on the limitation of liability.

4   The person providing the service shall be liable for a period of 20 years from the date of the service, and an injured party shall have a period of 10 years in which to start proceedings, the 10 years commencing when the damage was observed. This meant, in effect, a possible 30 years exposure.

5   A definition of damage as being that of death or injury to persons, damage to property, and what was called 'financial material' damage, which is financial damage resulting from the first two classes of damage.

The production of this directive caused something of a storm because of the inclusion of construction related services in this scope of the directive. The Union acceded to the representation from almost every member state and agreed to set up advisory panels to make proposals to the commission with regard to construction related services. The RIAI has a representative on one of the panels. It is to be hoped that the final proposals from the EU will be more realistic and will show more understanding of the practicalities of the building process.

At the moment there is some hope that a special directive will be prepared for the construction industry and it seems to be generally agreed that this would be preferable if the general directive is proceeding. There is also a possibility that the matter will not proceed any further as a number of member states are arguing that their existing domestic legislation is satisfactory.

9.7   **The Expert Witness**

An expert has been famously described by Mark Twain as 'some guy from out of town'. Architects, and indeed professionals generally, are regularly being sought as expert witnesses and it is suggested that there is a view that this requires the expert to give support to those that retain him and to give the evidence which would support his clients, and that in any event the responsibilities are not too great. This is a mistaken view. Perhaps the view quoted by the Master of the Rolls in the UK goes too far: 'Expert witnesses used to be genuinely independent experts. Men of outstanding eminence in their field. Today they are in practice hired guns. There is a new breed of litigation hangers-on whose main expertise is to craft reports which will conceal anything that might be to the disadvantage of their clients.'

The concern that is evident over the increase in the use of expert witnesses is not confined to this jurisdiction. The Master of the Rolls referred to above recently identified three main problems; excessive cost: lack of impartiality: and the emergence of an expert witness industry which her referred to as a 'great social ill'. In an attempt to curb some of these defects the concept of the single joint expert was proposed in the UK. The expert would be appointed by the Court and would be shared by all parties and the Court. The Court's permission would be required for the introduction of expert testimony. It is, however, hard to see such reforms being generally accepted without some form of regulation.

A very good summary of the position was given in the case of *National Justice Compania Naviera S.A. v Prudential Assurance Company Limited* [1993] THE TIMES, 5th March.

The Court said that expert witnesses in civil actions had a duty and responsibility to give independent and unbiased evidence. If an expert witness did not have experience in a certain area or had insufficient information to reach a properly researched conclusion then he should say so. The duties and responsibilities were:

1   The evidence should be the independent product of the expert uninfluenced by the exigencies of litigation.

2   The evidence is to be objective and within the expertise of the witness. An expert witness should never assume the role of advocate.

3   Facts or assumptions upon which the opinion is based should be stated together with any material facts which could detract from the concluded opinion.

4   An expert witness should make it clear when a question or issue fell outside his expertise.

5   If insufficient data is available then it should be stated that the opinion was provisional.

6   If an expert witness changes his mind after an exchange of reports then he must immediately communicate this to the other side and, where appropriate to the Court.

Reports given in civil actions should now follow the guidelines set out in a practice direction issued by the President of The High Court in 1993. These are intended to shorten the proceedings. It is recommended that written reports should be exchanged and, if possible admitted, between the sides thus removing the necessity of oral evidence. Copies of such reports should be made available to the Court. In a further development in 1966, Smyth J directed that all expert reports should identify, (i) qualifications, experience, etc, of witnesses, (ii) a summary of the report and (iii) the report proper.

9.8   Cases Referred To   *par.*

Chapter 10 – **Warranties and Opinions**

The previous chapter dealt with the overall responsibility of the design professionals, and of the contractor, and how this is constantly changing. This uncertainty has led to the development of the collateral warranty as it applies to the professionals and to a lesser extent has been a factor in the growth of the certificate, or opinion, of compliance.

10.1 **Collateral Warranties**

The cases listed earlier such as *D & F Estates v Church Commissioners* and *Murphy v Brentwood*, by causing liability, as far as professionals, contractors and others were concerned, to contract, particularly in England, might have been seen to be a good thing by the same professionals and contractors, employers (who become building owners) did not like this trend and set about redressing the balance by widespread use of the collateral warranty. A collateral warranty is a contract, and one that exists in conjunction with another, or 'principal' contract with one party common to both contracts. The word 'collateral' means alongside, or together with. Put simply, building owners were concerned that the previous widespread liability of their advisors or contractors was being eroded and they endeavoured to copper-fasten in contract what seemed to be disappearing in tort. A recent Scottish case (*Strathford East Kilbride Ltd v Film Design Ltd* [1997] THE TIMES, 1st December) confirmed the tortious position that an architect, who had a contract with a landlord, had no liability towards a tenant.

The growth of the collateral warranty in the construction industry is due to this uncertainty which resulted in the area of the legal relationship of tort and contract. As long as building owners in particular, could seek redress against those with whom they had no contract by suing in tort then there was no problem. These claims would be made in an action for negligence, which is a tort. A negligence action would arise if, say, an architect was held to have a duty of care towards a financial institution which buys a building he had designed, and if there is a breach of that duty and damage results, then the architect is liable to the financial institution, even though there is no contract between them. This remedy in negligence could be available to tenants as well.

But how is this duty of care established? Whether a duty of care existed or not depended on the Court's interpretation of the relationship between the particular plaintiff and the defendant. The Court had to establish whether the relationship between them was close enough to say that the defendant owed the particular plaintiff a duty to take care and whether it would be foreseeable that if the defendant did not take care that the plaintiff would suffer loss as a result.

Although the cause of action was established, the extent of the damages recoverable was not certain. Initially, when the Courts held that a duty of care existed in construction cases they said the only duty was a duty to avoid any defect which could be a danger. Therefore, the plaintiff could only recover if the defect was dangerous and not if it was a defect which merely lowered the quality of the building. Eventually the Courts began to say that plaintiffs could recover, even if the defects only meant that the building was of a poorer quality. The Courts also held that it was possible to recover damages for lost profit.

The point was soon reached where all consultants, contractors and sub-contractors involved in the construction industry were at risk from claims for negligence from a fairly wide range of potential plaintiffs including not only the people with whom they were in contract, such as a developer, but also subsequent owners and occupiers including tenants and sub-tenants.

On the other hand the persons owning or investing in buildings were afforded a very high level of protection as it was relatively easy to establish that the particular consultant or contractor owned a duty of care and if the duty of care was breached then the 'foreseeable consequences' were very wide. Collateral Warranties as a double safeguard were not seen as being very important. But when the Courts began to alter course, and start to restrict the range and scope of tortious remedies, owners and developers also changed course and began to promote the collateral warranty.

After the case of *Junior Books v The Veitchi Co* [1982] 21 BLR 66, the English Courts began to retreat from the previous very wide view of the extent of the duty of care and the type of damages that were recoverable when a duty of care could be established. This retreat became a rout in the next two cases. These cases were mentioned briefly in par. 9.4 dealing with the widening of liability but are examined here in some detail as they highlight the erosion of the wide scope of recovery under tort that previously protected building owners.

Firstly, *D & F Estates Ltd & Others v Church Commissioners for England and Others* [1988] 41 BLR 1: In this case defective plastering had been carried out by a sub-contractor to a main contractor. A lease-holder, claimed against the main contractor in respect of the costs of repair to the plastering actually carried out, future repair costs and loss of rent. As he had no contract with the main contractor, the plaintiff had to sue in tort. The plaintiff claimed that the main contractor had a duty to adequately supervise the work of the sub-contractor who did the plastering. The plaintiff failed to establish a duty of care, in this case, as the Court held that the claim here was for 'pure economic loss', as there had been no damage caused by the defective plaster either to other property or to any person. The Court held that to succeed in a claim for negligence there had to be some element of physical damage to property other than the defective item itself or some personal injury.

Secondly, in 1990, *Murphy v Brentwood District Council* [1990] 50 BLR 1, it was held that when carrying out its statutory functions of exercising control over building operations, a local authority was not liable in negligence to a building owner or occupier for the cost of remedying a dangerous defect in a building. The defect in question resulted from the negligent failure of the authority to ensure that the building was designed and erected in conformity with the applicable standards prescribed by the Building Regulations or bye-laws. The defect became apparent before it caused physical injury and therefore, the damage suffered by the building owner or occupier in such circumstances was not material or physical damage but 'pure economic loss' due to the expenditure incurred, either in remedying the structural defect to avert the danger or in abandoning the property because of its unfitness for use. Since a dangerous defect, when it became known, merely became a defect in quality, the Court said that to permit the building owner or occupier to recover this economic loss would logically lead to an unacceptably wide category of claims in respect of buildings which were defective in quality. Accordingly, the Court held that the authority owed no duty of care to the plaintiff when it approved the plans for what ultimately transpired to be a defective raft foundation in the plaintiff's house.

Following these decisions it became apparent that reliance on the tort of negligence for anyone who had an investment in property was not a particularly reliable source of protection and certainly in England it can now be said that negligence claims will rarely be successful unless there has been actual physical injury to the person or damage to property (other than the defective property itself). Economic loss will almost certainly not be recoverable. Par 9.4.1 deals in more detail with the latest trends and twists in the saga of economic loss as opposed to other forms of loss.

The differences between the state of the law as based on case law in England and Ireland has been commented on. The English decisions set out in the paragraphs above have not been followed in Ireland, but there are some signs that liability in tort might narrow. In *Ward v McMaster* [1989] ILRM 400, a plaintiff did recover economic loss but this was complicated by the duties of the local authority involved under the Housing Act 1966. A second case involving a local authority, *Sunderland v Louth County Council* [1990] ILRM 658 absolved the authority from any duty of care to ensure the suitability of a site when considering a planning application. It does seem that it will be more difficult in future in this jurisdiction to obtain redress on the same wide scale as before.

This recent restriction of tortious remedy, both here and in England, was responsible for the rise of the collateral warranty. The existence of the collateral warranty in the RIAI standard building contract forms does not owe its existence to the legal developments described, but is merely a common sense arrangement between the employer and a nominated sub-contractor. That warranty requires the sub-contractor to be directly responsible to the contractor for the quality of his work, and in return the employer undertakes to pay the sub-contractor directly if the contractor defaults. This section of the guide does not refer to that particular warranty but to the collateral warranty relating to the professional advisors.

When various bodies, mostly financial institutions in Britain, began to draft collateral warranties for professionals, they sought the most comprehensive, and in some views, penal guarantees.

10.2 Parties Seeking Collateral Warranties

It is understandable that any funding institution providing capital for a development will have a dominant motive in mind when looking for a collateral warranty, i.e. to protect the interest they are acquiring in the property. In a similar way, any purchaser of a development will be seeking protection through collateral warranties. They will want to have the right to make claims against those responsible for the design and construction of the development if something goes wrong. Again, a tenant of the property will also seek to protect himself as he will generally have an extensive and onerous repairing obligation under his lease. Therefore, funds, purchasers and tenants have an interest in common, i.e. they are all seeking to protect their interest and pass as much risk as possible back to the parties who designed and built the development, i.e. the professional consultants, contractors and sub-contractors. On the other hand, the professionals will be seeking what they regard as a reasonable half-way house between total liability and a workable compromise. But the difficulty is the negotiating power of the employer. There are some dangers to employers in imposing very severe terms, as Courts have long protected those that they regarded as having been unfairly forced, because of a poor bargaining position, into signing a particular contract such as a collateral warranty.

Employers were, in effect, forcing their professional advisors to go back to the bad old days of liability to 'everyone and forever'. It was, to a large extent, a force that could not be resisted, for the advisors needed the work and somewhere there would be an architect or engineer who would accept the employer's conditions. But not only were professional institutions concerned at this development, so also were the insurance companies who very quickly put limits on the kind of warranties that they would be prepared to back. Needless to say, an architect signing a collateral warranty without informing his insurers would have no cover for the extended risk. The scene that the employer was trying to create was that any subsequent claim against him, by a tenant of the building, by a financial institution, by a subsequent purchaser and so on, could be deflected towards the professional advisors, or the contractor.

10.3 The RIAI Form of Collateral Warranty

If an architect, in particular, finds that he has to sign a collateral warranty it should always be the RIAI form, which offers a reasonable measure of protection to the developer or his successor, while without at the same time imposing draconian obligations on the professionals. A vital component of this warranty is the clause (No. 7) referring to 'forbearance'. The core of a collateral warranty given by a professional to a client, or others, is that the professional agrees to be bound by the certainty of contract but that, in return, the uncertain and double hazard of tort is waived by the beneficiary of the warranty. The RIAI standard form of collateral warranty starts with the following statements:

General Notes

The purpose of a Collateral Warranty is to extend architects' responsibility, beyond their Employer, to another person or body. The beneficiary of such a warranty has direct legal access to the architects in claiming damages where faults arise.

Warranties should be entered into with the utmost care. The purpose of this warranty is to reasonably limit the extension of responsibility and to ensure that architects do not carry more than their reasonable share of any damages. This limitation is achieved principally by:

- *defining precisely the tasks to be undertaken and the responsibility of the architects*

- *prohibiting the assignment of the Beneficiaries interest in the Warranty to any other party*

- *placing a limit on the amount of damages that can be claimed form the architects and insuring that potential loss*

- *limiting the Warranty to six years*

- *ensuring that all parties to the contract sign warranties*

- *excluding consequential loss.*

At the moment the view of the RIAI is that, if a collateral warranty must be signed, it should:

1 Be signed by all members of the design team, main contractor, and nominated sub-contractor and should only operate when all have signed. If all the parties mentioned do not sign the warranty, the architect must ensure that his risk is limited to a stated percentage of the damages, as failure to do so would expose him to the full extent of the damages, under the joint and several provisions of the Civil Liability Act, 1961.

2   Be assignable by a client only to the beneficiary named and not be capable of being passed on to subsequent owners, lessees, tenants, etc. This seems now to be generally acceptable.

3   Be limited to six years. The RIAI form specifies that the six years will run from the date of the agreement, but some institutions endeavour to have the six year term run from the date of practical completion. This might not be reasonable in the case of large developments.

4   Be limited to a Schedule of Services based upon the RIAI Conditions of Engagement. These should be specified in the agreement.

5   The warranty should be restricted to the cost of making good physical damage to the development itself. Consequential damage could be quite horrific and must be excluded.

6   The warranty must be backed by an appropriate insurance policy. The form states that the liability of the architect will be limited to the amount of insurance cover in force, and if the architect can not obtain this cover for 125% of the standard rates in force he will not be obliged to insure.

It can be imagined that in a large development the number of parties involved who might wish to have a range of collateral warranties with a similar, or larger number, of other parties could be considerable. In one office development in Dublin over 200 such warranties were signed. This seems to be verging on the farcical.

10.4 Decennial Insurance as an Alternative

The ideal solution to the wide and confusing range of duties and liabilities of all the participants in the building process set out in the preceding nine paragraphs would seem to be a form of single comprehensive insurance, possibly decennial. This form of insurance would provide cover for the building itself, not for the consultants or contractor involved. The scope of the defects which might appear, known as 'latent defects', would be agreed in advance and would broadly cover repairing, renewing or strengthening the structural or water-proofing elements of the building. The policy would also provide cover for site clearance, and professional fees. It will, in short, cover any loss which occurs as a result of a design or construction problem. The cover would not require proof of fault, would be non-cancellable and would be freely assignable. It would be instituted by a single premium. The ideal length of time for the cover would appear to be 10 years for two reasons. Firstly, it has been estimated by the insurance industry itself that 95% of all latent defects appear within 10 years, and, secondly, 10 year or decennial insurance is a common concept in Europe and it is clear that our involvement in Europe is becoming closer and closer.

This cover is readily available and the cost of obtaining the cover has been estimated at around 1% of the contract value of the building, although it can be, as low as 0.5% depending on the technical survey which will be carried out by the insurers. This might seem expensive, but the overall protection provided to the building owner, and the removal of the time-consuming legal recovery route should be attractive. Not only that, but in a competitive property market, a new development which has decennial latent defects cover should have an advantage over the development without it, particularly as far as overseas buyers are concerned.

10.5 Opinions on Compliance

One of the more recent developments in the field of design and construction is the idea of the certificate of compliance. Up until 1964 there was no effective planning control and, except in the few local authority areas which operated building bye-laws, there was no control of building standards until 1992. This meant that the sale of properties was not effected by the existence or otherwise of planning permissions but after 1964 the standard requisitions on title issue by the Incorporated Law Society inquired into the status of the property under the Planning Acts. The led in turn to architects being asked to certify what the position was and the problems began to emerge. The reader is referred to John Gore-Grimes' book, KEY ISSUES IN PLANNING AND ENVIRONMENTAL LAW, for guidance on the detail required by the Law Society recommendations.

The first such problem was that few, if any, buildings were built in exact accordance with the planning permission drawings. The very nature of the process of producing working drawings for the contractor tends to introduce variations though sometimes of a very minor nature. Occasions also arose where there were substantial differences between the scheme as lodged with the planning authority and the scheme actually built. This led to architects certifying that the building did comply or, if it did not, that the differences were not significant. This procedure moved the file along and the very fact that a certificate existed was accepted by all as satisfying the requirements. This was the start of the use of words like 'substantial' in reference to certificates. It was remarked earlier in par. 2.4.12 that the courts have decided that exact compliance with planning permission drawings is not necessary.

Similarly, certificates were also needed in respect of building bye-laws in those local authority areas where such control existed. After the institution of Building Regulations in 1992, these were required on a countrywide basis. The problems that arose, however, in connection with buildings that had been erected in bye-law areas still subsists and sales of such properties are still dependant, to some extent, on the solicitors for the purchasers being satisfied as far as these problem areas are concerned. In the case of houses in particular it had soon become clear that very few architects, contractors, solicitors or owners were aware of the fact that exempted development under the Planning Acts if claimed by virtue of the Regulations in S.I. 65 of 1977 was not in fact exempt if bye-law approval had not been obtained. This was particularly prevalent where small extensions had been added on to houses or where garages had been converted into habitable rooms. This led to the issue of certificates which said that while bye-law approval had not been obtained it would have been granted had it been applied for. The fact, too, that the bye-laws were forty years out of date by the 1990s meant that large areas of the bye-laws were no longer relevant and waivers were being sought on a widespread scale. Certificates now began to say that bye-law approval had not been obtained but would have been granted if applied for, and that where the building did not conform with the bye-laws that a waiver would have been granted. Certificates were, in fact, becoming meaningless. The arrival of Building Regulations was the spur that has led to the regularisation of these certificates.

Along the way the name of the document was changed. Since the issue of a certificate by anyone is a statement that they are certain of the facts stated and as a large measure of personal judgement could be involved it was considered appropriate to alter the title of the document to an Opinion on Compliance. The opinions were generally qualified by the use of the phrase 'substantial compliance' to indicate that exact compliance was a rare event and substantial compliance was defined as meaning that any deviation in the case of the Planning Acts was of a minor nature that would not contravene the planning permission or the development plan and in the case of Building Regulations that any deviation would not merit the issue of enforcement proceedings.

The Royal Institute of the Architects of Ireland has now issued, in conjunction with the Incorporated Law Society, five standard forms of opinion for use by members of the Institute. They are to cater for:

a) an opinion with regard to the Building Regulations where a professional service has been provided at the design and construction stage

b) an opinion with regard to the Building Regulation for apartment buildings where a full architectural service is not being provided

c) an opinion with regard to the Building Regulations where a design only service has been provided and where a fire safety certificate is not required

d) an opinion where an exemption is being claimed under the Building Regulations

e) an opinion with regard to compliance or exemption in respect of the Planning Acts

f)   an opinion with regard to compliance or exemption in respect of the planning acts where bye-law approval was required whether it was obtained or not.

These six forms make it clear that the opinion is being given purely for the purposes of title and that it is not a report on the condition of the structure. Architects, provided that they are members of the Institute, should always use the standard forms. Architects who are not members of the Institute are not entitled to use these forms.

10.6   **Cases Referred To**   *par.*

D & F Estates V Church Commissioners [1988] 41 BLR 1   10.1
Junior Books v The Veitchi Company [1982] 21 BLR 66   10.1
Murphy v Brentwood District Council [1990] 50 BLR 1   10.1
Strathford East Kilbride Ltd v Film Design
      [1997] THE TIMES, December 1st   10.1
Sunderland v Louth County Council [1990] ILRM 658   10.1
Ward v McMaster [1989] ILRM 400   10.1

Index